62- ωₘ

THE OCCUPATION OF HAVANA

THE OCCUPATION

War, Trade, and Slavery

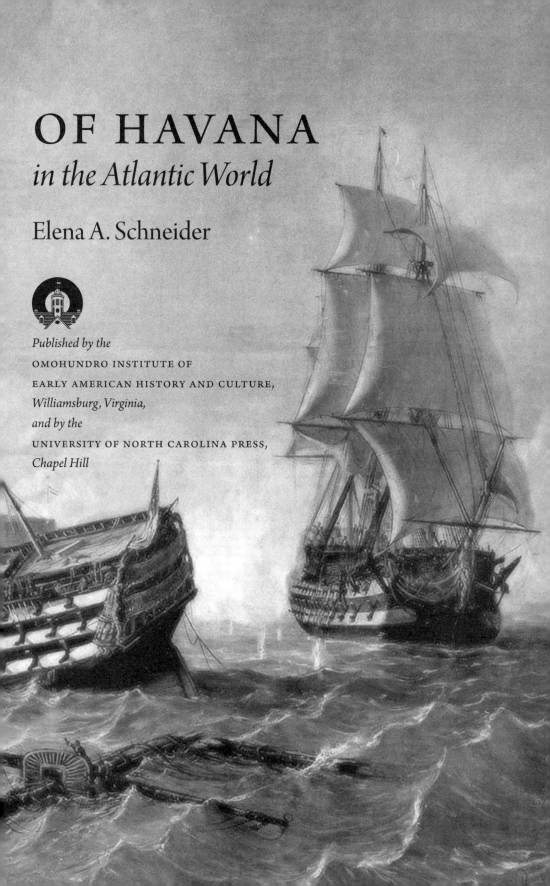

OF HAVANA
in the Atlantic World

Elena A. Schneider

Published by the
OMOHUNDRO INSTITUTE OF
EARLY AMERICAN HISTORY AND CULTURE,
Williamsburg, Virginia,
and by the
UNIVERSITY OF NORTH CAROLINA PRESS,
Chapel Hill

The Omohundro Institute of Early American History and Culture is
sponsored by the College of William and Mary. On November 15, 1996, the Institute
adopted the present name in honor of a bequest from Malvern H. Omohundro, Jr.

Cover illustrations: *The Capture of Havana, 1762: Storming of Morro Castle, 30 July.*
By Dominic Serres. 1770–1777. Oil on canvas. © National Maritime Museum, Greenwich,
London. Design of the Uniform of the Battalion of Morenos of Havana. By the *mulato*
painter José Nicolás de la Escalera. Permission, Spain, Ministerio de Educación,
Cultura y Deporte, Archivo General de Indias, Mapas y Planos-Uniformes, 25

Library of Congress Cataloging-in-Publication Data
Names: Schneider, Elena Andrea, 1977– author.
Title: The occupation of Havana : war, trade, and slavery in
the Atlantic world / Elena A. Schneider.
Description: Williamsburg, Virginia : Omohundro Institute of Early American
History and Culture ; Chapel Hill : University of North Carolina Press, [2018] |
Includes bibliographical references and index.
Identifiers: LCCN 2018023004 | ISBN 9781469645353 (cloth : alk. paper) |
ISBN 9781469645360 (ebook)
Subjects: LCSH: Cuba—History—British occupation, 1762–1763. |
Havana (Cuba)—History—Siege, 1762. | Blacks—Cuba—Social conditions—
History—18th century. | Anglo-Spanish War, 1739–1748—Campaigns—West Indies. |
West Indies—History—1756–1763. | Slave trade—Cuba—History.
Classification: LCC F1781 .S45 2018 | DDC 972.91/03—dc23
LC record available at https://lccn.loc.gov/2018023004

The University of North Carolina Press has been a member of the
Green Press Initiative since 2003.

For my parents, Ted and Fidela

Contents

Illustrations

MAPS

Abbreviations and Short Titles

ANC   Archivo Nacional de Cuba, Havana

AGI   Archivo General de Indias, Seville

       IG (Indiferente General)
       SD (Santo Domingo)

AGS   Archivo General de Simancas, Valladolid

AHN   Archivo Histórico Nacional, Madrid

BNE   Biblioteca Nacional de España, Madrid

BNJM   Biblioteca Nacional José Martí

BPL   Boston Public Library

BRP   Biblioteca del Real Palacio, Madrid

BL   British Library, London

HAHR   *Hispanic American Historical Review*

HSP   Historical Society of Pennsylvania, Philadelphia

JCBL   John Carter Brown Library, Brown University, Providence, R.I.

JNA   The National Archive at Spanish Town, Jamaica

LC   Library of Congress, Washington, D.C.

LCP   Library Company of Philadelphia

MHS   Massachusetts Historical Society, Boston

NYHS   New-York Historical Society

NYPL   New York Public Library

TNA   The National Archives, Kew, United Kingdom

       ADM (Admiralty)
       C (Court of Chancery)
       CO (Colonial Office)
       E (Exchequer)
       SP (Secretary of State Papers)

THE OCCUPATION OF HAVANA

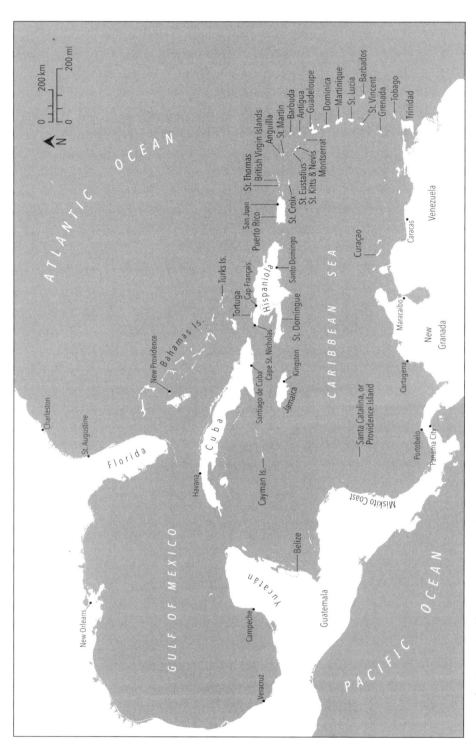

MAP 1 The Greater Caribbean Region. Drawn by Molly Roy

Introduction

The View from Havana

On the Sunday in June 1762 that a British war fleet appeared on Havana's horizon, María del Carmen had just recently bought her freedom. She likely earned the three hundred pesos that were necessary to do so on her days off from working for the man who owned her—by washing, cooking, cleaning, peddling, or selling her body in Havana's bustling urban economy. In Cuba, enslaved Africans could buy their freedom in installments, by a practice known as *coartación*. Just two months before British forces descended on Havana, María made her final payment. Now a moment of promise had suddenly turned into one of peril. How would she weather this invasion, and what would the possibility of the British seizure of Havana mean for her hard-won status? As María knew well, in British colonies purchasing one's own freedom was not permitted.[1]

She had not always been called María del Carmen. As a child in Jamaica, where she was born, she had a different name, given to her by her owner or perhaps her mother, most likely a native of Africa. At the age of eighteen, she was sold away from her home to a ship's captain from Cuba, who sailed her to Havana in the hold of his ship. There she was given a Spanish name and then sold again in the city where she would spend more than a decade. At the time that she purchased her freedom and British warships arrived offshore, she was thirty years old. Her youth had been spent in British Jamaica and her adulthood in Spanish Cuba, and now these two worlds of colonialism and slavery were violently colliding.

1. Manumission of Slaves, 1760–1765, Aug. 22, 1763, 161, JNA. Enslaved Africans sometimes received the sums to purchase their freedom from a free person of color who acted as sponsor. Because María del Carmen paid for her freedom in two installments, one of 250 pesos on November 16, 1761, and another of 50 pesos on April 29, 1762, it seems likely that she earned the money gradually rather than receiving it as a gift. See Alejandro de la Fuente, "Slaves and the Creation of Legal Rights in Cuba: Coartación and Papel," *HAHR*, LXXXVII (2007), 659–692; and Manuel Lucena Salmoral, "El derecho de coartación del esclavo en la américa española," *Revista de Indias*, LIX, no. 216 (1999), 357–374.

Sources do not tell us how María del Carmen survived the relentless cannonball bombardment or the outbreak of yellow fever that afflicted Havana during the six weeks that British forces besieged it in the summer of 1762. Nor do they tell us how she managed to navigate the eleven-month occupation that followed Havana's surrender, when British occupying forces ruled over Spanish Cuba's former capital. All we know is this: a year later, María del Carmen was on one of the many vessels departing Havana after the occupation ended. One month after Britain returned the city to Spain in the peace treaty that brought the Seven Years' War to a close, she was back in Jamaica. She was carrying with her the Spanish legal document certifying her free status—her *carta de libertad,* or freedom paper.

In Kingston, María del Carmen was able to get her Spanish legal document accepted as binding in the British colony, even though coartación was not a policy in Jamaica. The commercial worlds of Cuba and Jamaica were so closely linked that she managed to find a Jewish merchant there who knew the Havana notary who had penned her carta de libertad and would vouch for its authenticity to a government official. Thus, a woman whose personal history moved between British and Spanish islands found a way to take advantage of both the commercial circuits that ran between them and the transfer of sovereignty in Havana from Spain to Britain and back again. She had returned to the land of her birth and of her family no longer a slave.

At first glance, María del Carmen's story may seem little more than an interesting sidenote to the incident of imperial war and rivalry that is the primary subject of this book: the British invasion and occupation of Havana in 1762 and 1763, during the final stages of the Seven Years' War (1754–1763). But the interconnected world that María del Carmen's life reveals was both a cause and consequence of those events. Embedded in her manumission record in Jamaican archives is a history of Cuba's relations with the island of Jamaica and the Atlantic commercial system, centered on the slave trade. The Spanish ship's captain who bought her in Jamaica and sold her in Cuba, the silver pesos she earned in Havana to buy her freedom, the Jewish merchant in Kingston with ties to a Havana notary, the acceptance of a Spanish carta de libertad as valid in a British colony, all of those elements point to the emergence of a shared commercial space operating between Havana and Kingston along the contours of the slave trade. Havana's connections to Britain and British America at this time—and, through its slave traders and their captives, to West Africa—helped to drive the city's economic development and demographic growth, which in turn stoked British and British American desires to acquire the island and Spain's readiness to go to war to oppose their encroachments. Havana's engagements in the Atlantic world produced the British invasion and occupation, shaped the reactions of individuals on the island, and ultimately transformed long-standing Spanish policies regarding slavery and the slave trade as well as racial hierarchies on the island.

The Occupation of Havana is a *longue durée* history of the causes, central dynamics, and enduring consequences of an incident of eighteenth-century imperial warfare, the British invasion and eleven-month occupation of Havana at the end of the Seven Years' War. It situates the events in question within the narrative of a century of interactions between the Spanish and British empires and the evolving place of Cuba and its inhabitants in the Atlantic world, from the late seventeenth century to the onset of the Age of Revolutions. By focusing on the view from Havana before, during, and after this British campaign, the book offers a new understanding of the crucial role of the slave trade and African-descended peoples in the eighteenth century's imperial rivalries. It also revises our understandings of the place of slavery and the slave trade in the "Enlightened" imperial reforms that followed the end of the Seven Years' War and ushered in the Age of Revolutions.

When I began researching the British occupation of Havana, I did not expect to find people in the archives like María del Carmen. Her life defies expectations about the separateness of British and Spanish colonial space and the "British" and "Spanish" identities of the people who populated them. In fact, I wasn't even looking in the archive in Jamaica where she could be found. But I soon learned that merchants, privateers, slave traders, soldiers, smugglers, and the enslaved had long been sailing along the maritime routes that linked Havana to Kingston and other regions of the Atlantic world, well before British war ships appeared outside Havana's harbor. Neither empires nor imperial subjects were stable categories, and this long backstory of migration and exchange shaped the identities and responses of individuals in Havana to the British invasion and occupation of their city.[2]

2. Studies of interimperial migration and mobility in the Atlantic world have enriched our understanding of how individuals linked territories of rival colonial powers. Many of these works have focused on highly mobile, seafaring men. See, for example, Peter Linebaugh and Marcus Rediker, *The Many-Headed Hydra: Sailors, Slaves, Commoners, and the Hidden History of the Revolutionary Atlantic* (Boston, 2000); Julius Scott, "'Negroes in Foreign Bottoms': Sailors, Slaves, and Communication," in Laurent Dubois and Julius S. Scott, eds., *The Origins of the Black Atlantic* (New York, 2010), 69–98; and Scott, "The Common Wind: Currents of Afro-American Communication in the Era of the Haitian Revolution" (Ph.D. diss., Duke University, 1986); W. Jeffrey Bolster, *Black Jacks: African American Seamen in an Age of Sail* (Cambridge, Mass., 1997); Charlie Foy, "Maritime Populations," in Joseph C. Miller, ed., *The Princeton Companion to Atlantic History* (Princeton, N.J., 2015), 324–326; Ernesto Bassi, *An Aqueous Territory: Sailor Geographies and New Granada's Transimperial Greater Caribbean World* (Durham, N.C., 2016); and Jesse Cromwell, "More than Slaves and Sugar: Recent Historiography of the Trainsimperial Greater Caribbean and Its Sinew Populations," *History Compass*, XII (2014), 770–783. María's life offers a window onto lesser-studied itineraries, more personal and less commercial, that were nevertheless constitutive of these sites of Atlantic history. Her

These realizations informed my approach to reconstructing this history. From an early stage of the process, I envisioned this as an Atlantic story that would require research in multiple archives across a broad geographic and temporal frame. Focusing on colonial archives in only Spain or Cuba would reify imperial boundaries and make invisible people like María del Carmen, who moved between regions colonized by rival European crowns. Similarly, limiting my inquiry only to the period of the occupation would obscure how integrated and in fact mutually constitutive these supposedly separate imperial spaces actually were. This account thus relies on extensive multiarchival research into both the period before the British occupation, which is the least studied era in Cuba's past (roughly, 1600–1763), and the siege and occupation themselves. My goal is to restore the realities of an era in which connections and mobilities linked regions that historians still tend to treat as separate national and imperial units.[3]

There is another reason María del Carmen makes a fitting start. Her story recasts a momentous geopolitical conjuncture as a deeply personal struggle in the life of a woman born into slavery. Slave traders, the men and women in whom they trafficked, slaveholding whites, free people of color, sailors, soldiers, artisans, and servants—these were the individuals who built the British and Spanish empires and determined the outcome and legacy of a clash between them. This book thus combines a geopolitical and local lens, seeking out the relationship between imperial politics in London, Madrid, and Paris and the social and economic history of slaveowners and African-descended peoples in the Caribbean. I zoom in and out of Havana to show how imperial policy affected the lives of individuals, and individuals in turn shaped imperial policy. As we will see, the success or failure of this geopolitical contest— a clash between two competing imperial systems predicated on war, trade, and racial slavery—was determined by the actions of ordinary people in the Caribbean like María del Carmen.

In essence, the book represents a conceptual experiment in writing an Atlantic history of an event. It is a study of an event—rather, a series of events, both an invasion and an occupation—that relies on multiple, overlapping

---

migration and skillful navigation of multiple legal cultures is akin to that of Rosalie of the Poulard nation in Rebecca J. Scott and Jean M. Hébrard, *Freedom Papers: An Atlantic Odyssey in the Age of Emancipation* (Cambridge, 2012).

3. For Havana's importance in the Atlantic world in prior centuries, see Alejandro de la Fuente, with the collaboration of César García del Pino and Bernardo Iglesias Delgado, *Havana and the Atlantic in the Sixteenth Century* (Chapel Hill, N.C., 2008); and de la Fuente, "Sugar and Slavery in Early Colonial Cuba," in Stuart B. Schwartz, ed., *Tropical Babylons: Sugar and the Making of the Atlantic World, 1450–1680* (Chapel Hill, N.C., 2004), 115–157; and I. A. Wright, *The Early History of Cuba, 1492–1586* (New York, 1916).

temporal and spatial frames to tie together many different strands of history, historical actors, perspectives, and scales. William Sewell gives a helpful definition of a historical event, as opposed to just any old event, as a "sequence of occurrences that . . . is recognized as notable by contemporaries, and that . . . results in a durable transformation of structures." Because of Havana's strategic and economic value to European empires, the actions of individuals there had impacts that ranged broadly across different temporal and spatial scales and transformed structures both near and far. To do justice to this invasion and occupation and its many effects, I have tried to balance structure and event through the use of multiple storylines, a broad geographic lens, and the long timeframe that forms the spine of the book. Doing so has enabled me to incorporate both "British" and "Spanish" points of view, to foreground the integral part played by free and enslaved people of color, and to place all of the narrative on the Atlantic stage it requires.[4]

4. William H. Sewell, Jr., "Historical Events as Transformations of Structures: Inventing Revolution at the Bastille," in Sewell, *Logics of History: Social Theory and Social Transformation* (Chicago, 2005), 225–270, esp. 225, 228 (quotation). In general, during the period between the "conquest" and Age of Revolutions, Atlantic history has placed less emphasis on events and more on the movement of goods, peoples, ideas, and products throughout the Atlantic system. This tendency may be related to the influence of the Annales school and Fernand Braudel, who prioritized geography, climate, trade, migration patterns, and the ebb and flow of winds and currents across seas. In Braudel's famous work on the Mediterranean world, the realm of political events, or *histoire événementielle*, was the least important factor in historical change. See Fernand Braudel, *The Mediterranean and the Mediterranean World in the Age of Philip II*, trans. by Siân Reynolds (1940; rpt. New York, 1972), I, 21. On Atlantic history and microhistory, see Lara Putnam, "To Study the Fragments / Whole: Microhistory and the Atlantic World," *Journal of Social History*, XXXIX (2006), 615–630; Rebecca J. Scott, "Small-Scale Dynamics of Large-Scale Processes," *American Historical Review*, CV (2000), 472–479; James H. Sweet, "Mistaken Identities? Olaudah Equiano, Domingos Álvares, and the Methodological Challenges of Studying the African Diaspora," *AHR*, CXIV (2009), 279–306. In adopting multiple perspectives and story lines, I have taken my cue from Sweet, who has argued that "the 'truths' of Atlantic history cannot be confined to a singular genre of linear narrativity"; see Sweet, *Domingos Álvares, African Healing, and the Intellectual History of the Atlantic World* (Chapel Hill, N.C., 2011), 233. For the use of multiple narratives and perspectives in a work of Atlantic history, see also Inga Clendinnen, *Ambivalent Conquests: Maya and Spaniard in Yucatan, 1517–1570* (New York, 1987).
My approach has also been inspired by the many multifaceted studies of the Haitian Revolution—and slave rebellion in general—that follow the causes and impacts of events in and out of the Americas, Europe, and Africa. For examples of "Atlantic histories" of the Haitian Revolution, see C. L. R. James, *The Black Jacobins: Toussaint L'Ouverture and the San Domingo Revolution* (New York, 1938); Laurent Dubois, *Avengers of the New World: The Story of the Haitian Revolution* (Cambridge, Mass., 2004); David P. Geggus, ed., *The Impact of the Haitian Revolution in the Atlantic World* (Columbia, S.C., 2001); John K. Thornton, "'I Am the Subject of the King of Congo': African Political Ideology and the Haitian Revolution," *Journal of World History*, IV (1993), 181–214; and Thornton, "African Soldiers in the Haitian Revolution," *Journal of Caribbean History*, XXV, nos. 1–2 (1991), 58–80; Ashli White, *Encountering Revolution: Haiti and the Making of the Early Republic* (Baltimore, 2010); Scott and Hébrard, *Freedom Papers*; Sara E. Johnson, *The Fear of French Negroes: Transcolonial Collaboration in the Revolutionary Americas* (Berkeley, Calif., 2012); Susan Buck-Morss, *Hegel, Haiti, and Universal History* (Pittsburgh, 2009); Ada Ferrer, *Freedom's Mirror: Cuba and Haiti in the Age of Revolution* (New York, 2014); and James Alexander Dun, *Dangerous Neighbors: Making the Hai-*

The actions of individuals in Cuba had such wide-ranging impacts because the British siege and occupation of Havana was seen as profoundly significant at the time, even if today it is little remembered off the island of Cuba. María del Carmen had either the fortune or misfortune, or both, to live through a moment of great historical resonance. In the final years of the Seven Years' War—a war for empire that began in North America and went global—Britain sent a massive amphibious force to seize the city where she lived, the third most populous city in the Americas and one of its wealthiest. Following a string of prior conquests in Europe, North America, West Africa, India, and the Caribbean, this British naval campaign was part of a global strategy coordinated with an attack on Manila, the colonial capital of the Spanish Philippines. Britain's aim was to use Spain's late entry into the war on France's side to seize the crucial nodes that connected Spain to the global circulation of American silver and valuable Asian trade goods. The attack on Havana also promised to neutralize the largest and most strategic naval base in the Americas and potentially lead to the acquisition of a city and an island long coveted by Britons who sought markets for their goods and stepping-stones for trade.[5]

The battle plan had been rehearsed in numerous previous attempts to capture Spanish Caribbean territories, and this time British officials were determined to get it right. They mobilized a force of 28,400 soldiers, sailors, and enslaved Africans—more people than lived in any British American colonial city at the time—from Britain, British America, and the West Indies for this descent on the best-defended port in the Caribbean. Spanish soldiers and local militias from the island of Cuba, along with enslaved Africans who had been promised their freedom, fought off the attack for six suspenseful weeks, until British forces mined and blew up the fabled Morro fortress that stood at the entrance to Havana's harbor. In total, more than ten thousand lives were lost, the majority to an outbreak of yellow fever that laid waste to the opposing armies.[6]

---

tian Revolution in Early America (Philadelphia, 2016). The Occupation of Havana also builds on other studies of the local dynamics of imperial projects in the Caribbean: see, for example, David Wheat, Atlantic Africa and the Spanish Caribbean, 1570–1640 (Williamsburg, Va., and Chapel Hill, N.C., 2016); David Sartorius, Ever Faithful: Race, Loyalty, and the Ends of Empire in Spanish Cuba (Durham, N.C., 2013); and Anne Eller, We Dream Together: Dominican Independence, Haiti, and the Fight for Caribbean Freedom (Durham, N.C., 2016).

5. In the mid-eighteenth century, the most populous city in the hemisphere was Mexico City (approximately 110,000), followed by Lima (102,153), and Havana (50,000). For the population of Mexico City, see John Kicza, Colonial Entrepreneurs: Families and Business in Urban Mexico City (Albuquerque, N.M., 1983), 2; for Lima, see Adrian J. Pearce, "The Peruvian Population Census of 1725–1740," Latin American Research Review, XXXVI, no. 3 (2001), 99; and, for Havana, see Chapter 2.

6. In 1760, the population of Philadelphia was approximately 23,750, New York was 18,000, Boston was 15,631, Charleston was 8,000, and Newport was 7,500; see Carl Bridenbaugh, Cities in Re-

Despite its human and material costs, news of Havana's surrender was met with joyous bonfires, fireworks, balls, and providential sermons in British territories throughout the Atlantic world. In an address of thanksgiving delivered in New York, the Reverend Joseph Treat exclaimed, "What city, in all the Iberian dominions, is like unto this city, in riches and strength; And this is British property." British and British American merchants were eager to capitalize on the tremendous windfall presented by their sovereign's seizure of Havana. In the months after hostilities ceased, as many as seven hundred merchant ships sailed into Havana's harbor from North America, the West Indies, Britain, and Africa to sell food, merchandise, and enslaved Africans to eager buyers in the occupied city. Charles III of Spain was so humiliated by Havana's loss—contemporaries compared it to the defeat of Spain's celebrated Armada—that he was willing to give up all of Florida for its return in the peace treaty negotiated at the end of the war.[7]

There is no dearth of scholarship on the British siege and occupation of Havana, but there is a need for a new approach. Traditionally, histories of the siege—*"la toma de la Habana"* (the taking of Havana), as it is often called in Spanish—contextualize it within the parameters of the Seven Years' War. In contrast, studies of the occupation focus on its socioeconomic impact on Cuban sugar production in the years that immediately followed. But there is more to the story than just what occurred in Havana in the 1760s. By framing this study within a wider geographic and temporal landscape and engaging a deeper level of social history, the book yields a new set of arguments about the siege and occupation of Havana and the nature of war, trade, and slavery in eighteenth-century Cuba and the Atlantic world.[8]

---

volt: Urban Life in America, 1743–1776 (New York, 1955), 5. For the more than 10,000 dead, see J. R. McNeill, *Mosquito Empires: Ecology and War in the Greater Caribbean, 1620–1914* (New York, 2010), 186.

7. Joseph Treat, *A Thanksgiving Sermon, Occasion'd by the Glorious News of the Reduction of the Havannah* (New York, 1762), 9.

8. For discussions of the British invasion and occupation of Havana within the context of the Seven Years' War, see Francis Russell Hart, *The Siege of Havana, 1762* (London, 1931); David Syrett, ed., *The Siege and Capture of Havana, 1762* (London, 1970); David Greentree, *A Far-Flung Gamble: Havana 1762* (Long Island City, N.Y., 2010); Fred Anderson, *Crucible of War: The Seven Years' War and the Fate of Empire in British North America, 1754–1766* (New York, 2000), 497–518; Daniel Baugh, *The Global Seven Years War, 1754–1763: Britain and France in a Great Power Contest* (New York, 2011), 598–609, 632–639; and Hugh Thomas, *Cuba; or, The Pursuit of Freedom* (New York, 1998), 1–60. For Cuban and Spanish historiography on *"la toma de La Habana,"* see Pedro J. Guiteras, *Historia de la conquista de la Habana* (Philadelphia, 1856); Antonio Bachiller y Morales, *Cuba: Monografía histórica que comprende desde la pérdida de la Habana hasta la restauración española* (Havana, 1883); Emilio Roig de Leuchsenring, ed., *Como vio Jacobo de la Pezuela la toma de la Habana por los ingleses: Cuatro capítulos de su historia de la isla de Cuba y un fragmento de su diccionario geográfico, estadístico, histórico de la isla de Cuba* (Havana, 1962); Leuchsenring, ed., *Como vio Antonio J. Valdes la toma de la Habana por los ingleses: Libro quinto de su Historia de la Isla de Cuba y en especial de la Habana* (Havana, 1962);

First, as the life of María del Carmen illustrates, Havana was already a hybrid space before British warships forced their way into its harbor. The most powerful engine of that imperial integration was the trade in enslaved Africans; Britons coveted Spanish silver and used the slave trade and associated contraband to get it. British slave traders in Jamaica were Cuba's predominant source of enslaved Africans at the time, and in Cuba more than half of the population was of African descent. In Havana, enslaved Africans might speak the English they had learned in a British colony, and powerful merchants had commercial contacts in Kingston, Philadelphia, and London that had been brokered through the British slave trade. This finding contradicts a long-standing assumption, especially prevalent in the English-language scholarship, that credited the British occupation with busting open Spanish trade monopolies and catalyzing Cuba's sugar boom. Instead, Havana already had a powerful economic relationship with British slave traders and merchants that had allowed the city to grow strong and rich and made it a place coveted by the British. That relationship raised the ire of Spain, which fought a cycle of eighteenth-century wars to push back against British inroads.[9]

Secondly, the British slave trade to Cuba before the British invasion was larger than previously thought. This means that people of African descent occupied a greater variety of niches and played a more crucial role in the economy and society of eighteenth-century Cuba before its sugar boom than is often recognized. The Spanish crown relied on these Africans and their descendants to build Cuba's diversified economy and to serve in the militias and on the privateering ships that defended the island from repeated British incursions. Consequently, people of African descent were poised to play a critical part in the defense of Havana against British attack in 1762. Patterns of trans-

---

Guillermo Calleja Leal and Hugo O'Donnell y Duque de Estrada, *1762: La Habana inglesa: La toma de La Habana por los ingleses* (Madrid, 1999). For studies of the siege that have taken a somewhat longer historical view across the earlier decades of the eighteenth century, see Gustavo Placer Cervera, *Inglaterra y La Habana, 1762* (Havana, 2007); César García del Pino, *Toma de La Habana por los ingleses y sus antecedentes* (Havana, 2002); and McNeill, *Mosquito Empires,* 169–187. For studies that have dealt with the impact of the British occupation on Cuban sugar production, see, for example, Manuel Moreno Fraginals, *El ingenio: Complejo económico social cubano del azúcar,* I (Havana, 1964); Mercedes García Rodríguez, *La aventura de fundar ingenios: La refacción azucarera en la Habana del siglo XVIII* (Havana, 2004); García Rodríguez, *Entre haciendas y plantaciones: Orígenes de la manufactura azucarera en la Habana* (Havana, 2007); and Levi Marrero, *Cuba: Economía y sociedad,* 15 vols. (Madrid, [1972]–1992), VI, 120.

9. On hybrid spaces, see Jorge Cañizares-Esguerra and Benjamin Breen, "Hybrid Atlantics: Future Directions for the History of the Atlantic World," *History Compass,* XI (2013), 597–609. For histories that have credited the British occupation with busting open Spanish trade prohibitions and providing impetus to Havana's sugar boom, see, for example, Moreno Fraginals, *El ingenio;* Thomas, *Cuba;* Syrett, ed., *Siege and Capture of Havana;* Anderson, *Crucible of War;* and Baugh, *The Global Seven Years' War.*

imperial trade that had evolved over the preceding decades also meant that Havana's slave-trading elites were well equipped to exploit the commercial opportunities presented by the city's transfer to British sovereignty during its eleven-month occupation.[10]

Finally, the Spanish reoccupation of Havana in 1763 initiated a cascading set of changes that would remake Cuba and other areas of the Atlantic world—in more ways than historians have previously credited. For Spain, the sudden and disastrous loss of Havana altered ideas about what empires were and how the slave trade and people of African descent could help build them. No longer willing to rely on the British slave traders who had dominated the eighteenth-century trade, Spanish administrators embarked on a modernization project that transitioned Spain from a non-slave-trading nation to an eager investor in slavery's expansion in the decades that followed the Seven Years' War. In Cuba, these new pro-slave-trading policies of the Spanish government helped to set in motion a transformation that began to erode the traditional compacts between Africans and the sovereign that had been the foundation of Spanish colonialism. Though it hardly went as planned, this imperial policy shift helped Spain and Cuba become major slaving powers, catalyzing Cuba's sugar boom in the late eighteenth and early nineteenth centuries and flattening the variety of roles that people of African descent could play in the increasingly racialized landscape of the island. In the end, the men and women of African descent who fought and labored in Havana's defense—and their descendants—were betrayed by the changes their actions set in motion.

Seen in this light, the British invasion and occupation of a Spanish colonial space was not the radical rupture in Cuban history that it was once depicted as being. Instead, it represents the intensification of existing patterns and processes of interaction between Havana and its British neighbors that were directly connected to slavery, the slave trade, and populations of African descent. These dynamics played key roles in Cuba's economy and military before, during, and after the events that transpired in 1762 and 1763. It was Spain's novel response to events in Cuba—the decision to modernize

---

10. For studies of earlier eras that also argue for the crucial part people of African descent played in building Spanish colonialism, see Sherwin K. Bryant, *Rivers of Gold, Lives of Bondage: Governing through Slavery in Colonial Quito* (Chapel Hill, N.C., 2014); and Wheat, *Atlantic Africa*. On transimperial trade in the Greater Caribbean, see Wim Klooster, *Illicit Riches: Dutch Trade in the Caribbean, 1648–1795* (Leiden, 1998); and Klooster, "Inter-Imperial Smuggling in the Americas, 1600–1800," in Bernard Bailyn and Patricia L. Denault, eds., *Soundings in Atlantic History: Latent Structures and Intellectual Currents, 1500–1830* (Cambridge, Mass., 2009), 141–180; Linda M. Rupert, *Creolization and Contraband: Curaçao in the Early Modern Atlantic World* (Athens, Ga., 2012); Ernesto Bassi, *An Aqueous Territory: Sailor Geographies and New Granada's Transimperial Greater Caribbean World* (Durham, N.C., 2016); and Jesse Cromwell, *The Smugglers' World: Illicit Trade and Atlantic Communities in Eighteenth-Century Venezuela* (Williamsburg, Va., and Chapel Hill, N.C., 2018).

its empire through the expansion of slavery and the slave trade as a component of its ongoing rivalry with Britain—that led to a historic rupture on the island. Spain's process of reforming slavery and the slave trade was quite distinct and contrasted sharply with parallel processes in British, French, Portuguese, Dutch, and Danish polities in the wake of the Seven Years' War. Though Spain's imperial discourse was different from its rivals, its results would ultimately make Cuba look similar to neighboring Caribbean islands. Tragically, this chain of events also led to very painful transitions for the free and enslaved people of African descent who had found status and privilege for themselves in Cuba's social worlds before the advent of large-scale sugar plantation slavery at the end of the eighteenth century.[11]

As an intervention in the field of Atlantic history, *The Occupation of Havana* is part of a broader effort to emphasize the links between interconnected regions rather than solely to compare their differences. A long and rich tradition of discourse and scholarship has favored comparative approaches that emphasize imperial difference. This tendency has been especially pronounced when the topic of study is related to the Caribbean or to slavery; however, even studies of borderland regions in the Atlantic world more generally tend to compare neighboring imperial systems and depict the zones where they meet as points of rupture or contrast. The differences between imperial regimes matter, and this book emphasizes the way contemporaries sought to take advantage of divergences between various aspects of imperial culture, practice, and law (such as, for example, coartación). But, as the story of María del Carmen reveals, the divergent worlds of separate imperial historiographies do not accurately portray the converging world of the eighteenth-century Caribbean, where contested imperial zones developed close and mutually dependent relationships with one another during times of both war and peace.[12]

11. On this reform process across multiple European empires, see Pernille Røge, "A Natural Order of Empire: The Physiocratic Vision of Colonial France after the Seven Years' War," 32–52, esp. 35–36, 42, and Thomas Hopkins, "Adam Smith on American Economic Development and the Future of European Atlantic Empires," 53–75, esp. 66, both in Sophus A. Reinert and Røge, eds., *The Political Economy of Empire in the Early Modern World* (New York, 2013); Sophus A. Reinert, *Translating Empire: Emulation and the Origins of Political Economy* (Cambridge, 2011); John Shovlin, "War and Peace: Trade, International Competition, and Political Economy," 305–327, and Sophus A. Reinert, "Rivalry: Greatness in Early Modern Political Economy," 348–370, esp. 350, in Philip J. Stern and Carl Wennerlind, eds., *Mercantilism Reimagined: Political Economy in Early Modern Britain and Its Empire* (New York, 2014).

12. For emblematic comparative work on empires of the Atlantic world, see J. H. Elliott, *Empires of the Atlantic World: Britain and Spain in America, 1492–1830* (New Haven, Conn., 2006); Patricia Seed, *Ceremonies of Possession in Europe's Conquest of the New World, 1492–1640* (New York, 1995); Anthony Pagden, *Lords of All the World: Ideologies of Empire in Spain, Britain, and France, c. 1500– c. 1800* (New Haven, Conn., 1995); and Nicholas Canny and Philip Morgan, *The Oxford Handbook of the Atlantic World, 1450–1850* (New York, 2011). The canonical comparative work on slavery in the

The Occupation of Havana has three main parts, delineated by the events themselves: "Origins," "Events," and "Aftermaths." The first part examines the century before the siege of Havana and alternates between British and Spanish / Cuban perspectives. Chapter 1 charts British expansion into Caribbean waters claimed by Spain and developing conflict over commercial access to and political control over the island of Cuba. A deep-seated obsession with capturing Havana developed during these years of English and later British advance. In the early eighteenth century, the British-dominated slave trade to Spanish America and the contraband traffic that accompanied it led to conflicts with Spain that precipitated a cycle of wars. The Spanish monarchy sought exclusive political and commercial control over its overseas territories, yet, to its dismay, the local dynamics of these wars led to even more regional autonomy and integration. Through a cycle of eighteenth-century wars targeting Spanish America, British subjects developed closer commercial ties with Havana, and British commanders gained better knowledge of how to attack the city with each failed attempt.

Chapter 2 casts a "Havana-eye-view" on the way its residents positioned themselves inside and outside both British and Spanish sovereignty during the decades that preceded the British invasion. Well before the British war fleet began its siege of Havana, contraband and the British-dominated slave trade had already transformed the city into a hybrid space, mutually constituted with its British American neighbors. The African peoples brought to Cuba in predominantly British slaving ships were bought and sold as goods, yet, upon arrival, they and their descendants were also regarded as future loyal Spanish subjects, vital economic contributors, and crucial defenders of the king's realms in a climate of heightened imperial war and rivalry. Havana's merchants and landowners built a successful economy that profited from both trading with the enemy and making war against them through privateering and wartime transimperial trade. These prevailing patterns of war, trade, and slavery help to explain the reactions of individuals in Havana to the British siege and occupation of their city.

The second part, on the invasion and occupation, treats the two phases of the central events in Cuba as separate but parallel processes, with their own protagonists and outcomes. Chapter 3 focuses on the critical role of people of

---

Americas is Frank Tannenbaum, *Slave and Citizen: The Negro in the Americas* (New York, 1963); see also, for example, Laura Foner and Eugene D. Genovese, eds., *Slavery in the New World: A Reader in Comparative History* (Englewood Cliffs, N.J., 1969); and Ariela Gross and Alejandro de la Fuente, "Slaves, Free Blacks, and Race in the Legal Regimes of Cuba, Louisiana, and Virginia," *North Carolina Law Review*, XCI (2013), 1699–1756. This book builds off the model of "entangled history" proposed by Eliga H. Gould; see Gould, "Entangled Histories, Entangled Worlds: The English-Speaking Atlantic as a Spanish Periphery," *AHR*, CXII (2007), 764–786.

African descent during the siege. British war commanders had counted on a formidable defense of Havana from the Spanish soldiers stationed there, but what surprised them was the vigorous part played by free and enslaved people of color on the front lines of the defense. Not all people of African descent present at the siege acted in support of either the British or the Spanish war effort. But in general blacks in Havana made the siege so protracted that the British almost failed; its armies ended up losing more men to a virulent yellow fever outbreak than they had in the entire Seven Years' War in North America. The defense of Havana was so fierce that it took down a massive British army and severely limited plans for the occupation.

Chapter 4 focuses on Havana elites during the city's eleven-month occupation by British forces. Eager to trade for goods and enslaved Africans with their frequent commercial partners, Havana's elite residents ended up betraying those who had fought so hard to ward off the British attack. During the occupation, they cozied up to the British commander Lord Albemarle and seized commercial opportunities in the hybrid space they so often occupied, where layers of British and Spanish sovereignty overlapped. Ultimately, Albemarle's army was too weak and his governing practices were too corrupt for the occupation to have a lasting economic impact on Havana, but in the meantime the city's leading merchants and landowners managed to shape the period of British rule to their own advantage.

The third part moves across the fifty years after the occupation, exploring Spain's efforts to reconstitute its authority in Havana (Chapter 5) and the many reverberations of the occupation throughout broader Atlantic and global systems (Chapter 6). The actions of individuals in Cuba during this crucial episode of fighting and occupying revised understandings in the metropole that would go on to shape new policies with global ramifications. The exemplary service of black soldiers in defending Cuba from attack helped to convince the Spanish state of the "utility" of Africans for achieving its imperial ambitions and the wisdom of procuring, on its own, more populations of African descent for its overseas colonies. In addition, disloyalty among elites during the occupation convinced Spain that the way to tie the island better to its sovereign was to make more enslaved Africans available to these eager buyers.

Chapter 6 charts the wide-ranging impacts of new Spanish policies throughout the Atlantic world and then returns to the local story in Havana. Spain's Enlightenment-inspired reforms of the eighteenth century included new efforts to break into the slave trade, promote the military service of Spain's black subjects, and rationalize policies with regard to its populations of African descent in both Cuba and greater Spanish America. During this period, Spain took unprecedented measures to promote transatlantic human trafficking, including the annexation in 1778 of what would become its only sub-Saharan African colony, Equatorial Guinea, as well as the tightening of ties to the Spanish Philippines, which was seen as an essential source of goods for exchange in the slave trade. In the decades that followed the Seven Years' War, the men of African descent who had defended Cuba from British attack in 1762 sought the continuation and expansion of their many roles buttressing Spanish colonialism; however, white elites in Havana wanted new departures in Spanish imperial political economy and persuaded policy makers in Madrid to grant them. Their efforts remade the political economy of the island and more severely restricted the traditional privileges of free black soldiers and all people of African descent.

Through a chain of consequences, intended and unintended, that unfolded over the decades that followed, the invasion and occupation of Havana ended up strengthening slavery and white hegemony in Cuba. By the 1790s and early 1800s, the time of the Haitian Revolution, the Spanish colony of Cuba would look more like its Caribbean neighbors, and free people of color like María del Carmen would lose some of the leverage they had traditionally enjoyed by playing competing imperial systems off against one another. In the summer of 1762, however, that outcome was not visible on the horizon. In the events that transpired and the struggle over their interpretation, a clash of competing visions for the island's future had yet to unfold.

[handwritten marginal note: and it not would happened have anyway?]

PART I Origins

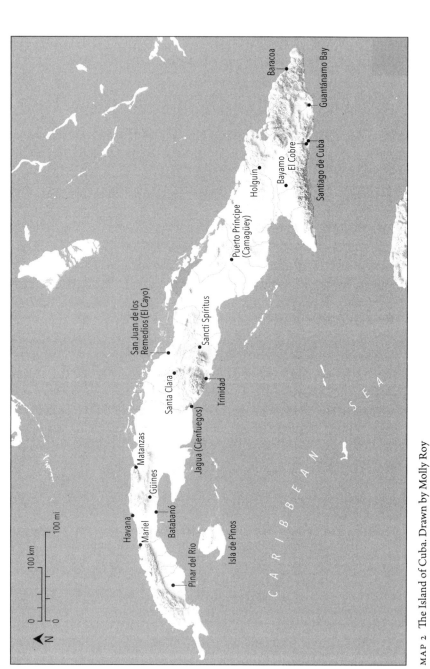

MAP 2 The Island of Cuba. Drawn by Molly Roy

1

. . .

Imagining the Conquest

A Deep History of British Plots against Havana

On the morning of June 6, 1762, a British squadron of thirty British warships and more than two hundred transport and support vessels arrived off the coast of Havana. This was one of the largest joint naval and army expeditionary forces ever assembled in the Americas. Aboard the vessels offshore were ten thousand sailors, twelve thousand soldiers, two thousand enslaved Africans, and six hundred free black militia, raised from all over Britain, British North America, and the West Indies. These were not just English, Irish, Scottish, North American, and West Indian subjects of the British crown but also soldiers and sailors from Africa, France, Germany, Portugal, Sweden, Italy, and even Spain. Among those caught within the expedition's net were a free black sailor from Curaçao and two Native American veterans of the siege of Quebec. The expedition's ranks included women as well as men. British officers had acquired enslaved women as their servants and forced mistresses and brought them on the Havana campaign. Other women in the squadron worked as nurses on the hospital ships, caring for the soldiers and sailors already wracked by yellow fever.[1]

1. For a full accounting of the expedition's numbers, see Chapter 3. For identities of the soldiers and sailors, see lists of deserters in the Havana Governor's Correspondence: AGI, SD, 1585 and 1586. For the free black sailor from Curaçao, see "Relación de los desertores ingleses y franceses que se hallan en el Castillo de la Real Fuerza," July 24, 1762, AGI, SD, 1586, no. 200. Henry Fletcher, an English officer at the siege of Martinique, claimed that Captain Kennedy's company had "two real Indians" who had joined the expedition from Quebec. Unless they fell sick in Martinique, they would have continued on the Havana campaign. See "Disposition for the Attack of the French Redoubts," Jan. 24, 1762, in "Seven Years' War Journal of the Proceedings of the 35th Regiment of Foot, by a British Officer, and Illustrated by a Military Engineer," Codex Eng 41, JCBL. On women with the expedition, see "Order Book Kept by Major Moncrieffe of the Voyage and Campaigns from New York, Martinique, Grenada, and Havanna," Frederick Mackenzie Collection, National Archives of Canada, Ottawa; "Orderly Book of the Havana Expedition," in *The Two Putnams: Israel and Rufus, in the Havana Expedition 1762, and in the Mississippi River Exploration 1772–73, with Some Account of the Company of Military Adventurers* (Hartford, Conn., 1931), 76; Anonymous letter, circa fall 1763, Establecimiento de rentas e intendencia de La Habana, AGS, Superintendencia de Hacienda, 2342.

In the diversity of its passengers and their far-flung origins, this military convoy off Havana marked a seminal moment in Atlantic history: the convergence of so many peoples from Africa, Europe, and the Americas in a single military force carrying out an attack against the most strategic and populous city in the Caribbean. Traditionally, the elaborate coordination required to bring this vast expedition together has been interpreted as the culmination of a global war eight years in the making. In 1762, the war that spawned the Havana expedition—the Seven Years' War—was actually eight years on. It had started, not with declarations of war in Europe, but a battle involving British, French, and Native peoples in the Ohio River valley of North America, had moved to Europe, and then gone global. By this point, the British fiscal-military state had reached a heightened level of efficiency, which made such a swift and sizable deployment possible. The advantage had already swung from France to Britain when, in August 1761, the Spanish king decided to enter into a secret family pact and ally himself with his fellow Bourbon monarch against Britain. When Britain found out, it declared war on Spain and launched coordinated attacks on Havana and Manila. The official instructions to commanders proclaimed the attacks a swift means to end the war by forcing Spain and France to the negotiating table with a dramatic blow to Spain's global commerce.[2]

The Seven Years' War provided the immediate context for this British assault on Havana—and the related, smaller one against Manila, undertaken jointly with the East India Company—but a plan the size and scope of Britain's Havana campaign could come together only after many years of plotting. By the standards of any era, but especially the eighteenth century, the expedition took shape with remarkable speed and precision. Any potential setbacks

2. For discussions of the Havana and Manila campaigns within the context of the Seven Years' War, see Fred Anderson, *Crucible of War: The Seven Years' War and the Fate of Empire in British North America, 1754–1766* (New York, 2000), 497–518; Daniel Baugh, *The Global Seven Years' War, 1754–1763: Britain and France in a Great Power Contest* (New York, 2011), 598–609, 632–639; and Richard Middleton, *The Bells of Victory: The Pitt-Newcastle Ministry and the Conduct of the Seven Years' War, 1757–1762* (London, 1985), 210. For a narrative of the build-up across the eighteenth century of the British "fiscal-military state" and its role in the expansion of British empire, see John Brewer, *The Sinews of Power: War, Money, and the English State, 1688–1783* (London, 1989), 205 (quotation). For Spain's entry into the Seven Years' War, see Vicente Palacio Atard, *El tercer pacto de familia* (Madrid, 1945); Anderson, *Crucible of War*, 484–502, esp. 484; Gustavo Placer Cervera, *Inglaterra y la Habana, 1762* (Havana, 2007), 62–63. According to Admiral Rodney's instructions, the king's aim was to make "some signal and effectual impression on the Spanish colonies in the West Indies"; see Admiralty to Rear-Admiral George Rodney, Feb. 5, 1762, in David Syrett, ed., *The Siege and Capture of Havana, 1762* (London, 1970), 23. For the king's instructions to Admiral Draper for the Manila expedition, see "George Rex, Secret Instructions to Our Trusty and Well-Beloved William Draper Esq. Brigadier General, Court of St. James, 21 January 1762," Petworth House Arhives, HMC 162, fols. 8–19, West Sussex Record Office, Chichester, U.K.

were anticipated in advance, as though it were a campaign that had been well rehearsed. Within three days of Britain's declaration of war against Spain on January 4, 1762, the Havana expedition's chosen land commander, George Keppel, third Earl of Albemarle, had received his preliminary orders. Within two short months, Albemarle and the sea commander, Sir George Pocock, sailed out of the British harbor at Spithead for the West Indies with four thousand troops, four battleships, one frigate, and sixty-four transport ships. Their orders were to join forces in the Caribbean with Admiral George Rodney, whose eight thousand men from Britain and North America, fresh from the capture of Quebec, were then engaged in a siege of Martinique.[3]

As a target, Havana was considered so important and the elements of speed and surprise so crucial that Rodney was instructed to abandon Martinique in favor of the Havana expedition if the French island had not yet surrendered. The plan was then to raise in Jamaica two thousand enslaved Africans to assist with the siege and an additional militia force of five hundred free men of African descent, for whom the expedition was carrying arms and uniforms from England. Fearing potential delays in Jamaica from planters reluctant to part with their enslaved workers, Albemarle purchased one hundred enslaved Africans while still at Martinique and dispatched an agent to Antigua and Saint Kitts, where he purchased and hired five hundred more enslaved blacks.[4]

Immediately upon the decision to attack Havana, the British secretary of state for the Southern Department, the Earl of Egremont, had written to Major General Jeffrey Amherst in North America to requisition four thousand North American troops. They were supposed to rendezvous with the Havana campaign off Cape Saint Nicolas on the northwestern coast of French Saint Domingue and then proceed to the assault on Havana. It had been determined that the best way to surprise Havana was to approach it by the uncommon and more dangerous route, navigating the Old Bahamas Channel along the north coast of Cuba against the current, from east to west (see Figure 1). The fleet thus had to rely on local pilots recruited from the British Bahamas and lead ships that set bonfires on the keys off the north coast to prevent the expedition from running aground at night. At the same time, colonial governors in New Jersey, New York, Rhode Island, and Connecticut were

3. "Pocock's Journal," Mar. 5, 1762, in Syrett, ed., *Siege and Capture of Havana*, 57; Syrett, "Introduction," ibid., xiii–xx; Francis Russell Hart, *The Siege of Havana, 1762* (Boston, 1931), 20; Anderson, *Crucible of War*, 516.

4. Admiralty to Rear-Admiral George Rodney, [Feb. 5], 1762, 23–26, Egremont to Major-General the Hon. Robert Monckton, Feb. 5, 1762, 26–28, Egremont to Governor William Henry Lyttelton, Jan. [4], 1762, 21, and Albemarle to Egremont, May 27, 1762, 137, all in Syrett, ed., *Siege and Capture of Havana*.

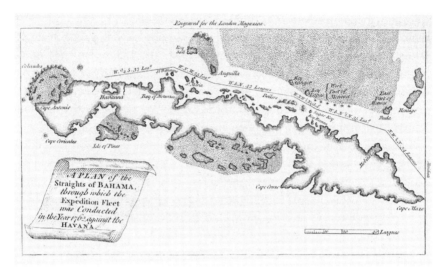

FIGURE 1 Map of the Route of Approach. From *London Magazine*, XXXII (January 1763), 41. After rendezvousing off Cape Saint Nicolas, Saint Domingue, in the Windward Passage, the fleet sailed across the north coast of Cuba through the perilous Old Bahamas Channel, against the winds and currents and through many shoals and keys. Local pilots were sent from the Bahamas and Jamaica to help guide the expedition, including three Spaniards and one free man of color; however, the lead ship, the *Richmond,* ended up sounding the channel itself in advance of the expedition. Courtesy, Cuban Heritage Collection, University of Miami

raising volunteer regiments to join the force. And, through networks of associates and subagents, merchants in London, Bristol, Philadelphia, Charleston, Bridgetown, Kingston, and other colonial ports were also spreading the word to send cargoes of goods and enslaved Africans to Cuba's capital city, which might soon be in British hands.[5]

As evidenced by the tremendous size and scope of the campaign, British war planners and many British subjects wanted to acquire Havana very badly, and they were willing to go to great lengths to achieve their goal. The British fleet's sudden arrival in Havana's waters had required swift and extensive coordination between Britain, North America, and the West Indies and the active support and involvement of not only the metropole but also a larger colonial system. Not all those involved were propelled by the same motivations, or equally helpful to the organizers, and far from all of those partici-

5. Albemarle's Secret Instructions, [Feb. 15], 1762, 33–36, Egremont to Major-General Sir Jeffrey Amherst, Jan. 13, 1762, 9–12, both ibid.; Lord Egremont to Governor William Shirley, Jan. 12, 1762, CO 117.1, fol. 9, TNA; César García del Pino, *Toma de La Habana por los ingleses y sus antecedentes* (Havana, 2002), 73; Placer Cervera, *Inglaterra y La Habana*, 120–126; Governor William Shirley to George Pocock, New Providence, Bahamas, Mar. 29, 1762, CO ADM 1.237, fol. 41, TNA.

pating were doing so by choice. But the campaign could not have coalesced without the many individuals across Britain and its colonies working together on a shared goal.

The largest and most ambitious British amphibious expedition of the Seven Years' War, the siege of Havana was more than just another battle in that protracted conflict between Britain and France—and now its Bourbon ally, Spain. Rather, the war presented a convenient opportunity in a larger, overarching British struggle to gain a foothold in Spanish America, an objective that was a driving force in its push for overseas expansion. From the age of the Elizabethan sea dogs to the 1760s, British ships had made a total of twelve attempts against Havana. The scope, conception, and aims of the Havana campaign of 1762 would not have been possible without plotting and prior attempts against Spanish America—some successful, others not—stretching across previous centuries. In fact, the British government was able to coordinate such rapid action against Havana in 1762 because the war plans it enacted had been formulated and fine-tuned during a series of earlier eighteenth-century wars against Spain, culminating in the Anglo-Spanish War of 1739.[6]

Across this period of British expansion and Spanish defense, the slave trade and commerce drew the two monarchs and their overseas territories into increasing connectedness and conflict. Knowledge gained through these interconnections made British subjects better able to target territories claimed by the Spanish monarch and ever more eager to do so. The inroads into Spanish America made by British explorers, merchants, slave traders, and settlers over the centuries roused opposition from Spain, snarling the two monarchies into wars in which Spain's British enemy kept trying to seize Cuba. It was because of the experience gained in all these escalating attempts—dealing with the challenges of amphibious siege warfare and the ravages of tropical disease on troops in the Caribbean climate—that British war planners and commanders were able to orchestrate the juggernaut that arrived offshore of Havana during the Seven Years' War. It was thus not just the Seven Years' War that brought a campaign of this size and scale to Havana but also underlying conditions of

---

6. David Greentree, *A Far-Flung Gamble: Havana 1762* (Long Island City, N.Y., 2010), 4, 76. Gustavo Placer Cervera and César García del Pino have contextualized the Havana campaign within a longer narrative of British attempts against Havana stretching back to Sir Francis Drake. Richard Pares linked the Havana campaign of 1762 to the hopes and projects of the War of Jenkins' Ear in *War and Trade in the West Indies, 1739–1763* (New York, 1936), 590. On the twelve prior attempts on Havana, see Cervera, *Inglaterra y la Habana*, 43. By contrast, no European power had attacked Manila since Spain's seizure, and the only previous attack had been that of the Chinese pirate and warlord Limahong in 1574. The Anglo-Spanish War of 1739 is commonly known as the War of Jenkins' Ear, especially in English. It merged with the War of the Austrian Succession and lasted until 1748.

Anglo-Spanish imperial connection and conflict that had set the two monarchies on a centuries-long collision course.

The ambition to annex Cuba was a deep and abiding preoccupation of the British political imaginary. The British colonial system needed markets to purchase the goods and enslaved Africans it brought to sell and stepping-stones to protect and expand its trade, and it was willing to go to great lengths to seize them in times of both war and peace. There was no single approach to empire driving eighteenth-century British expansion, but this fixation on the island of Cuba and its principal port reveals the way a desire for commerce blended with a desire for conquest in pursuit of the same goal. To explain the causes of Britain's expedition to invade Havana in 1762, it is necessary to understand the long history of early English imperial expansion into American territories claimed by Spain and the cycle of eighteenth-century Anglo-Spanish wars over trade and slavery that resulted.[7]

Early English Designs on Spanish America

The motivations behind the British campaign against Havana during the Seven Years' War have deep origins in early English expansion in the Atlantic world. Though more idealistic or intrepid origin stories may be cited, that expansion was driven by the desire to take the Americas and their riches away from Spain. In the wake of the Protestant Reformation, early English colonization developed as an anti-Spanish project. Leading the first forays of Elizabethan imperialism, Elizabeth I's notorious sea dogs, John Hawkins, Walter Ralegh, and Francis Drake, sought to plunder the great treasure of Spanish America and thus both enrich Protestant England and thwart Catholic Spain's ability to fund wars in Europe. In turn, their efforts shaped the contours of Spanish colonialism. In response to the threat from English, Dutch, and French pirating raids, in the late sixteenth century Philip II of Spain adopted the defensive system of treasure galleons and fortified Caribbean port cities. The treasure

---

7. Historians of eighteenth-century Britain have described its imperialism in different ways. See, for example, Steve Pincus, "Addison's Empire: Whig Conceptions of Empire in the Early 18th Century," *Parliamentary History*, XXXI (2012), 99–117. In the words of David Armitage, the British empire would be "Protestant, commercial, maritime, and free" (Armitage, *The Ideological Origins of the British Empire* [New York, 2004], 195). For notions of empire in eighteenth-century Britain, see, for example, J. H. Elliott, *Empires of the Atlantic World: Britain and Spain in America, 1492–1830* (New Haven, Conn., 2006), chap. 8; Anthony Pagden, *Lords of All the World: Ideologies of Empire in Spain, Britain, and France, c. 1500–c. 1800* (New Haven, Conn., 1995); and Sophus A. Reinert, "Rivalry: Greatness in Early Modern Political Economy," in Philip J. Stern and Carl Wennerlind, eds., *Mercantilism Reimagined: Political Economy in Early Modern Britain and Its Empire* (New York, 2014), 348–370, esp. 350.

galleons that gathered in Havana's harbor before convoying immense riches on their transatlantic passage back to Spain were a crucial component of the city's enduring allure.[8]

From their earliest forays into the Caribbean, English adventurers, including Hawkins, Drake, and Christopher Newport, used the sale of enslaved Africans as a wedge to force their way into protected Spanish American ports and markets. From the 1560s through the 1590s, Elizabethan contrabandists, pirates, and privateers robbed or purchased enslaved Africans from Portuguese slave traders and then sailed to the Spanish Caribbean, where they offered them for sale in an effort to coerce the opening of closed markets. Since the Treaty of Alcáçovas of 1479, which had divided the non-European, non-Christian world between Spain and Portugal, Spain had lacked a trading or territorial foothold in West Africa. Consequently, it relied on Portuguese and other foreign slave traders for the African laborers and subjects that made its colonial project possible. Exploiting this weakness, French and then English opportunists sought to lure Spanish subjects in the Americas into trade prohibited by their monarch with the promise of enslaved Africans they could not do without. This tactic turned out to be more of a false start than a continuous practice, but it established a pattern. From the start, English and Spanish expansion in the Atlantic world was entangled around the routes of the slave trade.[9]

English investors and adventurers, though, wanted more than just the immediate windfalls received from successful individual voyages. They also sought the acquisition of new territories in Spanish America that would provide strategic points from which they could prey on the Spanish galleons and

8. Kenneth R. Andrews, *The Spanish Caribbean: Trade and Plunder, 1530–1630* (New Haven, Conn., 1978); and Andrews, *Trade, Plunder, and Settlement: Maritime Enterprise and the Genesis of the British Empire, 1480–1630* (Cambridge, Mass., 1984), 9; Carl Bridenbaugh and Roberta Bridenbaugh, *No Peace beyond the Line: The English in the Caribbean, 1624–1690* (New York, 1972); Carla Gardina Pestana, *Protestant Empire: Religion and the Making of the British Atlantic World* (Philadelphia, 2009), 44, 63–65.

9. Andrews, *The Spanish Caribbean*, 108–133; Mark G. Hanna, *Pirate Nests and the Rise of the British Empire, 1570–1740* (Williamsburg, Va., and Chapel Hill, N.C., 2015), 39; Kris Lane, *Pillaging the Empire: Piracy in the Americas, 1500–1750* (Armonk, N.Y., 1998), 34–40; Gregory E. O'Malley, *Final Passages: The Intercolonial Slave Trade of British America, 1619–1807* (Williamsburg, Va., and Chapel Hill, N.C., 2014), 86–94; Paul W. Mapp, *The Elusive West and the Contest for Empire, 1713–1763* (Williamsburg, Va., and Chapel Hill, N.C., 2011), 271. There is a rich historiography on the foundational role people of African descent played building Spanish colonialism. Two publications that make that argument explicitly and focus on the sixteenth and early seventeenth century are Sherwin K. Bryant, *Rivers of Gold, Lives of Bondage: Governing through Slavery in Colonial Quito* (Chapel Hill, N.C., 2014), and David Wheat, *Atlantic Africa and the Spanish Caribbean, 1570–1640* (Williamsburg, Va., and Chapel Hill, N.C., 2016). This period loosely corresponds with the union of the crowns of Spain and Portugal between 1580 and 1640.

expand their trade in goods and humans with Spanish American settlements. The first English attempt at settlement in North America, Ralegh's ill-fated Roanoke Colony, was designed as a privateering base, established close to the routes of Spanish galleons exiting the Caribbean. Like the French, the Dutch, and the Danes, English subjects in the seventeenth century also opportunistically seized sparsely populated Spanish possessions, a practice they justified according to the principle of "effective occupation." Land deemed not properly utilized could be confiscated, the same logic British settlers would unleash against Native Americans in North America. Whether England and Spain or England and Native American nations were technically at war with one another during these offensive operations mattered little. Raiding, trading, invading, and occupying were all fundamental elements of English expansion, developed in tandem with their European rivals.[10]

Not only financial interests but also ideological ones drove early English expansionists forward. The Black Legend of Spanish colonialism provided motivation for these inroads, shaped their design, and influenced English attitudes across many centuries. As it did for Dutch Protestants in their wars against Spain, the Black Legend played an important part in mobilizing and fueling English animosity toward "Papist Spain." The publication of Bartolomé de las Casas's *Brief Account of the Destruction of the Indies*—with its numerous print runs in Amsterdam and London—fed propagandistic accounts of the essentially true horrors experienced by many indigenous peoples in the Americas at the hands of Spanish conquerors and colonizers. First published in England in 1583 as *The Spanish Colonie,* the text and its inherent condemnation of Spanish colonialism reappeared in print each time a war was declared against Spain or an expedition was launched. Las Casas's stories of Spanish brutality, illustrated by Dutch woodcuts depicting bloody and sensationalized scenes, convinced English readers of the moral rectitude of their project and the ease with which it could be accomplished. Despite their own use of enslaved Africans as an avenue into Spanish American markets, English adventurers imagined themselves as avengers and liberators of Spanish America's subjugated indigenous and African peoples, who, if given the opportunity, would rise up in arms and join them against their oppressors.[11]

10. For "effective occupation," see Pares, *War and Trade in the West Indies,* 4. The idea of *res nullius,* or "empty things," justified the seizure of lands if put to proper use by agriculture. See Pagden, *Lords of All the World,* chap. 3 (quotations on 76 and 77).

11. *The Spanish Colonie; or, Briefe Chronicle of the Acts and Gestes of the Spaniardes in the West Indies . . .* (London, 1583). See also its reissuance at the time of Oliver Cromwell's Western Design as *The Tears of the Indians: Being an Historical and True Account of the Cruel Massacres and Slaughters of Above Twenty Millions of Innocent People . . . ,* trans. J[ohn] Phillips (London, 1656). On the Black

The self-gratifying, moralizing notion that subjects of England would liberate the peoples of Spanish America filtered into battle plans and affected the actions of those who made decisions during campaigns. This thinking was bolstered by Sir Francis Drake's claim in the 1570s to have found willing allies in Panama among the indigenous and African maroon chiefs who shared his view of the Spanish as their enemies. The enduring memory of Drake's avowed collaboration led Sir Walter Ralegh to expect, falsely, that he would receive a liberator's welcome from the Native peoples of Guiana in 1595. Though it is a common conceit of invading armies to imagine themselves liberators, English attackers held onto this self-image with peculiar tenacity across the centuries. Because of it, they were prone to grossly underestimating the resistance they would face and thus risked tremendous losses among their own troops.[12]

After the eventual consolidation of successful settlement on the Chesapeake, English adventurers and the joint-stock companies that funded them went on to establish outposts around the fringes of the Spanish Caribbean at Saint Kitts (or Saint Christopher), Barbados, Nevis, Providence Island, Montserrat, and Antigua in the 1620s and 1630s (see Map 1). There they followed the Dutch and the French, who had occupied Spanish-claimed territory most prominently at Saint Eustatius (1600), Tobago (1632–1654), Guadeloupe (1635), and Martinique (1635). The short-lived English colony at Providence Island was planned as a beachhead for the founding of a great colony in Central America, which it was thought would draw settlers from the less promising settlement at Massachusetts Bay. The third of three Spanish attacks eliminated the English colony there in 1641, but the overall threat to Spanish

---

Legend, see Charles Gibson, *The Aztecs under Spanish Rule: A History of the Indians of the Valley of Mexico, 1519–1810* (Stanford, Calif., 1964); Christopher Schmidt-Nowara and John M. Nieto-Phillips, eds., *Interpreting Spanish Colonialism: Empires, Nations, and Legends* (Albuquerque, N.M., 2005); Walter S. Maltby, *The Black Legend in England: The Development of Anti-Spanish Sentiment, 1558–1660* (Durham, N.C., 1971); Carla Gardina Pestana, "Cruelty and Religious Justifications for Conquest in the Mid-Seventeenth-Century English Atlantic," in Linda Gregerson and Susan Juster, eds., *Empires of God: Religious Encounters in the Early Modern Atlantic* (Philadelphia, 2011), 37–57, esp. 44; Richard L. Kagan, "Prescott's Paradigm: American Historical Scholarship and the Decline of Spain," *American Historical Review,* CI (1996), 423–446; and Ricardo García Carcel, *La leyenda negra: Historia y opinión* (Madrid, 1992). Jorge Cañizares-Esguerra has argued that English Protestants initially saw New World expansion as a battle against a Spanish Catholic devil; see Cañizares-Esguerra, *Puritan Conquistadors: Iberianizing the Atlantic, 1550–1700* (Stanford, Calif., 2006), 8–9, 27–28.

12. Maroons are Africans who escaped from slavery and formed independent communities, sometimes mixing with indigenous inhabitants. For Sir Francis Drake in Panama, see Lane, *Pillaging the Empire,* 40–43; Andrews, *The Spanish Caribbean,* 139–141, 150–153; and Edmund S. Morgan, *American Slavery, American Freedom: The Ordeal of Colonial Virginia* (New York, 1975), 9–24. On Sir Walter Ralegh in Guyana, see his *Discoverie of the Large, Rich, and Beuutiful Empire of Guiana . . .* (London, 1596); and Karen Ordahl Kupperman, *Providence Island, 1630–1641: The Other Puritan Colony* (New York, 1993), 92.

settlements grew as the English interlopers gained footholds elsewhere in the region.[13]

Slowly and inexorably, English seventeenth-century efforts were resulting in a network of linked trading places in the Greater Caribbean region. These holdings encroached on Spanish-claimed territories but also fed off them like parasites. Following a proven strategy honed by other powers in the Mediterranean during the late Middle Ages and along the coast of West Africa in the fifteenth century, England's seizures of territory were effectively creating a chain of islands connected by favorable sea-lanes. These islands would facilitate access to the treasure galleons and trading places on this largely Spanish-controlled sea.[14]

In the early modern Age of Sail, European monarchs and their subjects coveted islands and their ports for many reasons. On long shipboard voyages, they were "like oases are to desert nomads." Pirates, traders, and adventurers all needed well-located stopping-off places where they could clean and repair their ships and take on more provisions. In the warm waters of the Caribbean, wooden vessels would rot in little more than a year if they were not careened, which entailed pulling a ship out of the water and tipping it on its side to scrape and repair the hull. For proper maintenance, every two to four months the barnacles, worms, plants, and other living creatures that had attached themselves to the ship had to be removed and the hull recoated with natural tar or pitch. A good, deep harbor was crucial for this work. Islands also offered sailors protection from enemy ships and hurricanes, and they provided merchants with hubs to warehouse their goods and gain valuable local information for coordinating trade.[15]

In all the plotting and targeting among imperial powers in the Atlantic, the island of Cuba and its principal port, Havana, were frequent objects of desire. Havana is situated at the entrance to the Bahamas Channels, which provide access to the Gulf Stream, the most convenient and fastest route for ships sailing from America to Europe. The advantages of its location were not lost on Philip II of Spain when he established the port as the meeting point of

13. Kupperman, *Providence Island*, ix, 1, 16.

14. John Gillis, *Islands of the Mind: How the Human Imagination Created the Atlantic World* (New York, 2004), 87–92. The "islands" in this network were on either land or sea. See S. Max Edelson, *The New Map of Empire: How Britain Imagined America before Independence* (Cambridge, Mass., 2017), 25.

15. Gillis, *Islands of the Mind*, 99; Lauren A. Benton, *A Search for Sovereignty: Law and Geography in European Empires, 1400–1900* (Cambridge, 2010), 162–221. On careening, see Peter R. Galvin, *Patterns of Pillage: A Geography of Caribbean-Based Piracy in Spanish America, 1536–1718* (New York, 1999), 84–85; and Richard Harding, "The War in the West Indies," in Mark H. Danley and Patrick J. Speelman, eds., *The Seven Years' War: Global Views* (Leiden, 2012), 299–300.

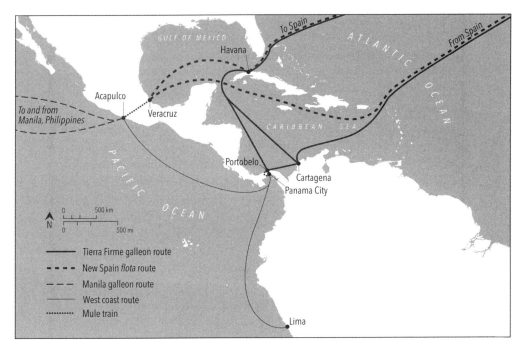

MAP 3 Routes of the New Spain Flota and the South American Treasure Galleons. The New Spain *flota* exchanged trade goods for Mexican silver at Veracruz. The South American (Tierra Firme) treasure galleons stopped at both Cartagena and Portobelo, where a large trade fair was held. The trade fairs at Portobelo and Veracruz were supposed to be annual, but they were in practice far less regular. Drawn by Molly Roy

the New Spain *flota* (fleet) and the South American treasure galleons before their return together in a convoy to Spain (see Map 3). This decision added to the city's appeal, as Havana was more accessible to pirates and privateers than Spain's inland territories in the Americas, and the fabled riches of Mexico and Peru, as well as trade goods from Asia, passed through its port annually. As the way station for Spain's treasure fleets, the colonial port represented the best potential point of access to all of Spanish America's gold and silver, which would be far more difficult to capture on the mainland where it was mined. Havana's attraction drew from its strategic location in this global circuitry of Spanish trade.[16]

Aware that the galleons heightened foreign interest in Havana, Spanish

16. Antonio García-Baquero González, *Cádiz y el atlántico (1717–1778): El comercio colonial español bajo el monopolio gaditano*, I (Seville, 1976), 145–151; Geoffrey J. Walker, *Spanish Politics and Imperial Trade, 1700–1789* (Bloomington, Ind., 1979), 4–5; Stanley J. Stein and Barbara H. Stein, *Silver, Trade, and War: Spain and America in the Making of Early Modern Europe* (Baltimore, 2000), 180–199.

kings sometimes referred to the city as Spain's "precious throat" to the kingdoms of New Spain and Peru, and, for this reason, "the most appealing port to foreigners and the principle object of the designs of the enemies of [the] Crown." It was Havana that connected the Iberian kingdoms to the sustenance that fed them and the air that filled their lungs—the gold and silver excavated from the mines of Peru and New Spain as well as trade goods from China, India, and Japan returning to Spain via the Manila galleon route. The galleons' haul enabled the Spanish monarchy's rise to dominance in Europe in the century between 1550 and 1650. Its riches funded Habsburg wars for territories in Portugal and its South American, African, and Asian dominions as well as the Low Countries, Sicily, and Naples. This lucre not only floated the Spanish monarchy but also flowed into the economies of Europe, its Atlantic colonies, and Asia, facilitating the global expansion of trade during the early modern era. Thus, the city came to symbolize for foreign crowns and the pirates, privateers, and merchants loosely affiliated with them the great riches of the Indies and of Asia, ripe for the taking. For the Spanish monarchy, it also represented the vulnerability that comes from being grabbed around the neck.[17]

Oliver Cromwell's Western Design

Though northern European attacks on Havana had a long history, the second half of the seventeenth century represented a turning point, as new kinds of offensive operations became possible. Oliver Cromwell's seizure of Spanish Jamaica in 1655—part of an operation known as the Western Design— marked a great advance in the ambitiousness of England's imperial goals vis-à-vis Spanish America as well as a transition to direct state sponsorship for expeditions instead of private backing. The Western Design also revealed the relentless character of England's targeting of Spanish America in that it was instituted when the two monarchies were not even at war with each other. In Cromwell's instructions to General Robert Venables, as his fleet of thirty-eight ships departed Portsmouth, England, in December 1654, he suggests as targets—rather diffusely—the island of Saint John's, the mouth of the River Orinoco on the coast of what is now Venezuela, and Havana. According to the

17. Real cédula, Madrid, June 10, 1717, in José Martin Felix de Arrate, *Llave del Nuevo Mundo: Antemural de las Indias Occidentales* (Havana, 1964), 67. For the reference to Havana as the throat connecting Old and New Worlds, see [Pedro Agustín Morell de Santa Cruz], *La visita eclesiástica: Selección e introducción de César García del Pino* (Havana, 1985), 6; García del Pino, *Toma de La Habana*, 57. For reference to Havana as "la llave de todas las indias y la más infestada y codiciada de enemigos, etc.," see Real despacho, Madrid, May 24, 1634, in Felix de Arrate, *Llave del Nuevo Mundo*, 68–69.

Council of State, though, "The taking of the Havana is so considerable we had thought of beginning the first attempt upon that fort and the island of Cuba."[18]

The acquisition of Jamaica altered English interactions with Spanish America in general and with the island of Cuba in particular in several fundamental ways. Despite a failed English campaign to take Hispaniola during the first phase of the Western Design, the eventual seizure and successful retention of Jamaica, in the heart of the Gulf of Mexico, bolstered English confidence about its providential mission. After the conquest of Jamaica, the idea that the border between English- and Spanish-speakers was a movable one gained further traction, as did the certainty that the English would continue to make inroads in Spanish territory.

Jamaica's acquisition inspired further geopolitical dreaming in England and its colonies, and Havana presented itself as a logical next target. Jamaica's proximity to Cuba and English privateers' and traders' increased exchanges and encounters with Havana enabled the English to refine their knowledge of the island—and their ideas for the best way to take it. In his 1671 translation of Arnoldus Montanus's *New and Unknown World,* a description of the newly "discovered" lands of the Americas and Australia and their peoples, the English geographer John Ogilby chose to add a letter to the original text's description of the island of Cuba, something he did for no other place. Purportedly penned by a Major Smith, who had been taken to Havana as a prisoner of war, the letter advocated attacking and annexing the port city. The Spanish, the author wrote, "much dread an old Prophecy amongst them, *viz. That within a short time the* English *will as freely walk the Streets of Havana, as the* Spaniards *now do"* (see Figure 2 [Plate 1]).[19]

Major Smith's proposed plan for an invasion of Havana was of early provenance, but it had enduring influence and thus merits attention. In 1666, En-

18. Carla Gardina Pestana, *The English Conquest of Jamaica: Oliver Cromwell's Bid for Empire* (Cambridge, Mass., 2017), 11, 57; Lane, *Pillaging the Empire,* 104; Oliver Cromwell's Instructions to General Robert Venables, Dec. 9, 1654, Vernon-Wager Manuscripts, LC.

19. John Ogilby, *America: Being the Latest, and Most Accurate Description of the New World . . .* (London, 1671), 336–337 (emphasis in the original). The Puritans of New England exemplified similar providential thinking, though their writings would have less impact on British battle plans in the Caribbean. At the end of the seventeenth century, the Bostonians Cotton Mather and Samuel Sewall imagined invading and converting Spanish America. Mather wrote and printed a tract, *La religión pura* (Boston, 1699), designed to convert Spanish America to Protestantism and make Mexico City the new capital of the Americas. Mather discussed plans to drop Spanish-translated Bibles in Havana, Santo Domingo, Puerto Rico, and Mexico. See Elliott, *Empires of the Atlantic World,* 217–218; Cotton Mather, *The Diary of Cotton Mather,* I, *1681–1708,* Massachusetts Historical Society, *Collections,* 7th Ser., VII (Boston, 1911), 206; Harry Bernstein, *Origins of Inter-American Interest, 1700–1812* (Philadelphia, 1945), 66–71. On the related topic of Puritan demonological thinking, see Cañizares-Esguerra, *Puritan Conquistadors.*

FIGURE 2 Engraving of Havana. From Arnoldus Montanus, *The New and Unknown World* . . . (Amsterdam, 1671). This illustration by Jacob Meurs appeared in both English and Dutch editions. It inspired numerous engravings and *vue d'optiques* in subsequent decades. Note the chain across the harbor and the two forts guarding the entrance to Havana's harbor, accurate details drawn from Major Smith's report in this otherwise fantastical northern European image. Courtesy of the John Carter Brown Library at Brown University

glish authorities in Jamaica had commissioned Smith to reestablish an English colony on Providence Island, off the coast of present-day Nicaragua—or, as the Spanish called it, Santa Catalina—in the wake of the buccaneer Edward Mansfield's brief recapture of the island from Spain. Among Smith's papers, now held in the Archive of the Indies in Seville, was a bundle of blank privateering commissions and the authorization to appoint captains "to attaque, fight with or surprise any vessel or vessels whatsoever you shall meet with to the southward of the Tropic of Cancer; and also, if you find it prudential to invade any of their lands, colony or plantations in America." A Spanish counter-raid launched from Panama soon captured Smith, his men, and his papers and took the would-be governor to Havana as a prisoner of war. There he remained undeterred in his quest, writing a letter outlining the best means of exploiting weaknesses in Havana's defenses and making the case for the value of its take-over. That letter was reprinted when Spain and Britain were at war in 1740 and

1741 and again in 1762. The prophecy he cited, that Havana would one day be English, would be invoked again in sources as varied as a Philadelphia newspaper, a London book, and a sermon delivered in Boston.[20]

Many of the elements that were common in seventeenth- and eighteenth-century texts predicting and plotting the conquest of Cuba—and that would come to embed themselves in the English imaginary—could be found in Smith's letter. They include the dream of future sugar plantations, hidden silver mines, and categorical maritime dominance of the Caribbean Sea. "This great Island is easie to be conquer'd," he wrote, "and would make the best Plantation, besides the prejudice it would be to the *Spaniard,* and the great advantage to our Nation." Describing the best possible plan of assault, Smith recommended landing two good regiments of soldiers from Jamaica to the west of the city, out of the range of the Morro Castle, when the Spanish treasure fleet was not in harbor. Before the fleet's return, the invaders would have enough time to take the city, settle planters to "Manure the Land," and build up defenses to stave off an attempted Spanish reconquest.[21]

According to Smith, the advantages of this acquisition would be many. Cuba had high-quality tobacco plantations and copper mines. He could not comment on whether it had mines for silver or gold, as the Spanish had supposedly dared not open any so close to the sea because of the threat of invasion. "I esteem . . . *Havana* . . . equivalent . . . to *Tangier* in the *Straights of Gibraltar;* and if we were at once Masters of both, it would without doubt so straiten the *Spaniards,* as absolutely to admit us a free Trade into their Ports of *America.*" Without Havana, Smith avowed in his letter, the Spanish would be "ruine[d]," unable to navigate "their great unruly Ships" through the Windward Passage on their voyage back to Spain.[22]

20. Ogilby writes that Captain Smith had been to Havana in 1665, which would be an error by one year. After Smith's capture, Henry Morgan captured Providence Island again during his 1670 raid of Panama. See "Expediente sobre la reconquista de la isla de Santa Catalina por el General Juan Pérez de Guzmán," 1666–1668, AGI, Panamá, 78; Donald Rowland, "Spanish Occupation of the Island of Old Providence, or Santa Catalina, 1641–1670," *HAHR,* XV (1935), 298–312; W. Noel Sainsbury, "The Two Providence Islands," *Proceedings of the Royal Geographical Society of London,* XXI (1876–1877), 148–149; Peter Earle, *The Sack of Panamá: Sir Henry Morgan's Adventures on the Spanish Main* (New York, 1981), 15; Lane, *Pillaging the Empire,* 112. Major Smith's prophesy is cited in: *American Weekly Mercury* (Philadelphia), June 12, 1740; *A Geographical and Historical Description of the Principal Objects of the Present War in the West-Indies . . .* (London, 1741), 173–175; Samuel Frink, *The Marvelous Works of Creation and Providence, Illustrated; Being the Substance of a Sermon Preached at the North Precinct in Shrewsbury; on Thursday the 7th of October, 1762, a Day of Public Thanksgiving, Occasioned by the Reduction of the Havannah* (Boston, 1763), 38. For a republication of Major Smith's letter, first published in 1762, see *A Description of the Spanish Islands and Settlements on the Coast of the West Indies . . . ,* 2d ed. (London, 1774); *London Evening Post,* Feb. 28, 1741, classified ads.

21. Ogilby, *America,* 336–337.

22. Ibid., 336.

In Smith's colorful account, the image of Havana was flexible and multi-faceted—which was perhaps part of its broad appeal to the English imagination as its details circulated and recirculated in the English-language press. The city was likened to a plantation, a Mediterranean port, a copper mine and possibly mines of gold and silver, a prophetic destiny, a rival's ruin, and a gateway to free trade throughout the Americas. In addition, seizing Havana and cultivating its soil seemed to imply magically and automatically acquiring the whole eight-hundred-mile-long island of Cuba, despite its great size. Yet what made the letter so compelling was the extent of its accurate detail accompanying the more wild conjecture. It reflected the observations of someone who had clearly been to Havana. The closeness of Jamaica and Cuba and the rising numbers of English adventurers in the region were putting both Havana and Cuba in greater peril.

In addition to Smith's ill-fated expedition to Providence Island, England's seizure of Jamaica sparked another series of smash-and-grab pirate raids in Spanish America almost a century after those carried out by the raiders' Elizabethan predecessors. In 1656, Jamaica's colonial governor Edward D'Oyley invited English and French buccaneers from Tortuga to make Kingston their home base. In return for protecting Jamaica from Spanish counterattack and a 10 percent cut of their takings, the buccaneers received both a good harbor well situated for attacks on Spanish America and a market for their stolen goods. D'Oyley's decision catapulted into action such notorious characters as Christopher Myngs and Henry Morgan. In the sixteen years between the English takeover of Jamaica in 1655 and the end of Henry Morgan's active career on the seas in 1671, eighteen cities, four towns, and more than thirty-five Spanish American villages were sacked. They targeted the mainland in Venezuela, Panama, and Mexico, as well as Santiago de Cuba and two cities in Cuba's interior, Puerto Príncipe (present-day Camagüey) and Sancti Spíritus. These pirates and their international crews were generally more interested in sacking and pillaging than establishing colonies; however, their swashbuckling exploits, described in texts like Alexander Esquemeling's *Buccaneers of America,* first published in English translation in 1684, fired the English imagination (see Figure 3). The pirate raids also helped to fund investment in Jamaican sugar plantations and African slavery, which made the English colony there more permanent. Sugar plantations guaranteed the colony's economic viability, as they had on the English island of Barbados, and they drew enough population ostensibly to thwart Spanish repossession.[23]

23. Subsequent to 1671, Jamaica-based pirates also raided Maracaibo in 1676, Santa Marta in 1677, Campeche in 1678, Portobelo in 1679, and Vera Cruz in 1683. See C. H. Haring, *The Buccaneers in the West Indies in the XVII Century* (London, 1910), 267; Galvin, *Patterns of Pillage,* 54; Nuala Zahedieh,

The Towne of Puerto del Principe taken & sackt
Part 2: Chap: 5:

FIGURE 3 Henry Morgan's Sack of Puerto Príncipe, Cuba. Depicted in Alexander O. Esquemeling's *Bucaniers of America; or, A True Account of the Most Remarkable Assaults Committed of Late Years upon the Coasts of the West-Indies*, I (London, 1684). The town was originally founded on the north coast of Cuba, but in 1528 it moved inland for protection from the attacks of indigenous peoples and an earlier series of pirate raids. Note the contrast in dress and appearance between the depictions of the pirates (right) and their Spanish opponents (left). Courtesy of the John Carter Brown Library at Brown University

After the capture of Jamaica, pirate raiding gave way to slave trading, which marked a transition from parasitic to symbiotic growth between British and Spanish territories. Through the African slave trade, English traders gained greater access to the port of Havana, the island of Cuba, and all of Spanish America. Soon after its capture by the English, Jamaica became a supplier of enslaved Africans to the region and a nexus of contraband trade with Spain's American settlements. Spanish America still had no transatlantic slave traders of its own and relied upon the Spanish monarchy's asiento system, whereby foreign merchants were permitted to sell enslaved Africans to its territories under a formal monopoly contract, the one legal exception to Spain's exclusive controls on American trade. As early as the 1660s, merchants from the Spanish colonial ports of Havana, Portobelo, and Cartagena began sailing into Kingston with cargoes of silver, seeking to purchase enslaved Africans directly from the English Royal African Company, outside the auspices of the asiento

---

"'A Frugal, Prudential, and Hopeful Trade': Privateering in Jamaica, 1655–1689," *Journal of Imperial and Commonwealth History*, XVIII (1990), 145–168, esp. 157; Hanna, *Pirate Nests*, 102–143, esp. 123, 138; Lane, *Pillaging the Empire*, 114–121; Nuala Zahadieh, "Trade, Plunder, and Economic Development in Early English Jamaica, 1655–1689," *Economic History Review*, 2d Ser., XXXIX (1986), 205–222, esp. 221.

contract. The English Navigation Acts technically prohibited such intercolonial commerce, but the king's Privy Council soon excluded the slave trade
from this ban, realizing it was a strategic way to acquire Spanish silver. English
traders and policy makers both agreed on this point, even though planters in
Jamaica resented having to compete with buyers from Spanish America for
African laborers.[24]

What made the African slave trade so attractive to English commercial
and political figures was that it offered a way to access Spanish silver that was
easier than capturing a Spanish treasure ship or launching a costly and difficult invasion of Mexico or Peru. As the Dutch West India Company had
learned during its recent occupation of Brazil (1630–1654), invading the mainland was costly, and retaining it, extremely difficult. Although the conquest of
the mainland remained far beyond the capacity of English adventurers and
armies, trafficking in enslaved Africans, one of the era's most expensive and
coveted commodities, could potentially open up the silver veins of Spanish
America.

For slave traders in Jamaica, the timing of England's seizure of their island
was fortuitous, as Spain and Portugal had recently split apart, cutting off Spanish America's access to Portuguese slave traders. After two decades of unreli-
able trading, in the 1660s the Spanish asiento was granted to Genoese and
Dutch merchants, who in turn struggled to meet elastic demand. The Dutch
were forced to contract for enslaved Africans in Jamaica when their own shipments from Curaçao fell short. This English subcontracting delivered large
quantities of silver to the hub of Jamaica and whetted the appetites of men of
commerce there for more slave trading with Spanish America. English rivalry
with the Dutch over the slave trade was so great it precipitated the founding
of the English Royal African Company and the outbreak of the Second Anglo-
Dutch War, during which English privateers attacked several Dutch slave trading stations on the coast of West Africa.[25]

The African slave trade became an effective means of tapping the wealth
of Spain's American possessions and also helped to open other branches of

24. O'Malley, *Final Passages*, 8, 12, 149, 160–162; Colin A. Palmer, *Human Cargoes: The British Slave Trade to Spanish America, 1700–1739* (Urbana, Ill., 1981), 1–10; Trevor Burnard and Kenneth Morgan, "The Dynamics of the Slave Market and Slave Purchasing Patterns in Jamaica, 1655–1788," *William and Mary Quarterly*, 3d Ser., LVIII (2001), 205–228; Stephanie E. Smallwood, *Saltwater Slavery: A Middle Passage from Africa to American Diaspora* (Cambridge, Mass., 2007), 172–173; José Luciano Franco, *Comercio clandestino de esclavos* (Havana, 1996), 4–13, 23–28.

25. O'Malley, *Final Passages*, 139–152, 160–170; Wim Klooster, *The Dutch Moment: War, Trade, and Settlement in the Seventeenth-Century Atlantic World* (Ithaca, N.Y., 2016), 7–9; Pestana, *The English Conquest of Jamaica*, 245.

trade. From 1661 to 1715, an estimated twenty-eight thousand enslaved Africans were exported from Jamaica, the majority to Spanish America. By the 1680s, the English Royal African Company was selling between 25 and 50 percent of the slaves it imported to the West Indies to Spanish subjects, largely through contraband channels. To build relationships with Spanish American merchants, merchants in Jamaica even offered arrangements by which Spanish American merchants could pay in bullion to local British agents in their home ports, plus a 35 percent fee, and then travel to Jamaica to pick up the enslaved Africans they had purchased without the risk of transporting Spanish silver on the open seas.[26]

Favorable arrangements like those described above facilitated the sale of English manufactured goods alongside enslaved Africans, making the slave trade a pathway to other restricted, contraband commerce. The resultant influx of Spanish silver helped to fund the development of Jamaica's sugar sector, fill royal coffers, and line the pockets of merchants in Jamaica and England. In an account of the island written in 1712, Jamaica merchant Robert Allen wrote that, when Spanish American trade was strong, "Jamaica flourished and abounded more in Spanish gold and silver than it ever did before."[27]

Jamaica's growth was dependent on the trade with Cuba, alongside other Spanish American territories. Across the late seventeenth and early eighteenth century, that trade bound the neighboring islands together, with goods, merchants, and enslaved Africans moving through networks connecting the two islands and their ports. Wealthy merchants from Havana and other Spanish American ports sailed into Port Royal in Kingston's harbor in search of enslaved Africans. Smugglers in Jamaica profited in this interstitial commercial space by using ties of religion and ethnicity to belong to both places. An eighteenth-century British report on trade in Jamaica referred to the pivotal role as intermediaries in this traffic of "Irish Roman Catholics and the Jews, who talk Spanish as natives." The report's author, Joseph Salvador, a Sephardic Jewish merchant from Kingston, testified that "many vessels pass between both states on short trips, who dexterously manage to belong to each nation,

---

26. The slave trade from Jamaica to Cuba before the British received the asiento is especially difficult to evaluate numerically. On its nature and volume, see O'Malley, *Final Passages,* 148–151, 353–357.

27. Adrian J. Pearce, *British Trade with Spanish America, 1763–1808* (Liverpool, U.K., 2007), 14–17; Nuala Zahedieh, "The Merchants of Port Royal, Jamaica, and the Spanish Contraband Trade," *WMQ,* 3d Ser., XLIII (1986), 591; Robert Allen, "An Essay on the Nature and Methods of Carrying on a Trade to the South Seas," 1712, Additional Manuscripts, 28140, fols. 20–28, esp. 24v, BL. Robert Allen went on to become a member of Parliament, and this 1712 tract on the importance of the trade to Havana and Spanish America from Jamaica was republished in 1762 during the debate over keeping Havana: *The Great Importance of the Havannah* . . . (London, 1762).

as it suits them best." Indeed, Cuba's coveted trade was drawing Spain's rivals in and allowing them to forge stronger links between Cuba and Jamaica.[28]

Anglo-Spanish Wars (1701–1748) and Conflict over the Asiento

In the early eighteenth century, the pace and intensity of imperial rivalry and Caribbean war making increased considerably, raising the threat to Havana. European competition for Spanish American markets led to a series of Anglo-Spanish wars, nested within broader European conflicts. The first of these contests, the War of the Spanish Succession (1701–1714), an overt struggle among European powers for control of the Spanish crown and its riches, triggered the hostilities that followed. Precipitated by the death of the last Habsburg king, Charles II, the war ended with Spain's loss of the Netherlands, its Italian territories, Gibraltar, and Menorca. By the end of the war, France had managed to place a fellow Bourbon on the Spanish throne and to carve out an increasing share of Spanish trade in Cádiz and the Pacific, spearheaded by the Compagnie de la Mer Pacifique. France's political and commercial gains, as well as its burgeoning sugar industry in Martinique, Guadeloupe, and Saint Domingue (the western half of Hispaniola, ceded by Spain to France in 1697), began to alarm its British adversaries. After 1713, this competition for Spanish American markets and territories—heightened by rivalry with France—propelled Britain and Spain into a cycle of further Anglo-Spanish wars.[29]

The first half of the eighteenth century became a near-constant state of war between Britain and Spain. Cumulatively, the early decades of the century through the outbreak of the Seven Years' War saw more years of war than of peace. Anglo-Spanish wars broke out in 1717, 1727, and 1739, and even those interwar years saw both sides authorizing privateering voyages and planning attacks on each other's settlements. Precipitating these wars was the under-

28. In 1682, for example, the governor of Jamaica reported the arrival of "one Don Gaspar de Montesdoco" [sic, probably Montes de Oca] from Havana seeking to buy 150 enslaved Africans, a request that could not be fulfilled at that time; see O'Malley, *Final Passages*, 147. For Joseph Salvador's report, see "Relations between Britain (Jamaica) and Spanish America," [1763], Add. MSS 38,373, 128–130, BL. See also Allan Christelow, "Contraband Trade between Jamaica and the Spanish Main, and the Free Port Act of 1766," *HAHR*, XXII (1942), 309–343, esp. 331.

29. In the British North American colonies, the War of the Spanish Succession was known as Queen Anne's War. By the end of the war, Portugal's rights to the Colônia do Sacramento, a major entrepôt of contraband trade in the Río de la Plata, had also been recognized. On the war, see Joaquim Albareda Salvadó, *La guerra de sucesión de España (1700–1714)* (Barcelona, 2010); and Henry Kamen, *The War of Succession in Spain, 1700–1715* (Bloomington, Ind., 1969). On its impact on commercial rivalries, in particular, see Kenneth J. Andrien and Allan J. Kuethe, *The Spanish Atlantic World in the Eighteenth Century: War and the Bourbon Reforms, 1713–1796* (New York, 2014), 35; Mapp, *The Elusive West*, 122–143.

lying structural conflict that Britain and its subjects wanted Spanish silver and access to its territories, and Spain had no intention of relinquishing them. The catalyst was the British receipt of the asiento contract to provide Spanish America with enslaved Africans.[30]

The British South Sea Company's acquisition of the asiento monopoly contract in 1713 was a concession in the Treaty of Utrecht at the end of the War of the Spanish Succession. The South Sea Company's penchant for contraband and British subjects' ongoing push for commercial and territorial inroads into Spanish America led to more discord than prior asientos with Portuguese, Genoese, Dutch, and French slave traders. The wars that resulted served as a petri dish for the growth of British plots against Spanish America and gave Britons additional reasons to want to attack Havana.[31]

The growth of Havana and the networks the city had built with foreign merchants through the slave and contraband trades heightened British desire for greater commercial access to the city. Though all of Cuba was coveted, Havana's size, its large, wealthy population, and its extensive silver reserves made it an especially desirable market for goods as well as enslaved Africans. Its residents' demand for slave labor gave British merchants in Jamaica an opening through which to promote this traffic alongside other branches of trade. Coincidentally, Britons' increased communication and exchange with Cuba elevated the quality of British intelligence about Havana, which fostered ever more informed plans to invade, attack, and acquire the city.

Spain's attempt to oppose these commercial inroads caused further friction that led to war. After the War of the Spanish Succession, Spanish administrators sought to implement several measures to better defend Spain's overseas

30. On the British asiento and the South Sea Company as a force that both connected the British and Spanish empires and drove them to war, see Adrian Finucane, *The Temptations of Trade: Britain, Spain, and the Struggle for Empire* (Philadelphia, 2016). British logwooders also desired territory in the Bay of Honduras and the Miskito Coast, a cause of strife between the British and Spanish crowns. For diplomatic aspects of this conflict, see Troy S. Floyd, *The Anglo-Spanish Struggle for Mosquitia* (Albuquerque, N.M., 1967); Robert A. Naylor, *Penny Ante Imperialism: The Mosquito Shore and the Bay of Honduras, 1600–1914: A Case Study in British Informal Empire* (Rutherford, N.J., 1989); Frank Griffith Dawson, "William Pitt's Settlement at Black River on the Mosquito Shore: A Challenge to Spain in Central America, 1732–87," *HAHR*, LXIII (1983), 677–706; and Barbara Potthast, *Die Mosquitoküste im Spannungsfeld britischer und spanischer Politik, 1502–1821* (Cologne, 1988).

31. Plots against Havana hatched during the War of the Spanish Succession, the Anglo-Spanish War of 1727, and their immediate aftermaths include the following: "Memorandum Advocating the Occupation by the English of Gibraltar and the Havana," sent to Sidney Godolphin, 1st Earl of Godolphin, Lord High Treasurer, 1705, Add. MSS 28058, fol. 31, BL; "Mr. A. Spotswood's Letter to Lord Townshend, 1727," Add. MSS 32694, BL; Robert Hunter to Lord Townshend, Nov. 12, 1726, fol. 14, and William Dummer, "A Short Sketch for Attempting the Havana," "Some Considerations about Forming a Descent in the West Indies," and "An Estimate of the Force and Its Charge for a Descent upon the Havana," 1730, all in Vernon-Wager Manuscripts, LC.

territories and to deter contraband trade with its rivals. One Spanish strategy to counteract contraband was the expansion of the *guardacostas,* or coast guard, that sought to intercept smugglers in Spanish American waters. Effectively, the guardacostas were privateers operating in times of peace. Under this system, colonial governors commissioned private individuals to outfit guardacosta ships that captured foreign vessels as prizes, which they could keep as compensation after payment of the royal *quinto* (20 percent tax). Their zealous seizures—both lawful and unlawful—threatened British trade with Spanish America and heightened diplomatic tensions between the British and Spanish governments.[32]

Privateers and their perceived abuses represented a flashpoint of an underlying struggle over commerce, slave trading, and imperial power. A mercantile faction in England was eager to exploit any reason to go to war with Spain because it saw war as means to both protect and expand British trade with Spanish America. The act of the British Parliament passed in 1739 that forbade trade with Spain while the two nations were at war only applied in Europe, thus giving tacit approval to the merchants' quest to use war with Spain to make further incursions into Spanish American markets.[33]

British commercial interests and their government considered trade with Spanish America worth going to war over. It was vital to the very survival of their Atlantic colonial system and enabled its expansion into other world oceans. British trafficking of both goods and enslaved Africans to Spanish America was big business, valued at approximately three hundred thousand pounds per year between 1713 and 1739. Abundant trade with Spanish America made Jamaica the primary supplier of bullion to Britain's North American colonies, thus solving their endemic monetary problems. Spanish American silver flowing into Jamaica also enabled Britain to increase its trade with China. Silver was the only commodity Chinese traders would accept for their coveted silks, spices, and other goods. By the late seventeenth century, Britain was drawing all the silver it needed for trade with Asia from the Spanish American market. By the 1730s, when the guardacostas were active, there

32. For a treatment of Spanish reform after the War of the Spanish Succession, see Kuethe and Andrien, *The Spanish Atlantic World,* 2, 31–132; and Pearce, *British Trade with Spanish America,* 8. On contraband trade and the complaints of Cádiz merchants, see George H. Nelson, "Contraband Trade under the Asiento, 1730–1739," *AHR,* LI (1945), 55–67, esp. 65; and Christelow, "Contraband Trade between Jamaica and the Spanish Main," *HAHR,* XXII (1942), 309–313. On the guardacostas, see Leslie Theibert, "Making an English Caribbean, 1650–1688" (Ph.D. diss., Yale University, 2013), 375–381, 387–390, 481–485; Kuethe and Andrien, *The Spanish Atlantic World,* 33, 118; John Robert McNeill, *Atlantic Empires of France and Spain: Louisbourg and Havana, 1700–1763* (Chapel Hill, N.C., 1985), 89–91; Walker, *Spanish Politics and Imperial Trade,* 150; Olga Pantaleão, *A penetração comercial da Inglaterra na America Espanhola de 1713 à 1783* (São Paulo, Brazil, 1946), 219.

33. Pares, *War and Trade in the West Indies,* 116–117.

were more British and British American traders doing business with Spanish America than at any time before.[34]

Disputes over inter-imperial trade, especially the slave trade, eroded diplomatic relations between Spain and Britain and formed a source of festering grievances between the nations' monarchs. The slave trade was a major boon to the British colonial project and a stimulus to Spanish American economies and societies, but it was an irritant to the Spanish crown, which wanted a monopoly in trade with its overseas possessions. The Spanish monarchy and its councillors perceived the slave trade to lie at the crux of the problem of contraband. Enslaved Africans were the most highly valued commodity smugglers traded, and a large amount of contraband trade went on "in the shadow" of the British asiento, a common phrasing in Spanish government correspondence. In both 1727 and 1739, Spanish complaints about the South Sea Company's abuses and arguments about its bookkeeping were germane to the breakdown of Anglo-Spanish negotiations and the onset of war.[35]

The unprecedented nature of the British asiento, as opposed to prior versions of the slave-trading grant, established an especially intimate and contentious relationship between Britain and Spain. When the British South Sea Company acquired the asiento, it gained coveted access to numerous Spanish American ports and the right to sell more than five thousand enslaved Africans per year there for a thirty-year contract.[36] The British and Spanish

34. The 300,000 GBP per year was a substantial increase over the 100,000 to 200,000 GBP per year in the period circa 1670–1713; see Pearce, *British Trade with Spanish America*, 18, 25. On the importance of Spanish silver to Jamaica and British North America, see Elliott, *Empires of the Atlantic World*, 226; Zahedieh, "The Merchants of Port Royal," *WMQ*, 3d Ser., XLIII (1986), 584. On the significance of Spanish silver to expanding trade with China, see Mapp, *The Elusive West*, 113–114; and Dennis O. Flynn and Arturo Giráldez, "Cycles of Silver: Global Economic Unity through the Mid-eighteenth Century," *Journal of World History*, XIII (2002), 391–427. On contraband trade in the 1730s, see Philip Woodfine, "'Suspicious Latitudes': Commerce, Colonies, and Patriotism in the 1730s," *Studies in Eighteenth-Century Culture*, XXVII (1998), 25–52, esp. 35.

35. For discussions of contraband "in the shadow of the slave trade" (*"a la sombra"* or *"en la sombra"*), see "Del rey a los oficiales reales en La Habana," Mar. 28, 1748, and "La junta formada sobre arbitrios en Indias," Dec. 31, 1740, both in AGI, SD, 2208. On Anglo-Spanish diplomatic disputes over the asiento, see Pares, *War and Trade in the West Indies*, 53; "Memorias de los cargos contra la Compañía y de las pruebas que hay de ellos," and "Translation of a Letter from a Merchant of Cadiz at Present in Madrid to His Friend a Merchant in London," 1728, both in AGS, Estado, 6878.

36. The estimate of "more than 5,000 enslaved Africans" is based on 4,800 *"negros piezas de indias."* Slave importations in the Spanish empire were counted, not by individual enslaved persons, but by what were called *piezas de indias*, or "pieces of the Indies." The origin of the phrase may have to do with the number of cloths from India exchanged for a person in West Africa. According to this system, a person between the ages of sixteen or eighteen and thirty-five equaled one *pieza*; two people between the ages of twelve or fourteen and sixteen or eighteen equaled one pieza; and three children between the ages of six and twelve or fourteen were counted together as two piezas. These calculations were used for taxation and pricing, and they varied according to gender and physical condition of the enslaved person. The contract also stipulated that two-thirds of the enslaved people

crowns each received a quarter stake in the company, which owed the Spanish monarch duties on each enslaved African imported, collected upon disembarkation in Spanish American ports. The company also received permission to send one ship annually to the trade fair with the Spanish flota at Veracruz or the galleons at Portobelo. Dutch, Portuguese, and French merchants all had held the asiento, but none could claim a coup so great as to be allowed to participate in the trade fairs. Equivalent to a territorial concession at the end of the War of the Spanish Succession, this commercial grant went along with Spain's cession of the island of Menorca and the port of Gibraltar and was equally if not more resented by its merchant monopoly in Cádiz.[37]

The British South Sea Company, which was created to receive the asiento, had an aggressive commercial agenda that was designed to make up the debt accrued in the War of the Spanish Succession with its revenues, either through slave trading alone or associated commerce. Although the British "permission ship" at the trade fairs was supposed to carry only five hundred tons of cargo, it frequently surpassed its allotted weight. Spanish reformers were trying to transition to a new system of smaller, more flexible register ships and phase out the flota, galleon, and trade fairs, and so they resented the permission ships for locking them into the old system. Even more, contraband trade was rampant both at the fairs and through the company's network of Spanish American trade factories.[38]

At stake in diplomatic disputes over the asiento were not only the disposition of imperial wealth but also the perceived internal security of empire. Under the terms of the asiento, British merchants were legally allowed to ensconce themselves in designated Spanish American ports, and foreign boats were permitted to sail into Spain's most strategic American harbors. This situation grew delicate during the incessant conflicts of the eighteenth century. In

---

should be male and nine-tenths of them should be over the age of sixteen. See Enrique López Mesa, "La trata negrera en el puerto de La Habana a mediados del siglo XVIII," *Sotavento*, III, no. 6 (Summer 1999), 19–31; and Carl Wennerlind, *Casualties of Credit: The English Financial Revolution, 1620–1720* (Cambridge, Mass., 2011), 218.

37. The king of Spain refused to send money to invest his quarter interest in the South Sea Company, so the company did it for him and charged interest. It claimed no profit on its voyages, though the one voyage whose accounts were examined did indeed make a very large profit. The company would not let the Spanish king inspect the accounts of any other voyages, which caused further disputes. See Pares, *War and Trade in the West Indies,* 53.

38. O'Malley, *Final Passages*, 168–170; Wennerlind, *Casualties of Credit,* 197–234; Abigail L. Swingen, *Competing Visions of Empire: Labor, Slavery, and the Origins of the British Atlantic Empire* (New Haven, Conn., 2015), 172–195. In the years of the British asiento, markets were often already flooded with smuggled British manufactured goods by the time the flota arrived; as a result, the flota's Cádiz merchant investors were losing money. Between 1721 and 1739, only six flotas sailed for Veracruz, and the galleons visited Cartagena and Portobelo only four times. See Kuethe and Andrien, *The Spanish Atlantic World,* 51, 106, 153; Walker, *Spanish Politics and Imperial Trade,* 71–74.

times of war as of peace, if British ships were allowed into Spanish American ports, Spanish authorities worried that they would have the opportunity to reconnoiter the relative preparedness of the fort in case of attack, the position of its defenses, and the location and extent of the food and water supply. Driven by fear and the desire for retribution, the Spanish monarch seized the company factors' property in Spanish American ports on the outbreak of war in 1717 and 1728, which became another source of great British complaint.[39]

Under the anxious conditions of on-again, off-again warfare between societies connected by the slave trade, the management of populations of African descent also became a site of diplomatic strife. Relying on the British in Jamaica to supply enslaved Africans to Cuba, for example, triggered the anxieties of Spanish officials. Agitated minds on the Council of the Indies in Spain and on the island of Cuba accused the South Sea Company of using the slave trade in a plot to acquire the island. According to the captain general of Cuba, the South Sea Company instigated a slave rebellion in 1727 in coordination with a planned naval attack by a British squadron under the command of Admiral Francis Hosier. The captain general alleged that the company had compelled an enslaved African they had sold on the island to start a rebellion just as the British warships arrived offshore. Spanish complaints about the incident persisted in diplomatic channels and were raised in a pamphlet, published in Madrid, Paris, and Amsterdam, that was designed to solicit European support shortly before the outbreak of war with Britain in 1739. In this appeal to potential allies, the Spanish author argued that the British asiento threatened Spain's ability to secure its own empire and control the colonial order in Cuba.[40]

This uprising of three hundred enslaved Africans on a plantation outside Havana had its own internal dynamics and local causes, despite its patronizing description in diplomatic correspondence. These men and women certainly had their own reasons to want to rebel, without being told to do so by Europeans. The idea that foreign enemies would incite the enslaved population to rebel, in coordination with a planned invasion, was a common trope in slave-

---

39. On the complexities of South Sea Company trade factors' experiences and identifications during their time in Spanish America, see Finucane, *Temptations of Trade*. On Spanish officials' concerns regarding intelligence gathered by factors about Spanish American ports' defenses, see "Los directores de la compañia de aquella ciudad," Aug. 4, 1744, AGI, SD, 2208; Penalosa to the Marqués de la Ensenada, Dec. 29, 1746, AGI, SD, 2208. On seizures of company property upon the outbreak of war, see Pares, *War and Trade in the West Indies*, 53.

40. Sr. Conde de Rotembourgo, Sept. 6, 1727, AGS, Estado, 6909; *Cotejo de la conducta de S.M. con la de el rey britanico . . . / His Catholick Majesty's Conduct Compared with That of His Britannick Majesty . . .* (London, 1739). For the arrival of Hosier's ships, see Levi Marrero, *Cuba: Economía y sociedad,* 15 vols. (Madrid, [1972]–1992), VI, 79.

holding societies, one that revealed more about feared vulnerabilities in the minds of the powerful than actual reasons the enslaved chose to rise up in arms. That said, meddling with each other's population of African descent was also a tactic attempted by both British and Spanish officials, and thus their fears of such machinations were not baseless.[41]

Mirroring such Spanish allegations, the British crown and councillors and its authorities in Jamaica accused their neighbors in Cuba of undermining their authority over their own populations of African descent. British colonial officials and polemicists regularly accused Spanish instigators of supplying the Jamaican maroons with arms in the war they were waging against colonial authorities — an accusation that quite likely was true. Also, in the 1680s the Spanish crown had begun a policy of offering freedom to the enslaved Africans of its Protestant rivals who ran away to Spanish lands and professed the desire to convert to Catholicism. With this policy, it sought to drain rival colonies of a vital source of labor. In groups as large as fourteen at a time, enslaved Africans in northern Jamaica stole boats and escaped to the south coast of Cuba to make a bid for their freedom. The practice sapped the wealth of slaveowners in Jamaica and cut into their ability to control their human capital. In a pamphlet published in London in 1739, a British sea captain who had been captured by Spanish privateers and taken prisoner in Trinidad, on the south coast of Cuba, decried these inflammatory practices, alleging that he himself had been "worse used than their Negroes" during his stint as a prisoner of war.[42]

When war began again in 1739, it was not a sudden rupture in a period of peace. Rather, it was an intensification of years-long hostilities between two rival colonial systems — predicated on war, trade, and racial slavery —

41. On the tropes by which slaveowners imagined rebellions of the enslaved, see Jason T. Sharples, "Discovering Slave Conspiracies: New Fears of Rebellion and Old Paradigms of Plotting in Seventeenth-Century Barbados," *AHR*, CXX (2015), 811–843. For an account of the 1727 slave rebellion in Cuba, see Manuel Barcia, *The Great African Slave Revolt of 1825: Cuba and the Fight for Freedom in Matanzas* (Baton Rouge, La., 2012), 45–46. In 1725, the British ambassador in Madrid warned that a proposal had been made to the Spanish king for launching an invasion of Jamaica that planned to use this same strategy; see "Extract of a Letter from Mr. Stanhope, His Majesty's Ambassador at Madrid to His Grace the Duke of Newcastle," June 22, 1725, Stowe MS 256, 11, BL.

42. *Cotejo de la conducta de S. M. con la de el rey Británico / The English Cotejo; or, The Cruelties, Depredations, and Illicit Trade Charg'd upon the English in a Spanish Libel, Lately Published . . .* [London, 1739], 6–7, 11, 13, 15 (quotation), 24. On Jamaican maroons' wartime relations with the Spanish, see Joseph Gálvez to the Govenor of Santo Domingo, Mar. 12, 1780, AGI, SD, 2082. On the Spanish policy of encouraging maritime marronage, see Linda M. Rupert, "Marronage, Manumission, and Maritime Trade in the Early Modern Caribbean," *Slavery and Abolition*, XXX (2009), 361–382, esp. 362; José Luis Belmonte Postigo, "'No siendo lo mismo echarse al mar, que es lugar de libertad plena': Cimarronaje marítimo y política trans-imperial en el caribe español, 1687–1804," in Consuelo Naranjo Orovio, ed., *Esclavitud y diferencia racial en el Caribe hispano* (Madrid, 2017), 43–70. For discussion of escapees from Jamaica in Cuba, see Consejo de Indias, Apr. 6, 1750, AGI, SD, 1130B.

that had grown deeply and dangerously enmeshed. The final war in this cycle, the War of Jenkins' Ear (1739–1748), was the most explicitly commercial and colonial war of the eighteenth century and the direct antecedent to the Seven Years' War. Tellingly, in Spain this Anglo-Spanish war was called the War of the Asiento, and British slave trading and related abuses were understood to have precipitated the conflict. The British named the war after Captain Robert Jenkins of Bristol, who allegedly had his ear sliced off by Juan León Fandiño, a Cuba-based privateer, off the coast of Havana. The British government pinned this Anglo-Spanish war on the "depredations" of the Spanish coast guard and privateers. The Spanish position was that the abuses of the South Sea Company slave traders and other contrabandists and interlopers were the primary cause of the war. Though Spain had threatened to do so many times before, in May 1739 it terminated the South Sea Company's asiento and refused to pay the ninety-five thousand pounds it owed for reprisals against company property. Urged on by the popular outcry in London against what were perceived as multiple abuses against British trade, the British government declared war on Spain in October of that year.[43]

For both Britain and Spain, the war provided a timely pretext for the pursuit of deep-seated imperial and commercial objectives vis-à-vis the other's empire. This conflict served as the testing grounds for the incredibly swift actions taken against Havana in 1762. Aside from one British victory at Porto-belo in 1739 and the triumphant seizure of the Manila galleon in 1743, the War of Jenkins' Ear was a series of mostly failed British operations—against Cartagena de Indias in what is now Colombia and Guantánamo, Cuba, in 1741 and Santiago de Cuba and Havana in 1748—that were dramatically improved on the next time around. Despite these failures, or in fact because of them, Britain's experience in the war is integral to explaining the ambitious scope, conception, and aims of the Havana campaign of 1762. The plots against Spanish America put forth during the War of Jenkins' Ear were not the first plans hatched, nor the first invasions botched. They were, however, the most influential on the chain of events that eventually brought Lord Albemarle's ships to the coast of Havana in June 1762.

43. The War of Jenkins' Ear, or the Anglo-Spanish War of 1739, merged with the War of the Austrian Succession and lasted until 1748. Historians of Britain traditionally blamed the "depredations" of the Spanish guardacostas for its outbreak, but now scholars generally concur that the actions of privateers were more pretext than underlying cause. See Pearce, *British Trade with Spanish America*, 24; Philip Woodfine, "The Anglo-Spanish War of 1739," in Jeremy Black, ed., *The Origins of War in Early Modern Europe* (Edinburgh, 1987), 193; and Pares, *War and Trade in the West Indies*, 23, 53. On the dispute between the Spanish monarch and the South Sea Company that led to declarations of war, see Woodfine, "The Anglo-Spanish War of 1739," in Black, ed., *Origins of War*, 186; Walker, *Spanish Politics and Imperial Trade*, 207.

Plots against Spanish America during the War of Jenkins' Ear

The War of Jenkins' Ear was the peak moment of the eighteenth century for the popular expression in the British press of territorial designs on Spanish America. The lead-up to the war saw a deluge of pro-war publications in Britain and British America about various plots to attack and acquire key points in Spain's empire. The British merchant community, their allies in Parliament, and the opposition popular press railed against Prime Minister Robert Walpole and galvanized support for a war of conquest against Spain, which they saw as the only suitable response to the recent "depredations" committed against their shipping by Spanish privateers. Among the pro-war group's objectives were Spanish plunder and potential markets for British merchants. In addition, it sought the annexation of Spanish lands as a blow to the enemy and as a means to protect and expand British trade and thus enhance the growth of its empire. The image of Havana was so malleable in this public discourse that it appealed to those that wished to acquire large, landed territories in Spanish America and those who only wanted further access to trade.[44]

Numerous proposals in the 1720s and 1730s championed taking and holding Spanish American territories. As the lesson of Jamaica had shown, trade could not be secured or protected without colonies nearby, not only way stations but also ports with hinterlands of their own, which could also be cultivated profitably by industrious British subjects. Though the Treaty of Utrecht of 1713 had granted Britain the asiento, many felt it had been a sham, depriving the nation of a much-deserved territorial concession in Spanish America. Authors harked back to the days of the Western Design with nostalgia, when "we *conquer'd* and we *kept*." Editors, authors, and publishers stoked readers' lust for lands, as well as marketed to it, by running descriptions of Spanish America highlighting the compelling reasons to acquire its most attractive ports and their hinterlands. This popular mobilization hastened Britain's declaration of war and left behind an abundant print record of the popularity of the idea of annexing Spanish American lands in mid-eighteenth-century Britain and British North America.[45]

---

44. The South Sea Company voted against the 1739 war because of the losses it would sustain through the interruption of its trade. See Kathleen Wilson, "Empire, Trade, and Popular Politics in Mid-Hanoverian Britain: The Case of Admiral Vernon," *Past and Present*, no. 121 (1988), 74–109, esp. 107; Steve Pincus, "Addison's Empire: Whig Conceptions of Empire in the Early 18th Century," *Parliamentary History*, XXXI (2012), 99–117.

45. *A Proposal for Humbling Spain . . .* , 2d ed. (London [1740]), 3, 53; *The Newsman's Interpreter; or, A Description of Several Spanish Territories in America; Particularly of Those Places against Which, It Is Supposed . . .* (Manchester, 1741). One British naturalist advocated for "the conquest" of Havana based on its supposedly healthier climate than the sugar islands; see Mark Catesby, *The Natural*

[But the gov't & parl[iamen]t of GB rejected territorial conquest in New Spain — The rhetoric was rejected, The capture of Havana was aimed at securing peace by attacking Spain, not

Imagining the Conquest • 45

In these public discussions, the familiar tropes of the Black Legend convinced Britons that acquiring lands in Spanish America would be relatively easy, which strengthened support for the war. A persistent theme in this literature was that British subjects would serve as the liberators of Spanish America—not only of their African and indigenous peoples but also of creole inhabitants—and thus rescue them from their subjugation to an oppressive and backward Spanish colonial master. This rhetoric led the British public to believe they could gain allies in Spanish American territories they attacked by appealing to the creoles' desire "to throw off the *Spanish* Yoke." Alternatively, they could offer arms to indigenous inhabitants or grant enslaved Africans freedom in exchange for their support. The belief that Britain's empire would grow by invitation—effectively, "annexation by consent"—smoothed over more complicated realities.[46]

In the heated climate of the War of Jenkins' Ear, a surprisingly public discourse developed about the most desirable target to attack and acquire in Spanish America (see Figure 4). Because of the speed with which British war planners leapt into action during the Seven Years' War, there was no similar protracted debate about which objectives to target in Spanish America during that later war. Rather, the lobbying in the press conducted during a war twenty-three years beforehand materially shaped strategic thinking behind the battle plans put into place in 1762. Plans were discussed and developed by government ministers, members of Parliament, merchants, planters, colonial governors, naval commanders, army generals, recruits, and the popular press. Merchants and colonial officials with experience in the region sent government ministers their proposals, and former prisoners of war and South Sea company factors brought back pilfered maps and their own recommendations. Publishers released "authentic" descriptions arguing for the most advantageous course of action and rallying the king and his councillors to seize the moment.[47]

History of Carolina, Florida, and the Bahama Islands . . . , 2 vols. (London, 1731–1743 [1729–1747]), II, xxxix. On the plots against Spanish America during this war, see also Mapp, *The Elusive West*, 270–282.

46. *The Present State of Revenues and Forces, by Sea and Land, of France and Spain, Compar'd with Those of Great Britain* (London, 1740), 33, 42, 48 (quotation). See also *Country Journal: or, The Craftsman* (London), June, 3, 1738. For the idea of "empire by invitation" or "annexation by consent," see Pares, *War and Trade in the West Indies*, 76.

47. South Sea Company factors in Cuba sent several intelligence reports and proposals for attacking Spanish America back to British authorities. See Proposals from Hubert Fassell and Henry Hutchinson, Oct. 25, 1739, Add. MSS 32694, fols. 47–48, BL; Leonard Cocke to Captain Digby Dent (Jamaica), Nov. 3, 1736, Vernon-Wager Manuscripts, LC. Many of Britain and the United States' extensive archival holdings of maps and materials from eighteenth-century Spanish America were pilfered by former prisoners of war. See "Plano del puerto de La Havana," 1741, Vz10/18, Royal Naval

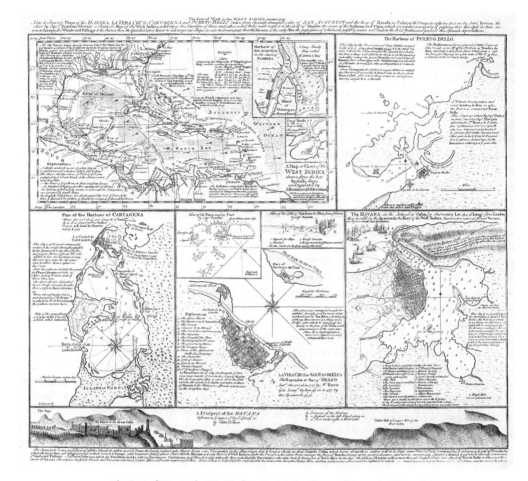

FIGURE 4 *The Seat of War in the West Indies Containing New and Accurate Plans of the Havana, La Vera Cruz, Cartagena, and Puerto Bello (taken from Spanish draughts), also of San Augustin and the Bay of Honda in Cuba* (London, 1740). By Emanuel Brown. Courtesy of the John Carter Brown Library at Brown University

Amid all this scheming, Havana emerged as a universally popular candidate for attack, though it was far from the only one discussed. Virtually all of Spain's overseas dominions were thought to be ripe for the taking. Other popular suggestions were Panama, Cartagena, Veracruz, Portobelo, Saint Augustine, and Peru. Stratagems hatched at the onset of the war advocated choking off Spanish trade by capturing and holding strategic ports in the Gulf

Museum, Portsmouth, U.K.; *A Geographical Description of the Coasts, Harbours, and Sea Ports of the Spanish West Indies . . .* (London, 1740).

of Mexico. In these early stages, there was also support for conquering territory that might make it possible to cut a swathe from the Caribbean to the Pacific, such as Buenos Aires or Darién, Panama, which the Scots had held and lost in the mid-seventeenth century. On the other side of the Pacific, Manila was also proposed, not only for the silver galleon that traveled there from Acapulco "with Eight or Ten Million Pieces of eight" but also for its potential as an entrepôt of Asian trade, if it could be garrisoned and kept. Many of the objectives discussed reflected Britain's growing global aspirations, but within this debate Havana continued to assert its potent appeal.[48]

There was concern not to discuss British war plans openly in Parliament, but, when the subject did come up, Havana was the first target on the lips of a member of Parliament. With some concern, the Spanish ambassador to London, Don Tomás Geraldino, reported back to his king in Madrid this talk about attacking Havana. His source in London had reported, "We shall continue to feel ourselves here with the hopes of taking not only the Havanna but even the rest of the Spanish dominions in America." The feasibility of such grandiose aims aside, British machinations against Spanish territories in the Americas, and against Havana in particular, were no mystery. They were everywhere in the British press, examples of which the Spanish ambassador scrupulously sent back to Madrid.[49]

Havana's popularity as a target rested on a powerful logic to Britons in the mid-eighteenth century, one that had been forged over centuries and that persuaded them that acquisition of the city would open access to vast amounts of Spanish silver. It was, they reasoned, the largest and richest city in the Caribbean, the stopping point of the treasure galleons and flota, and it had an excellent, geostrategically situated harbor, "one of the finest in the World." Like Jamaica, or Gibraltar in the Mediterranean (a frequent comparison), Havana's harbor was seen as a crucial stepping-stone to trade, one that would offer control of the region's sea-lanes and protect and bolster Britain's commerce with mainland Spanish America and its precious silvers and metals. As was often pointed out in the popular literature, the Spanish monarchy re-

48. For Buenos Aires, see *A Proposal for Humbling Spain,* 53; and *Country Journal: or, The Craftsman,* June, 3, 1738. For Darién, see ibid. For correspondence about proposed sites of attack, see Correspondence of the Duke of Newcastle, Add. MSS 32694, BL; Vernon-Wager Manuscripts, LC; Charles Wager, "Places Where the Spaniards May Be Attack'd (with a Proper Force) in Europe and the West Indies," June 5, 1738, 52v, and "Attempts That May Be Made, upon the Spanish Coast of Europe, or America," 1740, 57r–57v, both in Add. MSS 32694, BL.

49. J. Richmond to Tomás Geraldino, Nov. 15, 1739, AGS, Estado, 6908. During a debate in the House of Commons in November 1739, member of Parliament George Heathcote mentioned Havana first among potential targets, the others being Cartagena and Vera Cruz; see *The History and Proceedings of the House of Commons,* 1739 (London, 1742), 349.

ferred to Havana as the "key to the Indies"—a key was featured in its coat of arms—which made Havana, to British authors, "*The Key of all the West Indies, to lock up, or unlock the Door or Entrance to all America.*" "Were we Masters of this Port," another author conjectured, "it would force the Spaniards to allow us a free Trade to the Continent of America, where they sell our Commodities for ten Times the prime Cost in Spain."[50]

In part, Havana's allure might also have derived from its familiarity to British subjects and a popular imaginary already fixated on the port. Between travelers passing through, merchants, slave traders, ship's captains, and prisoners of war, it was the point of Spanish America most frequented by visitors. By the 1720s and 1730s, there was already a significant corpus of texts to draw on that offered tantalizing descriptions of Havana. Prior descriptions, maps, and drawings of the city, as well as schemes against it, were already in circulation and only had to be reissued. In a sign of striking continuity across time, Major Smith's hoped-for but still undiscovered gold and silver mines in Cuba and his fascination with the treasure galleons, for example, continued to be discussed. It was Smith's claim—still repeated almost a century later—that commodities in Spanish America were sold for ten times the cost in Spain. Similarly, the popular phrase about Havana as the key "to lock up, or unlock" American trade was taken from a text first published in London in 1648, *New Survey of the West Indies,* by Thomas Gage, the intellectual author of Cromwell's Western Design, who had visited the city in 1637.[51]

Part of the undying appeal of the desire to conquer Havana was the openness and flexibility of the ways it could be envisioned and the benefits that would likely accrue thereafter. For some, the acquisition of Havana opened up access to treasure ships' cargo of Spanish silver and the markets and mines of mainland Spanish America and especially Mexico. For others, Havana's capture was a springboard to capturing the island stretching to its east, imagined in one instance as "thinly inhabited with Indians not thoroughly reconciled

50. *Geographical and Historical Description,* preface, 2–3, 156–157, 165–166, 169, 170; *Newsman's Interpreter,* 38, 39, 41 (quotation), 42. For a similar claim that goods were sold in Spanish America for ten times the cost in Spain, see *Description of the Spanish Islands,* 104–105. For other proposals for capturing Havana, see the anonymous letter to Admiral Sir Charles Wager, "Scheme in Regard to an American Expedition against Spain," Jan. 14, 1739, J. Hamilton, "Proposal for Taking Cuba by a Force to be Raised in America," May 14, 1739, and Anonymous, "A Proposal for Taking Cuba by Attacking the Havana, Santiago de Cuba, and other Cities and Towns on that Island, and Subjecting the Whole to the King of Great Britain," all in Vernon-Wager Manuscripts, LC. For a proposal that emphasized the benefits of Cuban and Spanish American markets, see W. Hamilton, "A Proposal to Take the Island of Cuba, with Very Little Expense to England by a Force Raised in the American Colonies," Aug. 18, 1739, Add. MSS 32694, fol. 33, BL.

51. J. Eric S. Thompson, ed., *Thomas Gage's Travels in the New World* (Norman, Okla., 1958), 165–166, 176.

and naturalized to a Spanish arbitrary government" and in another as settled with seven blacks for every white. In either case, the island of Cuba was seen as easily conquered, as long as the British gave the indigenous population arms and promised the enslaved Africans their liberty. Several publications discussed the ease of capturing the rest of the island after Havana, which would serve as a valuable asset for the cultivation of sugar plantations or as a necessary counter to the machinations of the French in Hispaniola, who could potentially be contemplating expanding into eastern Cuba from their colony of Saint Domingue. Because the city's capture was depicted as providing entry into both trade to the west and sugar production to the east, the idea of attacking Havana was able to gain support among interest groups one would not normally associate with one another.[52]

Historians have argued that the West India interest, a powerful lobby of Caribbean sugar planters in British Parliament, had little enthusiasm for acquiring territory in Cuba and blocked this possibility because the island posed a threat as a rival sugar producer. Yet, even on the sugar island Jamaica, interest groups supported acquiring Cuba. Havana's economy was not yet dominated by sugar production; instead, it took part in a busy trade in enslaved Africans and also tobacco, wood, hides, and cattle that enriched Jamaica. Increasingly deforested, Jamaica needed timber for its sugar-boiling houses, and British logwooders set up temporary encampments on Cuba's south coast to remove the island's abundant hardwoods. The most committed Jamaican smugglers might prefer to continue to operate an unregulated and therefore duty-free trade with Cuba rather than have it come under British law and taxes, but Cuba's acquisition would provide other relief. If Britain should ultimately choose to seize eastern Cuba as well, Jamaican shipping would gain free navigation in the Windward Passage between Cuba and Hispaniola and protection from the famous harassments of Cuba's privateers at Havana, Trinidad, Santiago de Cuba, and Baracoa.[53]

By targeting Havana and potentially acquiring the island of Cuba, Britain would also release Jamaica, the Carolinas, the Bahamas, and Georgia from the ongoing threat of Spanish attack or counterattack. This aim was worthy in

---

52. *Country Journal: or, The Craftsman,* June 3, 1738; *Geographical and Historical Description,* 170; *A Dissertation on the Present Conjuncture Particularly with Regard to Trade, by a Merchant of Bristol,* 2d ed. (London, 1739), 23 (quotation); *Present State of the Revenues and Forces,* 42.

53. For the argument that the West India interest opposed Cuba's acquisition, see Pares, *War and Trade,* 77–82; Marrero, *Cuba,* VI, 126; Peggy K. Liss, *Atlantic Empires: The Network of Trade and Revolution, 1713–1826* (Baltimore, 1983), 18; Thomas, *Cuba,* 55–56. For arguments for acquiring Cuba voiced in Jamaica, see the discussion of Governor Edward Trelawny, below. For a discussion of British logwood encampments in Cuba, see, for example, Consejo de Indias, Nov. 26, 1776, AGI, Cuba, 1138, no. 16.

itself and might also make the island's retention more defensible to the other nations of Europe at the end of the war, or so it was thought. Without a foreign power next door, colonial authorities in Jamaica would also gain leverage against the maroons on the island, who would lose their ability to obtain arms from the Spanish. To the north, a joint Franco-Spanish force based out of Havana had attacked Charleston, South Carolina, in 1706, during the War of the Spanish Succession, and Cuba's privateers frequently haunted that port. The security of the Carolinas and also the Bahamas, which Spain had attacked twice, as well as of their shipping would be assured with the neutralization of Cuba and its soldiers and privateers.[54]

The British colony of Georgia, in turn, had great incentive to extinguish Havana's threat because rumors were swirling of an attempt on the colony to be launched from Havana. The Spanish king believed Georgia had been placed in territory that rightfully belonged to Spanish Florida. In April 1737, he instructed the captain general of Cuba to begin preparing an assault to destroy it. Perhaps reasoning that a strong offense was the best defense, in 1740 Governor James Oglethorpe of Georgia wrote to Prime Minister Walpole proposing an attack on Havana; he believed he could take the city with just two battalions as long as he had help from the British fleet and local Native allies. Oglethorpe ended up assaulting Saint Augustine later that year, and it was Spain's forces in Cuba that struck Georgia first, with almost two thousand soldiers besieging Gualquini, or Fort Frederica, on Saint Simons Island, in July 1742 (see Figure 5). The captain general of Cuba's plan involved inducing the enslaved population there to rise up in arms and join them, a familiar British stratagem that proved too difficult to implement. Though the invasion did not go as planned or cause the damage Spain intended, there was enough fear that another might follow to build support for a strike against Havana.[55]

54. *Geographical and Historical Description*, preface, 38, 170. In 1738, the Jamaican Assembly had finally managed to sign a peace treaty to end its first and most violent maroon war, spearheaded by maroon leader Cudjoe, who allegedly had been supplied with Spanish arms. As part of the peace treaty signed on January 2, Cudjoe agreed that he would aid the government's forces should the island come under enemy attack. See the treaty with Captain Cudjoe, maroon chief, Jan. 2, 1739, Jamaican Council Journals, IX, 1B/5/4/9, JNA. From Havana and Santiago de Cuba, attacks were launched on the Bahamas (1684, 1703, 1720) and Charleston, South Carolina (1706), the latter together with French troops. See David F. Marley, *Wars of the Americas: A Chronology of Armed Conflict in the Western Hemisphere, 1492 to the Present*, 2d ed., I (Santa Barbara, Calif., 2008), 345–346, 350, 370.

55. Woodfine, "The Anglo-Spanish War of 1739," in Black, ed., *Origins of War*, 146; Andrien and Kuethe, *The Spanish Atlantic World*, 146–148; Pares, *War and Trade*, 29–56; Walker, *Spanish Politics and Imperial Trade*, 205–207; Larry E. Ivers, *British Drums on the Southern Frontier: The Military Colonization of Georgia, 1733–1749* (Chapel Hill, N.C., 1974), 72–73; Marley, *Wars of the Americas*, 207; James Oglethorpe to Robert Walpole, Jan. 25, Apr. 2, 1740, CH (H) correspondence 2942, 2948, Cambridge University Library, cited in Philip Woodfine, *Britannia's Glories: The Walpole Ministry and the 1739 War with Spain* (Woodbridge, U.K., 1998), 179 n. 175. On the Spanish raid on Gualquini,

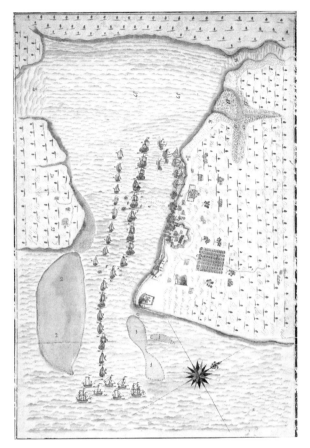

FIGURE 5 Map of the Spanish Attack on Gualquini (Saint Simons Island, Georgia). By Engineer Antonio de Arredondo, 1742. Havana Governor Francisco Cagigal de la Vega planned to foment a rebellion among the local enslaved population in Georgia and even sent African interpreters to help implement this unsuccessful scheme. Courtesy, Biblioteca Nacional de España, Madrid

Farther north, British North Americans, without whose manpower a descent on the island would be impossible, demonstrated a sustained and fervent popular enthusiasm for taking possession of Cuba. In fact, British colonials in North America were the ones who most consistently advocated for the annexation of the entire island. British North Americans exercised no decision-making power in the war, but British war planners knew that without the northern colonists they did not have enough soldiers to conceive of making an attempt on Havana or any other part of the island. While merchants

Georgia, see Allan J. Kuethe, *Cuba, 1753–1815: Crown, Military, and Society* (Knoxville, Tenn., 1986), 9; and Marley, *Wars of the Americas,* 395–396. On the plot to induce rebellion among Georgia's slaves, see "The Governor General of Cuba Appoints the Governor of Florida Commander of the Expedition against Georgia, and Issues His Orders for the Conduct of Operations," in Georgia Historical Society, *Collections,* VII, pt. 3 (Savannah, Ga., 1913), 32–35; Jane Landers, *Black Society in Spanish Florida* (Urbana, Ill., 1999), 38.

in the northern colonies spoke of the boon it would be to acquire greater markets for the region's products, poor whites in the northern and mid-Atlantic colonies were tantalized by the prospect of gaining a plantation or land grant on the island of Cuba. This dream was a product of the struggling colonists' own social and economic ambitions, inspired by what they had heard or seen of the island or the West Indies in general, as well as the flow of English pamphlets, newspapers, and magazines that crossed the Atlantic. British North American colonial governors, who were soon pressured to raise as many volunteers as possible in order to provide sufficient manpower for an attempt on Cuba, promoted the possibility of land grants for those willing to sign on. A recruiting pamphlet in New York for a 1740 expedition to Guantánamo, Cuba, promised "an easy conquest" and that Spaniards would "fly before you and leave their houses, their negroes, their money, plate, jewels, and plantations, to be possessed by you and your posterity forever." With such arresting images of seizing the wealth, property, and enslaved Africans of Cuba, the island had the most potential of all targets for raising North American recruits.[56]

At the heart of all the sometimes amazing plans for Spanish American annexation, whether by conquest, consent, invitation, or instigation, was a disjuncture between the size of British imperial ambitions and the limited ability of British man and sea power at midcentury to achieve what they proposed. To make up the gap, an array of creative, experimental, and potentially problematic solutions were devised, particularly in London, far from the imagined American theater of war. From London, Spanish America was a place only partially and fragmentally understood, pieced together from dispatches and reports from those returning from the colonies. British perceptions of the region's creole, indigenous, and African-descended populations, particularly how easily they could be manipulated to achieve desired ends, were tenuous. Yet what were sometimes fantastical British imaginings would directly influence the course of British military campaigns.

By the time war broke out, the expectation that Havana would be attacked was palpable throughout Britain and its colonies in North America and the West Indies. As the *Boston Gazette* observed, "The Nation, not in the least

56. William Bradford, *A Supplement to the New York Gazette,* Apr. 14, 1740, LCP. See also Jill Lepore, *New York Burning: Liberty, Slavery, and Conspiracy in Eighteenth-Century Manhattan* (New York, 2005), 21, 235. On Cuba as a market for North American commerce, see New York governor George Clarke, Speech to the Assembly, June 30, 1740, CO 5.1094, fol. 144, TNA; *By the Honourable Joseph Talcott Esq; Governour of His Majesty's Colony of Connecticut . . . A Proclamation* [Call for Volunteers], May 13, 1740, New London, Connecticut, New-York Historical Society. On schemes of land bounties to encourage enlistment in case of raising North American troops for an expedition against the Spaniards, see Anonymous Letter to Admiral Sir Charles Wager (Whitehall), February 1739, Vernon-Wager Manuscripts, LC.

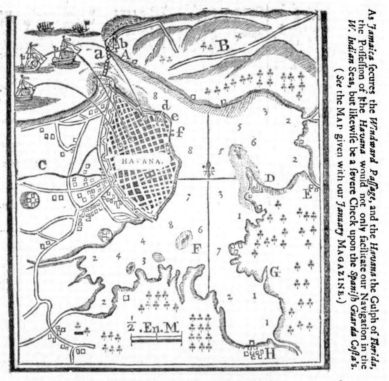

The village of Guanabacoa is located incorrectly in the legend; however, other details, such as the guns of the Morro and the city's water source, are accurate. Courtesy, Northwestern

Explanation of the foregoing P L A N.

A *The Battery called,* 12 Apoſtles.
B *The Road from the eaſtern Caſtle, which lies on the Coaſt 5 Miles from the Town.*
C *The River* Lagida, *which falls into the Sea near the weſtern Caſtle at about 5 Miles diſtance.*
D *Noſtra Sennora de la Regla.*
E *Venta, or Inn de Marimelena.*
F *Iſla de mugeres.*

G *La* Doctora.
H *Guanabacoa Village.*
a *The Boom and Chain a-croſs the Harbour*
b *The M ro Caſtle of* 52 *Guns.*
c *Fort St* Maria, *or de la*Punta, *of* 30 *Guns.*
d El Fuerte *where the Governour reſides with* 22 *Guns.*
e *The Mole.*
f *The point Gate and ſmall Fort.*

FIGURE 6 "Plan of the City of Havanah." From *Gentlemen's Magazine*, X (March 1740), 149. The village of Guanabacoa is located incorrectly in the legend; however, other details, such as the guns of the Morro and the city's water source, are accurate. Courtesy, Northwestern University / Hathitrust Digital Library

doubting of Success, foretold, as a Thing certain, the Conquest of the Havannah." A few months after Britain's and Spain's mutual declarations of war, two
popular British magazines, *Gentleman's Magazine* and the *London Magazine,*
published military maps of Havana accompanied by detailed prescriptions
for how an assault should be conducted (see Figure 6). The extent of the detail the articles and maps conveyed—including the Morro Castle's fifty-two
guns, soundings of the harbor, and the chain and boom raised across the harbor mouth every night—revealed the input of merchants or prisoners of war
who had spent time in Havana. The tactics proposed were also eerily similar
to battle operations that would later be conducted in 1762. They entailed landing an army a few miles to the east of the port, gaining control of the fortress
called La Cabaña, and from there taking the Morro Castle and, ultimately, the
city. Now that the plan had been set, the British army and navy needed only
to put it into action.[57]

"The Seat of War" in the West Indies

Once war was declared and the action moved to the West Indies, the Caribbean became a British training ground for offensive operations against the
most-coveted ports of Spanish America. If delusions were rampant before the
War of Jenkins' Ear, the conflict provided a powerful lesson in the practical
costs of attacking Cuba. When the "seat of war," as it was called, moved to the
Caribbean, decisions about which parts of Spanish America to target were left
to those on the scene: naval commanders, army generals, and local governors
conferring in councils of war held at the base of operations in Jamaica. By necessity their plans were more pragmatic and less fantastical, tempered by the
realities of manpower, weather and wind patterns, hurricanes, disease, provisions, ammunition, and available ships. Officials in Jamaica would also, of
course, harbor less-fanciful notions of Cuba. It was an island known to them
through networks of trade, privateering, and prisoner exchange, and whose
home fires they could see burning at night from Jamaica's northern shores.

The desire to target Havana drove the early phase of tactical operations. As

57. *Boston Gazette,* Jan. 26–Feb. 2, 1741, [2]; *London Magazine, or Gentleman's Monthly Intelli-*
gencer, IX (April 1740), 192–193; *Gentleman's Magazine,* X (March 1740), 149. In April 1740, the *New*
England Weekly Journal ran brief descriptions of Havana and Cartagena, the two cities "being at this
day the subject of much conversation" (Apr. 1, 1740, [2]). In February 1740, the Philadelphia paper
the *American Weekly Mercury* printed an extract of a letter from Antigua reporting that a fleet of ships
had been sighted on its way to join Admiral Vernon in Jamaica "on some great design, tho' it is cred-
itably reported, that they are going to make a Descent on *Cuba* and that the *Havannah* will be the
first Place they'll attack." The reprinted letter was dated Jan. 2, 1739 (*American Weekly Mercury,* Feb.
26–Mar. 4, 1739–1740, [3]).

soon as the British naval squadron in Jamaica was alerted to the imminence of war, two months before it was officially declared, Commodore Charles Brown left Port Royal with seven warships to cruise around Cuba. One of these, the *Shoreham,* under the command of Captain Edward Boscawen, reconnoitered approaches to Havana—destroying two Spanish sloops and capturing a third—and established a blockade of the port.[58]

At the war's beginning, a Pacific campaign was postponed in order to concentrate resources on a more sizable expedition in the Caribbean. George II's instructions to Vice Admiral Edward Vernon, on his departure for the Caribbean from Portsmouth in July 1739, were "to commit all sorts of hostilities against the Spaniards in such manner as you shall judge the most proper." The Duke of Newcastle wrote to naval commander Lord Cathcart that he found American commanders' support of Havana as a "practicable" target heartening and that they would be able to provide as many as three thousand troops. In a private letter, he expressed his hope that the commander would undertake a siege of the city, which would be "the greatest and most glorious work of all." Lord Cathcart's instructions were to attack Havana first and foremost when he arrived in the Caribbean with his eight thousand British troops.[59]

Governor Edward Trelawny of Jamaica was an important and influential early advocate for Havana as the most promising British target, calling it potentially "a most valuable possession to the crown." So great was Trelawny's enthusiasm for a Havana expedition, he volunteered to be named a colonel and to leave Jamaica to take part in the offensive, despite his posting as governor and his confessed lack of military experience. Because Havana was the base of the Spanish *guardacosta,* which had preyed on Jamaican merchant ships and privateers, Trelawny thought it would be particularly sweet revenge if it were "the first to fall, a sacrifice to our just resentment." Although an expedition against Darién, Panama, was also being considered in 1739, Trelawny saw it as "but piddling with respect to the Havana." Havana's acquisition, he declared, promised to "drive the Spaniard out of the West Indian seas and make their possessions in America worthless. . . . If we had that, we could have what we would besides almost at pleasure, as we should be masters of the whole seas."[60]

58. Marley, *Wars of the Americas,* 251.

59. For Admiral Vernon's instructions, see King George II to Vice Admiral Edward Vernon at Portsmouth, "Instructions to Wage War upon the Spanish in the West Indies, Capture the Galleons, etc. and Secret Instructions to Vice Admiral Vernon to Report to England on Best Practicable Place for Attacking Spaniards in West Indies," July 16, 1739, Vernon-Wager Manuscripts, LC. For Newcastle's hope of targeting Havana, see Newcastle (private) to Lord Cathcart, Aug. 14, 1740, Add. MSS 32694, fol. 472, BL.

60. Edward Trelawny to the Duke of Newcastle, Aug. 8, 1739, Despatches, Jamaica to England, 1739–1755, JNA.

For Cuba, Trelawny had in mind a take and hold policy because of the island's strategic geographical and commercial advantages. He proposed that the North American colonies send down men and provisions and that a landing with six thousand men should be made to the west of the port, as recommended by Major Smith, followed by a ground invasion. According to his reckoning, the aid of the North American colonies, coupled with the superiority of British shipping, would enable Britain to "keep [Havana] against all the powers of Europe, who have not strength enough in the West Indies to retake it." Trelawny knew that targeting Havana would make it easier to recruit North American volunteers. As he wrote, "There is a vast spirit by all accounts in those of the Northern Colonies who in their imagination have swallowed up all Cuba."[61]

Admiral Vernon, by then in Jamaica, believed that an attack on Havana would be too difficult to attempt at that early moment in the war in the fall of 1739. Guided by intelligence from the South Sea Company's factor previously stationed in Panama, he decided instead that Portobelo was inadequately defended and would make an ideal first target. It could lead to the capture of any galleons in the harbor and severely disrupt Spanish trade. Taking Portobelo by surprise, Vernon and his six ships shelled the city for a mere two days before Panama's governor raised the white flag. Despite its international reputation as a center for and symbol of Spanish American trade, the port mainly served as a destination for mule trains coming from Peru to the trade fairs. Although Portobelo was effectively an easy victory taken before other more important ports could be attempted, its acquisition was a victory celebrated as avidly in Britain as though the admiral had marched into the grand Zócalo of Mexico City itself and claimed it for Britain, along with the viceroyalty's fabled silver mines. "Vernon's triumph" was commemorated with popular demonstrations, songs, toasts, plays, books, commemorative medals, and the renaming of Green's Lane in London as Portobello Road.[62]

61. When Trelawney later considered Saint Domingue as a target, on France's entry into the war, he thought the island should be invaded only to destroy its sugar works. See Trelawny to the Duke of Newcastle, March 1747/8, Despatches, Jamaica to England, 1739–1755, fol. 349; Trelawny to Sir Charles Wager, Aug. 8, 1739, and Trelawny to Wager, Aug. 29, 1740, Vernon-Wager Manuscripts, LC. See also Pares, *War and Trade in the West Indies*, 89.

62. On the decision *not* to target Havana in 1739, see Edward Vernon, *Original Papers Relating to the Expedition to the Island of Cuba* (London, 1744), 7. On the celebration of "Vernon's triumph," see Kathleen Wilson, *The Sense of the People: Politics, Culture, and Imperialism in England, 1715–1785* (New York, 1998); and Wilson, "Empire, Trade, and Popular Politics in Mid-Hanoverian Britain: The Case of Admiral Vernon," *Past and Present*, no. 121 (November 1988), 74–109. After the euphoria of Vernon's victory at Portobelo, the green light was given to Anson to head to the Pacific. He failed to capture Peru or the Philippines, and his expedition experienced great hardships, but he did seize the fabled Manila galleon; see Glyn Williams, *The Prize of All the Oceans: The Dramatic True Story of*

FIGURE 7 A British Medal Minted in Anticipation of Admiral Vernon's Capture of Cartagena in 1741. On the back is printed "Vernon conquered Cartagena" (B) while the front identifies Vernon's next target as Havana (A). The exact same template was used for coins to celebrate the capture of Portobelo in 1739, the only change being the name of the city on the back. Despite early false reports of Cartagena's capture, the British siege of the city was a failure. © National Maritime Museum, Greenwich, London

After Vernon's return to Jamaica from Portobelo, Trelawny advocated most avidly for moving on Havana next, as a fitting bookend to the victory in Panama. With that objective in mind, in June 1740 Vernon arrived off the coast of Havana with fifty-seven ships, though not enough men to launch an attack, and spent two months cruising around western Cuba, surveying the coastline. By this point, the British had lost the chance to catch the city before its defenses had been put on alert, as the alarm had already been raised in Havana over a rumored attack. A Spanish privateer had intercepted a Jamaican ship carrying a letter in which "some fool had wrote to his correspondent in England that they were in daily expectation of 50,000 men from England to attack the Havana." This warning gave the governor of Havana and the captain general of Cuba time to muster militia and put the city in excellent condition to resist an attack.[63]

What followed, however, was, not an assault on Havana, but the siege of Cartagena of 1741, an engagement that proved a colossal and embarrassing failure for Vernon and a triumphant victory for the Spanish defenders (see Figure 7 [Plate 2]). Meant to capture another strategic Spanish Caribbean

---

Commodore Anson's Voyage Round the World and How He Seized the Spanish Treasure Galleon (New York, 2000).

63. García del Pino, *Toma de la Habana*, 28–29; Edward Boscawen to Vernon, Nov. 27, 1740, Governor Juan Francisco de Güemes i Horcasitas to Charles Brunies, Marquis de Larnage of Saint Domingue, Mar. 12, 1741, both in Vernon-Wager Manuscripts, LC.

port and unlock access to the mines of Peru, the siege of Cartagena can also be seen as a dress rehearsal for the Havana campaign of 1762 — the kind of dress rehearsal that goes so badly it ensures an infinitely better opening night. Rebuffed by the strength of the city's defenses and the skill of its defenders and reeling from the effects of yellow fever on his men, Vernon was forced to retreat after six weeks of fighting. After regrouping in Jamaica, he turned to Cuba again, weighing anchor for Santiago de Cuba, where he briefly established a foothold on the island of Cuba at a point less difficult to attack than Havana. Vernon seemed to think that doing so would protect him from criticism after the failures at Cartagena and Havana.

Admiral Vernon and General Thomas Wentworth made a landing in July 1741 in Guantánamo Bay, which they renamed Cumberland Bay, and established a fortified encampment there called George Stadt. Although their original plan was to try to use the encampment at Guantánamo as a launching point for an assault on Santiago de Cuba, Vernon redirected the objective toward creating a more permanent settlement on the eastern end of Cuba, which might open up the Windward Passage and halt the operations of Santiago de Cuba's privateers. Bickering among the commanders and local resistance conspired to thwart this attempt to take Cuba from what was considered the easier eastern side. In many respects, the campaign at Guantánamo, like the one at Cartagena, represented the implosion of several strands of Britons' expansive imperial dreams. In relatively quick succession, Vernon had failed in attempts to conquer Cartagena and Santiago de Cuba and lost, by one estimate, more than twenty thousand men, the vast majority to yellow fever.[64]

Vernon was promptly removed from his post as commander of British naval forces in the Caribbean, but victories also eluded his successor, Admiral Sir Charles Knowles, who launched naval assaults against both Santiago

64. Charles E. Nowell, "The Defense of Cartagena," *HAHR*, 477–501, esp. 492; Gonzalo M. Quintero Saravia, *Don Blas de Lezo: Defensor de Cartagena de Indias* (Bogotá, 2002), 221–222; J. R. McNeill, *Mosquito Empires: Ecology and War in the Greater Caribbean, 1620–1914* (Cambridge, Mass., 2010), 154. See also Blas de Lezo, "Diario de lo acontecido en Cartagena de Indias desde el día 15 de marzo de 1741 hasta el 20 de mayo del mismo año," AHN, Estado, 2335; Cristobal Bermúdez Plata, *Narración de la defensa de Cartagena de Indias contra el ataque de los ingleses en 1741* (Seville, 1912); José Manuel Rodríguez, *El almirante Blas de Lezo: El vasco que salvó al imperio español* (Madrid, 2005). The British knew about Guantánamo's potential as a naval base, thanks to the account of a ship's pilot from New Spain picked up by a prisoner of war in Havana and taken to a London printer; see [Caleb Smith], *A Geographical Description of the Coasts, Harbours, and Sea Ports of the Spanish West Indies* . . . (London, 1740). See also Olga Portuondo Zúñiga, *Una derrota británica en Cuba* (Santiago de Cuba, 2000), 132, 134–135, 162; Richard Harding, *Amphibious Warfare in the Eighteenth Century: The British Expedition to the West Indies, 1740–1742* (Suffolk, U.K., 1991), 127, 133, 135. For estimates of the death toll, see McNeill, *Mosquito Empires*, 167.

FIGURE 8 A Contemporary British Sketch of the Naval Encounter off Havana in 1748.
This depiction shows Knowles's squadron burning Commander Reggio's ship, rather than
Reggio successfully running off Admiral Knowles. Both sides claimed this naval encounter
as a victory. © National Maritime Museum, Greenwich, London

de Cuba and Havana in 1748. The attempt on Havana, mounted by Knowles
shortly after the navy's second failure at Santiago de Cuba, was little more than
an afterthought and took place after news of the war's end had reached the
West Indies. Ending the campaign, not with a bang, but a whimper, Admiral
Knowles engaged in an inconclusive sea battle off the coast of Havana with the
Spanish commander Andrés Reggio, who successfully protected the Spanish
treasure galleon from Knowles's attack (see Figure 8). Though Knowles managed instead to seize the battleship *Conquistador*—of some symbolic value—
and proudly sail it into Port Royal, Jamaica, both sides would claim victory.[65]

Havana, Santiago de Cuba, and Cartagena eluded the grasp of British
admirals during the War of Jenkins' Ear, but British war commanders learned
useful lessons in those campaigns that they yearned to apply. Four years after
Vernon's removal from the West India command, his name was erased by
George II from a list of officers in the Royal Navy. In a lament to the House of

65. García del Pino, *Toma de la Habana*, 40; Cervera, *Inglaterra y la Habana*, 41–42; Portuondo
Zúñiga, *Una derrota británica*, 183.

Commons in February 1743, Vernon blamed his defeats at Cartagena and Santiago de Cuba on the failure of supplies to arrive in a speedy fashion. If supplies and reinforcements had gotten to him in time, he claimed, he would have gone after Havana, the prize that got away. Instead, the slow arrival of more land and sea forces gave the enemies time to fortify themselves against his operations and make themselves "more powerful than We." Given the needed resources, Vernon said he would surely have "touch'd the Enemy in the most sensible Part (I mean the Island of *Cuba* and the *Havana*)."[66]

Conclusion

A deep history of Anglo-Spanish conflict and codependence forged the conditions that brought the massive British expedition to Havana during the Seven Years' War. In the late seventeenth and early eighteenth century, the slave trade and related commerce drew these rival monarchs' colonies into close and tense relations with each other, which embroiled them in a cycle of wars. During these wars, Britons kept plotting to take Havana and learning how to do it better, one new informant or failed attempt at a time.

The Anglo-Spanish War of 1739 can be read as a testing ground for British forces, allowing them to work out their model of combined land and sea operations in fits and starts, with more failures than successes. For the next war between Britain and Spain in 1762, and the next expedition against Havana, the prior attempts on Guantánamo and Cartagena provided at once a rehearsal, a hard lesson about the gap between imagination and reality, and an incentive for redemption at the next opportunity. In both efforts, all the difficulties for British commanders of putting the ambitious schemes of the war planners to work had manifested themselves. As it turned out, neither the taking nor the holding part of a strategy of take and hold was so easy after all. The Spanish defenses in Cartagena and Santiago de Cuba were much stronger than expected. Amerindians, blacks, and creoles were not as easily won over to the British side as it was thought. And yellow fever could take a devastating toll on troops newly arrived in the Caribbean, who lacked immunity to the disease and experienced a mortality rate as high as 85 percent. Clearly, Britain needed to have better intelligence, to move faster, and to raise troops more efficiently. Carrying out a successful campaign against Havana would have to be done quickly, and it would require a staggering number of sailors and soldiers. Finally, it would have to be mounted with enough speed to succeed be-

66. *Boston Post-Boy,* Apr. 18, 1743, [1]. See also Placer Cervera, *Inglaterra y la Habana,* 39; Portundo Zuñiga, *Una derrota británica,* 63–65.

[handwritten: Yes, why the long peace?]

fore Cuba's governor could raise its militias and Spain had time to reinforce its troops — and before disease could take its toll on British troops.[67]

After the war's end, the South Sea Company asiento, which had been such a cause of strife between Britain and Spain, was terminated, and a period of détente between Spain and Britain followed. The Seven Years' War was notable for the long shadow Spain's absence cast across its first years, what historians have called the "Seven Years' Peace." It was not to last. In 1759, Charles III ascended the Spanish throne and began pursuing a more aggressive agenda to counteract British commercial inroads into his realms. Spain is often depicted as France's dupe for being talked into entering the Seven Years' War as its ally when prospects of a resounding British victory were clear and peace negotiations had already begun. But Charles III's decision to go on the offensive drew from a logic based on more than just this one war. The Spanish king interpreted the Seven Years' War within the context of a longer, overarching struggle with Britain over sea-lanes, territorial possessions, markets, and the trade in enslaved Africans. After the results of the last war, Charles III also had reason to be confident in his prospects, as well as the strength of his most-prized overseas possessions.[68]

For Britain, Spain's late entry into the war gave it something all nations crave: an opportunity to refight a war that had gone badly and to learn from its mistakes. British plotting against Havana, seemingly a national pastime, began well before Spain entered the conflict, as early as the fall of 1760. When word of the French-Spanish accord leaked to Britain in October, the king and his ministers formally resolved to attack "Cuba, Louisiane, and the Manillas." William Pitt, leader of the House of Commons who wanted to fix the errors of the War of Jenkins' Ear, so aggressively pushed for immediately declaring war on Spain that he ended up being forced from office by Lord Bute, his rival in the war cabinet. Yet even Bute ended up rushing to push the plan into effect.[69]

---

67. McNeill, *Mosquito Empires*, 37; P. D. Curtin, "'The White Man's Grave': Image and Reality, 1780–1850," *Journal of British Studies*, I (1961), 94–110, esp. 99.

68. According to the terms of the Bourbon family compact, the two monarchies would settle their differences with Great Britain together, respecting each other's mutual interests, and, if the war had not ended by May 1, 1762, Spain would enter on France's side. The Spanish plan was to try to avoid war until well into 1762 in order to get the treasure fleet home and to prepare imperial defenses. See Vincente Palacio Atard, *El tercer pacto de familia* (Madrid, 1945); Anderson, *Crucible of War*, 484–502, esp. 484; Placer Cervera, *Inglaterra y la Habana*, 62–63; Finucane, *The Temptations of Trade*, 146–157; Jean McLachlan, "The Seven Years' Peace, and the West Indian Policy of Carvajal and Wall," *English Historical Review*, LIII (1938), 457–477.

69. The King to Lord Bute, Jan. 6, 1762, in Syrett, ed., *Siege and Capture of Havana*, 3. Olaudah Equiano reported a rumor in Spithead of a fleet outfitting for a secret attack on Havana as early as the fall of 1760 in *The Interesting Narrative of the Life of Olaudah Equiano, or Gustavus Vassa, the African*, I (London, [1789]), 152. Equiano speculates that the death of George II on October 25 might have pre-

The Havana campaign was launched by war commanders in the British government, but it was also supported, developed, honed, and championed by many individuals around the British Atlantic world for a very long time, and their experience strengthened its execution. The popularity of the planned Havana campaign, the longevity of its appeal, and the general support for it among the troops and colonial governors who would have to enact it reflect the long history of Britain's and Spain's codependence in the Atlantic world and deep-seated British imperial and commercial ambitions vis-à-vis the Spanish empire. Some recruits imagined themselves growing rich from Havana's spoils after the city's capitulation; others, from the land bounties they expected on a newly British isle. The division of booty—an important element to solidify before such an expedition in order to ensure cooperation between naval and army forces—had been determined by a template laid out by Queen Anne back in 1702 in the plans for an attack on Havana during the War of the Spanish Succession. The capture of Havana was a quest at least sixty years in the making. Britain now hoped it would at last claim this great prize.[70]

---

vented the expedition. Another surprise attack, against Havana, Panama, and Manila, was planned as early as spring of 1761, before Spain allied itself with the French; see Middleton, *Bells of Victory,* 205.

70. This was to be a joint British and Dutch attack on Havana or Martinique, to be led by the Earl of Peterborough. See Admiralty to Pocock, Feb. 18, 1762, in Syrett, ed., *Siege and Capture of Havana,* 45–46.

2

• • •

Havana at the Crossroads

War, Trade, and Slavery, circa 1700–1762

On the morning of June 6, 1762, the governor of Havana and captain general of Cuba, Juan de Prado, was awakened and summoned to the Morro fortress to take a look at something troubling that his lieutenant had sighted on the horizon. A small boat rowed Prado from the walled city to the entrance to Havana's harbor, where he climbed the rocky promontory to the fort's lookout point. Through a spyglass, he could see a large British fleet offshore, what one eyewitness described as "a forest of ships." The ships were still four leagues, or more than thirteen miles, out to sea—just distant shapes on the horizon. Havana's governor was quite accustomed to seeing British ships passing en route from Jamaica to the Bahamas Channel, where they would catch the Gulf Stream and sail to the North Atlantic. Brushing off this fleet as nothing more than the annual mercantile convoy making its way from Jamaica to London, Prado expressed his displeasure with his lieutenant for raising the alarm, dismissed his concerns (although he left a pilot behind to keep watch), and rowed back across the bay to Havana to attend Sunday mass.[1]

Within two hours, church bells across the city were clanging to warn residents of an impending British attack. The pilot on watch had reported that several British warships had turned in toward the beach at Cojímar, east of the city, and were lowering launches to make a landing. By that evening, the rest of the convoy had also changed direction, and now more than two hundred ships were bearing down on Havana. It was without a doubt a powerful armada coming to lay siege.[2]

1. Pedro Manuel de Olañeta, "Diario del sitio y rendición de la plaza de la Habana al Ingles," 1762, Miscellaneous Manuscripts, MS 352, XV, box 83, folder 1662, Sterling Memorial Library, Yale University; "Breve resumen de lo acaezido en el sitio de La Havana," Additional Manuscripts 13974, BL; Juan Miguel Palomino, "Noticias de la Habana que refieren como la ganaron los Ingleses el año de 1760," MS 10818/33, BNE; "Diario de lo ocurrido en la Habana durante el sitio de 1762," Real Academia de la Historia, Madrid.

2. "Diario del Capitán Don Juan de Casta del sitio de la ciudad de Havana," 1762, Theodorus Bailey Meyers Collection, NYPL; "Diario militar de las operaciones ejecutadas en la ciudad, y

Prado's false assessment of the danger would later be held up as a sign of his incompetence, yet his failure that morning to grasp what he was seeing was understandable. The size, sophistication, and swift deployment of the British expedition were unlike anything Havana had experienced. The attack reflected a tremendous leap in Britain's capacity to quickly mobilize man and sea power since the last battle between Britain and Spain off Cuba's shores, during the War of Jenkins' Ear. And, although rumors of a new conflict between Britain and Spain had filtered into Havana from several sources that spring, the British navy had intercepted Prado's official instructions from Madrid regarding the mutual declarations of war between Britain and Spain.[3]

Nevertheless, even knowing that war was likely would not have given Prado reason to panic. Despite the profusion and persistence of British designs on the city, the failure of British forces to launch a direct attack on Havana and Britain's setbacks elsewhere during the War of Jenkins' Ear had fostered the sense that Havana was so well fortified no fleet would attempt an assault. News had reached Havana that British forces had captured the French Caribbean islands of Guadeloupe, Martinique, and Dominica during earlier moments of the Seven Years' War, but their defenses could not compare to Havana's. M. Villiet d'Arignon, a French traveler who visited Havana in 1746, concurred with this sentiment in his description of the city and its impressive arsenal, shipyard, fortifications, and large garrison of soldiers. After a month's stay in Havana, he wrote that it was "the best defended of all places in America" and called it "impregnable."[4]

Certainly it was not a surprise to see British ships offshore, even and especially during wartime. Since Britain's acquisition of Cuba's neighbor Jamaica in 1655, and increasingly during the prior decades of the eighteenth century, British ships had contributed to a busy maritime traffic along the north coast of Cuba. Even more, they had been frequent visitors to Havana's harbor. Among the sailors and officers on board those warships Prado spied offshore that morning were men who had sailed into Havana's port on other

---

campo de la Habana (Prado)," June 6, 1762, in Amalia A. Rodríguez, ed., *Cinco Diarios del sitio de La Habana* (Havana, 1963), 70–71.

3. *Proceso formado por orden del Rey Nuestro Señor por la Junta de Generales que S.M. se ha dignado de nombrar a este fin sobre la conducta que tuvieron en la defense, capitulación, pérdida, y rendición de la plaza de la Habana, y esquadra, que se hallaba en su Puerto el Mariscal de Campo Juan de Prado . . .*, 2 vols. (Madrid, 1763–1765), I, BNE; David Syrett, "Introduction," in Syrett, ed., *The Siege and Capture of Havana, 1762* (London, 1970), xx; "Diario militar de las operaciones ejecutadas en la ciudad, y campo de la Habana (Prado)," June 6, 1762, in Rodríguez, ed., *Cinco Diarios*, 70–71; Francis Russell Hart, *The Siege of Havana, 1762* (Boston, 1931), 11.

4. "Voyage du Sr. Villiet d'Arignon, a la Havane, la Vera-Cruz, et le Mexique," in *Voyages intéressans dans différentes colonies françaises, espagnoles, anglaises, etc.* (London, 1788), 299–348 (quotations on 300, 301).

ships in the past few years. Prado's predecessor, Francisco Cagigal de la Vega, had even felt comfortable allowing Admiral Charles Knowles to pay a visit in 1756 when he was on his way back to London after the end of a term as governor of Jamaica. This visit occurred just seven years after Knowles himself had launched a failed attack on the city.[5]

But to thoroughly understand Prado's nonreaction to the sight of the British fleet, as well as the shared confidence in Havana that the city would not be attacked, it is necessary to begin well before the invasion. For the populations of the city and its surroundings, a deep history of interactions with the British in the region framed their response to the siege and occupation of their city. Before the siege, Havana had already developed a mutually constitutive relationship with the Anglo-American commercial system, centered around the slave trade. That relationship entailed a combination of making war with the British and trading with them in goods and persons. These relations of war, trade, and slavery were integral to the kind of society that developed in Havana, and they were also a reason the city was attacked. A history of war making and slave trading with the British had made Havana the strongest military outpost and the richest and most populous city in the Caribbean. At the same time, it had also drawn British merchants and spies into the port in search of Spanish silver and the key to unlock the city's defenses.

The sine qua non of Havana's military strength and economic growth was its population of African descent. People of African descent made up more than half of Havana's population of fifty thousand people at midcentury, and they provided the foundation to the city's society and economy. Blacks shaped Havana's social worlds, powered its military, constructed its defenses, and built its economy. Like their white counterparts, some of these men and women descended from ancestors who had been on the island since the sixteenth century. Others had arrived more recently, often on board British slave ships. The economy in general and its agricultural sector in particular depended on new arrivals of enslaved Africans to grow. As a result, Havana elites and local officials courted closer relations with British merchants, smugglers, and asiento factors who could secure their access to more enslaved Africans.[6]

---

5. Among those British subjects with the expedition who had been to Havana before was Captain Alexander Innes, known to U.S. historians as a British spy during the American Revolution; see B. D. Bargar, "Charles Town Loyalism in 1775: The Secret Reports of Alexander Innes," *South Carolina Historical Magazine*, LXIII (1962), 125–136. For Innes's prior presence in Havana, see "Correspondencia official con los gobernadores, Isla de Cuba," 1759, AGI, SD, 1194. For his presence with the 1762 expedition, see Captain Alexander Innes, *Hampton Court* in Havana Harbor, June 4, 1763, ADM 106/1124/9, TNA.

6. Cuba's first census was not conducted until 1774, so there are competing estimates for the city's population at mid-eighteenth century. The information for this estimate was gathered by Bishop

Relying on the British slave trade and the city's large population of people of African descent, Havana's merchants and landowners built up a successful economy centered around slavery, services, and Atlantic exchange that operated in the interstices of the Anglo-Spanish rivalry and often profited handsomely from conflicts between the imperial powers. Hostilities broke out with unrelenting frequency during this period, and the city lived under the threat of British attack, but Havana had grown accustomed to the state of war. Its residents of both European and African descent had learned to seize wartime opportunities to pursue their own social and economic interests. While under Spanish rule, Havana's residents leveraged proximity to the British in Jamaica to become a surprisingly autonomous, self-governing, and open trading place that knew how to prosper from the business of war, despite the seeming contradictions of trading with the enemy.

As we will see, Havana's growth was fueled in three key ways: by slave trading, smuggling, and war making—both with and against its British neighbors. Regional commerce and the slave trade brought the city into conflict with its Spanish sovereign, as the trade in persons and goods built strong ties between Havana's population and its British American neighbors, despite the desires of Iberian officials and merchants to keep Spain's subjects in America separate and to monopolize their trade. Paradoxically, rather than curtailing relations with the British, the Anglo-Spanish wars pulled Havana into greater contact with the goods, ships, and people of Spain's rival. The cycle of conflicts in the eighteenth century—and the War of Jenkins' Ear, in particular—created a boom time in Havana, one that led to tremendous economic growth and also fed assumptions later, during the Seven Years' War, that the city was so strong it would never be attacked. The city of Havana thrived at the crossroads between making war against the British and trading for goods and people with them, and only rarely, as on that Sunday in June 1762, did those two functions come into direct conflict.

Morell in 1754–1757 and includes the *extramuros* (extramural) neighborhoods of Guadalupe, Regla, and Jesús del Monte; see "La visita del Obispo Morell," AGI, SD, 534, fols. 55r–56r; Levi Marrero, *Cuba: Economía y sociedad*, 15 vols. (Madrid, [1972]–1992), VI, 47–48. See also estimates of forty thousand to fifty thousand in John Robert McNeill, *Atlantic Empires of France and Spain: Louisbourg and Havana, 1700–1763* (Chapel Hill, N.C., 1985), 35–39; and "Declaración de Juan Ignacio de Madariaga," Apr. 14, 1763, AGI, SD, 1587. For studies of the population of African descent in Cuba in earlier eras, see David Wheat, *Atlantic Africa and the Spanish Caribbean, 1570–1640* (Williamsburg, Va., and Chapel Hill, N.C., 2016); and Alejandro de la Fuente, with the collaboration of César García del Pino and Bernardo Iglesias Delgado, *Havana and the Atlantic in the Sixteenth Century* (Chapel Hill, N.C., 2008), 147–185.

A Military Bastion and a Place of Commerce

It is a long-standing assumption in the historical literature that Havana before the siege was primarily a military stronghold awakened to regional commerce only by the arrival of British and British American merchants during the occupation. This was simply not the case. Such a reading of eighteenth-century Havana is the result of looking backward from the sugar boom of the 1790s — seeing what came before as sleepy, economically stagnant, "pre-plantation" history — and failing to recognize western Cuba's diversified, outward-facing, slave-powered economy in the mid-eighteenth-century Atlantic world. In fact, it was Havana's relationship of exchange with its neighbors and the interplay between its military and commercial functions that made it so strong and such an attractive target. In the decades before the British invasion of 1762, Havana was both a military bastion and a thriving and open trading center, precisely the characteristics that made the city so coveted by the British — and also that helped them gain, over time and through ongoing contacts, the knowledge to target it successfully.[7]

Although it was more than merely that, Havana was indeed a center of Spanish military power in the Americas. There was reason for Prado to believe that Havana was so well fortified it would not be attacked. Consider, for example, the city's built defenses. To keep foreigners and their ships out of Havana, Spanish authorities developed one of the most elaborate fortification systems of any American port. Such an investment in imperial security was necessary because of the crucial role the city played in the global circulation of goods and capital that funded the Spanish monarchy and because of its relentless targeting by enemies of Spain. Philip II had commissioned the Italian military engineer Giovanni Battista Antonelli to build Havana's fortresses in the late sixteenth century as part of a comprehensive plan for the defense of the Spanish Caribbean. Havana's Morro fortress was famed for its batteries, one of which had been dubbed "the Apostles" for its twelve guns trained on the entrance to the harbor. It also had fifty-two cannons placed along the parapet ringing the castle. Because it was across the bay from the city, the fort had

---

7. Owing to the scarcity of research in the period before 1763, even distinguished historians of Cuba have shared the assumption that Havana at mid-eighteenth century was "under-populated," "underdeveloped," "sluggish," and "closed in on itself and closed out of the world." See Franklin W. Knight, *Slave Society in Cuba during the Nineteenth Century* (Madison, Wis., 1970), 3; Robert L. Paquette, *Sugar Is Made with Blood: The Conspiracy of La Escalera and the Conflict between Empires over Slavery in Cuba* (Middletown, Conn., 1988), 30; Louis A. Pérez, Jr., *Cuba: Between Reform and Revolution*, 3d ed. (New York, 2006), 25, 27, 38–48 (quotation on 44).

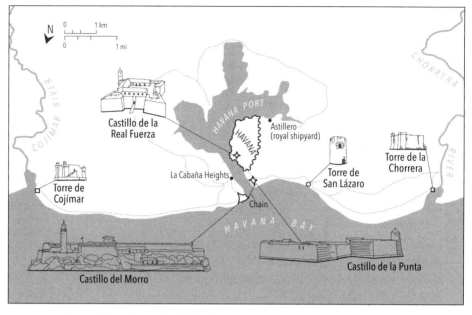

MAP 4 Havana Forts. Drawn by Molly Roy

the necessary infrastructure for stocking food and providing its own water—storage rooms and wells—as well as for housing a large garrison.[8]

"The Moor's Castle," as the British and North American press liked to call it, was just part of the network of fortifications designed to protect Havana against the kind of surprise that Governor Prado received in 1762. At the entrance to Havana's bay, the Morro Castle sat across the water from another fort, the star-shaped Castillo San Salvador de la Punta. Together they guarded the narrow strait leading into the harbor. The Morro and Punta functioned in coordination with Havana's oldest fort, completed in 1577, the Castillo de la Real Fuerza, which was located on the city's Plaza de Armas. Havana's three forts communicated with a string of smaller Mediterranean-style fortress towers erected east and west of the city to guard its two main rivers, at Cojímar and Chorrera, and to keep watch along the north coast. Like all the principal Spanish urban centers in the Greater Caribbean region, Havana was also a walled city, ringed by walls of stone and mortar five feet thick and more than thirty feet high (see Map 4 and Figure 9 [Plate 4]).[9]

8. Gustavo Placer Cervera, *Inglaterra y la Habana, 1762* (Havana, 2007), 75; Francisco Pérez Guzmán, *La Habana: Clave de un imperio* (Havana, 1997), 9; Tamara Blanes Martín, *Fortificaciones del Caribe* (Havana, 2001); and Martín, *Castillo de los Tres Reyes del Morro de la Habana: Historia y arquitectura* (Havana, 1998).

9. Although they sound alike, *morro* (meaning a prominent rock or, in this case, Havana's for-

FIGURE 9 *The Morro Castle and the Boom Defense Before the Attack.* By Dominic Serres. 1770. Oil on canvas. This is one of a series of eleven paintings of Havana by Serres depicting both the naval engagements during the siege of Havana and scenes of the city. Based on a sketch by Elias Durnford, a military engineer present during the invasion and occupation of Havana, this is one of the earliest existing images of Havana. Born in France, Serres was a sailor in his youth and, according to accounts, spent time in Havana as a prisoner of war. © National Maritime Museum, Greenwich, London

Prado could be confident that Havana's human defenses were also formidable. Between Spanish warships in the harbor and Havana's permanent regular garrison of troops, the city regularly hosted the largest number of sailors and soldiers in the Americas. The upsurge in troop levels since the beginning of the Seven Years' War had been so large that in 1760 there was an outbreak of yellow fever, or *vómito negro* (the black vomit), among the troops in Havana. Yellow fever often preyed on large groups of newcomers to the tropics, such as European-born soldiers, who lacked immunity to the mosquito-born disease. But, as of May 1762, Prado still had 4,781 Spanish soldiers and sailors in Havana at his disposal, including soldiers at the garrison and sailors aboard the Spanish warships then in port. In June of that year, Prado also had on hand more local militia than Spanish professional soldiers. These included 2,142 men, organized in four Havana companies separated by the prevailing racial classifications of the day—*morenos* (blacks), *pardos* (mulattos), and whites. The series of wars in previous decades had shaped Havana's militias

tress) and *"moro"* (Moor) are not the same word in Spanish, nor are they etymologically related. For "the Moor's Castle," see, for example, "References to the Annexed Plate," *London Magazine,* XXXII (March 1763), 116; and *Pennsylvania Gazette* (Philadelphia), May 26, 1743, [3]. On Havana's forts and walls, see Placer Cervera, *Inglaterra y la Habana,* 81.

into experienced forces that could be relied on to defend the city and to serve on offensive operations against British America.[10]

Besides its fortifications and large numbers of troops, another point of great military strength in Havana was its naval shipyard—the largest in the Americas. Originally established in the seventeenth century, Havana's shipyard was revamped by the Bourbon monarchy in its effort to update the navy in response to the escalating British threat. Ships made of cedar, oak, and other resistant woods from Cuba were considered superior to those made in Spain's other two shipyards, both in Iberia. They also cost half as much to produce as those made in Spain because of locally available timber and the cheap labor of the enslaved Africans and free artisans of color who constructed them. The ships built in Cuba lasted thirty years, as opposed to the twelve or fifteen years ships built in Spain were expected to last, and they reportedly needed to be careened and repaired less frequently and absorbed ammunition shot better without splintering. Between 1730 and 1750, the Havana shipyard produced twenty-nine ships, including twenty-two that had sixty cannons or more (see Figure 10). On the day that Lord Albemarle's convoy turned toward Havana, nearly a third of the Spanish navy was in Havana's harbor, including twelve warships of sixty cannons or more, and two more ships were on the stocks.[11]

As elaborate and strong as its military design was, Havana's strategic function was carried out within a city that had grown into a thriving, prosperous commercial hub. In fact, the Spanish monarchy's investment in Havana's defenses had helped drive the development of its expanding economy. The shipyard, the garrison of Spanish soldiers permanently stationed at Havana, and the fortifications, which required ongoing maintenance to stay in good repair, called for continued royal expenditures in Havana. When the numbers of professional Spanish troops stationed in Havana rose during times of war,

10. Prado to the Marqués de Sobremonte, June 23, 1762, AGI, Ultramar, 169. The Spanish professional troops numbered 1,325 infantry, 52 artillerymen, and 172 *dragones* (cavalry); "Estado que manifiesta el número de plazas," June 7, 1763, CO 117.2, fol. 34. The most thorough analysis of troop numbers in Havana at the time of the British attack may be found in Placer Cervera, *Inglaterra y la Habana*, 99–102. On the susceptibility of European-born soldiers to yellow fever, see J. R. McNeill, *Mosquito Empires: Ecology and War in the Greater Caribbean, 1620–1914* (Cambridge, Mass., 2010).

11. Allan J. Kuethe and José Manuel Serrano, "El astillero de la Habana y Trafalgar," *Revista de Indias*, LXII (2007), 763–776; G. Douglas Inglis, "The Spanish Naval Shipyard at Havana in the Eighteenth Century," *New Aspects of Naval History: Selected Papers from the 5th Naval History Symposium* (Baltimore, 1985), 47–58; David Greentree, *A Far-Flung Gamble: Havana 1762* (Long Island City, N.Y., 2010), 10; José Martin Felix de Arrate, *Llave del Nuevo Mundo: Antemural de las Indias Occidentales* (Havana, 1964), 91; Marrero, *Cuba*, VIII, 17; "Estado que manifiesta el número de plazas," June 7, 1763, CO 117.2, fol. 34, TNA; "A List of the Ships-of-War That Were in the Harbour of the Havana . . . and Surrendered with the City on the 12th of August," in Syrett, ed., *Siege and Capture of Havana*, 289; "Ships at the Havanna," Aug. 12, 1762, and "Dimensions of the Spanish Ships of War That Surrendered with the Havana," Aug. 12, 1762, CO 117.2, fols. 11, 23–24, TNA.

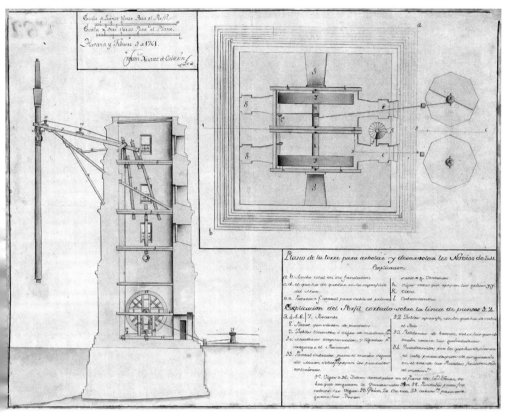

FIGURE 10 "Plan of the Tower for Inserting and Removing Masts at the Royal Naval Shipyard of Havana, Feb. 9, 1761." By Francisco Juárez de Calderín. When British forces occupied Havana in 1762, they were impressed by the level of technology they encountered at the shipyard. Technicians who worked at the shipyard also designed Havana's snuff mills. Permission, Spain, Ministerio de Defensa, Archivo Cartográfico y de Estudios Geográficos del Centro Geográfico del Ejército

so did the crown's spending in the local economy to feed them. An increase in productivity at the naval shipyard—inspired by the threat of war—meant more wages for many of its workers and more profits for local dealers in wood and other necessary materials. When the crown invested in repairing Havana's fortifications, day laborers earned wages and the owners of enslaved Africans received hiring-out fees for loaning the people they owned to work on the projects.[12]

Because revenues from taxes were insufficient to cover these military costs,

12. Havana's earlier history of commercial growth, operating inside and outside the city's imperial function serving the treasure fleet, may be found in de la Fuente, *Havana and the Atlantic.*

royal investments in Havana's defenses were made via the *situado,* an annual subsidy of silver transferred to Havana from New Spain. During the 1750s, the Havana treasury took in an average of just 162,000 pesos annually from local taxes, but the situado averaged 323,000 pesos annually. Historians have traditionally considered the size of the situado Havana received as an indication of the sleepiness of Havana's economy at the time and the city's dependence on New Spain. They point to the island's inability to provide sufficient revenue to fund its own upkeep and its reliance on infusions of silver from Mexico. However, it would be unreasonable to expect Havana to produce enough tax revenue itself to construct ships for the Spanish navy, to protect the wealth of Mexico, Peru, and the Philippines as the fleet made its way through Havana and back to Spain, and to defend the rest of the island and Florida, which fell under its military jurisdiction as well. The direct investments from the Spanish crown were not merely propping up a stagnant economy. To the contrary, they stimulated the further growth of a dynamic private sector and redirected Spanish American silver into local hands.[13]

The Havana shipyard, a site of direct imperial financing via the situado, provides a window into how royal investment led to the growth of the private sector. In the 1730s, when construction was at its peak in the shipyard during the preparations for the War of Jenkins' Ear, the situado reached as high as 700,000 to 1.1 million pesos. This financing both stimulated the domestic economy of western Cuba and promoted exchange with other areas of the Atlantic world. Funded by the situado, the shipyard's day-to-day activities were conducted by local merchants it commissioned, including (after 1740) the Royal Havana Company (RHC), a monopoly company of predominantly Cuba-based merchants. In turn, those merchants contracted with British American merchants based in New York for needed shipbuilding supplies like rigging.[14]

13. For Havana's annual tax revenue, see Allan J. Kuethe and G. Douglas Inglis, "Absolutism and Enlightened Reform: Charles III, the Establishment of the *Alcabala,* and Commerical Reorganization in Cuba," *Past and Present,* no. 109 (November 1985), 120. The amount of the situado is a calculated annual average for 1750–1757 and 1759, the years for which it is available; see Kuethe, "Guns, Subsidies, and Commercial Privilege: Some Historical Factors in the Emergence of the Cuban National Character, 1763–1815," *Cuban Studies,* XVI (1986), 123–138, esp. 130, Table 1; Carlos Marichal and Matilde Souto Mantecón, "Silver and Situados: New Spain and the Financing of the Spanish Empire in the Caribbean in the Eighteenth Century," *HAHR,* LXXIV (1994), 587–613. Other scholars have argued that the situado was a way revenue from one area of empire was redirected and repurposed in its fastest-growing sectors and regions; see Regina Grafe and Alejandra Irigoin, "A Stakeholder Empire: The Political Economy of Spanish Imperial Rule in America," *Economic History Review,* LXV (2012), 609–651.

14. The only year the situado fell below this level was 1734, when Mexico sent only 309,000 pesos. See Marichal and Souto Matecón, "Silver and Situados," *HAHR,* LXXIV (1994), 594, 612–613; Kenneth J. Andrien and Allan J. Kuethe, *The Spanish Atlantic World in the Eighteenth Century: War and the Bourbon Reforms, 1713–1796* (New York, 2014), 116. For purchases made in British North

Havana's royal shipyard was also a major employer of skilled and unskilled laborers who logged the wood the ships were made from, built and decorated the vessels, and smelted the cannons for them in the iron foundry. Between dockworkers, craftsmen, blacksmiths, and other laborers, one contemporary estimated that three thousand people labored at the shipyard, the majority of them enslaved and free men of African descent. Its activity also spread out into the surrounding countryside, where teams of enslaved loggers chopped down and transported the cedar trees and hardwoods that made Havana ships of such high quality. Representing the ripple effects the shipyard had on the local economy, at least one creole family managed to make a fortune in the logging industry. Additionally, the fields newly cleared by logging provided arable land for tobacco farms, which were well located close to the capital.[15]

In a similar public-private dynamic, Havana residents had developed over the centuries a thriving service economy around the Spanish treasure fleet. During the months that the galleons waited in Havana before forming a convoy for their transatlantic voyage, the city's population could rise by as many as three to four thousand people. Life in Havana was traditionally divided into what residents called *tiempo de flota* ("time of the fleet") and *tiempo muerto* ("dead time"), when the population would drop and the pace of life would slow. So embedded were these phrases in Cuba's lexicon that in the nineteenth century the phrase *tiempo muerto* would be used to refer to the times between *zafras,* or sugar harvests.[16]

During *tiempo de flota*, locals profited from providing passengers and sailors passing through Havana with the housing, clothing, food, drink, sex, and other entertainment they sought in the city's streets, its many taverns and inns, and its large marketplace. As the Italian traveler Gemelli Careri commented about a visit to Havana in 1698, living there was "extremely expensive" — a man could scarcely live on less than two pieces of eight a day,

America for the shipyard, see, for example, Consejo de Indias, Mar. 28, 1748, AGI, SD, 1130A, and Consejo de Indias, Apr. 29, 1750, no. 7, AGI, SD, 1130B.

15. Alejandro de la Fuente, "Economía, 1500–1700," in Consuelo Naranjo Orovio, ed., *Historia de Cuba* (Madrid, 2009), 59–68, esp. 64; Allan J. Kuethe, "Havana in the Eighteenth Century," in Franklin W. Knight and Peggy K. Liss, eds., *Atlantic Port Cities: Economy, Culture, and Society in the Atlantic World, 1650–1850* (Knoxville, Tenn., 1991), 17–18; Arrate, *Llave del Nuevo Mundo,* 92. On logging for the royal shipyard and later conflict with the sugar industry, see Reinaldo Funes Monzote, *From Rainforest to Cane Field in Cuba: An Environmental History since 1492* (Chapel Hill, N.C., 2008), 15–126.

16. De la Fuente, *Havana and the Atlantic;* Enrique López Mesa, "Esclavitud, prostitución, y represión en la Habana, siglos XVI–XVIII," *Caliban: Revista cubana de pensamiento y historia* (May–August 2012), http://www.revistacaliban.cu/articulo.php?numero=13&article_id=142. De la Fuente has argued that, even during the height of the treasure fleets, the idea that the city was dead between their arrivals was distorted (de la Fuente, *Havana and the Atlantic,* 66).

especially when the galleons were in port. With the city's high rents, providing lodging for visitors, who regularly stayed as long as six months at a time, was a lucrative pursuit. Because prices in the city were so notoriously high, there was also money to be made providing sustenance for visitors and locals, as well as salt pork and beef for consumption aboard ship. By one mid-eighteenth-century estimate, the city slaughtered more than one hundred swine and processed sixty head of cattle a day—for meat and for hides—in two slaughter-houses, one reserved for the garrison.[17]

The wealth produced in Havana's burgeoning service economy, compounding over time, drove the development of its vast hinterland and helped to create an elite class of merchants and ranchers invested in the production of food, agricultural commodities, and urban services. Many Havana residents were so successful they were able to extend their landholdings across large expanses of western Cuba as well as to construct multiple residences within city walls. Unlike other colonies in Spanish America, in Cuba the capital's city council retained the right to disburse land and charter towns, which gave it significant power to develop and control an area that stretched across the western part of the island. In the mid-eighteenth century, Pedro Agustín Morell de Santa Cruz, on his arrival in Havana to take up the new bishop's seat, was struck by how the city had grown into the surrounding territory. "Like locusts," he wrote, residents of Havana had "spread throughout all the lands in its jurisdiction, where they had built their houses, farms, sugar plantations, and tobacco farms, whose dust flew all over the universe." Because Cuba is an island, even *hatos* (ranches) deep in Havana's backcountry were closely connected to both the metropolitan market and other ports on the coastlines that opened up to regional Caribbean trade.[18]

As the economy diversified and the city developed its hinterland and its trade networks off the island, the Havana service economy shifted to serve not just the sailors and passengers in port but also all those drawn to Havana by the economic opportunity their intermittent presence brought. As the city grew, the population swings caused by the arrival of the fleet had a diminishing impact. The fleets themselves became less regular in the mid-eighteenth century, when they were replaced by smaller register ships, which sailed somewhat more frequently. By then, maritime activity in the region had al-

17. Giovanni Francesco Gemelli Careri, *Giro del Mondo*, VI (Naples, 1708), 175 (*"carissimo"*); Arturo Sorhegui D'Mares, *La Habana en el Mediterráneo americano* (Havana, 2007), 89. Havana residents preferred to eat pork, and they used the lard for cooking. For estimates on swine and cattle, see Arrate, *Llave del Nuevo Mundo*, 84.

18. *Relación de la visita ecclesiástica de la Isla de Cuba*, Oct. 4, 1758, AGI, SD, 534, 68v. On the vast geographic range of Havana's wealthiest residents' landholdings in the sixteenth century, see Sorhegui D'Mares, *La Habana en el Mediterráneo americano*, 96–107.

ready driven the development of a populous urban settlement in Havana, with a booming service sector and surrounding regions that provided products for both the city's urban economy and the export market—chiefly hides, tobacco, cattle, mules, lumber, sugar, foodstuffs, and copper from the mines of eastern Cuba.[19]

Havana's successful landowners relied on enslaved labor to grow rich by producing a diversity of goods to sell in the Atlantic economy. In addition to trading commodities and services in Havana's marketplace, merchants and landowners enjoyed profits from developing contraband trade. Lumber, cattle, mules, hides, salted meats, and tallow were especially popular in the trade with foreigners along Cuba's south coast, as neighboring Jamaica and French Saint Domingue had shifted to producing sugar almost exclusively and prices for other products on those islands were high. Although some of Havana's richest residents began to invest in the sugar industry at midcentury, the island's economy remained diversified. By the middle of the eighteenth century, for example, only one-sixth of the enslaved Africans on the island worked on sugar plantations.[20]

All of the economic activity in Havana and its hinterland concentrated the population of Cuba in the western half of the island. Havana's rate of growth was out of proportion with the rest of the island. The population within city walls had grown by as much as one-third in the thirty years between 1718 and 1748. By 1757, approximately 50 percent of the population of Cuba lived in Havana and its outskirts, and the capital's population was at least four times as large as that of Santiago de Cuba, the island's second largest city. British war plotters could be excused for conflating Havana with the entire island of Cuba and wanting very badly to get their hands on the city, not only to destroy the Spanish military outpost but also to have it as a trading entrepôt, with its large reserves of silver and its lucrative market for enslaved Africans, foodstuffs, manufactured goods, European cloth and clothing, and luxury goods

19. Between 1717 and 1762, only nine of the New Spain floats made the rounds (with none between 1735 and 1757) and four galleons for Cartagena and Portobello. The new system of register ships also sailed infrequently. According to Antonio García-Baquero, between 1717 and 1738 twelve *registros* sailed to Havana and Santiago de Cuba from Cádiz, with twenty-seven returning. See García-Baquero González, *Cádiz y el Atlántico (1717–1778): El comercio colonial español bajo el monopolio gaditano* (Seville, 1976), 159, 170; Kuethe and Andrien, *The Spanish Atlantic World*, 106, 153–155.

20. Levi Marrero, *Historia económica de Cuba: Guía de estudio y documentación* (Havana, 1956), 276–277; Mercedes García Rodríguez, *La aventura de fundar ingenios: La refacción azucarera en la Habana del siglo XVII* (Havana, 2004); Alejandro de la Fuente, "Esclavitud," in Naranjo Orovio, ed., *Historia de Cuba,* 144. According to an account written in 1749, at that time in Havana's vicinity there were 62 sugar *ingenios* with 21 being built; 3,800 *estancias, caleras* (lime kilns), *tejares* (tile manufacturers), and tobacco *vegas;* and 494 cattle ranches; see Bernardo Joseph de Urrutia y Matos, *Cuba: Fomento de la Isla,* ed. Levi Marrero (Puerto Rico, 1993), 6.

from all corners of the globe. Ironically, the Spanish investments in the island, which had stimulated the development of Havana's local economy, had been intended to keep foreigners out of this strategic port. Now the dynamic economy that had developed was drawing them in—from Africa, Europe, and the rest of the Caribbean—like never before.[21]

Havana's transformation in the eighteenth century was driven by a private commercial sector that grew alongside and superseded the public military sector. For Havana residents at midcentury, the local demands of commerce had outpaced the imperial demands of defense. Both halves of Cuba's economy, though, relied entirely on the slave trade and the island's sizable population of African descent. Spain's colonial project in Cuba was built on the backs of free and enslaved Africans, who, in the eighteenth century, were increasingly arriving in British slaving ships.

Havana's Population of African Descent

Eighteenth-century Havana's economic growth and military strength would not have been possible without a large population of African descent. An overwhelming majority of the toiling classes, they worked in many sectors of the economy, in both the city and the countryside. As in prior generations, Havana's enslaved population was "a precondition and function" of its growth. More than in the society that would evolve at the peak of sugar plantation slavery in Cuba, people of African descent, enslaved and free, filled a variety of niches in the city and its hinterland's diversified economy. Their labor made Havana an alluring British target; it supported every aspect of the city's livelihood, from agriculture to ranching to shipbuilding to copper mining, from construction to logging, and from transportation to domestic service.[22]

In Havana's bustling urban economy, blacks dominated painting, sculpting, shoemaking, and the skilled artisan crafts like blacksmithing, in which, as one observer noted, "few whites are employed." According to the chronicler José Martín Félix de Arrate y Acosta, one of the first historians of the city, the skills of pardos and morenos as cobblers, tailors, bricklayers, and carpenters were well known as well as their work in silversmithing, sculpting, painting,

21. Actas capitulares del Ayuntamiento de la Habana, Feb. 11, 1718, Aug. 8, 1748, Archivo del Museo de la Ciudad de La Habana; Sorhegui D'Mares, *La Habana en el Mediterráneo americano*, 27. Because Havana's first census was not until 1774, comparative figures for the island's population have been estimated from Ramón de la Sagra, *Historia económico-política y estadística de la isla de Cuba* (Havana, 1831), 3.

22. De la Fuente, *Havana and the Atlantic in the Sixteenth Century*, 43. As David Wheat has argued, Africans and African-descended peoples constituted demographic majorities in many areas of the Spanish Caribbean before 1600, including Havana and its hinterland; see Wheat, *Atlantic Africa*, 4.

and woodworking. Women of color, both enslaved and free, predominated in Havana's vast service sector, running and cleaning the city's many taverns and inns and working as cooks, washerwomen, water carriers, seamstresses, nurses, midwives, maids, wet nurses, prostitutes, and street vendors. On the ranches, truck farms, and sugar and tobacco plantations that surrounded the city, men and women of African descent were the primary labor force. The economy they helped to build served Havana's own large urban population, the Spanish treasure fleet when it came into port, and a variety of regional trading partners from Kingston to Veracruz and from Caracas to Philadelphia.[23]

Like the woman discussed in the Introduction, María del Carmen, many of these people's lives defy expectations of Caribbean slavery based on the plantation colony model. In urban Havana, the diversified economy produced many service-sector jobs that blurred the lines between slavery and freedom, and, as those lines blurred, opportunities for manumission arose. Street vendors and cart pushers in the city, for example, were sometimes free and sometimes enslaved day laborers, or *jornaleros,* hiring themselves out and paying a daily or weekly fee to their owner. Their status could be somewhat confusing, as commented on pointedly in the city ordinances, in that they "walked around like free people, working and occupying themselves in whatever they wanted." The dynamism and liquidity of the urban economy, recirculating as much Spanish silver as it did, gave enslaved people the ability to earn silver pesos. Consequently, the city was home to a sizable population of free people of African descent who had earned the money to purchase their freedom or had received help from free people to do so through Cuba's practice of *coartación.* Less frequently, owners also manumitted their enslaved Africans, especially women who were the mothers of their owners' children. Practices like these had resulted in a large and multilayered population of African descent, with distinctions that were often fuzzy between the free and enslaved.[24]

Besides making Havana's economy run, people of African descent also performed functions critical to the island's defense, such as constructing ships for the Spanish imperial navy. Alongside much smaller groups of convict and forced indigenous laborers from Mexico known as *guachinangos,* en-

23. "Noticias del estado de Cuba," 1775, MS/21430/6, 11–12, BNE; Arrate, *Llave del Nuevo Mundo,* 96–97. Despite the long-standing narrative of tobacco as a white smallholders' crop, made famous by Fernando Ortiz (Ortiz, *Contrapunteo cubano del tabaco y el azúcar* [Havana, 1940]), more recent work has shown the predominance of the labor of free and enslaved people of African descent in tobacco agriculture as well. See Enrique López Mesa, *Tabaco: Mito y esclavos: Apuntes cubanos de historia agraria* (Havana, 2015); and Charlotte A. Cosner, *The Golden Leaf: How Tobacco Shaped Cuba and the Atlantic World* (Nashville, Tenn., 2015).

24. "Ordenanzas de La Habana," June 6, 1777, Manuscritos de América, II-2460, 26v, BRP; de la Fuente, "Esclavitud," in Naranjo Orovio, ed., *Historia de Cuba,* 132–144.

slaved Africans built the fortifications in Havana that made Prado confident it would not be attacked. They also erected and maintained Santiago de Cuba's own elaborate fortresses and those of other ports on the island. In response to pirate raids by Spain's French, Dutch, and British enemies, militia companies of free people of color had been established island-wide since the end of the sixteenth century. During times of both war and peace, Cuba's population of African descent manned privateering vessels that menaced British shipping and served as soldiers for offensive and defensive military actions.[25]

Havana's city council and its most prominent white residents spoke of its militias of African descent as a point of particular pride, and they readily relied on them during wartime. In one of the earliest accounts of the island, published in Madrid in 1761, Arrate, who also served as a *cabildo* (city council) member and *alcalde* (royal constable), extolled the military talents of the city's population of pardos and morenos: "A talent for greater things has been discovered in them," he wrote, "and spirits more appropriate for war, which they have proven in expeditions they have made, with credit to the nation and the fatherland." These militias had proven their mettle during earlier cycles of Anglo-Spanish (and French) war, including attacks on the Bahamas (1703, 1720), Pensacola (1719), and the attempt on Charleston, South Carolina (1706).[26]

25. *Guachinango* is an indigenous Nahuatl word generally used in Cuba to mean Native peoples or sometimes mestizos, sent from New Spain, to labor on the fortifications. Often they had been convicted of a crime. Sometimes they were also called *forzados*; see Emilio Roig de Leuchsenring, ed., *La dominación inglesa en la Habana: Libro de cabildos, 1762–1763* (Havana, 1962), 116–117; Celía María Parcero Torre, *La pérdida de La Habana y las reformas borbónicas en Cuba, 1760–1773* (Valladolid, Spain, 1998), 154; and Ruth Pike, "Penal Servitude in the Spanish Empire: Presidio Labor in the Eighteenth Century," *HAHR*, LVIII (1978), 21–40, esp. 35. Free and enslaved people of African descent had been protecting Havana since the French pirate Jacques de Sores's attack in 1555. Black militias existed in Havana, Puerto Príncipe, and Sancti Spíritus from at least as early as 1630. Authorities also armed and organized black subjects into militias in Santiago de Cuba, Bayamo, Baracoa, and Trinidad. See Pedro Deschamps Chapeaux, *Los batallones de pardos y morenos libres* (Havana, 1976), 17–18, 20–21; María del Carmen Barcia, *Los ilustres apellidos: Negros en la Habana colonial* (Havana, 2009), 235–237; Herbert S. Klein, "The Colored Militia of Cuba, 1568–1868," *Caribbean Studies*, VI, no. 2 (July 1966), 17–27, esp. 18; Jane Landers, "Transforming Bondsmen into Vassals: Arming Slaves in Colonial Spanish America," in Christopher Leslie Brown and Philip D. Morgan, ed., *Arming Slaves: From Classical Times to the Modern Age* (New Haven, Conn., 2006); 120–145; and Landers, *Atlantic Creoles in the Age of Revolutions* (Cambridge, Mass., 2010), 138–174.

26. Arrate, *Llave del Nuevo Mundo*, 97: " . . . descubriéndose en ellos ingenio para más grandes cosas, y unos espíritus más a propósito para la guerra, lo que han comprobado en las expediciones que se han ofrecido, con crédito de la nación y de la Patria." In 1714, after the end of the War of the Spanish Succession, the Spanish king issued a royal proclamation to prevent the king's pardo troops from being insulted or mistreated in any way, in recognition of the self-sacrifice and zeal with which these "ancient and especially meritorious" companies served the crown: May 20, 1714, AGI, SD, 337. See also Klein, "The Colored Militia," *Caribbean Studies*, VI, no. 2 (July 1966), 18; Barcia, *Los ilustres apellidos*, 238–239.

During these earlier wars, the pardos had more experience than the morenos serving abroad and were more famous for their martial reputation, but the Havana city council expressed confidence in all of Havana's troops of African descent. In fact, its first preparations for war in 1739, on the eve of the War of Jenkins' Ear, entailed a proposal to raise a company of one thousand or more "trustworthy, able, and brave blacks"—only blacks were mentioned at this juncture—to protect the plaza. The cabildo both recognized their skill and potentially also anticipated fewer objections to being mustered from free militiamen of color than from white militia, of which there were fewer in the city anyway. Although the numbers of militia fluctuated, during his *visita* of 1754–1755 Bishop Morell described the presence of more black than white militia companies in Havana.[27]

Just months before the British siege began, the governor of Havana and captain general of Cuba had decided to reorganize the militias of color on the island and to upgrade the company of pardos to a battalion, owing in part to their exemplary performance keeping watch at home and serving in military action abroad during the War of Jenkins' Ear. Among the soldiers of African descent in Havana at the time were veterans of the Spanish attack on Georgia in 1742. In 1748, other members of the pardo militia had gone to sea on several warships under the command of Andrés Reggio, fending off Admiral Knowles's ill-conceived attempt on Havana. Some had even been captured as prisoners of war during that naval engagement. Reflecting the prestige of Havana's militias of color and the importance of their role defending the city, the city ordinances of 1755 stipulated that, although enslaved blacks could not carry swords around the city, *"negros horros"* (freed blacks) could bear arms "because there are in this *villa* many that are *vecinos* [residents] and officers, and because it is a port." Free men of color in Cuba had a long tradition of volunteering to fight for Spain in exchange for the elevated status, rights, and privileges associated with serving the king in war.[28]

27. "Cabildo extraordinario de 10 November 1740," in "Actas capitulares," 1739–1743, Archivo del Museo de la Ciudad de La Habana, 223v ("Negros de confianza, habilidad, y valor"). Of thirty-one companies, Morell counted ten units of pardos and nine of morenos; see "Relación de la visita eclesiástica de la isla de Cuba," 1754–1756, AGI, SD, 534, 54v–55r.

28. "Ordenanzas de la Habana," June 6, 1777, Manuscritos de América, II-2460, fols. 26r–26v, BPR. The ordinances are recopied from 1640 and dated 1755, then signed off in another hand by the Marqués de la Torre in June 1777. In Santiago de Cuba and Bayamo, in addition to Cuatro Villas (Trinidad, Villa Clara, Sancti Spíritus, and San Juan de los Remedios), three other battalions of soldiers of color were created. See Deschamps Chapeaux, *Los batallones,* 25–26; Jacobo de la Pezuela, *Diccionario geográfico, estadístico, histórico, de la isla de Cuba,* II (Madrid, 1863), 251; "Libro de servicios de los pardos libres de La Habana" and "Libro de servicios de los morenos libres de La Habana," June 1765, AGI, SD, 2093. On the traditions of free black militias in Cuba, see Deschamps Chapeaux, *Los batallones,* 20–21, 26; and Landers, *Atlantic Creoles,* 138–174. For prior battle experiences

Leveraging their indispensability to both the military and the economy, some free people of color had managed to attain relatively high status in Havana's social worlds, acquiring property and even enslaved Africans of their own. Free people of color founded Havana's oldest standing church and were members of Catholic religious brotherhoods (*cofradías*) as well as the city's twenty-one *cabildos de nación*, which were mutual aid societies associated with specific African nations. Whites in Cuba enforced purity of blood regulations that kept people of African descent from serving in government offices and otherwise policed the boundaries of race, but less vehemently than they would in later eras.[29]

Over generations, militia service helped propel free families of color into notably elite status. The captain of the battalion of free pardos, Antonio Flores, provides a case in point. A carpenter, Flores initially volunteered in 1708, during the War of the Spanish Succession, as a common soldier and climbed his way up the ranks. Flores's service during the wars of these decades included privateering, guarding the forts surrounding Havana and the settlement at Pensacola, Florida, raiding Gualquini, Georgia, in 1742, and being held as a prisoner of war for eighteen months in France. As a battalion commander, he added the aristocratic prefix "de" to his last name and managed to send his sons to primary and secondary school, despite official exclusions for children of color. In 1759, Flores petitioned the crown for his sons' right to enroll at the university if they wished and to enter any professions they might desire. At that time, his petition to the crown was denied, but it is telling that Flores stated that the rise of militia officers' sons to prominent socioeconomic posi-

---

of Havana's militia of *pardos libres*, see "Libro de servicios de los oficiales y sargentos del batallon de pardos libres de esta plaza, hasta fin de diciembre de 1763," AGI, SD, 2117. At least two members of the militia of pardos libres, *teniente* Josef Joaquin Borroto and *subteniente* Vicente Pimenta, had been taken prisoner by Admiral Knowles's forces in 1748. Pimenta had been serving on the ship *El Conquistador* that Knowles captured. See "Libro de servicios de los oficiales y sargentos del batallon de pardos libres de La Havana, hasta fin de diciembre de 1771," AGI, SD, 1136A , fols. 468, 480.

29. For examples of free women of color buying enslaved women of the same ethnicity, see Protocolo Fornari, tomo 1763, Venta real, July 13, 1763, fol. 365, Protocolo Regueira, tomo 1763, Venta real, Mar. 26, 1763, fol. 567, both in ANC. In 1638, free blacks founded Havana's oldest standing church, the Iglesia de Espiritu Santo, in honor of Divino Paráclito; see Joaquín E. Weiss, *La arquitectura colonial cubana: Siglos XVI/XVII* (Havana, 1979), 121–122. During his visita of 1755, the bishop of Cuba recorded the presence in Havana of twenty-one cabildos de nación, associated with ten different African nations: *carabalí* (five), *mina* (three), *lucumí* (two), *arará* (two), *congo* (two), *mondongo* (two), *gangá* (two), *mandingo* (one), *luango* (one), and *popó* (one); see Dec. 6, 1755, AGI, SD, 515, no. 51. For the history of the cabildos as they evolved in the late eighteenth and nineteenth century, see Matt D. Childs, "Re-creating African Ethnic Identities in Cuba," in Jorge Cañizares-Esguerra, Matt D. Childs, and James Sidbury, eds., *The Black Urban Atlantic in the Age of the Slave Trade* (Philadelphia, 2013), 85–100; and Philip A. Howard, *Changing History: Afro-Cuban Cabildos and Societies of Color in the Nineteenth Century* (Baton Rouge, La., 1998).

tions was a common occurrence in Cuba. As his petition attested, his own command had "exalted and ennobled him."[30]

Both Arrate and creole author and lawyer Nicolás de Ribera regarded Havana's free population of color as fundamentally loyal. In fact, their existence confirmed to these men the civilizing mission of Spanish colonialism. In their efforts to persuade the crown to expand the slave trade to the island, Havana's leading white residents celebrated the extent to which free blacks managed to become valuable Spanish subjects. In his lengthy description of the island of Cuba written in 1757, Ribera lobbied for opening the slave trade based on the claim that even African-born *bozales* flourished under the influence of Spanish slavery in Cuba, as opposed to the British islands, where they treat Africans "like beasts" and do not "instruct them in religion." Rather, in Cuba, he argued, they came to be good Catholics, form families, buy their own freedom, buy property, and even sometimes become rich. Remarkably, he found, within just a few years of their arrival in the Americas, African-born bozales learned to speak Spanish and to take up arms and defend the territory if they were instructed and trained. The sons of bozales, he wrote, "could only be distinguished from Spaniards by color."[31]

With statements like these, which are striking compared to those that would come later, Ribera was at once acknowledging the high status some creoles of African descent achieved in Havana and justifying the practice of African slavery in order to argue for its expansion. To his mind as well as others of his status, slavery in Cuba was an improving institution that evangelized and supposedly civilized Africans, much like Spanish subjects on the mainland claimed that colonialism there had improved America's indigenous peoples.

As Ribera's appeal to expand the slave trade makes evident, Havana's residents' demand for enslaved Africans had outpaced the traditional provisions for slave trading permitted by the Spanish crown. In fact, the gap between Havana elites' demand for enslaved Africans and the numbers legally available for sale was so great it was causing increasing tension with the monarch. The Spanish king owned his own royal slaves who were used to maintain the fortifications and work at the shipyard, but colonial authorities also depended on local slaveowners' lending out day laborers for royal projects. When Juan

30. Expediente de Don Antonio Flores, 1760, AGI, SD, 1455, no. 5. On Antonio Flores and his family, see Ann Twinam, *Purchasing Whiteness: Pardos, Mulatos, and the Quest for Social Mobility in the Spanish Indies* (Stanford, Calif., 2015), 152–158; Klein, "The Colored Militia of Cuba," *Caribbean Studies*, VI, no. 2 (July 1966), 17–27, esp. 26, 29; Deschamps Chapeaux, *Los batallones*, 26, 56–60; Barcia, *Los ilustres apellidos*, 355–356; and Landers, *Atlantic Creoles*, 152–154, 162.

31. Nicolás Joseph de Ribera, *Descripción de la isla de Cuba*, ed. Hortensia Pichardo Viñals (Havana, [1975]), 137–143, esp. 143.

de Prado arrived to take over the position of governor of Havana and captain general of Cuba in February 1761, he brought a royal order to fortify the Cabaña heights across the bay from the city, known since the day of Giovanni Battista Antonelli as a weak point in the event of an attack. Despite the long-standing custom by which local slaveowners loaned their enslaved Africans for royal projects, Havana's leading residents refused his request, citing a shortage of workers for their own tobacco farms and sugar plantations. After appealing to Veracruz to send more guachinango laborers, he decided to commission prominent local merchant and slave trader Juan de Miralles to sail to foreign colonies in search of more enslaved Africans to purchase for the island. In the meantime, however, Prado had no choice but to abandon the project, as there were not enough enslaved Africans available to commence this crucial work.[32]

The Slave Trade and Contraband

Havana's ability to grow in size and strength, and even to feed itself, relied on not only investment by the Spanish monarchy but also the slave and contraband trades with foreign merchants. The slave trade was the prime mover of this system. Because it was largely people of African descent who worked to defend the city and produce much of its wealth, the city depended on the slave trade to function. The trade in persons was the most valuable branch of trade in Havana, and it enabled the city to grow as quickly as it did. By 1750, well before Cuba's sugar boom, a Havana lawyer and former member of the Audiencia (high court) reported that "nothing is undertaken on the island that doesn't need blacks." Making enslaved Africans more affordable and available for purchase, he added, was "one of the political issues of greatest importance on our island."[33]

Historians' characterization of eighteenth-century Cuba as sleepy and inward-facing derives in part from a low estimate of the volume of the slave trade to Cuba in the first half of the eighteenth century. In general, few histori-

---

32. "Papeles aprehendidos entre los de Don Joseph García Gago, Secretario del Governador, y de la Junta formada en la Habana," "No. 474: Relación simple de la comisión dada a Don Juan de Miralles para la negociación, y compra de negros en las colonias estrangeras," I, and ""Defensa del Mariscal de Campo Don Juan de Prado," II, in *Proceso formado de orden del Rey Nuestro Señor por la Junta de Generales*, BNE.

33. "Resumen de los intereses y posibles aumentos de la isla de Cuba . . . por el Doctor Don Bernardo Joseph de Urrutia y Matos, cathedratico de Prima de Canones de la Insigne Pontifica y Real Universidad de La Havana, oydor honorario de la Audiencia y Chancilleria Real de la Isla Española del Consejo de Su Majestad . . . ," 1750, AGI, Ultramar, 986, no. 1; Urrutia y Matos, *Cuba*, ed. Marrero. When whites used the label *negros*, or "blacks," the meaning was usually implied to be "slaves."

ans have tried to assess the slave trade to Cuba before 1762, seeing it as the time before the trade reached considerable volume. Cuba's slave trading increased precipitously at the end of the eighteenth century during the island's sugar boom and reached massive proportions (more than seven hundred thousand people) during the nineteenth century; both of these periods have understandably been the focus of far more study. Before the trade took off in 1790, the number of African arrivals in Cuba was also far smaller than the hundreds of thousands of enslaved Africans imported to the British and French Caribbean islands, then at the peak of their own sugar production. The work that has been done to estimate Cuba's trade before 1762 has been piecemeal and problematic because so much of the trade was contraband, thus leaving few or no records behind. Moreover, the trade occurred on short, intra-American voyages from foreign colonies, rather than on the longer, transatlantic voyages that were the focus of historians' first efforts to document the trade.[34]

For the first half of the century, however, new research places the documented number of Africans who arrived in Cuba between 1701 and 1762 at around forty thousand people. This number is larger than previously thought and will likely grow as more research is conducted and trade records from exporting regions in other empires continue to be consulted. Yet it is probably still far lower than the actual number of people brought to the island. As indicated above by the statement about the slave trade being of the greatest political importance in Cuba, the trade at mid-eighteenth century was already fundamental to the society and economy that developed on the island.[35]

---

34. Few historians have estimated African arrivals in Cuba before 1762, and the estimates that do exist reflect little consensus and significantly underestimate the number of arrivals. In 1811, a junta studying the trade in Cuba estimated that 25,000 enslaved Africans had entered the jurisdiction of Havana by 1763, and 35,000 entered the province of Oriente, for a total of 60,000 enslaved Africans in all of Cuba; see "Nota sobre introducción de negros bozales en la Isla de Cuba y el estado y actual distribución de las gentes de color libres y esclavos en ella," 1811, MS 14,613/23, no. 6, BNE. Alexander Humboldt used that same estimate of 60,000 for the entire period from 1521 to 1763 (Humboldt, *The Island of Cuba,* trans. J. S. Thrasher [New York, 1856], 217). José Antonio Saco cited more than 4,000 enslaved Africans between 1740 and 1760, a number that corresponds with the Royal Havana Company asiento and that Hubert H. S. Aimes also uses (4,986 for 1740–1760). Hugh Thomas estimated 5,000 enslaved Africans legally imported from 1740 to 1760 and perhaps 5,000 through contraband. See Saco, *Historia de la esclavitud de la raza africana en el Nuevo Mundo* (Barcelona, 1879), 312; Aimes, *A History of Slavery in Cuba, 1511–1868* (New York, 1907), 23–24; Thomas, *Cuba, or the Pursuit of Freedom* (1971 rpt. New York, 1998), 31. The monumental *Trans-Atlantic Slave Trade Database* (www.slavevoyages.org) has focused on transatlantic voyages, as its name indicates. For a new effort to assess the intra-American slave trade, see Gregory E. O'Malley, *Final Passages: The Intercolonial Slave Trade of British America, 1619–1807* (Williamsburg, Va., and Chapel Hill, N.C., 2014). For a reassessment of the importation of enslaved Africans into Spanish America, see Alex Borucki, David Eltis, and David Wheat, "Atlantic History and the Slave Trade to Spanish America," *American Historical Review,* CXX (2015), 433–461.

35. For this new estimate for the slave trade to Cuba and its interpretation, see David Eltis and

Acknowledging that the slave trade to Cuba before the British siege of Havana was larger than once thought revises several long-standing assumptions about early-eighteenth-century Cuba. First, it affirms the growing scholarly consensus that during every stage of Spanish presence on the island of Cuba the colonial project was built through the traffic in enslaved Africans and exploitation of their labor. Secondly, it changes how we view the strength and dynamism of the links between Cuba's population of African descent and African society, politics, and culture in the eighteenth century. And, finally, it alters our understanding of the relationship of Cuba to the Atlantic — and, in particular, British Atlantic — commercial system in the era before its sugar boom.[36]

In the seventeenth and eighteenth centuries, slaveowners in Cuba exploited the presence of subjects of their crown's European rivals in the region — particularly the British, the dominant transatlantic slave traders of the era, but also Dutch, French, and Danish merchants — to purchase the enslaved Africans they desired to grow and develop the economy. Sometimes this commerce occurred through the crown-sanctioned asiento monopoly trade and sometimes through the channels of contraband and other forms of wartime regional trade. Because British Jamaica was the major source of enslaved Africans in the region during the eighteenth century, Havana elites' demand for more enslaved Africans compelled them to broker ties with their British American neighbors. In so doing, they built a dynamic, diversified, and interdependent economy that allowed them to evade and gain leverage against political authorities in Spain.

The British asiento was a powerful bond cementing relations between Cuba and Jamaica, but also between Cuba and other points in British America. Conditions of the asiento permitted the importation, free of duties, of one barrel of flour per enslaved African. Often the barrels of flour that arrived in Havana accompanied enslaved Africans on the same ships, but it was also permissible for the barrels to come on another vessel hailing from another point of origin, such as British North America. The concession for flour in the asiento helped Havana to feed its expansive population, whose demand was never adequately met by New Spain, and it also opened another avenue by which the city's merchants could build their regional trade within and beyond Spanish monopolies.[37] Via the asiento slave trade, flour shipments arrived in Havana from

Jorge Felipe González, "The Rise and Fall of the Cuban Slave Trade: New Data, New Paradigms," and Elena A. Schneider, "Routes into Eighteenth-century Cuban Slavery: African Diaspora and Geopolitics," in Alex Borucki, Eltis, and David Wheat, eds., *From the Galleons to the Highlands: Slave Trade Routes in the Spanish Americas* (Albuquerque, N.M., 2019).

36. Schneider, "Routes into Eighteenth-Century Cuban Slavery," in Borucki, Eltis, and Wheat, eds., *From the Galleons to the Highlands*.

37. According to the terms of the agreement, the asiento holder was allowed to bring in enough

Martinique, South Carolina, Providence, Philadelphia, and New York from 1730 to 1762. Scholars have cited the American Revolution as North American merchants' legal entry into the flour trade to Cuba, but under the asiento British American flour was permitted there earlier.[38]

Contraband trade was not a new phenomenon in the eighteenth century, but its volume grew along with the size of Havana's economy, the strength of its residents' purchasing power, and the growth of foreigners' presence in the region. In the eighteenth century, merchants and smugglers in western and southern Cuba reached out to British and British American traders as their most frequent commercial partners. As one minister in the Spanish court commented in a report in the 1760s, extinguishing contraband in Cuba had become impossible. While finding a way to moderate it would be very good, he acknowledged, "this matter is as bottomless as the ocean, and a sea of such breadth that land is never discovered." By way of response, the Spanish government in Cuba relied on a practice of granting pardons *(indultos)* every couple of years for all who were in possession of enslaved Africans illegally introduced onto the island of Cuba. In exchange for the payment of duties after the fact, local officials branded the enslaved individuals with the mark of the Spanish crown and pronounced them legalized possessions of their owners. This brutal practice represented the Spanish government's attempt to generate tax revenue and to accommodate to a situation that had slipped beyond its control — and in which its own officers were often complicit.[39]

food on each ship to feed its human cargo and then sell what was regarded as excess on the open market. In practice, flour rarely if ever was given to the enslaved, who were instead given plantain and cassava to eat and the hardtack *bizcocho* rather than bread. Populous Havana was supposed to depend for its flour supply on shipments from New Spain, but those shipments never met the city's needs, and its European-descended population preferred wheat bread over corn. The importation of excess barrels of flour, a common occurrence, was explained away by traders who claimed the corresponding enslaved Africans had died in transit. See Enrique López Mesa, "La trata negrera en el puerto de La Havana a mediados del siglo XVIII," *Catauro: Revista cubana de antropología*, II, no. 3 (January–June 2001), 148–158, esp. 153.

38. Ibid., 154. J. R. McNeill has argued that after 1748 flour shipments from British North America became more frequent, though I would argue that the increase came during the War of Jenkins' Ear. See McNeill, *Atlantic Empires of France and Spain*, 177. James A. Lewis contends that the failure of New Spain adequately to provision Cuba during the American Revolution was what gave entrée to North American flour shipments in the Cuban market; see James A. Lewis, "Nueva España y los esfuerzos para abastecer La Habana, 1779–1783," *Anuario de Estudios Americanos*, XXXIII (1976), 501–526. For links between Cuba and Philadelphia, forged through the flour trade in the 1760s and 1770s, see also Linda K. Salvucci, "Atlantic Intersections: Early American Commerce and the Rise of the Spanish West Indies (Cuba)," *Business History Review*, LXXIX (2005), 781–809; Sherry Johnson, "El Niño, Environmental Crisis, and the Emergence of Alternative Markets in the Hispanic Caribbean, 1760s–70s," *William and Mary Quarterly*, 3d Ser., LXII (2005), 411–440; and Johnson, *Climate and Catastrophe in Cuba and the Atlantic World in the Age of Revolution* (Chapel Hill, N.C., 2011).

39. Joseph de Abalos to Don María Bucarely, Feb. 17, 1768, AGI, SD, 1156, no. 14: "Es este asumpto tan insondable como el oceano, y un mar de tal anchura que no se le descubre la tierra." On contra-

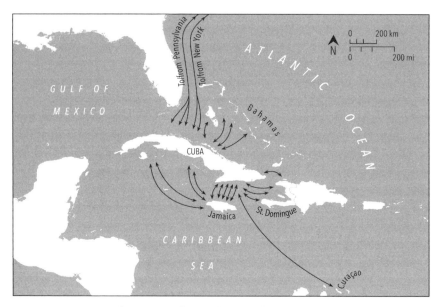

MAP 5 Major Routes of Interimperial Contraband Trade. Drawn by Molly Roy

It was not just Havana, of course, but the whole island of Cuba that participated in contraband trade through a variety of routes of exchange. We can get a fairly good sense of the trade's overall contours even if by necessity it is more in qualitative than quantitative terms (see Maps 2 and 5). According to officials' reports, British American traders from New York, Pennsylvania, and New Providence in the Bahamas predominated on the north coast of the island. The majority of traders who arrived on the island's south coast sailed from British Jamaica, French Saint Domingue, and Dutch Curaçao. Closer to the eastern end of the island at Santiago de Cuba, French traders from Saint Domingue were more prevalent than British, and there were instances when French smugglers brought enslaved Africans to Cuba from Jamaica as well. In the middle of the island, along the south coast, the town of Puerto Príncipe was known to have several resident British merchants who operated a busy trade with Jamaica, exporting livestock and importing cloth and manufactured goods.[40]

band slave trading in Cuba, see José Luciano Franco, *Comercio clandestino de esclavos* (Havana, 1996). For *indultos de negros de ilícita introducción,* which were also sometimes issued as a sign of good faith upon the swearing in of a new governor, see, for example, AGI, SD, 2209. On this topic, see also López Mesa, "La trata negrera," *Catauro,* II, no. 3 (January–June 2001), 148–158.

40. Spanish records documenting contraband trade consist of anonymous reports to the crown, accounts of efforts to combat contraband and prosecute its practitioners, and passing references to

Contraband activity on the southern coast of Cuba did not operate in its own sphere, as the economies there — especially from Trinidad to the west — were inextricably linked to Havana's. The vast geographic range of Havana's largest landholders enabled them to benefit from trade on the south coast. In addition, the town of Batabanó, only thirty miles from Havana on the narrow southwestern end of the island, functioned in large part as the capital's second port. Batabanó often received ships carrying goods, or enslaved Africans, that were then transported to the capital on foot or by horse or mule train. Besides traders, travelers to and from Havana also used the port. Those going from Havana to Trinidad, Santiago de Cuba, Cartagena de Indias, Spanish Santo Domingo, and other destinations primarily made their way overland from Havana to Batabanó and then sailed from there. When Juan de Prado arrived on the island to assume the governorship of Havana and the captain generalcy of Cuba in 1761, he landed at Batabanó and made the journey to Havana by horse.[41]

Trade with foreign merchants also occurred openly in Havana's bay to a greater extent than historians have heretofore acknowledged. In the eighteenth century, Havana's port officials still retained the custom of pulling a massive chain across the mouth of the harbor at night, although by this point this was done more to prevent the entry of contraband goods than to protect against pirate attacks. Nevertheless, as colonial officials' reports reveal, canoes filled with smuggled textiles and other goods still managed to slip in beneath the chain at night. Then, once prohibited goods made their way into port, or anywhere in Havana's vicinity, Havana residents from all rungs of the social order — men and women, Europeans and Africans, rich and poor — had a hand in the contraband trade. Locals passed bags and barrels of prohibited merchandise over, under, and through the city's walls and down its streets in numerous ingenious ways. According to reports, women rode horses through the gates with saddle bags packed with contraband silk fabrics and other cloth, and Spanish and French sailors surreptitiously moved sacks of goods around the city.[42]

---

restricted foreign goods in the possession of Spanish colonial subjects; see, for example, Miguel de Altarriba to Julián Arriaga, Mar. 8, 1765, AGI, SD, 2188; Don Juan Horcasitas to Consejo de Indias, Mar. 28, 1743, AGI, SD, 2208. For the British traders in Trinidad, see "Don John Further Displayed: Being a Supplement to Considerations on the American Trade," London, 1740, Baker Business Library, Harvard University, Cambridge, Mass.

41. López Mesa, "La trata negrera," *Catauro*, II, no. 3 (January–June 2001), 152; Juan B. Amores, *Cuba en la época de Ezpeleta (1785–1790)* (Pamplona, Spain, 2000), 198–199, 221. For traffic between Batabanó and Havana, see, for example, Consejo de Indias, Nov. 21, 1749, AGI, SD, 1130A, no. 10. For Prado's arrival in Havana, see Prado to Consejo de Indias, Feb. 21, 1761, AGI, Ultramar, 169.

42. Consejo de las Indias, May 31, 1769, no. 14, and Consejo de las Indias, Sept. 26, 1769, no. 21,

Smugglers also conjured up excuses to sail directly into the bay, where they would sell cloth, manufactured goods, or enslaved Africans clandestinely, or even quite openly, under the noses of often-complicit royal officials. Since the American Treaty of 1670, Spain had been forced to permit British ships to receive help and "refreshments" when storms or enemies drove them into its American ports. Thus, common reasons foreign traders cited for entering Havana's harbor were that their ship was taking on water, they needed water or wood, or they were suffering from damage caused by a storm and had a dire need to stop and make repairs. The pretext of needing water and wood became such an obvious — and universally recognized — excuse to slip into harbor with contraband that in 1748 one royal official in Havana commented, "Foreigners act like idiots when it is convenient for their business." Even when royal officials inspected foreign ships looking for clandestine goods, smugglers often found that offering bribes and concealing contraband — in barrels of flour, for example — proved effective.[43]

Cuba's contraband trade was not just a function of foreigners pushing their way into Havana with the help of locals. Despite prohibitions, Spanish subjects in Cuba also frequently sailed out to trade in neighboring colonies. One study of British contraband in the Caribbean and the Gulf of Mexico from 1748 to 1778 found that, among Spanish ships sailing directly into British American ports to participate in contraband trade, more were from Cuba than from any other part of Spanish America. An anonymous report to the Spanish crown pointed out that it was not unheard of to find nineteen or twenty ships from Cuba docked in Kingston at any given time. During disruptions in the all-important asiento slave trade, Cuba's captain general even blurred the line between contraband and sanctioned trade by permitting large landholders and merchants in Havana and Santiago de Cuba to sail to a foreign colony to

both in AGI, SD, 1136; Consejo de las Indias, Nov. 29, 1749, AGI, SD, 1130A, no. 14; Consejo de las Indias, Feb. 5, 1750, AGI, SD, 1130B, no. 2; Consejo de las Indias, Feb. 5, 1750, AGI, SD, 1130B, no. 2. Jesse Cromwell provides a window into the means and methods by which goods moved inland and officials conspired in their sales in *Choppy Waters: Smuggling in the Development of Commerce and Community in Eighteenth-Century Venezuela* (Williamsburg, Va., and Chapel Hill, N.C., 2018).

43. Juan Thomas de la Barrera, Antonio Rivero, Diego Peñalver y Angulo, and Manuel Cagigal de la Vega to Ensenada, Oct. 20, 1750, AGI, Escribiania, 70C: "Los extrangeros se hacen bobos cuando conviene para su negocio." On the American Treaty of 1670 and Anglo-Spanish Caribbean commerce more broadly, see Richard Pares, *War and Trade in the West Indies, 1739–1763* (Oxford, 1936), 30; Allan Christelow, "Contraband Trade between Jamaica and the Spanish Main, and the Free Port Act of 1766," *HAHR*, XXII (1942), 309–343, esp. 330; James A. Lewis, "Anglo-American Entrepreneurs in Havana: The Background and Significance of the Expulsion of 1784–1785," in Jacques A. Barbier and Allan J. Kuethe, eds., *The North American Role in the Spanish Imperial Economy, 1760–1819* (Manchester, U.K., 1984), 112–126, esp. 120. Many cases of smuggled contraband can be found in AGI, SD, 1130B, and AGI, SD, 1194.

purchase enough enslaved Africans to replenish their own workforces, plus a few hundred more to help finance the trip.[44]

Acknowledging the extent to which Havana residents had already built commercial ties with British colonies in the early eighteenth century casts the arrival of the British expedition of 1762 in a markedly different light. As elsewhere in Spanish America, locals in Havana relied heavily on smuggling and contraband trade to meet their commercial needs, thus knitting together a "transimperial Greater Caribbean" of communication and exchange. What made Havana stand out was that it was such a strategically critical Spanish possession; it was the site of its only shipyard in the Americas, the base of its American navy, and its largest and most strategic garrison of troops as well as a well-populated city better connected to the metropole than, for example, Río de la Plata or even Cartagena de Indias. All this, and it was also a city that engaged in a high volume of prohibited trade with Spain's enemies. Transactions with foreigners in a port of such geopolitical military importance were a special concern for the Spanish crown, increasingly so during times of war; the possibility that these foreigners might be spying on Havana's naval base made the monarchy anxious about their presence. Yet both Havana and many parts of Cuba depended heavily on British traders. Regional trade in both goods and humans — in almost all cases technically prohibited by Spanish law — was the island's lifeblood.[45]

The South Sea Company Asiento

When the British South Sea Company gained the contract for the slave trade in Spanish America in 1713, it allowed British merchants and more enslaved Africans into Havana, hastening population growth and economic development in Cuba. British subjects, through the asiento, found ways to weave themselves into the fabric of Havana's economic and political life. Because Havana's merchants and landowners needed enslaved Africans for their agricultural and service-industry pursuits, they actively courted these relationships with the South Sea Company factors to improve their access to enslaved Africans and other commercial networks off the island in spite of Spanish

44. Hector R. Feliciano Ramos, *El contrabando inglés en el Caribe y el Golfo de México (1748–1778)* (Seville, 1990), 166. On ships from Cuba in Kingston's harbor, see Intendencia de la Habana, 1764, AGS, Hacienda, 2342. The granting of private asientos was a long-standing practice sanctioned by the crown in 1751; see Arriaga to the Marqués de la Ensenada, Dec. 11, 1753, AGI, SD, 2209.

45. Ernesto Bassi, *An Aqueous Territory: Sailor Geographies and New Granada's Transimperial Greater Caribbean World* (Durham, N.C., 2016), 4. For patterns of contraband in Cartagena de Indias, see also Haroldo Calvo Stevenson and Adolfo Meisel Roca, eds., *Cartagena de Indias en el siglo XVIII* (Cartagena, Colombia, 2005).

legal constraints. Because the asiento represents a unique case study of trade both within and beyond the parameters of Spanish policy, how it worked in practice merits special attention. In miniature, Havana's South Sea Company trade factory demonstrates the way Havana residents leveraged the asiento to build up a multifaceted trade with British America and other regions. And, just as Spanish officials had feared, as a shared interest between subjects of the British and Spanish crowns developed around the slave trade Britain's increased access to Havana also gave it crucial information it could use to target the city.[46]

The South Sea Company factory in Havana was especially busy, more so than the company's operations at Veracruz and Cartagena de Indias, two Spanish Caribbean ports that served larger inland territories. Despite two interruptions owing to war, between 1715 and 1734 the company brought 6,062 enslaved Africans into Havana as well as 503 enslaved Africans into its factory at Santiago de Cuba. The South Sea Company was especially eager to sell enslaved Africans in Havana because buyers in the city had more liquidity to pay for enslaved Africans in Spanish silver, as opposed to products of the land, which the company also accepted in payment, but less eagerly.[47]

In Havana, the South Sea Company factors also profited from an especially busy sideline contraband trade. In fact, the volume of contraband trading in Havana was so great that company officials feared it risked alienating the Spanish court and the Council of the Indies and jeopardizing Britain's asiento to all of Spanish America. A British merchant in Jamaica reported that the private smuggling trade with Cuba had dropped off since the South Sea Company had acquired the asiento, explaining, "For their sloops and vessels being

46. Adrian Finucane's book considers how South Sea Company factors stationed throughout Spanish America both connected British and Spanish empires and drove them to war; see Finucane, *The Temptations of Trade: Britain, Spain, and the Struggle for Empire* (Philadelphia, 2016).

47. "Observations on the Trade and Navigation in That Part of America Which Is Generally Called the Trading Part of the West Indies," [1739 or 1740], Add. MSS 32694, fol. 64, BL; "Razón de los negros introducidos en el puerto de la Habana desde que se inició el Asiento hasta el 1 de marzo de 1734," AGI, Contaduría, 268; "Cuenta general del trato de negros en Santiago de Cuba desde 1715 hasta el 24 de junio de 1722," AGI, Contaduría, 266; Mercedes García Rodríguez, *Los ingleses en el tráfico de esclavos en Cuba, 1715–1739* (Havana, 2006), 26–27, 303. According to García Rodríguez and Jean O. McLachlan, the factory in Santiago de Cuba ceased importing slaves after that time. See McLachlan, *Trade and Peace with Old Spain, 1667–1750* (Cambridge, 1940), 82. In Santiago de Cuba in 1719, the company even officially closed down a factory when its residents could not pay for slaves in currency. The 6,062 enslaved Africans sold in Havana were counted as 5,114⅓ *"piezas de indias."* In comparison, in Veracruz between 1716 and 1731 records indicate 1,464 "piezas de Indias" were received, and 2,808 "piezas" arrived in Cartagena between December 1714 and 1730. For Veracruz and Cartagena, see Elena F. S. de Studer, *La trata de negros en el Río de la Plata durante el siglo XVIII* (Buenos Aires, 1958), 231–232. On the preference of British slave traders in Jamaica for Spanish buyers, because they often paid in pieces of eight, see O'Malley, *Final Passages,* 162.

permitted to introduce negroes into the Spanish ports, do at the same time, though not on the company's account, carry on a considerable private trade, which is winked at by the Governors and royal officers, who as it is said generally buy their cargoes by persons they appoint for that purpose." To the author's dismay, the South Sea Company's rival smuggling trade benefited from the support and involvement of the highest levels of colonial officialdom.[48]

South Sea Company factors in Havana took full advantage of their right to establish homes and factories in Spanish American ports as well as to send agents inland to sell slaves. Article 35 of the asiento permitted company agents to rent land in order to "refresh and maintain the health of the disembarked slaves." On these lands, they could also cultivate agricultural products, ostensibly to sustain the enslaved Africans as they awaited sale. In practice, however, several factors in Havana managed to acquire sizable agricultural estates. Although two of these landholding factors were expelled by Spain at the outbreak of the War of Jenkins' Ear and had their lands and possessions seized, at least one of the British company's agents remained and was able to naturalize in Havana and help develop the nascent sugar industry in Cuba.[49]

That South Sea Company factor was Richard (Ricardo) O'Farrill, who came to possess various properties and sugar estates in Havana, some purchased while a factor and others gained afterward. A native of Montserrat of Irish Catholic background, O'Farrill arrived in Havana in 1715 to replace the French asiento factor before him. Three years later, in response to food shortages in the city, the governor of Havana gave O'Farrill permission to import 698 barrels of flour from Jamaica and Barbados, a concession that helped him build a local fortune independent of the company. O'Farrill then left the South Sea Company and solicited his naturalization as a vecino, or resident, of Havana, which he was granted in 1722. Shortly after O'Farrill's naturalization, his son brought over to Cuba from Jamaica a shipment on his own account of 236 enslaved African men and women and 260 barrels of flour, in addition to his father's personal possessions, household furnishings, and materials for constructing what would be, up until 1780, the largest sugar plantation on the island.[50]

48. On concerns that contraband in Havana was jeopardizing the Spanish asiento, see "Some Consideration Offered to Prevent the Farming of the Factory on the Island of Cuba," Shelburne Papers, XLIII, 279–283, William L. Clements Library, Ann Arbor, Mich.

49. Asiento agreement between Britain and Spain, Mar. 26, 1713, AGI, SD, 2208.

50. Mercedes García Rodríguez, "El monto de la trata hacia Cuba en el siglo XVIII," in Consuelo Naranjo Orovio and Tomás Mallo Gutiérrez, eds., *Cuba, la perla de las Antillas: Actas de las I jornadas sobre "Cuba y su Historia"* (Madrid, 1994), 298; Marrero, *Cuba*, VI, 174; Rafael Fernández Moya, "The Irish Presence in the History and Place Names of Cuba," *Irish Migration Studies in Latin America*, V (2007), 189–198; Julio David Rojas Rodríguez, "La familia O'Farrill y sus negocios en África" (paper presented at "The Slave Trade to Cuba: New Research Perspectives," Havana, Cuba, June 9, 2016); Manuel Moreno Fraginals, *El ingenio: Complejo económico social cubano del azúcar* (Barcelona, 2001),

What made O'Farrill's naturalization possible was the welcome he received from Havana's richest, most powerful families, who quickly embraced him as one of their own. In 1720, he married María Josefa Arriola y García de Lodoño, the widow of an important landholder and the daughter of an official of the royal treasury and founder of the royal navy's shipyard in Havana in 1713. Merchants often strive to marry well in local society, and Havana was known as a city in which foreigners "land from all parts," despite Spanish prohibitions on their presence in its American realms. Nicolás de Ribera captured Havana's open attitude toward integrating foreigners when he commented they "become like Spaniards with time." In this case, O'Farrill benefited from a combination of his Catholic faith and Havana residents' desire to expand the slave trade to the island. That he joined them from the British enemy they manufactured ships to fight against did not matter — O'Farrill gave Havana elites interested in investing in sugar access to more enslaved Africans and perhaps the technology and machinery necessary to enter into that industry. O'Farrill's wife served as a cultural broker with the host society, and both his personal fortune and members of Havana's elite milieu prospered.[51]

The South Sea Company factors in Havana after O'Farrill left his post, Wargeant Nicholson and Hubert Fassell, also bought a large estate and further facilitated the trade of Havana's wealthiest residents, in addition to selling them enslaved Africans. Nicholson and Fassell's landholding, called El Inglés, was located close to the site where the enslaved disembarked from the company's ships. On its grounds, they ran a sugar mill and tobacco factory, which were worked by enslaved laborers the company had for sale but who labored for them as long as three years at a time before their disposition in the local market. George Wane, master of a British ship that put in at Havana in the spring of 1738, commented on the elaborate establishment: "In short your factory appears to me like the house of a minister of state." In the 1720s and the 1730s, Nicholson and Fassell exported snuff, logwood, and mahogany planks from Havana to Jamaica, Amsterdam, and Hamburg. The factors also partnered with another Jamaican merchant, William Cowley, to use the asiento ships to transport hides from Cuba to London for sale. Shortly before the

---

16. In her study of South Sea Company factors in numerous Spanish American ports, Adrian Finucane has shown that some factors decided to "defect" to the Spanish empire, though none became as wealthy and prominent in a Spanish American city. See Finucane, *Temptations of Trade,* 53–54, 63–68, 81–83, 102.

51. "Voyage du Sr. Villiet d'Arignon," in *Voyages,* 301: *"grand concours d'etrangers qui y abordent de toutes parts"*; Ribera, *Descripción de la Isla de Cuba,* ed. Pichardo Viñals, 70; Kuethe and Andrien, *The Spanish Atlantic World,* 108. Bishop Morell mentioned marriages with *"vagos extrangeros,"* which had concerned his predecessor, in his 1755 visita: "Relación de la visita ecclesiástica," Oct. 4, 1758, 53, AGI, SD, 534.

War of Jenkins' Ear, they sent a large shipment of Havana snuff to agents in Amsterdam who sold it all at public auction, thus defying the Spanish monopoly on Cuba's tobacco trade. In the early years of the British asiento, so much Havana snuff was making its way through various routes off the island and into northern European markets that the price in Amsterdam dropped almost by half.[52]

Not only did the asiento factors facilitate Havana residents' trade throughout the Atlantic system but they also shielded their capital accumulation from Spanish taxation and enforcement. Across the eighteenth century, Havana elites used asiento factors like Nicholson and Fassell, as well as trade contacts they made in Kingston, to remit silver and jewels back to Spain, often via London. Doing so had the dual benefit of avoiding the royal *quinto* and concealing from Spanish authorities the earnings they were making in extralegal regional trade. In addition to these services, Nicholson and Fassell also mortgaged estates for royal officials in Havana and offered bribes to the governor and other officials in charge of checking for contraband on ships that entered and departed the harbor.[53]

As part of this mutually beneficial relationship, the governor of Havana protected the factors from agents of the Spanish Church and state concerned about their commercial or Protestant religious activities in Havana. When the Inquisition or the king sought to counteract the factors' growing entrenchment in Havana society, the governor and elites protected them. Members of Havana's city council even testified on the factors' behalf to shield them from disciplinary action from South Sea Company officials in London, who were concerned about the extent of their personal business dealings in Cuba outside sanctioned company affairs. This shielding of South Sea Company factors drew criticism from witnesses in Havana, who reported to authorities in Spain

52. Letter of George Wane, Havana, Apr. 11, 1738, Shelburne Papers, XLIV, no. 220, Clements Library; "Memorandum relative to the Campeache Trade by Peter Burrell," Shelburne Papers, XLIII, no. 80, fol. 275. A property named El Inglés still appears on a map dated 1773 and was located near the royal shipyard, not far from the Jesuits' former *hacienda;* see "Defensa de la Habana y su Castillo por Don Silvestre Abarca," 1773, MS 9/5406, Real Academia de la Historia, Madrid; García Rodríguez, "El monto de la trata," in Naranjo Orovio and Mallo Gutiérrez, , eds., *Cuba,* 300–301, 305. For the export of hides, see Campbell v. Orts, C 111.200, TNA. For the export of snuff, see Campbell v. Orts, Exhibit E, Muilman and Sons to John Bland, Jr., Sept. 14, 1764, C 111.200, TNA. The factors also exported snuff to Hamburg; see "Memorandum relative to the Campeache Trade by Peter Burrell," Shelburne Papers, XLIII, no. 80, fol. 275, Clements Library.

53. British sources from the 1760s and 1770s refer to this practice of remittances as established and ongoing. See Salvador to [unknown symbol], Jan. 28, 1766, Add. MSS 38339, fols. 225–227, BL, in Christelow, "Contraband Trade between Jamaica and the Spanish Main," *HAHR,* XXII (1942), 331; "Tract on the Spanish Trade, in a Letter from Lieutenant Governor Dallings," Apr. 11, 1773, CO 137.68, TNA; "Memorandum on the Spanish Trade," Shelburne Papers, XLIV, fols. 12–18, Clements Library; Feliciano Ramos, *El contrabando inglés,* 204.

the problem of "the union and alliance of the Governor with the asiento factors." The presence of these factors was an asset to local commerce, however, and the governor, colonial officials, and city council members willingly protected them in order to enhance their trade networks with British American territories and, via the slave trade, West Africa.[54]

Although O'Farrill might have married into Havana society and ended up developing the island's sugar industry, other factors acted more as Spanish officials feared they would. South Sea Company factors in both Havana and Santiago de Cuba sent spying reports back to London on activities such as privateering and military preparations for the attack on Georgia. After he was driven out of Havana by the War of Jenkins' Ear, Hubert Fassell joined in the war plotting against Havana. In October 1739, two years after he left the city, he wrote a letter to British admiral Sir Charles Wager, claiming he was prompted to write by the talk in London that the city was being seriously considered for attack. Warning of the necessity of a large squadron of men to take the city and the tremendous difficulties disease would pose for any expedition, he sought to introduce a degree of realism and sophistication into Britain's war plans. But Fassell's loyalty to the crown was hardly pure. Whatever he could do to help advise the admiral he would do, he said, not just for "the benefit of the nation" but also for the recovery of "a landed estate" he owned on the island.[55]

The War of Jenkins' Ear: "The Happiest Time"

The series of eighteenth-century Anglo-Spanish wars in the region disrupted the asiento, displaced South Sea Company factors, and facilitated further

54. Cartagena de Indias, June 18, 1734, Testimony of Don Antonio de Luna, AHN, Inquisición, 1599, ex. 14. For instances of factors who came into conflict with the Inquisition in Santiago de Cuba and elsewhere in Spanish America, see Finucane, *Temptations of Trade,* 97–98, 100–101. On the collusion of the governor with the factors, see Report of Don Miguel de Tapia Cotategui, Sept. 6, 1728, AGI, SD, 1499. For Nicholson and Fassell's financial dealings in Havana, see Campbell v. Orts, C 111.200, TNA. For the amount spent on bribes, see Colin Palmer, *Human Cargoes: The British Slave Trade to Spanish America, 1700–1739* (Urbana, Ill., 1981), 60, 72; García Rodríguez, "El monto de la trata," in Naranjo Orovio and Gutiérrez, eds., *Cuba,* 297–312, esp. 302, 305.

55. "An Exact Account of the Expedition That Was Carried on by the Spaniards at Havana and Intended against the Colony of Georgia," Shelburne Papers, XLIII, no. 63, fols. 213–215, Clements Library; Leonard Cocke to Captain Digby Dent (Jamaica), Santiago de Cuba, Nov. 3, 1736, Vernon-Wager Manuscripts, LC; Finucane, *Temptations of Trade,* 94; Hubert Tassell [Fassell] of the Havana to Captain S. Bonham, Jan. 12, 1732, Add. MSS 32776, fol. 294, BL. Just two days after Fassell wrote his letter, he submitted a more fantastic and elaborate plan for an attack on Callao, Peru, followed by a march on Lima that involved disseminating pamphlets written in Spanish about the benefits of British rule. See Hubert Fassell to Admiral Sir Charles Wager, Oct. 24, 1739, Vernon-Wager Manuscripts, LC.

plotting against Havana. Paradoxically, however, rather than disturbing relations of contraband and slave trading between Cuba and British America, war provided an opportunity for Havana residents to expand regional trade under their own auspices. Anglo-Spanish war became a time when Havana residents pursued their own economic interests with increasing autonomy, even as they engaged in military action on behalf of their crown. With normal transatlantic trade routes disrupted, local authorities needed more than ever to reach out to Cuba's neighbors for food supplies and for their very economic survival. Opportunism spurred other residents of Cuba, both public officials and private individuals, into higher volumes of contraband trade. As a result, the wars brought many foreign goods, merchants, sailors, and enslaved blacks into the city, even subjects of Spain's enemies. Havana elites used wartime to pull the city into closer relations of trade and diplomacy with British America and also make it a more open port, one that was more closely linked with British America before the invasion than historians have heretofore acknowledged.

The cycle of Anglo-Spanish warfare across this period was quite lucrative for Havana. The wars both integrated the city into the regional economy and gave it greater autonomy from political authorities at the Spanish court and the Council of the Indies and from merchant monopolies in Cádiz. Although all the wars of this period had similar effects, the War of Jenkins' Ear brought the most gains to the city. The intensified rate of contraband and privateering made the War of Jenkins' Ear a boom time for Havana, a trade fair, a tiempo de flota. Nicolás de Ribera called the war "the happiest time." Despite anxiety at its onset about the interruption of trade, he wrote, "never had it been so rich or populated as then." "The Island began to abound in money." The Spanish government's heightened investment in the city, owing to its role as a crucial staging ground for Spain's American military operations, was partly the reason for the increased prosperity. With Havana serving as the base for the royal armada in America, warships and sailors were concentrated in the city. The number of Spanish troops stationed at the garrison rose, as did Spanish expenditures to feed them. Thus, the posting of more Spanish troops to the city necessitated an increase in regional trade, particularly with North American mills, for enough flour and bread to feed the garrison, either coordinated directly or via Jamaica. But the boom time of the War of Jenkins' Ear was also driven by the initiatives of Havana residents themselves to expand their networks of regional trade.[56]

56. Ribera, *Descripción de la isla de Cuba*, ed. Pichardo Viñals, 113–114: "la Epoca más feliz de aquella Ysla, pues nunca se havia visto tan rica ni poblada, como entonces" (115), "Empezo la Ysla á abundar en dinero" (114). For a similar phenomenon during the war in Cartagena de Indias, see

As war broke out in 1739, one of Havana's most prominent merchants, Martín de Aróstegui, arrived in Madrid with powers of attorney from a leading coterie of Havana merchants and ranchers to lobby for the founding of a Havana-based monopoly company. Chief among his concerns was the lack of sufficient outlets to connect Cuba's goods to markets and the scarcity of enslaved Africans needed to power the island's economy. As a result of Aróstegui's mission, the king chartered the RHC in 1740, which was granted a partial monopoly on the island's commerce and the slave-trading asiento to the island in exchange for providing a variety of services for the Spanish crown. Its duties reflected the blending of military and commercial functions that was the hallmark of the Havana economy. Among its many tasks, the company would manufacture warships in Havana (an expensive and money-losing venture, as it learned), provision and arm the Spanish forts in Florida, transport troops, arm privateers, and create the *guardacostas* to intercept contraband. In return, it received freedom from certain duties and a number of privileges, such as a monopoly on tobacco exports to the royal factory in Seville. By design it was set up both to meet the needs of Cuba's economy better and to combat contraband with foreign colonies, a cause of increasing concern in Spain and a precipitant to the war with Britain.[57]

Havana's most powerful men of commerce used the RHC to expand regional trade during wartime. Like the Royal Caracas Company in Venezuela, the RHC was designed to emulate the practices of Spain's British, Dutch, and French competitors and to meet strategic needs in a climate of increased imperial rivalry and warfare. Unlike the Royal Caracas Company, which was founded by peninsular merchants and based in San Sebastián — or in fact any other monopoly company in any empire at the time — the RHC was locally controlled in an overseas territory. Despite the word "royal" in its name, the king himself held only one hundred shares, which would never amount to more than a 7 percent interest in the company. Half of the RHC's shares were in Havana, half in Spain, and the creole merchants who served as its directors convened meetings of the company's officials in Cuba. Leveraging this local control, Havana elites built on advantageous relationships with merchants in Jamaica and British North America that they had fostered through contraband trade and the auspices of the British asiento. Those creoles holding posi-

Casey S. Schmitt, "Virtue in Corruption: Privateers, Smugglers, and the Shape of Empire in the Eighteenth-Century Caribbean," *Early American Studies*, XIII (2015), 80–110.

57. Montserrat Garate Ojanguren, *Comercio ultramarino y ilustración: La Real Compañía de La Habana* (Donostia-San Sebastián, 1993), 22–23.

tions of power in the RHC sought to emulate and usurp the South Sea Company in the island's commerce.[58]

Although the RHC was supposed to have agents in only Spanish and Spanish American ports, the Havana leadership stationed a representative in Kingston who contracted for shipments of enslaved Africans, manufactured goods, and foodstuffs from merchants there. The delegate the RHC chose was Pedro de Estrada, a wealthy Havana merchant, owner of "one of the most beautiful houses" on Havana's Plaza Nueva and four *haciendas* outside the city. The British consul at Cádiz described Estrada as "a French gentleman" of sizable capital, married, naturalized, and long resident in Havana. Like the South Sea Company factors in Havana, Estrada and the RHC agent who succeeded him in Kingston participated in a lucrative sideline trade in manufactured goods and foreign cloth, outside the legal parameters of the company's contract.[59]

During the war and the immediate postwar period, the RHC's slave trading far superseded the conditions and volume of the slave-trading asiento that the Spanish crown had granted it and the estimates historians have traditionally made for the slave trade under its control. According to the asiento's terms, enslaved Africans were supposed to be brought into Puerto Rico by friendly or neutral powers, such as the French or Dutch, and then transshipped to Havana. Royal authorities sought to bar foreign merchants, with their spies and contraband goods, from such critical ports as Havana. Instead, Estrada arranged for enslaved Africans and provisions to be delivered to Cuba directly in British ships, undertaken at the Jamaican merchants' own risk and arriving either at the port of Havana or in Batabanó on the island's south coast. One of the Jamaican merchants Estrada did business with was the wealthiest in Jamaica at the time, Edward Manning, who later stationed his own agent, Charles Robertson, in Havana to fulfill slave trading contracts. These ships also brought the customary barrels of imported flour that were allowed alongside the enslaved Africans as well as other foodstuffs to help meet demand in

58. Garate Ojanguren, *Comercio ultramarino e ilustración*, 11–60. On the Royal Caracas Company, see also Cromwell, *Choppy Waters*; and Roland Dennis Hussey, *The Caracas Company, 1728–1784: A Study in the History of Spanish Monopolistic Trade* (Cambridge, Mass., 1934).

59. The founders of the RHC were among those listed in confidential South Sea Company documents as principal contacts in Havana during the 1730s. See "Memorandum on the Spanish Trade," Shelburne Papers, XLIV, fol. 7, Clements Library; "Los directores de la compañía de aquella ciudad," Aug. 4, 1744, AGI, SD, 2208. For the agent of the RHC in Kingston, see also Trelawney to Newcastle, Aug. 16, 1744, Nov. 15, 1745, CO 137.57, TNA. For discussion of the impact of the RHC on the local economy in Havana, see Ribera, *Descripción de la isla de Cuba*, ed. Pichardo Viñals, 114–115. On Estrada's house, see "Remarques sur la Havane," Pierre Eugene du Simitière Papers, West Indies No. 4, LCP. For the comments of the British consul at Cádiz, see James Cornerford to Wargeant Nicholson, Campbell v. Orts, July 7, 1752, C 111.200, TNA.

Havana during wartime, such as pigs, lard, cheese, and salted cod in addition to foreign cloth and manufactured goods.[60]

The RHC did such brisk business that between February 1743 and October 1747 it imported 4,484 enslaved Africans into Havana, nearly as many enslaved Africans in just three and a half years as the 4,986 historians have ascribed to the company for the twenty years it held an asiento. Some of the early shipments hailed from Dutch Curaçao and Saint Eustatius and from French Martinique, but more than 90 percent of the enslaved Africans had embarked from Jamaica. By the time its asiento had expired in 1760, the RHC had imported more enslaved Africans than the South Sea Company had during the decade before. Indeed, company records indicate that it made a significant profit on the slave trade.[61]

In addition to expanding Cuba's slave trade, the RHC also transacted with merchants from other British and British American ports who sailed into Havana's harbor to fulfill their contracts. In 1747 and 1748, merchants from New York and Liverpool were among those who traveled to and from Havana on the RHC's account. Charles Allen of New York had been hired to bring in shipbuilding materials as well as provisions and other goods worth eighteen thousand pesos. Another New York merchant, William Walton, the most prominent British or British American merchant dealing with the RHC, was charged with the sensitive task of provisioning the Spanish fort at Saint Augustine in Florida with food and even munitions during wartime. Referred to in Spanish records as either Guillermo Walton or "an individual from New England," he had established contracts to provision the Saint Augustine garri-

---

60. "La Junta formada sobre arvitrios en Indias para el actual armamento," Dec. 31, 1740, and "Memorial aprobado en 29 marzo de 1741, en Retiro, por Joseph de la Quintana, en lo qual cedió por Don Martín de Ulibarrí y Gamboa," Mar. 15, 1741, both in AGI, SD, 2208; López Mesa, "La trata negrera," *Catauro*, II, no. 3 (January–June 2001), 148–153. On Edward Manning, see Trevor Burnard and Kenneth Morgan, "The Dynamics of the Slave Market and Slave Purchasing Patterns in Jamaica, 1655–1788," *WMQ*, 3d Ser., LVIII (2001), 205–228, esp. 221–222; Andrew Rutledge, "Enemies Bound by Trade: Jamaica, Cuba, and the Shared World of Contraband in Atlantic Empires" (Ph.d. diss., University of Michigan, 2018).

61. They made 112,242 pesos, a considerable profit from the trade; see López Mesa, "La trata negrera," *Catauro*, II, no. 3 (January–June 2001), 153. Other company records affirm that the RHC brought in more enslaved Africans, even just in the first ten years, than the South Sea Company asiento; see "Resumen de negros introducidos en la Habana desde 1741–1751," AGI, Ultramar, 986, no. 2. Though Greg O'Malley has found a certain degree of drop-off in Jamaica's slave trading to Spanish America during the War of Jenkins' Ear, other sources indicate an increase in inter-island slave trading ("Jamaica: Account of Negroes Imported and Exported between the 1st Day of July 1739 and 1 July 1749," CO 137.25, fol. 87, TNA). The total for this period is cited as 69,140 enslaved Africans, 54,463 of which were sold to the island's planters and 14,677 of which were reexported after duties were paid in Jamaica. For the years 1743–1747, 36,731 Africans were brought into Jamaica, with 27,816 remaining and 8,915 finding themselves put to sea again to be sold elsewhere. See O'Malley, *Final Passages*, 296, 361, 364.

son since 1726, during a prior Anglo-Iberian war. It must have been lucrative indeed because in 1752 he built the Walton House mansion on Pearl Street, considered the most impressive residence in Manhattan in its day.[62]

Once the war had ended, the RHC continued to operate with this local autonomy, tapping into regional networks of trade during the postwar period despite an effort by its Cádiz-based shareholders to reprimand the Havana leadership. Charles Robertson continued to reside in Havana, showing up in company records as late as 1757, and British ships continued to sail into the harbor with cargoes of enslaved Africans, barrels of flour, and foodstuffs. In 1761, not much more than a year before the British war fleet arrived offshore of Havana, a British slave ship sailed into Havana's harbor with two hundred enslaved Africans on board, brought on the RHC's account.[63]

Historians of the siege of Havana have traditionally given much credence to the idea that the Knowles report, made in 1756 by the governor of Jamaica on his way back to London, provided the British expedition of 1762 with the intelligence it needed to mount its later attack. Yet there were multiple other sources. Scottish lieutenant general David Dundas, in his memoir of the siege of Havana, recollected that he had information on the port from "an English trader who had long lived there." Secretary of state for the Southern Department, the earl of Egremont, had also received from a British merchant a detailed description and map of Havana, with soundings of the bay and the size and location of each of its cannons, dated September 1760. These spying reports could have been provided by this slave ship's captain, or perhaps by Charles Robertson, or by any number of other merchants coming in and out of the Bay of Havana.[64]

62. "Memorial of William Walton, of the City of New York, Merchant," *El Escribano*, III, no. 3 (July 1966), 14–22; John Austin Stevens, Jr., *Colonial Records of the New York Chamber of Commerce, 1768–1784* (New York, 1867), 56–62. Allen and the merchant from Liverpool, John Cooper, show up in Spanish government records because of problems that arose with their contracts or suspicions that they were engaging in contraband on the side (Consejo de las Indias, Apr. 29, 1750, no. 7, and Sept. 25, 1750, no. 22, both in AGI, SD, 1130B; Consejo de Indias, Oct. 30, 1749, AGI, SD, 1130A, no. 5). Often individuals from New York were identified as being from "Nueva Inglaterra" in Cuban sources from this period. See Consejo de Indias, Año de 1745, Resumen de carta, Havana, Aug. 4, 1744, Los directores de la compañía de aquella ciudad, AGI, SD, 2208.

63. Garate Ojanguren, *Comercio ultramarino e ilustración*, 119–124. For "Carlos Robertson" mentioned as "residente" in Havana in 1757, see "Testimonio de diligencias de la armazon de negros," 1757, AGI, SD, 2209B. For the British slave ship in 1761, see "El Governador participa la entrada en aquel puerto de un navio mercante ingles con 200 cabezas de negros de cuenta de aquella Real Compañía," Mar. 11, 1761, AGI, SD, 2209.

64. "Lieutenant-General David Dundas's Memorandum on the Capture of Havana," September 1800, in Syrett, ed., *Siege and Capture of Havana*, 315; Anonymous to Egremont, September 1760, Petworth House Archives, 2955, and Map of Havana, Petworth House Archives, 5120, West Sussex Record Office, Chichester, U.K.

Through the RHC, Havana merchants managed to seize the opportunity of wartime to serve their own economic and local interests within the officially sanctioned structures of Spanish colonialism. This history must be taken into account in order to understand the response of Havana's merchant classes to the British invasion and occupation of 1762. In his explanation of the "happiest time" of the War Jenkins' Ear, however, Ribera cited more than just the royal injections of cash into the economy and the trade that flourished during the war. He also drew attention to all the people and goods that were brought into port by the linked ventures of privateering and prisoner exchange. According to Ribera, "The island abounded with cheap flour, cod, clothing, and other things, and over all, it was enriched with sailors and beautiful ships." Indeed, intensification of Caribbean warfare led to increasing connections between Havana and other American ports, thus contradicting how imperial wars were supposed to draw clearer lines between British and Spanish territories.[65]

Privateering and Prisoner Exchange

The actions of Havana's privateers during the War of Jenkins' Ear occasioned a tremendous circulation of goods, people, and capital through the city that contributed to economic growth that spilled over into the postwar period. Privateers brought captured boatloads of British money, goods, and enslaved Africans to Havana. More than other places on the island, Havana came into closer contact with the peoples, goods, and ships of its neighboring colonies during times of war than in times of peace. In various ways, wartime trading patterns and the business of privateering and ransoming ships — auctioning them off, taking, holding, and exchanging prisoners, and resolving the many disputes that these activities engendered — expanded Havana's trade and created heightened levels of communication and exchange.

Although it is seldom seen this way, privateering really functioned as another form of regional trade through which Havana's merchants profited during wartime and the immediate postwar period. The practices of privateering and prisoner exchange, which went hand in hand, brought more foreigners into the port during periods of war and helped Havana operate in the region with considerably more autonomy. Privateering often inspired multiple rounds of contraband trade, as prisoner-exchange missions, which followed on the heels of capturing and impounding a ship, were openly acknowl-

---

65. Ribera, *Descripción de la isla de Cuba*, ed. Pichardo Viñals, 114: "Abundaba la Ysla de harinas mui baratas y de yacalao y de algunas ropas y de otras cosas, y sobre todo se enriquecía de marineros y de bellas embarcaciones."

edged as opportunities to engage in contraband trade as well. Through this circulation of captured goods, ships, and people, Havana residents expanded their trading during wartime, and, rather than keeping enemies out, they drew more subjects of Spain's enemies into the port during times of war. As with the establishment of the South Sea Company in Havana, the presence of foreigners in the city was a double-edged sword. Allowing foreigners in enriched the city and helped it to grow, but it also risked drawing in more British subjects who might further whet Britain's appetite for taking over the city or provide information to enable an attack.

In the years leading up to the War of Jenkins' Ear, Spanish privateering conducted primarily from Cuba, Puerto Rico, Florida, and Santo Domingo was blamed for precipitating the conflict, and during the war privateers played an outsized role in the fighting. Many years before the official declarations of war, Spain had declared a virtual open season on British ships sailing in the region. Between 1739 and 1741, Spanish privateers reportedly seized well over three hundred ships heading to or sailing from British American ports. Privateers from Spanish America roamed as far north as New England and as far east as the Gulf of Guinea in West Africa; they attacked British ships off the coasts of South Carolina, New York, and Long Island. In fact, before settling in Havana the merchant Pedro de Estrada made his fortune privateering along the coast of the Carolinas out of the port of Saint Augustine, Florida.[66]

Like their counterparts in other Cuban ports, such as Trinidad, Bayamo, and Santiago de Cuba, Havana residents eagerly answered the king's call to prey upon the ships of its enemies in American waters. In doing so, they invested their money into outfitting ships for privateering voyages, joined the crews of privateering vessels, and reaped profits through their share of the captured goods. In his description of Havana at the time, Nicolás de Ribera wrote, "Everyone was talking about arming corsairs." A British shipmaster putting into Havana in the spring of 1738 declared the city "a nest of pyrates," and the British trade factors in Havana commented on the volume of seized goods they saw coming into port.[67]

During the war, the governor of Havana and the captain general of Cuba

66. Herminio Portell Vilá, *Historia de Cuba en sus relaciones con los Estados Unidos y España*, I, *(1512–1853)* (Havana, 1938), 52–53; Hernán Venegas Delgado, *Trinidad de Cuba: Corsarios, azúcar, y revolución en el Caribe* (Havana, 2005), 25; Petition of Don Pedro de Estrada, Havana, Nov. 24, 1762, AGI, SD, 1506; Peggy K. Liss, *Atlantic Empires: The Network of Trade and Revolution, 1713–1826* (Baltimore, 1983), 32. Another source has it that between 1739 and 1741 Spanish privateers seized 329 British merchant ships; see *A List of Merchant Ships Taken by the Spaniards* [n.p., 1742].

67. Ribera, *Descripción de la isla de Cuba*, ed. Pichardo Viñals, 114: "No se hablaba en la Ysla, sino de armar corsarios"; Letter of George Wane, Apr. 11, 1738, Shelburne Papers, XLIV, no. 220, Clements Library.

and the RHC together gave out more than 130 letters of marque to privateers sailing out of Havana and Santiago de Cuba. In 1746, the *South Carolina Gazette* reported that Havana alone had seventeen privateers preparing to cruise along British American coastlines during that summer. Like their counterparts elsewhere in Spanish America, Cuba-based privateers and pirates—the line between them was often slim, or situational—were a mix of individuals of European and African descent, born in the Americas and Spain. The most famous and prolific privateer in the Americas, the man who cut off Jenkins' Ear, was a Spaniard operating out of Havana, Juan León Fandiño. Other privateering captains of the era and the ordinary sailors manning their ships included men of African descent, whose marginalization in other realms led them into this high-risk but potentially high-reward activity. During the war, members of Cuba's black militias also served on privateering vessels. Privateers or sailors of color ran the risk of being sold as slaves if they were captured in a foreign ship. The Spanish crown often complained that its free sailors of African descent were knowingly sold into slavery by British privateers.[68]

Collectively, privateers operating throughout the region made Havana a crucial hub because they brought many boatloads of people and goods from foreign colonies into the city for sale. Between 1743 and 1745, for example, twenty Cuba-based privateers captured seventy-seven British and North American ships, which brought hundreds of prisoners and cargoes valued at millions of pesos into Havana. After capturing a foreign ship at sea, the Spanish corsair would bring its prize into port—to Saint Augustine, for example, but often Havana, where buyers had more currency to chase goods at auction. There royal officials would rule on whether the seizure had been just, and the captured goods would be auctioned off. After the privateer's share, five-sixths of the proceeds were deposited in royal coffers for the king and one-sixth for the judges and ministers. Because wealthy Havana was such an attractive destination for selling captured British ships, privateers from Puerto Rico and other Spanish American ports also took their prizes there.[69]

68. Marrero, *Cuba*, VI, 111; Joyce Elizabeth Harman, *Trade and Privateering in Spanish Florida, 1732–1763* (1969; rpt. Saint Augustine, Fla., 2004), 35; Shelburne Papers, XLIV, nos. 58–58, fols. 321–355. On complaints about sailors from Cuba *"de color quebrado"* being sold into slavery by British privateers, see "Testimonio remitido por Don Juan Francisco Horcasitas," Havana, Oct. 24, 1745, AGI, SD, 1130A.

69. Jacobo de la Pezuela, *Historia de la Isla de Cuba*, 2 vols. (Madrid, 1868–1878), II 583–587; Portell Vilá, *Historia de Cuba*, 53; Marrero, *Cuba*, VI, 192; Jonathan Dennis to Court Directors, Nov. 2, 1731, Shelburne Papers, XLIV, no. 62, fols. 329–355, Clements Library. In reports in the *South Carolina Gazette*, June 25–July 2, 1741, three Englishmen who escaped from Saint Augustine reported that the Spanish had taken and sent to Havana thirty-six vessels, the majority of which had been captured on the southeastern coast of North America; see Harman, *Spanish Privateering*, 36–37.

Privateers and their seizures of property thus provided an economic windfall for the royal treasury in Havana, further lubricating the machinery of Havana's wartime economy. Between September 1738 and December 1742, the royal accounts in Havana gained a staggering 734,559 pesos from the auctioning of captured British (and two Dutch) ships and the seizure of the British asiento factor's goods and property in Havana. This amount was as much as the situado during the peak years of shipbuilding during the 1730s. One historian has made the credible claim that over the course of the entire war privateers brought 2 million pesos of revenue to the royal treasury. The currency raised through these auctions was used to pay the wages of Spanish troops in Havana's garrison, laborers working on fortifications in Havana and elsewhere on the island, and two companies of free pardo militiamen who had been sent to reinforce troops in Florida in 1742.[70]

These auctions of seized British ships both reveal the wealth of Havana merchants and enhanced it further. Auctions of captured prizes became bidding wars in Havana's heavily monetized economy. Havana merchants who frequented the auctions, or bought the goods later on the open market, could buy the latest model of merchant ships, the manufacture of which was forbidden by the Spanish crown. They also gained access to an array of goods from all over the world at a time when many British and other foreign goods were prohibited from being shipped to them from Cádiz. Records remain for the inventory of one packet boat, *The Trial* from the Carolinas, captured in January 1745 by the infamous Basque corsair Pedro de Garaicoechea off the north coast of Cuba, and they show a lengthy list of items in the boat's cargo. The goods, auctioned off over nine successive days in Havana, were purchased by the merchant Don Joseph de Laguardia for 51,996 pesos. In a testament to the high prices in the city and the purchasing power of the Havana residents, he paid 72 percent more than the cargo's official valuation of 30,230 pesos. Along with twenty-five enslaved Africans, the purchase included silver cutlery, locks, sundials, compasses, combs, soap, hats, and a vast collection of cloth. Laguardia, who would go on to become a director of the RHC, then proceeded to sell the enslaved Africans and goods on the open Havana market at a profit.[71]

70. Pezuela, *Historia de la Isla de Cuba*, II, 392. For the 734,559 pesos, see Caja de La Havana, no. 1, 1738–1756, AGI, Contaduría, 1170. This amount was also more than the considerable sum gained between October 1739 and July 1741 by Santiago de Cuba, Cuba's second-largest privateering base: 106,994 pesos.

71. AGI, SD, 2025, in Marrero, *Cuba*, VI, 190–192; Pares, *War and Trade in the West Indies*, 121. In an argument similar to one that could be made for Havana, Harman contends that Saint Augustine, Florida, relied on privateering to feed itself during the War of Jenkins' Ear; see Harman, *Trade and Privateering*, 37–40, 70.

The circulation of goods through privateering exchange also increased demand for Cuban exports throughout the region. Products from Cuba were picked up by British, French, and Dutch corsairs and dispersed to many locations on the Atlantic rim, where buyers developed a taste for Spanish American commodities. Among British captures in January 1749 was a register ship, just off the Azores, returning from New Spain and Cuba, a frigate carrying the best of that year's tobacco harvest in Cuba. After making its capture, the British merchant ship promptly sailed with its prize to Boston, where those Boston consumers who had not yet tried Havana tobacco soon would. In a sign of how privateering could move goods around when other trade conduits were choked off by warfare, sometimes corsairs even facilitated trade between Havana and other Spanish American territories. Spanish colonial authorities regularly auctioned off goods captured in British ships that were of Spanish American origin.[72]

Contesting the seizure of a ship allowed foreign captains to sail into Havana to appear in court or to reclaim their property, opening further pathways for the city's residents to trade. Once a prize ship had been brought into Havana, its captain had the right to defend himself and appeal the seizure in Havana's Spanish court. More often, however, a captain would petition to his own government, which would be more inclined to believe that he had been unjustly captured. Should a British ship's captain be successful in making his case to British authorities in London, they could appeal to the Spanish crown, and the captain might be issued a decree that would entitle him to reclaim his goods at the place where they had been impounded or auctioned off. No matter what the outcome, contesting a seizure or following up on its status provided a good excuse to sail into port and engage in more contraband trade, thus making the expensive journey worthwhile.[73]

As evidenced by the auctioning off of the cargo of *The Trial*, privateering was also another way for Havana residents to expand their slave trading during the war. Many ships captured at sea carried human cargo below decks, and these men, women, and children were considered prizes to be sold at auction. On captured vessels, free sailors of African descent could also be sold or ransomed into slavery. Alongside the activities of the RHC and contraband trade, these practices provided a wartime slaving windfall that brought Africans and creoles from other areas of the Americas to Havana. In fact, the demand for enslaved Africans was so great that some privateering practices ex-

72. Marrero, *Cuba*, VI, 192–193.
73. Harman, *Trade and Privateering*, 47; Pares, *War and Trade*, 25–26.

plicitly targeted enslaved Africans in Jamaica. During the War of Jenkins' Ear, small craft from the south coast of Cuba ran nighttime raids on plantations on the north coast of Jamaica, where they allegedly stole enslaved Africans and either seized or damaged boats and other property. Jamaican planters complained that this "manner of privateering" was "robbing the seaside settlements of considerable numbers of negroes." In some instances, the enslaved Africans had likely run away themselves, but Spanish records do confirm the persistence of these slave raids.[74]

Closely associated with privateering was the practice of prisoner exchange, which circulated additional numbers of foreigners into wartime Havana and facilitated further trade. During the War of Jenkins' Ear and its aftermath, the activities that fostered the most interaction—and forged the closest ties—between Spanish and non-Spanish colonies were the capturing, holding, ransoming, and exchanging of prisoners. Owing to the prolific activity of its privateers, Havana built a large population of foreign prisoners during the War of Jenkins' Ear. Drawn by the lucrative market for auctioning off prizes, privateers frequently elected to sail their captured ships to Havana and would deposit the captured sailors there. Crews of ships that were captured—officers, captains, common sailors, whether merchant marine or royal navy—were taken by their captors to one of their neighboring ports, where they were either sold as slaves or held until they could be ransomed or exchanged for an enemy prisoner of the same rank. Some of these prisoners of war were merchants, who would gain familiarity with the port and return later to trade once they had been ransomed.

The prolonged holding of large numbers of enemy prisoners in Havana reached its peak during the War of Jenkins' Ear. In the spring of 1743, when Philadelphia-based privateers managed to ransom and bring back 80 British American prisoners from Havana, they claimed that 200 of their imprisoned countrymen remained behind. Other North American newspaper reports from 1741 and 1743 put the number of British prisoners in Havana at around 250. There were so many British prisoners that they altered the dynamics of

74. Jacobo de la Pezuela estimated that Havana gained six hundred enslaved Africans via privateering, but that estimate would not include contraband and seems low; see de la Pezuela, *Historia de la Isla de Cuba*, I, 392. On Cuba-based privateers' slave raiding, see Venegas Delgado, *Trinidad de Cuba*, 25; Edward Trelawny to the Duke of Newcastle, Feb. 17, 1740, Despatches, Jamaica to England, 1739–1755, duplicate, fol. 75, JNA; "The Humble Address of the Governor, Council, and Assembly of the Island of Jamaica, to This King's Most Excellent Majesty," May 8, 1747, Jamaican Council Journals, 1738–1747, JNA. On complaints from Jamaican planters, see Trelawny to the Right Honourable Lords of Trade and Plantations, Jan. 19, 1748, CO 137.25, TNA. This practice was ongoing in the 1760s; see "Cartas escritas al teniente Governador de P. Príncipe," 1766–1769, AGI, Cuba, 1077.

the city. When a RHC ship that had been captured by British corsairs near Cádiz was brought into Havana after it had been ransomed, British prisoners reportedly celebrated in the streets.[75]

Between 1747 and 1749, according to records in Seville, 920 new prisoners were taken into Havana from ships that hailed from all over North America and the West Indies. Most of their ships had been captured by Cuba-based privateers, though some of these prisoners had been seized from ships suspected of contraband. Of the 920 prisoners, nearly half came off ships from British West Indian ports south of Havana that had likely been making their way north back to Europe, and 30 percent had been removed from ships that identified themselves to Spanish authorities as having been staged in seaports to the north, in New Providence (Bahamas), New York, Philadelphia, and the Carolinas. Havana's wealth, its ability to feed a larger population, and the amount of work its fortifications required meant that it had the capacity to absorb all these prisoners of war and had uses for their labor. Many of the prisoners were forced to perform physical labor for low wages or no pay at all under harsh conditions, and their incidence of disease was quite high, yet their experience in Havana might also have been better than it would have been elsewhere.[76]

Capturing, ransoming, and exchanging these prisoners, during the war and for a short period afterward, increased the traffic of foreign ships into ports and facilitated further trade. Reliable and recent information about prices in Havana, brought back with returned prisoners of war, gave merchants in Boston, Bridgetown, and Charleston added incentive to risk the journey. The presence of these prisoners in port afforded an excuse for ships to enter in order to exchange or ransom prisoners, a customary privilege permitted during wartime and shortly thereafter, as long as those ships flew a flag of truce. Because so many prizes were hauled into Havana for sale, its population of prisoners

75. Marrero, *Cuba*, VI, 76; Portell Vilá, *Historia de Cuba*, I, 40. On the Philadelphia privateers' report, see *Boston Gazette*, Apr. 19, 1743, [3]. For the report of 250 prisoners, see John Murray, Benjamin Paine, and Thomas Poole, "Charles-Town, South-Carolina, September 26," *Pennsylvania Gazette* (Philadelphia), Oct. 22, 1741, [2]; *Boston Post-Boy*, Feb. 28, 1743, [3]. For the British prisoners' celebrating in the streets, see "Consultas, decretos, y ordenes originales de la Habana y Cuba," 1741–1750, AGI, SD, 1130B.

76. AGI, Contaduría, 1164, in Marrero, *Cuba*, VI, 111, 190. After a joint French and Spanish privateering raid on Charleston, South Carolina, during the War of the Spanish Succession, the town could not afford to feed the 320 prisoners (white, black, Indian, "French," and "Spanish") they had captured and instead sent many of them to Virginia; they were then to continue on the king's fleet to England, where their fate would be decided. Facing similar challenges, Virginia debated whether to allow those to settle who would take an oath of loyalty but ended up landing many of them on barren stretches of coastline near Saint Augustine, Florida, and on the north coast of Hispaniola. See Harry S. Mustard, "Defense of Charles Town against the French and Spaniards in 1706," 1963, 56–67, South Carolina Historical Society, Charleston.

FIGURE 11 *Watson and the Shark*. By John Singleton Copley. 1778. Oil on canvas. This view is from inside Havana's harbor, looking out toward the opening of the bay. Visible in the background are the royal shipyard and the walled city (to the left) and the Morro (to the right). The incident depicted occurred in 1749, when the unlucky swimmer Brook Watson was serving as a cabin boy on a Boston merchant ship visiting Havana. After losing his leg to this shark, Watson went on later in life to become a prominent and successful businessman in Britain, a member of Parliament, a director of the Bank of England, a founder of Lloyd's of London, and lord mayor of London. According to estimates, black sailors like the one dramatically depicted here made up 20 percent of the Anglo-American merchant marine in the eighteenth century. Courtesy, National Gallery of Art, Washington, D.C. / Bridgeman Images

was especially high, and, hence, so was the traffic of flag-of-truce ships from Britain and British North America. Flag-of-truce ships were often nothing but a ruse for contraband trade. The visit of one such flag-of-truce ship from Boston in 1749, at the end of the War of Jenkins' Ear, might well have led to an incident depicted in a famous painting of Havana's harbor, John Singleton Copley's *Watson and the Shark* (1778), which shows a group of British American sailors on a rowboat inside Havana's harbor (see Figure 11 [Plate 3]).[77]

77. Tellingly, given how often the ships engaging in prisoner exchange were British, these ships were called *facatruzes* in Spanish, a Hispanicization of the English phrase "flag of truce." Similarly, the phrase used for prisoner exchange was also corrupted from the English: both the port pidgin *cange de prisioneros* and the invented Spanish verb *cangear*, for "exchange" or "change." Ships' mas-

Throughout the war, intelligence from British prisoners who had been held in Havana arrived in North American and British West Indian ports, quite likely carried by the flag-of-truce ships. The information they brought back included updates on the numbers of troops stationed in Havana. It was in this way that New York, Philadelphia, and Charleston first received news of the successes and failures of the 1741 expedition against Guantánamo attempted by Admiral Edward Vernon and General Thomas Wentworth. This exchange worked both ways, however, as complaints were regularly made that arms, ammunition, provisions, and intelligence were being conveyed to the Spanish via British flag-of-truce ships.[78]

Reports from the enemy's ports not only revealed useful information for those plotting attacks but also created permanent links between colonies in the Atlantic world. The knowledge and experience that prisoners of war gained while held in a foreign port often built lasting connections that carried over into peacetime. Several merchants who operated across imperial lines after the war had served some time as a prisoner in an enemy port and then later returned to carry on active trading relationships in that city. Holding populations of foreign prisoners also promoted cross-cultural contact and the flow of information between the territories of rival sovereigns. During their tenure in an enemy port, prisoners had the opportunity to learn the local language, customs, and topography; to make contacts with merchants, servicemen, or seamen; or to spy on behalf of their own government. On their return home, many published accounts of these foreign places in newspapers and books. Indeed, the first slave narrative published in British North America, a remarkable captivity memoir written by an enslaved sailor from Massachusetts named Briton Hammon, recounts nine years that the author spent in Havana after being brought there by a Spanish sailor and ransomed by the governor. It can be no accident that the account was not published in Boston until 1760, when British American sailors were again finding themselves captured at sea and talk began to return to the possibility of targeting Havana. Havana's very integration with British America had stoked Britain's desire to take the island

---

ters sometimes purchased supposed prisoners of war to have a pretense to sail into enemy harbors and exchange them. Admiral Knowles decried this practice among merchants "from Rhode Island and Providence" in Saint Domingue, but it was more widespread than that. See Account of Admiral Knowles, *Cornwall*, in Port Royal Harbour, Jamaica, Apr. 6, 1748, Despatches, Jamaica to England, 1739–1755, fol. 361, JNA.

78. For reports on the number of troops, companies, and battalions stationed at Havana, see *Boston Post-Boy*, Feb. 28, 1743, [3]; *Boston Weekly News-Letter*, Mar. 25, 1743, [1]. For intelligence about preparations in Havana to attack Georgia, see CO 5.1054, TNA. For a report from prisoners in Havana on the progress of the Guantánamo campaign, see, for example, *Pennsylvania Gazette*, Oct. 22, 1741, [2].

and—through the flow of British prisoners in and out of the port—improved the intelligence that informed its plans to do so and the popular enthusiasm that made recruiting possible.[79]

Conclusion

In the first half of the eighteenth century, Havana had outgrown its imperial functions and outpaced the commercial regulations of the Spanish empire. Although Spain wished to keep Havana separate from its British neighbors, local forces increasingly integrated the city into the regional system. The large and diverse population of Havana residents had their own ideas about how best to insert themselves into broader economies. Although the island continued to profit from infusions of silver from New Spain and the metropole, it increasingly found itself at cross purposes with royal authorities, especially in the realms of commerce and the slave trade; its greatest point of collaboration with Madrid and Cádiz was in the waging of war. In broad terms, the chief grievances of the city council and Havana's elite were economic rather than political, for the reigning political climate in practice afforded them a considerable degree of local autonomy, which they readily exploited. This situation also gave Spanish subjects in Cuba incentives to broker relationships with the subjects of other crowns and to invent their own solutions to trade, migration, and development rather than follow metropolitan dictates.

A crucial nexus of that connection between Cuba and British territories was the trade in enslaved Africans, which presented a conundrum for Spain. People of African descent, both enslaved and free, filled a variety of niches in Cuba's economy and military and were essential to the island's development and defense. Free people of color had proven their reliability as soldiers and privateers serving the Spanish king. Consequently, they were poised to play a critical role in the defense of Havana against British attack in 1762. Patterns of inter-imperial trade that had evolved over the preceding decades also meant that Havana's slave-trading elites were well equipped to exploit the commercial opportunities presented by the city's transfer to British sovereignty during its eleven-month occupation. Yet, before the siege, Spain bristled at the increasing bonds the RHC and Havana's commercial classes and large landowners were building with their neighbors in Jamaica and elsewhere in British America in order to expand their trade in goods and humans.

79. *A Narrative of the Uncommon Sufferings, and Surprizing Deliverance of Briton Hammon, a Negro Man* ... (Boston, 1760). For a general study of the conditions for prisoner laborers in Spanish American ports, see Ruth Pike, "Penal Servitude in the Spanish Empire: Presidio Labor in the Eighteenth Century," *HAHR*, LVIII (1978), 21–40.

By the time Prado rowed out to the Morro to see the British ships on the horizon, Havana had become both deeply enmeshed in a developing regional economy and increasingly confident that it would not be attacked. Havana and its extensive hinterland in western Cuba were thriving at the crossroads of exchange with a broad network of ports: Veracruz, Caracas, Kingston, Bridgetown, New Providence, Guarico (Saint Domingue), Curaçao, Charleston, Philadelphia, New York, London, Amsterdam. As a possession of the Spanish crown, the city had also been at war with the sovereigns of many of those places. Havana's merchants and local leaders had learned that war was good for business, fostering regional autonomy and exchange with neighbors. Its commercial wealth and military strength on the border of the British and Spanish empires made it vulnerable, though it hardly felt that way.

Understanding the extent to which commercial activity bound Cuba to British colonies before the British expedition of 1762 reframes our understanding of the events surrounding that expedition. Even more, it calls into question histories that have normally analyzed colonial economies separately, in their respective imperial boxes. Cuba played a larger role than previously imagined in the eighteenth-century Atlantic economic system. As we have seen, the connections between Cuba and Britain and British America were broad and deep, and the relationships they established took many different forms, involving sectors of society inside and outside the capital city.

From the perspective of the island of Cuba, the relentless war making of the eighteenth century bound American colonies more tightly together in relationships formed around military engagement, piracy and privateering, prisoner exchange, contraband, diplomacy, slave trading, and migration. War had strengthened the circuits of regional trade and human trafficking, even though many of the conflicts between Britain and Spain had arisen over British commercial encroachment, via the slave trade, into Spanish-governed territories such as Cuba. Well before the British expedition arrived offshore in June 1762, interconnections between Cuba and its British and British American neighbors had both caused wars between Britain and Spain and been intensified by these wars. Now, with the arrival of Lord Albemarle's massive fleet off the shore of Havana, something was about to change.

All of Havana's social sectors were involved in the siege and occupation of Havana, but, when the British attacked, Havana's military sector would come to the fore, and the commercial sectors would fade more to the background. The opposite would occur during the occupation. In both cases, though, the framework that structured Havana residents' reactions was built over earlier decades of war making, slave trading, and exchange with Cuba's British neighbors.

PART II Events

3

· · ·

A City under Siege

The Battle for Havana

By mid-July 1762, just over a month into the siege of Havana, the massive British expedition launched against the city was faltering. Despite excellent intelligence and carefully honed plans, the fate of the campaign was beginning to look as inescapable as that of the failed operations at Cartagena and Guantánamo during the War of Jenkins' Ear. Havana's resistance had been much fiercer than anticipated, and capturing the Morro fortress had proved far more difficult than expected. Rains had accompanied the arrival of the British fleet, disease-carrying mosquitoes had hatched, and Britain's forces were falling ill in staggering numbers to yellow fever. Nearly five thousand soldiers were reported sick either in their encampment or on the hospital ships, and more than one thousand British attackers had died from wounds and disease. After failing to make their scheduled rendezvous with the expedition in the Windward Passage southeast of the island, between Cuba and Saint Domingue, four thousand expected North American provincial troops had still not arrived. Frustrated, the expedition's land commander, Lord Albemarle, wrote to his superior, Lord Egremont, in London: "If the North Americans do not arrive, and very soon, I shall be at a loss at how to proceed." As many of his generals and the suffering soldiers concurred, it looked as though they would have to abandon the campaign in a matter of days.[1]

Had the British withdrawn at this point and given up their attempt to take

---

1. Albemarle to Egremont, July 17, 1762, CO 117.1, fols. 96–98, TNA; *An Authentic Journal of the Siege of the Havana by an Officer* . . . (London, 1762), July 4, 1762, 22: "The Morro was now found to be *tuffer* work, and the *Spaniards more resolute than was at first imagined.*" For troop returns in mid-July, see CO 117.1, fol. 94, TNA; HA 67/969/58, Suffolk Record Office; Erica Charters, "The Caring Fiscal-Military State during the Seven Years War, 1756–1763," *Historical Journal,* LII (2009), 933. One source claims five thousand soldiers and three thousand sailors were sick by the end of July; see *An Authentic Journal of the Siege of Havana by an Officer,* July 23, 24, 26, 27, 1762, 32. On the state of the operation, see Fred Anderson, *Crucible of War: The Seven Years' War and the Fate of Empire in British North America, 1754–1766* (New York, 2000), 500; James Miller, "Memoirs of an Invalid," Transcripts of the Amherst Papers, Packet 54, fol. 43, Library and Archives of Canada.

Havana, it would not have been for lack of trying. After more than a month
under heavy fire, British forces had managed to move within striking distance
of the Morro fortress, considered by those who had designed the plan of attack
the key to seizing the city. For almost two weeks, their approach had made the
fort a living hell for its defenders, with tens, then hundreds of bombs raining
down in a single day. One Spanish naval officer inside remarked that a shelling so intense had "scarcely been seen in history." So many had died inside
the Morro it was impossible to keep count, and the survivors were reduced
to throwing the rotting bodies into the sea below. Only the steady arrival of
more men, ferried to the Morro on ships from the walled city, had allowed
the Spanish to hold the fort for so long. When at last British guns silenced the
Morro's cannons and the soldiers drew close, to their dismay they discovered
a large ditch had been dug just in front of the fortress, which would make it
impossible for troops to climb the ramparts to enter the fort. Seeing no other
option, Major General William Keppel, Albemarle's brother and divisional
commander, made the decision to begin digging tunnels into the limestone
promontory under the Morro and plant a mine that would blow up the fortress from below.[2]

Governor Juan de Prado would later deem the explosion of a mine under
the Morro, deployed without warning, a shocking violation of the rules of
war. Unprecedented in Caribbean siege warfare, Keppel's decision was an
act of desperation to salvage the siege and avoid the repetition of the failure
at Cartagena in 1741. During the critical moment at Cartagena, when British
troops stormed the port's twenty-four-gun Castillo San Felipe de Barajas, a
series of errors had turned a moment of expected triumph into a disaster, forcing them to retreat without capturing the castle and to give up the siege. After
twenty years of recriminations for that botched operation at Cartagena and
six weeks of grueling warfare in Havana, British commanders saw no way in
but the extraordinary action of blowing up the Morro fortress from below.[3]

Buoyed by the much-delayed arrival of the North American troops two
days before, at two o'clock on July 30, after forty-four days of hard fight-

2. Pedro Manuel de Olañeta, "Diario del sitio y rendición de la plaza de la Habana al Ingles,"
July 1, 1762, Miscellaneous Manuscripts, MS 352, XV, box 83, folder 1662, Sterling Memorial Library,
Yale University; Sonia Keppel, *Three Brothers at Havana, 1762* (Wiltshire, U.K., 1981), 67.

3. Juan de Prado to Juan Ignacio Madariaga July 30, 1762, and Prado to Don Carlos Caro, July
30, 1762, AGI, Ultramar, 169, no. 28; Charles E. Nowell, "The Defense of Cartagena," *HAHR*, XLII
(1962), 498; José Manuel Rodríguez, *El almirante Blas de Lezo: El vasco que salvó al imperio español*
(Madrid, 2008), 226; Blas de Lezo y Olavarrieta, "Diario de lo acontecido en Cartagena de Indias
desde el día 15 de marzo de 1741 hasta el 20 de mayo del mismo año," AHN, Estado, 2335; J. R.
McNeill, *Mosquito Empires: Ecology and War in the Greater Caribbean, 1620–1914* (New York, 2010),
160–161, 167.

FIGURE 12 *The Capture of Havana, 1762: Storming of Morro Castle, 30 July*. By Dominic Serres. 1770–1777. Oil on canvas. © National Maritime Museum, Greenwich, London

ing, British forces exploded the mine. With a thunderous boom, the fabled sixteenth-century fort's southeastern bastion blew up, sending into the air a cloud of smoke and debris and several unfortunate Spanish sentinels. Once the dust settled, it was apparent that a breach had been opened, exposing the 780 men inside defending the fort. Two thousand British soldiers began moving up the hill, with their advance party charging over the rubbish and rubble and storming into the Morro, swords in hand. Faced with this onslaught, many of the terrified and disoriented men inside the fort sought to flee, climbing down rope ladders and crowding into boats or jumping into the water to swim back across the bay to the protection of Havana's city walls (see Figures 12 and 13 [Plate 8]).[4]

About what happened next accounts do not concur. From outside the

4. Olañeta, "Diario del sitio," July 30, 1762, Miscellaneous Manuscripts, MS 352, XV, box 83, folder 1662, Sterling Memorial Library; "Diario de Juan de Prado," in Amalia A. Rodríguez, ed., *Cinco diarios del sitio de la Habana* (Havana, 1963), 108–111; David Syrett, ed. *The Siege and Capture of Havana, 1762* (London, 1970), 270–274.

FIGURE 13 "The Breach of the Moro Castle, July 30, 1762." Engraving by Pierre Canot and Thomas Mason, based on a sketch by naval lieutenant Philip Orsbridge and a painting by Dominic Serres. Orsbridge served onboard the *Orford*. Courtesy, Anne S.K. Brown Military History Collection, Brown University Library

Morro, by the River Almendares to the west of the city, a volunteer soldier from Connecticut described a struggle for the fort. After hearing "a very grand explosion in oure faver," he saw the Spanish flag come down from the Morro's flagpole and the British flag hoisted up. Then the British flag came down, and the Spanish flag went back up. A minute or two later, he saw the Spanish flag come back down. During this struggle, the Spanish commander, naval officer Don Luis Vicente de Velasco, took a bullet in the lung that would prove fatal. Many of the other officers and soldiers were killed in the fighting or as they sought to escape. Several hundred troops surrendered and were taken prisoner. Others hid in the lighthouse, beneath the flagpole. When three of the British lieutenants who had led the charge paused to congratulate one another, the hidden men shot two of them dead. As a reprisal, the surviving officer, Lieutenant Charles Forbes, of the First or Royal Regiment of Foot, attacked the lighthouse and, rather than take any prisoners, had all the men they found there put "to the sword." After six weeks of bitter struggle, the Morro was now in British hands, virtually ensuring Havana's capture.[5]

No moment better encapsulates the bitterness of the struggle for Havana or the contingency of British victory than the mining and storming of the Morro. The decision to explode the mine and to treat those inside with no mercy demonstrated how badly the British wanted to capture the island and how fiercely the siege had been contested. Despite all their preparations, British forces were surprised by the tremendous resistance they met from the defenders of Havana, not only Spanish soldiers and sailors and ordinary militia from the island but also a foe they understood less well: members of Cuba's population of African descent. The morning the mine went off, one British officer encamped before the Morro, who had also fought in the siege of Martinique, wrote to his father that the enemy "have so far made a very noble and brave defense." They consisted, he wrote, "of several regiments and negroes innumerable."[6]

In the days that followed the storming of the Morro, the killing in the lighthouse became the source of a rumor in Havana that British forces had "put to the knife" the blacks and *mulatos* they found inside the fort, instead of taking them prisoner, because they "wanted to take their lives in revenge" for their role in the defense. According to the minutes of the Havana *cabildo* (city council), many blacks in the city ran away shortly after the Morro was stormed, "terrified by the insults the enemy committed during the taking of the plaza."[7]

Perhaps not surprisingly, British sources do not mention any racial component to the deaths, nor do they agree about the number of Spanish fatali-

---

5. Roswell Park, "A Journal of the Expedition against Cuba," ed. Julian Park, *University of Buffalo Studies*, I, no. 4 (December 1920), 231–244 (quotation on 242); Richard Cannon, *Historical Record of the First, or Royal Regiment of Foot* . . . (London, 1847), 147; *An Historical Account of His Majesty's First, or the Royal Regiment of Foot,* comp. Joseph Wetherall (London, 1832), 105.

6. Captain Nicholas Delacherois, 9th Foot, to his brother Samuel Delacherois, July 30, 1762, Acc. No. 7805-63, May 1757–July 1774, National Army Museum, London.

7. This interpretation of events was reported in both a letter of Juan Miguel Palomino to a correspondent at court and the Havana cabildo minutes. There are three extant copies of Palomino's letter ("put to the knife" / "pasaron al cuchillo"): "Carta de Don Juan Miguel Palomino a Don Nicolas de Ribera, vecino de Madrid, fecha en La Havana a 28 de agosto de 1762 sobre la toma de aquella plaza por los ingleses," C.M. Pérez, BNJM; "Copia de una carta escrita en la Habana a un correspondiente de la corte," Additional Manuscripts 13976, fol. 298–299, BL; Juan Miguel Palomino, "Noticias de La Habana que refieren como ganaron los Ingleses el año de 1762," MS 10818/33, BNE. For the cabildo minutes reporting the rumor and subsequent flight ("terrified" and "wanted"), see "Expediente tocante a la aprovación que la ciudad de la Habana solicita de las providencias que dio para la captura de los negros que se huyeron de ella por miedo de que los ingleses les quitasen la vida," 1763, AGI, SD, 1457, no. 6; Emilio Roig de Leuchsenring, ed., *La dominación inglesa en la Habana: Libro de Cabildos, 1762–1763,* 2d ed. (Havana, 1962), 114, 119. Slaveholding members of the cabildo had reason to pin blacks' flight on British atrocities, but they were not the only source for accounts of blacks being murdered at the Morro.

ties. Several soldiers and an officer recorded in their journals that 400 or more men inside the Morro "were slaughtered on the spot," whereas Major General William Keppel's official return cites only 130 men killed outright and 213 drowned while trying to escape or shot and killed in boats, for a total of 343 dead, 37 wounded, and 326 taken prisoner. It is strongly probable that blacks were among those killed in the lighthouse, and the shooter who angered the British lieutenant could potentially have been a member of Havana's *pardo* militia, although there were Spanish soldiers and sailors present as well. What Carl von Clausewitz famously referred to as the "fog" of war means that we can probably never know what truly happened in the Morro that afternoon. What made this rumor credible, however, is the nature of the battle that had taken place over the preceding forty-four days.[8]

Throughout the siege, people of African descent stood on the front lines of the battle. Although they played a variety of roles fighting alongside and supporting Spanish soldiers and sailors and Cuba's white militias, they sustained a disproportionate number of the fatalities. British combatants commented on the stubbornness of the Spanish defense of the Morro and the preponderance of men of African descent defending it and launching counterattacks. They had reasons to unleash violence against the remaining men they found there. In a letter to a correspondent in Madrid, a Havana lawyer named Juan de Palomino interpreted the murder of black troops at the Morro as an act of revenge for the many brave and "barbarous" assaults (a term frequently used by whites to describe the military actions of nonwhite fighters) they had launched against British soldiers during the six weeks of fighting.[9]

8. For accounts of 400 or more Spanish troops killed in the Morro, see John Sinclair, Commonplace Book, 1762–1801, fol. 9, Special Collections, Perkins Library, Duke University, Durham, N.C.; Park, "Journal of the Expedition against Cuba," ed. Park, *University of Buffalo Studies,* I, no. 4 (December 1920), 231–244; Keppel to George Pocock, July 30, 1762, in Syrett, ed., *Siege and Capture of Havana,* 273; and "Mackellar's Journal," July 22, 1732, ibid., 259. For Keppel's official return, which listed 2 "negro officers" and 94 "negroes" inside the Morro when it was stormed, see State of the Garrison of El Morro When Taken by Storm, July 30, 1762, ibid., 272. David Dundas estimated that the Spanish lost 1,000 men total in the defense of the Morro; see Dundas's Memorandum on the Capture of Havana, ibid., 325. Spanish accounts of who was in the Morro when it was stormed do not concur. One Spanish captain stated that the Morro contained 250 soldiers, 300 marines and militiamen, 100 "*morenos* with lances and machetes, and 100 blacks [slaves] for labor" ("cien morenos con lanzas y machetes, y cien negros para las faenas"); see Olañeta, "Diario del sitio," July 30, 1762, Miscellaneous Manuscripts, MS 352, XV, box 83, folder 1662, Sterling Memorial Library. Juan de Prado gave a loose estimate of 300 regular Spanish troops, 50 marines, and an unspecified number of militiamen of all colors and blacks (slaves) dedicated to labor; see "Diario de Juan de Prado," in Rodríguez, ed., *Cinco diarios,* 109. For the "fog" of war, see Carl von Clausewitz, *On War,* ed. and trans. Michael Howard and Peter Paret (Princeton, N.J., 1989), 140.

9. *Archibald Robertson: His Diaries and Sketches in America, 1762–1780,* ed. Harry Miller Lydenberg (1930; rpt. New York, 1971), 55–56; "Carta de Don Juan Miguel Palomino," C.M. Pérez, BNJM:

Blacks have been virtually erased from most histories of the invasion, and certainly from its popular memory. However, they played a key part in enabling Havana to hold off the British invaders for so many weeks—long enough for yellow fever to spread and take a devastating toll and for the siege almost to fail. The critical role of people of African descent in the battle over Havana was an outgrowth of the part they played in the city's everyday life, heightened by the extraordinary developments of the siege. Over the prior decades of Anglo-Spanish warfare, Spain's subjects in Cuba of African origins had made themselves essential to the state's ability to wage war, especially as soldiers in its militias. Now their actions shaped this crucial battle fought at least in part over the circuits of the slave trade that brought Africans to the island, a battle that was the result of more than a hundred years of plotting against Havana.

The siege of Havana might have been the largest mobilization of enslaved Africans in any American battle before the Haitian Revolution. Not only the Spanish but also the British forces relied on them. Albemarle brought, in total, more than twenty-four hundred enslaved Africans with him as well as approximately six hundred free black soldiers. At least three thousand enslaved Africans came into Havana from elsewhere in Cuba to join the defense efforts of the population already there. All war—but especially early modern siege warfare—requires a tremendous amount of manual labor, and these campaigns reflected their Caribbean context in that they relied on the labor of Africans and African-descended peoples. This mutual dependence on black soldiers and laborers instilled a sense of vulnerability in whites on both sides, and black loyalty became a shared object of concern for white commanders during the campaign. Partly, their sense of vulnerability derived from the contours of the slave trade in eighteenth-century Cuba, which had knit the two societies together through networks of migration and trade and compromised the security of both Cuba and Jamaica against the enemy's machinations. The other source of whites' sense of vulnerability during the siege was inherent in the institution of racial slavery. As Olaudah Equiano wrote, "When you make men slaves, you . . . compel them to live with you in a state of war." Both the British and the Spanish forces depended on enslaved laborers, just as they depended on them during times of peace, but now the stakes were higher. The

---

"La razon que tuvo el ingles de matar a los negros y mulatos del Morro, consistió en las correrias que estos le hicieron bárbaramente, pues 20 se descolgaron del fuerte en una occasion, no más que con sus machetes, y a pesar de los fuziles se metieron en una trinchera, mataron a los que no huyeron, y huvieran clavado la artilleria varios honradissimamente, disminuyendo las fuerzas del enemigo a costas de sus vidas."

resolution of a global war and the possession of American territories hung in the balance.[10]

The reactions of people of African origins to the imperial conflict between Britain and Spain were as varied as their personal histories and positions in those colonial societies, but, because Africans moved between British and Spanish spaces during times of both war and peace, on some level their loyalty was always in question. Within the parameters of the battle between Britain and Spain, violent conflict — and the perceived threat of it — between people of African descent and people of European descent broke out on both sides. Besides those who volunteered or were forced to fight for one crown or the other, other people of African descent ran away on foot or by ship, deserted to the other side, pretended to be British, pretended to be Spanish, spied, robbed, raped, sacked and plundered, murdered whites, and continued to fight even after Havana's formal capitulation. Loyalty to one crown or the other could be heartfelt or a strategic alliance, depending on the person and the circumstances he or she faced. At several critical points during the invasion, white commanders exhibited profound anxiety about their ability to control the black soldiers or workers on whom they intimately relied. Just like the rest of Havana's population, people of color sought to exploit the possibilities, despite the extreme danger, of this geopolitical conflict on a grand scale. Ultimately, their actions would shape the outcome of a battle many years in the making and the culmination of a global war.

Spanish Defenses

After his initial surprise at the arrival of the British fleet offshore on June 6, Governor Juan de Prado was optimistic about the chances for Havana's defense. In written appeals to Spanish colonial officials in the region and French allies in Saint Domingue asking for aid that never came, he nonetheless predicted a Spanish victory. As he noted, the season of the year had already precipitated the onset of yellow fever among the British troops. The Spanish military strategy of "delay and hold" did not necessitate matching British troop numbers but called for just having enough men to buy time for a month or so until the disease could take its toll on the attackers.[11]

10. Olaudah Equiano, *The Interesting Narrative and Other Writings*, ed. Vincent Carretta (1995; rpt. New York, 2003), 111.

11. Prado wrote to officials in New Spain, New Granada, Santiago de Cuba, and Santo Domingo, in addition to those at Saint Domingue. See "Correspondencia del Governador de la Habana con el de Cuba antés de la invasión inglesa, previniendole lo conveniente a precaución, y después de ella, sobre que le socorriesse," in *Proceso formado de orden del Rey Nuestro Señor por la Junta de Generales que S.M. se ha dignado de nombrar a este fin sobre la conducta que tuvieron en la defense, capitulación,*

There were legitimate reasons for Prado's optimism. Despite the depletion of his own ranks by disease, as of May 1762 Prado had a force of approximately fifteen hundred Spanish regular troops, twenty-one hundred militiamen, and four thousand sailors at his immediate disposal within Havana city walls. Between those troops and Cuban militias hailing from towns in the immediate vicinity of Havana—Guanabacoa, Santa María del Rosario, Bejucal, Güines, and Batabanó—Prado had more than ten thousand troops to draw on. Disease was a factor for the Spanish forces as well as the British, but it was not an unfamiliar one. In Havana, smaller outbreaks of yellow fever happened annually, and major epidemics often accompanied war and the preparations for it. Since the accession of Charles III to the Spanish crown, the build-up of troops in Havana had precipitated a yellow fever outbreak among the new arrivals beginning in 1760 and reaching mass proportions during the siege. According to Prado, the *vómito negro,* or black vomit, affected soldiers, sailors, and even natives on the island, as it had in prior wars. Though disease hampered the defense and caused profound loss of life, it would imperil the attackers' many new arrivals to the region more than it would the defenders. Troop levels and battle plans were designed in expectation of this factor, and enough healthy soldiers and sailors remained in Havana, combined with the city's formidable complex of fortifications, to buttress Prado's confidence.[12]

Prado placed a Spanish naval captain with experience in the Mediterranean and at Gibraltar, Don Luis Vicente de Velasco, in command of the Morro. Velasco was a brave and determined leader of the Spanish sailors and soldiers under his command, but it was Cuba's multiracial militia forces that would come forward to provide the essential manpower for the defense, despite initial distrust and disparagement among Spanish military commanders new

---

pérdida, y rendición de la plaza de la Habana, y esquadra, que se hallaba en su Puerto el Mariscal de Campo Juan de Prado . . . , 2 vols. (Madrid, 1763–1765), I, 4, BNE.

12. On the yellow fever outbreak in Havana, see Prado to Julián de Arriaga, Nov. 12, 1761, AGI, SD, 1581; Levi Marrero, *Cuba: Economía y sociedad,* 15 vols. (Madrid, [1972]–1992), VI, 123–124; "Confesión del Mariscal de Campo Don Juan de Prado," in *Proceso formado de orden del Rey Nuestro Señor por la Junta de Generales,* I, 9, BNE. According to Prado's letter of November 1761, 750 people were sick in Havana, and 187 had died since the summer of 1761. Havana had also experienced major epidemics of yellow fever in 1709, 1715, 1730, 1731, 1733, 1738, and 1742; see McNeill, *Mosquito Empires,* 175. Historians disagree about the number of Spanish troops at Havana, but these are estimates based on the last review of troops, conducted ten days before the British attacked. Numbers above have been rounded. The Spanish regular troops consisted of 1,325 infantry, 52 artillerymen, and 172 *dragones* (cavalry). Though sailors numbered 4,458 initially, they had been reduced by sickness. The militia inside Havana's city walls included 2,142 men. See "Estado de la tropa de infantería, artilleros y dragones sacado de la revista que se les pasó en La Habana el 27 de mayo de 1762 y la que existía el 6 de junio en la plaza, firmado por Antonio Ramírez de Estenoz," AGI, SD, 1585. The most thorough analysis of troop numbers may be found in Gustavo Placer Cervera, *Inglaterra y la Habana, 1762* (Havana, 2007), 99–102.

to Cuba, including Velasco himself. The militia launched multiple counter-attacks against the British, protected Havana's flanks, kept open its supply lines, took hundreds of British prisoners, and thwarted their advances on the city's exposed, western side. As the soldiers proved their mettle and the battle wore on, Velasco himself asked that more local troops be sent to the Morro fortress in order to make sallies against the enemy because of their "great skill and resolve with the machete."[13]

The militias were particularly important because the defense of Havana would be conducted entirely on land, despite the fact that nearly one-third of the entire Spanish navy was in port at the time. Prado called together a *junta de guerra* of experienced commanders present in Havana to direct the city's defense, and one of their first decisions as a group tilted the battle toward a land fight. In an attempt to imitate the successful defense of Cartagena and to protect the Spanish squadron, Prado and the junta de guerra immediately ordered three Spanish warships sunk at the mouth of the harbor to make it impassable to British ships. They also had a strong boom constructed across the entrance to the bay. These maneuvers were designed to block or at least slow British entry into the port, although they would also render the Spanish fleet useless during the siege. The many sailors in port were switched to shore duty, and the onus for the defense shifted to the land forces, even though the junta had less tactical knowledge of battles on land than at sea.[14]

During the course of the siege, militia companies of whites, free blacks, and free mulatos came into Havana from virtually every locale on the island except Bayamo and Santiago de Cuba, where men were reserved for fear of another attack. They hailed from as far away as Trinidad, Puerto Príncipe, Villa Clara, Sancti Spíritus, and Cayo. Given the shortage of weapons in the capital, Prado was insistent that they bring as many of their own arms as possible. The com-

13. *Proceso formado de orden del Rey Nuestro Señor por la Junta de Generales*, I, BNE; César García del Pino, *Toma de la Habana por los ingleses y sus antecedentes* (Havana, 2002), 92. For an example of disparaging comments about the abilities of the militias, from early in the siege, see Prado to Caro, June 9, 1762, AGI, Ultramar, 169: "Los ánimos de las milicias y demas cuerpos de mulatos, y negros que la experiencia a acreditado de poquíssima utilidad." For an example of British troops expressing admiration of Velasco, see John Sinclair, Commonplace Book, 1762–1801, fol. 9, Perkins Library, Duke University.

14. The members of the junta included the commander of the Spanish squadron, the Marqués del Real Transporte; six naval captains; the former governor of Cartagena de Indias, Don Diego Tabares; and the former viceroy of Peru, the Conde de Superunda—the latter two were both in Havana by chance on their way back to Spain after their terms of service had ended. Lorenzo de Montalvo attended several of the juntas. Also caught in Havana during the British siege was the new governor designated for Manila, carrying plans to strengthen its defenses; see Nicholas Tracy, "The British Expedition to Manila," in Mark H. Danley and Patrick J. Speelman, eds., *The Seven Years' War: Global Views* (Leiden, 2012), 465. For the members of the junta de guerra and their decisions, see *Proceso formado de orden del Rey Nuestro Señor por la Junta de Generales*, I, BNE.

panies of men of color were less likely to have their own firearms, and some
carried machetes or lances instead.[15]

In total, several thousand free men of color came forward to serve in militias
as soldiers and artillerymen in Havana's defense. The commander of Spanish
ground forces reported that between twenty-seven hundred and three thousand militiamen, both white and free men of color, and four hundred to five
hundred militiamen categorized as black came into the city to aid in its defense, though this is likely a low estimate. A partial pay docket for those militia troops from Havana and its surroundings fighting under the command of
Don Luis Joseph de Aguiar, in charge of land forces on the western front of the
battle, suggests an even higher percentage of troops of color. Payment rolls reveal an increasing percentage of black versus white militia over the course of
the siege and nearly twice as many black as white militia receiving rations and
pay in the final days before the mine exploded at the Morro.[16]

Unlike British forces, which were newer at raising black troops and militias,
Spanish authorities in Cuba had been relying on black soldiers and the institution of the colonial militia for centuries. During the defense of the city, it is no
surprise that they played an essential role. Havana's black militias were able to
serve with such skill because they were an experienced fighting force. Among
the militia companies were many veterans of the War of Jenkins' Ear, including one company of free blacks from Trinidad under the command of Captain
Crispin, "of proven valor . . . with experience in privateering."[17]

There are many reasons that black militias' role in the defense of Havana
has so often been effaced. Traditionally, many readers and writers of this history have seen this battle as a clash between British and Spanish forces engaged in a European imperial war, rather than as a military engagement conducted with a multitude of diverse actors in a hybrid Caribbean space. In a
corrective to this view, Cuban national history championed the role of local

15. Prado to the Marqués de Sobremonte, June 23, 1762, AGI, Ultramar, 169.

16. Juan Ignacio de Madariaga, "Socorros introducidos en la plaza de La Habana durante el sitio,"
Apr. 20, 1763, AGI, Ultramar, 169; "Cuenta y relación de raciones de la tropa que se hallava sobre las
armas con motivo del sitio puesto a esta plaza por la nación británica en los puestos del Horcón,
San Luis Gonzaga, y sus avanzadas al mando del Coronel Don Luis Joseph de Aguiar," June, July,
and August 1762, AGI, SD, 1842. Don Luis Joseph de Aguiar was one of the only officials on the city
council *(regidores)* who took an active military role in the defense of Havana. See "Biografias . . . ," in
Rodríguez, ed., *Cinco diarios*, 231.

17. Madariaga to Prado, July 15, 1762, AGI, SD, 1581, no. 23 (quotation). On the traditions of free
black militias in Cuba, see Deschamps Chapeaux, *Los batallones de pardos y morenos libres* (Havana,
1976), 20–21, 26; and Jane G. Landers, *Atlantic Creoles in the Age of Revolutions* (Cambridge, Mass.,
2010), 138–174. For prior battle experiences of Havana's militia of pardos libres, see "Libro de servicios de los oficiales y sargentos del batallon de *pardos libres* de esta plaza, hasta fin de diciembre de
1763," AGI, SD, 2117.

militia and the humble white creole Pepe Antonio, the mayor of Guanabacoa
and militia commander who took many prisoners before his death at the hand
of British forces. Accounts of the siege, however, have paid less attention to
the role of the militias of people of African descent. Their occlusion derives
from a long practice of erasing the contributions of people of African descent
to the history of the Americas, compounded by the difficulties of recovering
the experience of common soldiers in the fog of war.[18]

In the chaos of the battle, Spanish military commanders stopped keeping careful tallies of white, pardo, and *moreno* militiamen, racial distinctions
that would be recorded in calmer circumstances. This seeming lack of records
makes the specific contribution of free men of color harder to trace in historical documents. Accounts and correspondence produced during the siege also
tend to have been written by either colonial officials or soldiers and sailors
hailing from Europe or North America. Thus, they carry typical biases, particularly in the beginning of their accounts, when the authors were newly arrived in the Caribbean. Outsiders to Havana had little understanding of the
multiple roles that people of African descent played in Spain's military machinery. For that reason, they could be poor observers and interpreters of local
realities in Cuba. By casting a wide net for sources such as journals and correspondence, in addition to the official reports of commanders, and then putting
British and Spanish accounts in conversation with each other, it becomes possible to see what participants in the battle knew well: local forces and especially people of African descent were a preponderance of those laboring and
fighting to protect Havana, especially during the bitter end of the siege.

18. Accounts of the siege written by historians of Britain and its empire tend to focus on the protagonism of British commanders and often the tremendous and senseless sacrifice of their men. See,
for example, Francis Russell Hart, *The Siege of Havana, 1762* (Boston, 1931); Anderson, *Crucible of
War*; and Daniel Baugh, *The Global Seven Years' War, 1754–1763: Britain and France in a Great Power
Contest* (Harlow, U.K., 2011). Accounts written by historians of Spain and Cuba have often focused
on the tragic heroism of Spanish naval captain and commander of the Morro, Don Luis Vicente de
Velasco, or the humble creole militia soldier from Guanabacoa, Pepe Antonio, a protonationalist
figure popularized in many Cuban accounts of the siege. In the former category, see, for example,
Guillermo Calleja Leal and Hugo O'Donnell y Duque de Estrada, *1762, La Habana inglesa: La toma
de La Habana por los ingleses* (Madrid, 1999). In the latter category, see Juan Florencio Garcia, *Pepe
Antonio: Biografía del héroe popular cubano* (Havana, 1962). Historians of Cuba César García del Pino
and Pablo J. Hernández González have paid the most attention to the role of local militias and black
soldiers in the defense of Havana of any scholars of the siege thus far; see García del Pino, *Toma de la
Habana*; and González, *La otra guerra del inglés: Cabildos, milicianos, y casacas rojas en la Cuba de 1762*
(San Juan, P.R., 2011). Gustavo Placer Cervera includes black soldiers in his narrative of the siege but
somewhat less centrally; see Cervera, *Inglaterra y la Habana* and Placer Cervera, *Los defensores del
Morro* (Havana, 2003). J. R. McNeill's account, *Mosquito Empires*, focuses on yellow fever as the criti-
cal factor determining the outcome of the siege. On archives, history, and erasure, see, for example,
Michel-Rolph Trouillot, *Silencing the Past: Power and the Production of History* (Boston, 1995); and
Marisa J. Fuentes, *Dispossessed Lives: Enslaved Women, Violence, and the Archive* (Philadelphia, 2016).

One explanation historians have cited for the pivotal role played by local forces was that they were more likely to be resistant to yellow fever than their European counterparts. But lack of disease alone cannot account for the critical part they played. So many local militiamen and enslaved Africans came forward to fight that they outnumbered Spanish regular forces in the city's defense, and they distinguished themselves in battle even in comparison with the professional army and navy they fought alongside. Furthermore, British and Spanish commanders noted that no one escaped the effects of disease; individuals born in the Americas and people of African descent on both sides fell ill during the siege. At the onset of the fighting, in fact, the sick in Havana included the commander of the militia of pardos, Antonio de Flores, one of the most famous soldiers in Havana at the time and a veteran of privateering raids during the War of the Spanish Succession and the raid on Georgia during the War of Jenkins' Ear. Flores was so frustrated by sitting out the battle that he assisted the defense from the sidelines by helping to direct the construction of defensive batteries on the city walls.[19]

Though Havana's land forces were capable and willing, Prado was aware of the one great weakness in Havana's defenses—the hilltop behind the Morro known as La Cabaña, across the bay from the city proper, which he had neglected to fortify since he had assumed office. Not only had he failed to raise enough enslaved Africans to complete this project, but one of the two engineers assigned to the task had died of yellow fever soon after his arrival in Havana. In the initial moments after British ships arrived offshore, Prado hastily rushed together a party of blacks, sailors, and students from the Jesuit college to occupy and fortify the Cabaña. During the confusion of the first days of the siege, however, the junta de guerra panicked that the Cabaña was still indefensible and made the fateful decision to abandon it. In the middle of the

19. On the role of yellow fever in the Havana campaign and differential immunity, see McNeill, *Mosquito Empires*, 142, 157, 169–191. On the debate about acquired versus inherited immunity to yellow fever among people of African descent, see ibid., 44–46; Sheldon Watts, "Yellow Fever Immunities in West Africa and the Americas in the Age of Slavery and Beyond: A Reappraisal," 955–967, and Kenneth F. Kiple, "A Response to Sheldon Watts . . . ," 969–974, both in *Journal of Social History*, XXXIV (2001). Lieutenant-General David Dundas wrote that, though they were thought to be immune, the blacks on the expedition from the West Indies "partook of the sickness in a considerable degree." He also wrote that "there seemed to be no particular distinction in health between those that came direct from Europe and those that after serving long in America came last from Martinique." Members of the expedition likely also suffered from malaria and dysentery, among other diseases. See "Dundas's Memorandum on the Capture of Havana," in Syrett, ed., *Siege and Capture of Havana*, 324. On Antonio de Flores, see "Libro de servicios de los oficiales y sargentos del batallón de pardos libros de esta plaza, hasta fin de diciembre de 1763," AGI, SD, 2117 (Commandante Pedro Menedes is listed as "governando un batallón por enfermedad del comandante Antonio de Flores," 65); "Expediente de Don Antonio Flores," AGI, SD, 1455, no. 5; "Ordenes de Don Antonio Flores," July 25, 1762, AGI, SD, 2082.

night on June 9, under orders, the men spiked the cannons they had dragged up the hill, or pushed them into the harbor, and retreated, leaving only a small contingent of militiamen to defend the locale, which British forces overran and occupied a few days later, on June 13. By the end of the first week, those in charge of Havana's defense were left facing the grim consequences of this failed enterprise, along with their controversial decision to sink the Spanish warships; and yet the British siege had only just begun.[20]

The British Attack

Despite eight grinding years of global war and memories of great losses during the last one, the British war planners had managed to amass one of the largest forces assembled in the history of the Americas and speed them to Havana before Governor Prado received official word from Madrid of the outbreak of war. The forces that converged on Havana included approximately 16,000 soldiers, 10,000 sailors, and 2,400 enslaved Africans, for a total of 28,400 men, in addition to several hundred additional men and women supporting the expedition. The strategy of British war planners was to rush as many bodies as possible to Havana for the siege before the city had time to prepare and the hurricane season began in August. These tactics had evolved through Britain's prior conflicts with Spain, just as Spain had developed its own counterstrategies in answer to British attacks, defending its American territories with local garrisons, colonial militias, and elaborate fortifications. Earlier encounters with the Caribbean environment—and its biggest scourge for many newcomers, yellow fever—had also shown British commanders that success in battle was predicated on being able to withstand tremendous losses long enough for the will, water, or food supplies of the besieged to give out and force a surrender.[21]

20. "Defensa del Mariscal de Campo Don Juan de Prado," in *Proceso formado de orden del Rey Nuestro Señor por la Junta de Generales,* II, BNE; "Diario del Capitán Don Juan de Casta del sitio de la ciudad de Havana," 1762, Theodorus Bailey Meyers Collection, NYPL; "Dundas's Memorandum on the Capture of Havana," in Syrett, ed., *Siege and Capture of Havana,* 317; "Breve resumen de lo acaezido en el sitio de La Havana," Add. MSS 13974, BL; "Carta del Jesuita Thomas Butler," Dec. 12, 1763, C.M. Pérez, no. 26, fol. 15, BNJM; García del Pino, *Toma de La Habana,* 79–80.

21. Syrett, "Introduction," xix, xxxiv, "Abstract of the General Return of His Majesty's Forces under the Command of Lieutenant-General Lord Albemarle," May 23, 1762, 126, "A List of His Majesty's Ships and Vessels . . . ," n.d., 134–135, all in Syrett, ed., *Siege and Capture of Havana.* Remarkably accurate intelligence in Cuba informed them, via deserters and spies in Jamaica, of the number of soldiers and sailors amassed against them; see "Razón rubricada del Gobernador de Cuba de lo que se decía en Jamaica sobre las fuerzas destinadas contra La Havana," AGI, SD, 1585, no. 94; and Olañeta, "Diario del sitio," June 9, 1762, Miscellaneous Manuscripts, MS 352, XV, box 83, folder 1662, Sterling Memorial Library. The number of troops on the Cartagena expedition of 1741 was roughly equivalent to the forces assembled for the Havana campaign. McNeill cites 29 ships of the line, 186

Having seen the horrific impact of tropical disease during the last conflict with Spain, British commanders and their authorities in Westminster considered the ability to raise large numbers of not only North American troops but also black troops and auxiliaries, both enslaved and free, to be essential for success in this Havana campaign. Lord Albemarle's thinking and that of British officialdom was that men "seasoned" in the Americas would be less susceptible to tropical disease than recruits from Europe. Albemarle was so convinced of the necessity of enslaved laborers to the siege, he professed that he could not do without them. As in previous campaigns, enslaved Africans were to be used for the harder physical labor, such as moving artillery and building up provisional batteries, which was thought to weaken the immune system and make workers more vulnerable to disease. Seen as more expendable or, erroneously, as inherently immune to tropical disease, enslaved Africans would be used to protect the health of white sailors and soldiers.[22]

British commanders were less experienced raising enslaved blacks and free black troops than their Spanish counterparts, and the process did not go smoothly. Though orders had been sent to Jamaica to raise 2,000 enslaved Africans for the siege, planters resisted lending out their human property, especially after the losses sustained during the War of Jenkins' Ear. In order to assure compliance, a royal official had to confirm that they would receive as compensation both hiring-out pay and reimbursement of the full appraised value of the enslaved recruit should he be killed, taken by the enemy, lost, or injured and unable to work. Given that the massive slave insurrection known as the Coromantee War had just ended, Jamaica's slaveowners potentially tried to send on this venture the men they had the most difficulty controlling and were most willing to lose. In order to ensure they would not be dangerously militarized upon their return, members of the colonial assembly insisted that their enslaved Africans sent on the Havana expedition be used, not as "shot negroes" and soldiers, but rather as "pioneers," who did more support

---

vessels of all descriptions, 15,000 sailors, and about 29,000 men in all, including sailors (*Mosquito Empires*, 154).

22. Before an awareness of the role of mosquitoes in disease transmission, the popular thinking was that sweating and self-exertion made people more vulnerable, but there was a widespread understanding that those new to the tropics fell at a faster rate. See McNeill, *Mosquito Empires*, 69–72; Philip D. Curtin, "'The White Man's Grave': Image and Reality, 1780–1850," *Journal of British Studies*, I (1961), 94–110, esp. 99. From Albemarle's arrival in Barbados in April, he repeatedly emphasized the necessity to the expedition of sufficient numbers of slaves and free blacks, considering the matter "an article of the most serious nature, upon which (considering the violent heats) the health of the soldiery and even the success of the expedition may greatly depend" (Albemarle to Robert Monckton, Apr. 21, 1762, in Syrett, ed., *Siege and Capture of Havana*, 94). As he insisted, "I cannot do without them" (Albemarle to Pocock, Apr. 27, 1762, ibid., 100).

The people who waged war

work and would not be outfitted with firearms. Sir James Douglas, the man in charge of coordinating Jamaican conscripts, complained that slaveowners sent people that were "sick, lame, or insufficient for the public service," and some ran away during the march across the island to the transport ships waiting to board them in Port Royal. These delays meant that only 1,245 men sailed in the first group from Jamaica, although 600 enslaved workers were sent later, arriving in Cuba shortly before the mining of the Morro. In anticipation of Jamaican planters' recalcitrance, Albemarle had already purchased 100 enslaved Africans at Martinique, and he had dispatched an agent to Antigua and Saint Kitts to purchase or hire out 500 more.[23]

Five hundred members of the free black militia of Jamaica were also recruited to join the expedition, despite their avowed concern that they would not be ransomed if captured but would instead be enslaved by the enemy. Overtures to the Jamaican maroons proved fruitless — they were unwilling to sail to Cuba and join this expedition against the Spanish — but Albemarle still managed to assemble a vast and diverse force. In addition to these forces, Albemarle proceeded to Havana with the expectation that North American provincial troops, who were being recruited in New York, New Jersey, Rhode Island, Connecticut, and South Carolina, would join them shortly as well. By the calculations of those in Westminster and on the ground in the Caribbean, Albemarle had enough manpower to proceed to the assault on Havana and the promise of more arriving soon to make it a success.[24]

23. Jamaican Council Journals, August 1756–April 1762, Apr. 13, 15, 1762, JNA. Jamaican slave-owners also insisted that the hiring-out pay for the slaves who were killed or lost be calculated and rendered to them until the day of the slave's disappearance or death (CO 140.42, TNA). Initially, they also complained that they were being paid hiring wages that were two-thirds less than the proprietors of Antigua had been paid for their slaves who went on the Martinique expedition (William Henry Lyttelton to Lord Egremont, May 23, 1762, CO 137.61, fol. 116v, TNA). On Sir James Douglas's pessimistic view: "I have been on three different expeditions with negroes attending them, the last at Martinico confirmed me in the opinion of their being of very little utility, therefore would be for going on without them, the delay of staying for them will not answer for what service they can do" (Sir James Douglas to Admiral Pocock, May 5, 1762, ADM 1.237, fol. 34, TNA); Lyttelton to the Lords Commissioners of Trade and Plantations, June 15, 1762, CO 137.32, 154v, TNA; Douglas to Lyttelton, June 2, 3, 1762, William Henry Lyttelton Papers, William L. Clements Library, Ann Arbor, Mich. For the purchase of enslaved Africans for the expedition in Martinique, Antigua, and Saint Kitts, see Albemarle to Egremont, May 27, 1762, in Syrett, ed., *Siege and Capture of Havana*, 136–138. On the Jamaican Slave Rebellion of 1760–1761—also known as Tacky's War or the Coromantee War— see Vincent Brown, "Slave Revolt in Jamaica, 1760–1761: A Cartographic Narrative," http://revolt .axismaps.com.

24. "Copies and Extracts of Letters from Governor Lyttelton to Commodore Forrest, the Earl of Albemarle, Sir James Douglas, etc. concerning the Corps of Free Negroes and 2000 Slaves Raised in Jamaica for the Late Expedition against the Havannah," CO 137.61, fols. 147–158, TNA; Lyttelton to the Lords Commissioners of Trade and Plantations, May 12, 1762, CO 137.32, fols. 114–116, TNA. This was a sizable number of black militiamen given that Jamaica was under suspected threat of a siege from combined French and Spanish forces. According to one report, Jamaica's militia forces num-

Once the expedition arrived in Havana's waters, the British planned to exploit the key weakness in the city's fortifications at La Cabaña. Based on intelligence they had received, the expedition's engineer, Patrick MacKellar, and the land commanders Albemarle and William Keppel agreed that Havana had too many troops defending it to approach the city directly on its exposed western side, the tactic favored long ago by Major Smith. Even before the Spanish ships had been sunk to block access to the harbor, a frontal naval assault through the mouth of the bay had been considered too risky, given the number of warships in the harbor and the narrowness of its mouth. Instead, the British design of attack was to land troops both to the east and the west of Havana in order to surround the city and approach it by land. In a coordinated assault, they would attack the city simultaneously from both sides, although operations would be focused on the heights of the Cabaña and the Morro fortress. Gaining possession of both would mean the British could fire cannons directly down into the city and force its surrender.[25]

At six o'clock in the morning on June 9, protected by the covering fire of eleven warships and three bomb vessels positioned outside the harbor, nearly four thousand soldiers and engineers rowed to shore in flat-bottomed boats, struggling to keep their musket locks dry in a torrential downpour (see Figure 14). By noon the day after this landing to the east of Havana, the British had managed to neutralize forts at Cojímar and Bacuranao, despite the opposition of "600 men in arms" stationed there to defend them, described by one participant as "a considerable number of peasants and Negroes." Two days

[margin note: June 9]

---

bered 5,398, of which 830 were free blacks. The population of the island at the time was reported to be 15,000 whites exclusive of the regular troops, 4,000 free blacks and mulattos, and approximately 146,464 enslaved Africans (William Henry Lyttelton, "Report on the State of the Island of Jamaica Anno 1763 in Answer to Questions from the Lords Commissioners for Trade and Plantations," July 9, 1763, CO 137.33, fols. 59v, 60r, TNA). On the recruitment of enslaved Africans and black militia in Jamaica during both the War of Jenkins' Ear and the Seven Years' War, see Daniel E. Walker, "Colony versus Crown: Raising Black Troops for the British Siege on Havana, 1762," *Journal of Caribbean History*, XXXIII, nos. 1, 2 (1999), 74–83; and Maria Alessandra Bollettino, "Slavery, War, and Britain's Atlantic Empire: Black Soldiers, Sailors, and Rebels in the Seven Years' War" (Ph.D. diss., University of Texas at Austin, 2009), 95–139, esp. 122. According to Bollettino, only 139 black militiamen from Jamaica ended up serving.

Half of the North American contingent consisted of regulars of the 46th and 58th regiments and the New York independent companies and the other half were provincials raised from New York, New Jersey, Rhode Island, and Connecticut, according to quotas set by relative population, and three companies of regulars enlisted in South Carolina, who were later added. The slowness of their arrival had to do with the difficulty of gathering volunteers, wary of the tremendous loss of life on prior failed expeditions to the West Indies during the War of Jenkins' Ear, and several shipwrecks off the north coast of Cuba; see David Syrett, "American Provincials and the Havana Campaign of 1762," *New York History*, XLIX (1968), 375–390; Hart, *Siege of Havana*, 20, 30–31.

25. "Thoughts upon the Siege of the Havana by Lieutenant-Colonel Patrick Mackellar," in Syrett, ed., *Siege and Capture of Havana*, 151–157; Syrett, "Introduction," ibid., xxii.

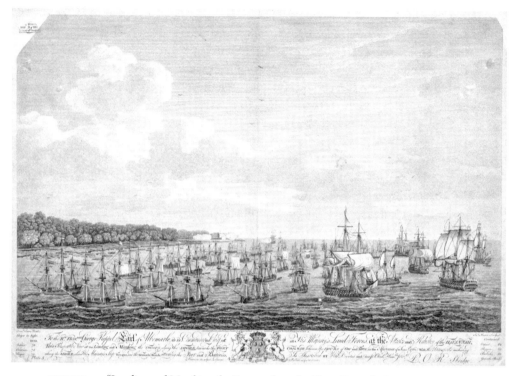

FIGURE 14 "Landing and Marching the Troops along the Shore Towards the Fort Cojimar . . . , June 7, 1762." Engraving based on a painting by Dominic Serres and an original sketch by Lieutenant Philip Orsbridge. Courtesy, Library of Congress, Washington, D.C.

later, Admiral George Pocock and Colonel William Howe led warships and marines in a mirroring action to the west of Havana, at the Chorrera River, where British soldiers would seek to divert Havana's forces and cut off the main supply of water to the city.[26]

Immediately, British soldiers on the western side advanced inland to the village of Guanabacoa (see Map 6). After fending off the defensive reprisals of six or seven hundred troops from the cavalry and local militia, they captured the town. Inside Havana's jurisdiction but essentially its own village, Guanabacoa had already been abandoned by its residents when British soldiers arrived. The British planned to use Guanabacoa as a base of operations as they moved their men through the woods toward the rocky limestone heights of the Cabaña and the Morro and as a source of provisions and, they hoped,

26. *Authentic Journal of the Siege of the Havana*, June 7, 1762, 10 ("600 men in arms"), 12–15; "Mackellar's Journal," June 7, 1762, in Syrett, ed., *Siege and Capture of Havana*, 168 ("a considerable number"); David Greentree, *A Far-flung Gamble: Havana, 1762* (Oxford, 2010), 36–38; Placer Cervera, *Inglaterra y la Habana*, 141–142; García del Pino, *Toma de la Habana*, 77.

water. They looted the church, stabled their horses in its chapels, and, as a Spanish captain alleged in his journal, gave the women traveling with the regiment the religious vestments to wear. In the meantime, from Guanabacoa, on June 11, Colonel Guy Carleton's troops were able to overrun the Cabaña, which they called "the Spanish Redoubt." Under heavy Spanish fire from the Morro and the warships anchored in the harbor, the British battery nevertheless began shelling the city.[27]

For the next seven weeks, the British expedition attacked Havana on three simultaneous fronts—the Cabaña, the Morro, and the city's flanks to the west and south (see Figure 15). Designed to break Spanish resolve, the shelling of the city from the Cabaña rained down hundreds of bombs on Havana in a single day. Artillery from the Cabaña also targeted the Morro fortress, which British forces were slowly approaching on its opposite, seaward side with the support of the naval fleet. As they moved toward the Morro, British troops cleared trees to open up a line of advance and constructed batteries meant to knock out its guns (see Figure 16 [Plate 6]). This work was incredibly demanding and slow, conducted under constant enemy fire and far from any water supply. Enslaved Africans built a wooden road up the hillside to cart the cannons into place. Trenches could not be dug to protect the cannons in the rocky earth before the Morro, so instead soldiers, sailors, and enslaved workers filled thousands of sandbags on the beach and carried them up the hill. While this work progressed, soldiers encamped at the Chorrera River advanced on Havana to its west, diverted the river that was its main water source into a marsh, and sought to disrupt its supply routes to the interior of the island.[28]

Even as he waged this intense military assault, Albemarle began conducting a "hearts and minds" campaign designed to impress upon Spain's creole subjects in Cuba the benefits of British rule and induce them to submit to it

27. "Dundas's Memorandum on the Capture of Havana," 316–317, "Mackellar's Journal," June 11, 1762, 186 ("the Spanish Redoubt"), Albemarle to Pocock, June 11, 1762, 182, all in Syrett, ed., *Siege and Capture of Havana; Authentic Journal of the Siege of the Havana*, June 11, 1762, 13; Olañeta, "Diario del sitio," June 8, 1762, Miscellaneous Manuscripts, MS 352, XV, box 83, folder 1662, Sterling Memorial Library; Greentree, *A Far-Flung Gamble*, 42.

28. On the shelling of the city from the Cabaña, see *Proceso formado de orden del Rey Nuestro Señor por la Junta de Generales*, I, BNE; García del Pino, *Toma de la Habana*, 86; "Camp before Havana," July 14, 1762, Richard and William Howe Collection, Clements Library. On the British plan of attack, see Celía María Parcero Torre, *La pérdida de la Habana y las reformas borbónicas en Cuba (1760–1773)* (Valladolid, Spain, 1998), 98–112; C. Martínez-Valverde, "Operaciones de ataque y defensa de la Habana en 1762," *Revista general de Marina*, CLXIV (May 1963), 706–727; Emilio Roig de Leuchsenring, ed., *Como vio Jacobo de la Pezuela la toma de la Habana por los ingleses . . .* (Havana, 1962); and Antonio Bachiller y Morales, *Cuba: Monografía histórica que comprende desde la pérdida de la Habana hasta la restauración española* (Havana, 1962).

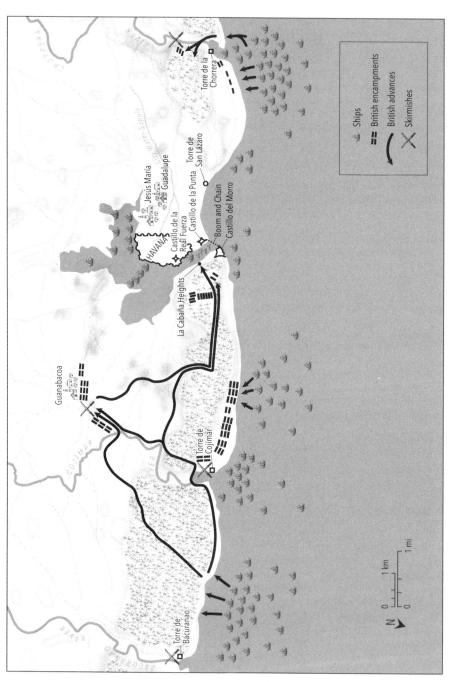

MAP 6 The British Invasion, June 6–June 15, 1762. Drawn by Molly Roy

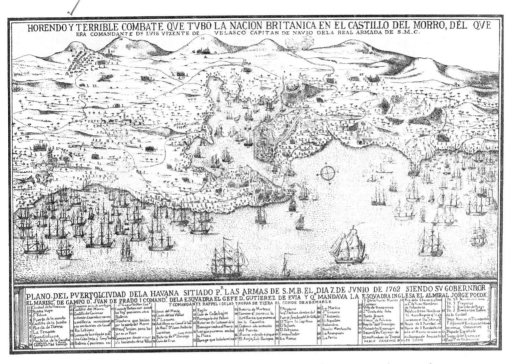

FIGURE 15 *The Horrendous and Terrible Battle That the British Nation Waged against the Morro Castle, of Which Don Luis Vicente de Velasco, Captain in the Royal Navy of his Catholic Majesty, was Commander.* By Lacalle y Gutiérrez. 1894. Escoto Cuban Collection, MS Span 52. Though produced on the eve of the U.S. invasion of Cuba in the nineteenth century, this map demonstrates quite clearly British tactics during the siege of 1762. Note the two-pronged British attack, which made landings at Cojímar (left) to the east of the city and Chorrera (right) to its west. Courtesy, Houghton Library, Harvard University

willingly. As much as military tactics had advanced, the idea that the Spanish would submit willingly to British liberators still persisted. As soon as the expedition had a foothold on land, Albemarle sent a series of letters, translated into menacingly stilted Spanish, to be distributed among the population. They assured the people that their property and freedom of religion would be protected under British rule, but they also promised destruction and pillage if the city's inhabitants continued to resist. Although these documents were modeled after manifestos planned for Peru and deployed in Guantánamo during the War of Jenkins' Ear, in many ways they resembled more closely the *requerimiento* that Spanish conquistadors used in the sixteenth century, a pro forma statement read aloud to Amerindians requiring their surrender. In Albemarle's letter, titled "Spanish Manifesto on Landing," he threatened that he possessed enough arms and troops "to destroy and ruin the entire country" but added

FIGURE 16 *The Capture of Havana, 1762: The English Battery before the Morro Castle.* By Dominic Serres. 1770. Oil on canvas. This painting gives a false sense of the British soldiers' leisure as they manned the cannons at the Grand Battery, opposite the Morro. The wall of fascines, or bundled sticks, protecting the cannons caught fire during the first week of July, destroying the battery after two weeks of grueling work to construct it. Wikimedia Commons

reassuringly that "the magnanimous and pious heart of the King my Master does not want to make innocents unhappy and does not regard them as his enemies (if they don't arm against his troops)." Reactions inside the city walls, however, revealed that Havana residents were indeed afraid of Albemarle's troops. The siege itself presented ample threats. The forces amassed offshore and the bombs being launched at the city triggered memories of pirate raids of yore and powerful impulses of self-preservation. This campaign was something entirely different from their most recent experiences of war.[29]

Panic in the City

As soon as it was confirmed that the enormous British fleet spotted offshore that first morning was indeed warships sent to launch an assault on Havana,

29. "Tres cartas originales del Conde de Albemarle persuadiendo a los naturales de la Isla de Cuba que prestasen la obediencia al Rey de la Gran Bretaña con fecha de 13 de junio," AGI, SD, 1585, no. 27; "Spanish Manifesto on Landing," CO 117.1, fols. 241, 245, TNA; Guillermo de Blanck, ed., *Papeles sobre la toma de la Habana por los ingleses en 1762* (Havana, 1948), 52–53.

panic broke out inside the city walls. The city had not been raided since the assault of the French buccaneer Jacques de Sores in 1555. Because Havana had seemed an unassailable target for two centuries, a powerful sense of complacency had settled in, and, in the meantime, its population had grown exponentially. Now, as the Spanish naval captain Juan de Casta wrote in his journal, "All the city was a great confusion." On June 8, Juan de Prado ordered all women, children, and old and infirm residents — all those unfit to bear arms — to evacuate the city within six hours. He also commanded Havana's large population of religious personnel, including the bishop, to remove themselves from the city and the reach of British bombs. Militiamen were sent to escort the cloistered nuns of Havana into safety in the interior, away from British attacks, on what was a long and difficult march along muddy roads.[30]

Besides those ordered to evacuate, many others chose to flee Havana and its surroundings. In fact, so many people fled the city that its population dropped from fifty thousand to only twenty thousand, and Prado issued a ban on subsequent departures. Among those electing to leave the city, especially once the bombardment started, were Havana's most prominent residents. The majority of those who owned ranches and plantations retreated to the countryside. Spanish naval captain Juan Ignacio de Madariaga, who was in charge of the defense outside city walls, claimed that some of these men came up with "pretexts to [go] home to their houses" in the country. Even those on the cabildo made themselves scarce as well, with only a few notable exceptions. Prado noted that, of the cabildo members, none "died, nor was hurt because they wanted nothing to do with picking up a rifle."[31]

Havana's elite residents packed their furnishings, mattresses, and pots and pans into carriages and coaches and onto mules and mule carts or had them carried out of the city by enslaved Africans. They also took with them a tremendous quantity of silver coinage — as much as 3.5 million pesos, according to testimony after the occupation. For comparison, the *situado* from Spain to all of its islands in the Caribbean was generally less than 3 million pesos

30. "Diario del Capitán Don Juan de Casta," 1762, Theodorus Bailey Meyers Collection, NYPL; "Carta del Jesuíta Thomas Butler," Dec. 12, 1763, C.M. Pérez, no. 26, BNJM; "Carta que en 12 de diciembre de 1763 escribió un padre jesuíta de La Habana al prefecto Javier Bonilla de Sevilla . . . ," *Memorias de la Sociedad Patriótica de la Habana,* VIII (Havana, 1839), 298–323, esp. 301–302.

31. Olañeta, "Diario del sitio," June 10, 1762, Miscellaneous Manuscripts, MS 352, XV, box 83, folder 1662, Sterling Memorial Library; Prado to Madariaga, July 10, 1762, AGI, Ultramar, 169 ("pretexts"); "Confesión del Mariscal de Campo Don Juan de Prado," in *Proceso formado de orden del Rey Nuestro Señor por la Junta de Generales,* I, 76, BNE ("died"). On the population drop, see "Cartas originales de Don Juan Ignacio Madariaga a Don Juan de Prado," June 16, 1762, ibid., 27; Placer Cervera, *Inglaterra y la Habana,* 173. Except for Don Luis Joseph de Aguiar and Don Laureano Chacón, who were made colonels of militia troops and participated actively in the defense outside the city, none of the city council members were to be found in the immediate vicinity of the city.

annually, and the entire output of Mexico's silver mines at the time was 11.7 million pesos a year. Of the wealth taken out of Havana, 800,000 pesos belonged to the royal treasury, but the rest was privately held, confirming what British attackers imagined and Spanish observers remarked, that Havana was "una ciudad llena de plata" (a city full of silver). Although they loaned some money to the war effort by paying soldiers' wages, for example, and offering relief to indigent evacuees from the city, Havana's richest merchants and landowners largely removed themselves and their enormous sum of silver and sought refuge inland. Whatever would come of the siege, virtually all the city's wealthiest residents would wait it out elsewhere.[32]

Though enslaved soldiers and laborers would play critical roles in the Spanish defense, in the initial moments of the siege many enslaved Africans who lived in Havana took advantage of the chaotic atmosphere in the city to flee from the capital. In so doing, they were both avoiding the impending violence and seizing the opportunity to escape from their owners. Throughout the course of the British campaign, there were complaints of bands of people identified as runaway slaves stealing food or conducting raids against refugees from the city. One source lamented that families fleeing Havana were equally besieged by the attacks of the enemy and those of blacks, who in open territory outside the city were "no less fierce enemies." Eager to try to assert control, Prado promulgated an edict declaring harsh punishment for the "excesses" that blacks and mulatos were allegedly committing at night.[33]

Those who fled upon the arrival of the British expedition also included deserters from Spanish and local militia forces stationed in Havana, Guanabacoa, and Matanzas, the largest nearby port, just sixty miles to the east. At the

32. Olañeta, "Diario del sitio," June 10, 1762, Miscellaneous Manuscripts, MS 352, XV, 83, folder 1662, Sterling Memorial Library. On the situado to the entire Caribbean, see Carlos Marichal and Matilde Souto Mantecón, "Silver and *Situados:* New Spain and the Financing of the Spanish Empire in the Caribbean in the Eighteenth Century," *HAHR,* LXXIV (1994), 587–613, esp. 590. On the output of Mexico's silver mines, see John Tutino, *Making a New World: Founding Capitalism in the Bajío and Spanish North America* (Durham, N.C., 2011), 550. For "a city full of silver," see "Memoria sobre los motivos que ocasionaron la fundación de la Compañía de La Habana," Dec. 21, 1770, Coleccion Mata Linares, LXXV, 613–618, Real Academia de La Historia, Madrid. On loaning money to the war effort, see "El cabildo secular, copia," Aug. 26, 1762, AGI, SD, 1356. For mention of the alms regidores supplied to poor families and those of men serving in militias, see Prado to Madariaga, June 13, 1762, AGI, SD, 1581, no. 1. On Spanish subjects' practice of loaning their money to the king during war, see Viviana Grieco, *On the King's Power and His Subject's Money: The Political Culture of the Viceroyalty of the Río de la Plata, 1776–1809* (forthcoming).

33. "Diario del Capitán Don Juan de Casta," 1762, Theodorus Bailey Meyers Collection, NYPL; "Carta de Don Juan Miguel Palomino," C.M. Pérez, BNJM ("no less fierce enemies"), and "Copia de una carta escrita en la Habana a un correspondiente de la corte," Add. MSS 13976, fol. 298–299, BL; "Noticias de la Habana que refieren como la ganaron los ingleses, August 29th, 1762," MS 10818/33, BNE. "Ordenes, vandos, disposiciones, y otras providencias políticas y de buen govierno dadas por Don Juan de Prado, durante el sitio de la Habana," June 13, 1762, AGI, SD, 1584, no. 473 ("excesses").

beginning of the siege, Prado wrote to Juan Ignacio de Madariaga complaining that fugitives from the Havana militia who had deserted into the countryside were among those committing crimes of opportunity against Havana refugees. Of the residents who had fled Havana, the *extramuros* (outside the city walls) neighborhood of Guadalupe, the village of Guanabacoa, and other neighboring regions, he declared with dismay that their actions represented a "notorious abandonment of the principal object they ought to attend to in the defense of the *patria*." Yet many of those who fled had no roofs over their heads when they left and were facing flooded conditions after the rains. One of the first orders of the defense had been to set fire to the straw huts in the predominantly free black neighborhood of Guadalupe to deprive British forces of cover should they approach from the west. Another two hundred houses outside the city walls had been demolished for their wood, which was used to build up the ramparts atop the city walls. In these conditions, it was the decision to stay and fight that should stand out as surprising.[34]

In the first days of the siege, Havana and its surroundings felt like a world turned upside down. More than forty lepers had broken free from quarantine and were wandering loose. Because it had rained nonstop for eight days, stretches of road were impassable by horse, mule, or carriage, with knee-deep mud that sucked at feet, hooves, and wheels. The sight of families on the road, exposed to the raids of runaway slaves, and formerly cloistered nuns with sacred relics clutched to their chests, losing their shoes in the mud as they scrambled to escape to the interior, struck one observer as apocalyptic. There were reports throughout the siege of both white and black *"pícaros," "vagabundos," "viles,"* and *"cobardes"* (cowards) committing robberies and raping the women sent out of the plaza into the countryside. In his journal of the siege, one Spanish sailor claimed that, on June 22, six men, identified as both black and white, had been apprehended who had not only robbed people and raped women but also allegedly murdered and dismembered their female victims.[35]

34. "Cartas originales de Don Juan Ignacio Madariaga a Don Juan de Prado," June 16, 1762, in *Proceso formado de orden del Rey Nuestro Señor por la Junta de Generales*, I, 27, BNE; Prado to Madariaga, June 17, 1762, AGI, SD, 1581 ("notorious abandonment"); Actas Capitulares de Matanzas, 1760–1769, fols. 44, 53, Archivo Histórico Provincial de Matanzas, Cuba; Urbano Martínez Carmenate, *Historia de Matanzas (Siglos XVI-XVIII)* (Matanzas, Cuba, 1999), 96; Ambrosio de Justis de Sayas to Prado, June 19, 1762, AGI, SD, 1586, no. 64. On the destruction of houses extramuros, see "Diario del Capitán Don Juan de Casta," Theodorus Bailey Meyers Collection, NYPL; "Diario del manuscrito de Madrid," June 22, 1762, in Rodríguez, ed., *Cinco diarios*, 27; Olañeta, "Diario del sitio," June 10, 1762, Miscellaneous Manuscripts, MS 352, XV, box 83, folder 1662, Sterling Memorial Library.

35. Roig de Leuchsenring, ed., *La dominación inglesa*, 122–123; Olañeta, "Diario del sitio," June 8, 1762, Miscellaneous Manuscripts, MS 352, XV, box 83, folder 1662, Sterling Memorial Library; "Carta que en 12 de diciembre de 1763 escribió un padre Jesuíta de la Habana al Prefect Javier Bonilla, de Sevilla," Document No. IV, in Roig de Leuchsenring, ed., *La dominación inglesa*, 254–255; "Cartas

Such accounts reflect the very real danger that women, in particular, faced during this invasion as well as heightened anxieties about the general breakdown of law and order on the arrival of the British war fleet. As city authorities and refugees feared, Havana was on the verge of becoming a lawless and dangerous place, with racial hierarchies inverted and the upheaval encouraging violence and opportunism. One man who had been left behind to protect the sacred relics in the church of Guanabacoa was hanged for stealing them himself and attributing the theft to the British. Three black men were whipped for supposedly robbing an abandoned house. In the early days of the siege, before a defense could be organized, that same Spanish sailor wrote again in his journal: "Even worse than the aforementioned destruction caused by the British was what our own *havaneros* have done, whites as well as blacks."[36]

The Call to Arms

The chaos in the initial hours and days after the arrival of the British ships triggered fears of another slave rebellion like the one that broke out in 1727, when Admiral Francis Hosier's ships cruised offshore during a prior Anglo-Spanish war. In response to the rapid depopulation of the city and the sense of impending crisis among Spain's own subjects, on June 9 Prado decreed that enslaved Africans who came to Havana from agricultural estates to help defend the city would be rewarded with their freedom. When questioned about why he had made this decision, Prado testified that he had wanted to preempt any British maneuver to turn the enslaved population against the Spanish and, as he put it, because of their great numbers (and hence whites' vulnerability) in Havana's hinterland.[37]

Prado's assessment that British troops would appeal to Cuba's enslaved Africans to rise up against their masters in return for manumission was driven more by age-old fears than eighteenth-century realities. British commanders had discussed using this strategy during the Guantánamo campaign of

originales de Don Juan Ignacio Madariaga a Don Juan de Prado," June 16, 1762, in *Proceso formado de orden del Rey Nuestro Señor por la Junta de Generales,* I, 27, BNE (quotations); "Diario del manuscrito de Madrid," in Rodríguez, ed., *Cinco diarios,* June 22, 1762, 27. Additionally, Casta reported that at least one "black" was hanged for allegedly raping a young woman.

36. "Diario del manuscrito de Madrid," in Rodríguez, ed., *Cinco diarios,* June 22, 27, 1762. On the church at Guanabacoa, see "Cartas originales de Don Juan Ignacio Madariaga a Don Juan de Prado," June 20, 1762, in *Proceso formado de orden del Rey Nuestro Señor por la Junta de Generales,* I, 28, BNE. On the abandoned house, see Olañeta, "Diario del sitio," June 27, 1762, Miscellaneous Manuscripts, MS 352, XV, box 83, folder 1662, Sterling Memorial Library.

37. One account of the siege claimed it was the junta's idea, not Prado's, though he took credit for it. See Prado to Arriaga, May 4, 1763, AGI, SD, 2209; "Breve resumen de lo acaezido en el sitio de La Havana," Add. MSS 13974, BL.

1741, the Guadeloupe campaign of 1759, and no doubt others, but, as experience had demonstrated, the significant number of enslaved troops relied upon by the British themselves rendered unworkable any offer to free the enemy's slaves while denying the same to their own. As evidenced by the halting process of recruiting enslaved Africans in Jamaica, British commanders already had reason to question their ability to control this population. By this point in the mid-eighteenth century, with the growth of British slaveholding and the transformation of Barbados and Jamaica into sugar-producing islands with large black demographic majorities, what the British had always considered Spanish America's great Achilles heel—its large population of enslaved Africans—had become their own.[38]

However Prado judged the threat of slave rebellion in the initial days of the siege, it seems unlikely that enslaved Africans were initiating a coordinated rebellion against whites in the region. What appeared to be targeted attacks against whites were probably desperate acts of survival. Many of Havana's black inhabitants, like its white residents, chose to flee into the interior, but, unlike whites, they generally had less money and fewer resources to rely on as they went. To get by, they might have chosen raiding and robbery to get the food, money, and supplies they needed. Some escaping enslaved Africans might have perpetrated acts of vengeance against white men or women during the chaotic flight from the city; however, those in Havana who ran away from the British invasion generally followed a pattern also seen in Spanish Jamaica, when the English invaded in 1655, and in Suriname, when the Dutch took over in 1667. Mass escapes of enslaved Africans, referred to by historians as incidents of grand marronage, often occurred during moments of geopolitical crisis and division within the white ruling order. Many of these individuals might have been choosing to escape both sides in the conflict altogether and to head for the hills to live on their own in maroon communities, rather than continue in a state of slavery or to wage war against British enemies or their former owners.[39]

Despite the misperceptions that informed it, Prado's proclamation offer-

38. During the British occupation of Guantánamo in 1741, Governor Edward Trelawny of Jamaica had written to the Duke of Newcastle that to offer the enemy's enslaved Africans freedom without promising the same to one's own on the expedition "must naturally occasion great heart-burning if they are not made free, too." At that time, he had recommended promising the enslaved laborers working for the British their freedom as well "to secure the fidelity of these negroes," though this option was not exercised. See Trelawny to Newcastle, May 29, 1741, Despatches, Jamaica to England, 1739–1755, fol. 188, JNA.

39. Herbert S. Klein and Ben Vinson III, *African Slavery in Latin America and the Caribbean*, 2d ed. (New York, 2007), 176. On the formation of Jamaican maroon communities during the English invasion and conquest, see Carla Gardina Pestana, *The English Conquest of Jamaica: Oliver Cromwell's Bid for Empire* (Cambridge, Mass., 2017), 194–214.

ing enslaved Africans their freedom in return for joining in the fighting was the single best decision he and the junta de guerra made during the entire defense of Havana. Prado's decree was crucial because it gave enslaved Africans throughout the island an incentive to come to Havana and defend the city while so many of its residents were fleeing. Without this offer and those who took it up, Havana would not have had nearly enough soldiers and workers to stave off the British attack as long as it did — so long it nearly failed. During the course of the siege, the city's black majority grew, as many individuals of European descent removed themselves to safety and enslaved Africans and militias came from all over the island to work or fight. Joseph Antonio Moreno, an enslaved man in Puerto Príncipe reported that, as soon as the British began their invasion, a proclamation was made in his town that all enslaved Africans who presented themselves in Havana's plaza would be declared free in return for their services. In his own words in a later testimonial, given that assurance, he "ran" the 150 leagues to present himself in Havana.[40]

Reportedly, Prado ordered owners of agricultural estates to allow half of their enslaved Africans to go to Havana to aid its defense, and they came into the city from more than a hundred estates. However they came, their owners invariably took credit for sending them and did so based upon the time-honored tradition by which they were paid hiring-out fees for their human property's labor. One owner of a sugar plantation outside Havana claimed to have sent in twenty-five of his "best" enslaved Africans, armed with machetes and hoes, to participate in the defense of the Cabaña and the Morro. In an act that was probably not typical among plantation owners, he said that he later released his twenty-five remaining enslaved Africans as well. Another plantation owner wrote that he sent thirty enslaved Africans, "all of good disposition," to militia commander Coronel Don Luis Joseph de Aguiar to join in the defense. The timing of the call for reinforcements was fortuitous, as the sugar harvest, or *zafra,* had just ended, making it easier for the area's sugar plantations to spare their workers. The imminent threat from the British also made slaveowners less recalcitrant than those in Jamaica and more willing than they themselves had been previously when asked to provide workers to reinforce the Cabaña.[41]

40. Petition of Joseph Antonio Moreno, n.d., AGI, SD, 2208. The distance was closer to 100 leagues, or 350 miles, depending on the roads taken.

41. "El cabildo secular," Havana, Aug. 26, 1762, AGI, SD, 1356; "Servicios y exercicios literarios del Doctor Don Carlos del Rey, Presbytero, Domiciliario de la Habana," AGI, SD, 1357 ("best"); "Relación de los méritos y servicios de Don Joseph Cypriano de la Luz, Correo Mayor que ha sido de la isla de Cuba y regidor perpetuo por Su Majestad de la cuidad de San Cristobal de la Habana," AGI, IG, 2821 ("good disposition").

Reliance on the labor of black people was something the British attack and the Spanish defense of Havana had in common. Men and women of African descent prepared food and cared for the sick on both sides of the conflict, including in the Morro fortress itself. Working for the British, black militia and enslaved laborers cleared trees to open a line of advance on the Morro, dug trenches, made fascines, hauled artillery, and foraged for food across enemy lines. The Spanish defense relied even more heavily on blacks as both war workers and soldiers, laboring and fighting in tandem with Spanish soldiers and sailors and white creoles from the countryside. Havana's economy and its military could not operate in either war or peace—nor could the island of Cuba even feed itself—without the labor of its black population, and this moment of imperial war was no exception.[42]

So many enslaved Africans went to Havana to offer their services, despite the extreme danger in the city, that Governor Prado lost count over the course of the siege. He later estimated that eight hundred or nine hundred of these men perished in the fighting. Their losses were likely so great because in many cases they served as soldiers and support workers in the city and Morro fortress during the peak of the bombardment. Enslaved Africans and free blacks bore the brunt of the casualties, out of proportion to their numbers on the island, and the rate at which they fell intensified during the brutal final weeks of the siege. In one particularly grim account, a Jesuit present noted that one bomb that landed in the walled city killed fifteen blacks in a single strike.[43]

Lured by the promise of their freedom, many enslaved Africans sought to ensure it by making their way to the front lines of the battle despite the grave danger. In his diary of the siege, Prado qualified his promise of manumission

42. *The Two Putnams, Israel and Rufus, in the Havana Expedition 1762, and in the Mississippi River Exploration 1772–73, with Some Account of the Company of Military Adventurers* (Hartford, Conn., 1931), 88. Women also served as nurses on the British hospital ships and as personal servants, forced mistresses, and slaves of British officers. On women at the Morro, see "Diario del manuscrito de Madrid," July 3, 1762, in Rodríguez, ed., *Cinco diarios,* 31. "Fascines" were bundles of long sticks used to shore up trenches or ramparts, particularly around artillery batteries. On the labor of blacks on behalf of the British expedition, see Order Book of Major Moncrieffe of Voyage and Campaigns from New York, Martinique, Grenada, and Havana, Frederick Mackenzie Collection, Library and Archives of Canada. On the manual labor of blacks in Havana, see Olañeta, "Diario del sitio," June 6 and 8, 1762, Miscellaneous Manuscripts, MS 352, XV, box 83, folder 1662, Sterling Memorial Library.

43. For Prado's reference to "losing count," see Prado to Madariaga, Apr. 20, 1763, AGI, Ultramar, 169. It was estimated they hailed from around one hundred different agricultural estates ("más de cien ingenios"); see "Testimonio de Don Ignacio de Ayala y el Ayuntamiento de esta Ciudad de La Habana," Aug. 26, 1762, AGI, SD, 1356. Of Don Carlos del Rey's twenty-five enslaved Africans, reportedly six died, ten retreated to the interior of the island to continue in His Majesty's service, and only nine returned to the plantation. According to Don Joseph Cipriano de la Luz, seven of his thirty enslaved workers died, and two were injured beyond the ability to work. See "Carta del Jesuíta Thomas Butler," Dec. 12, 1763, C.M. Pérez, fol. 15, BNJM.

by stating that it would apply only to those enslaved Africans that earned it through their efforts. What that meant, precisely, and how it was understood by the men volunteering would become a point of contention after the siege. But many of the men who arrived at the plaza ready to fight seem to have thought it meant taking a role on the front lines. As Juan Ignacio de Madariaga commented just ten days before the explosion of the mine under the Morro, it was necessary to restrain the crowds at the docks vying to make their way to the Morro, which they perceived to be "the most distinguished and high-risk" site of the battle.[44]

According to the governor's language in his diary of the siege, the most "capable" among the enslaved Africans who came to Havana were to be used in the exercise of arms, whereas African-born *bozales* would be used in ends "more fitting of their understanding," such as manual labor. Enslaved Africans unloaded cannons from the Spanish warships in the harbor, hauled them to the city, the Cabaña, the Morro, and the Punta fortress, and mounted them on the walls to protect the city. A team of more than one hundred bozales with a black creole captain was put to work logging and transporting large quantities of wood, which was needed for building and repairing parapets on the walls of the Morro and the city. In general, bozales ended up doing more support work and had fewer opportunities to earn their freedom; as in times of peace, freedom remained more within the reach of better-acculturated creoles.[45]

Yet, despite such distinctions between the free and enslaved people of African descent, bozales and creoles, and war workers and soldiers, these categories tended to break down in the urgency of the siege. As the Morro, the Cabaña, and the city itself were heavily shelled by the British, constant labor was required to remount the cannons and rebuild the wooden parapets behind which the defenders found cover as they returned fire. Havana's carpenters were free men of African descent, and the defense relied on several carpenters who were members of the battalion of *pardos libres* to make vital repairs to the city's walls and its forts at night during breaks from enemy fire. While a number of free black militia members did support work, some enslaved men

44. "Diarios de las operaciones del sitio de la Habana en 1762 formados por el Governador de ella Don Juan de Prado y por el Gefe de Escuadra Marqués del Real Transporte," in *Proceso formado de orden del Rey Nuestro Señor por la Junta de Generales*, I, 9, BNE; "Papeles que entrega el Capitan de Navio Don Juan Ignacio Madariaga," July 20, 1762, AGI, Ultramar, 169, no. 23.

45. "Diarios de las operaciones del sitio de la Habana en 1762 formados por el Governador de ella Don Juan de Prado y por el Gefe de Escuadra Marqués del Real Transporte," in *Proceso formado de orden del Rey Nuestro Señor por la Junta de Generales*, I, 9, BNE; "Diario del Capitán Don Juan de Casta," 1762, July 30, 1762, Theodorus Bailey Meyers Collection, NYPL. This logging squad resembled those used with royal slaves for the shipyard; see "Cuenta presentado por Don Miguel Calvo de la Puerta del caudal de Real Hazienda que administró durante el sitio de la plaza," AGI, SD, 1842, fols. 15r–18r.

were able to insert themselves into militias made up of free blacks. Others joined ad hoc companies of recruits, under white commanders, that formed throughout the siege as individuals arrived from the interior and assembled in Havana. Wartime necessity presented opportunities free and enslaved blacks eagerly seized.[46]

The enslaved proved especially successful at capturing British prisoners, which provided them with an economic boon unlike anything available during peacetime. During the first week of the siege, it was announced that, no matter what a person's skin color or legal status, if he could capture a British solider the Spanish king would reward him with thirty reales. Ten reales was the prize for capturing a sailor. Both amounts were much greater than day laborers earned at the time. Blacks in Cuba knew the terrain well and excelled at ambushing and capturing British troops, an expertise outside the realm of traditional eighteenth-century European modes of warfare. Many observers commented on the skill displayed by men of African descent in taking British prisoners as well as their tremendous motivation for doing so. Through the eyes of the Spanish sailor who kept a diary of the siege, blacks performed *"diabluras,"* or daring feats without fear for their safety, as though they were possessed by the devil, to capture the enemy and obtain this prize of thirty reales. Early in the siege, Prado tried in vain to instruct the *"paisanos"* in the rules of warfare "between cultured nations" so they would not violate them in their zealous pursuit of prisoners. Rather than take prisoners, sometimes these men killed the British soldiers they encountered. One group of twelve blacks making a raid from the Morro on June 22 managed to kill ten British soldiers with their machetes, bringing back their red coats, hats, and guns as proof.[47]

Some of the men who captured British soldiers and sailors did not even have weapons, but they still achieved success. One enslaved man named Joseph Antonio Barreto, who was serving in the Morro, described being sent by the official in charge to fight the British "man to man" without any weapon.

46. "Libro de servicios del batallón de pardos libres de La Habana," 1771, AGI, Cuba, 1136A; Prado to Madariaga, July 17, 1762, AGI, Ultramar, 169: "Han entrado 194 negros esclavos de las compañias de Trinidad, el Cayo, y Sancti Spíritus, y hoy 164 entre negros y gente blanca de Arroyo de Arenas, que en todos se compone el número de 258 hombres."

47. "Diario del manuscrito de Madrid," June 13, 29, 1762, in Rodríguez, ed., *Cinco diarios*, 25, 29 (quotation); Olañeta, "Diario del sitio," June 22, 1762, Miscellaneous Manuscripts, MS 352, XV, box 83, folder 1662, Sterling Memorial Library. On instructing the "paisanos" in the rules of war, see Prado to Madariaga, June 17, 1762, AGI, SD, 1581. In the late seventeenth century, enslaved Africans in Havana earned four daily reales if they were a man and three if they were a woman (Alejandro de la Fuente, "Esclavitud, 1510–1886," in Consuelo Naranjo Orovio, ed., *Historia de Cuba* [Madrid, 2009], 139). These rates seem to have changed little by the mid-eighteenth century; see, for example, "Cuenta presentado por Don Miguel Calvo de la Puerta del caudal de Real Hazienda que administró durante el sitio de la plaza," AGI, SD, 1842, fols. 15r–18r.

As he testified, he was able to "capture a prisoner by the hair" and march him back to his commanding officer. On Havana's flanks, one sortie of blacks on July 5 reportedly took four hundred British prisoners, and another sortie captured another one hundred. By early July, the Spanish might have held as many as eight hundred prisoners at Managua, to the south of Havana. There were so many that some prisoners and deserters had to be held on ranches and plantations, in monasteries and convents outside the city, and even on ships anchored in the harbor.[48]

In most cases, it is difficult to know whether enslaved combatants were Africa- or America-born, but one of the most celebrated triumphs of the defense of Havana was achieved by a group of enslaved soldiers under the command of one of their own, an enslaved African-born man, Andres Gutiérrez. On June 26, thirteen enslaved Africans surprised an advance party of British soldiers moving through the woods toward the Morro fortress. Armed with only machetes against troops carrying firearms, they killed one British soldier, took seven prisoners, and chased off the rest. In recognition of their valor, in the midst of the fighting the governor of Havana awarded the men their immediate freedom in the name of the Spanish king and ordered that their owners be compensated with funds from the royal treasury. Prado commented to Don Carlos Caro, a Spanish military commander operating on the outskirts of the city, that the news of this success had raised the spirits of the troops from Spain as well as the *gente del país*. In response, the Havana governor subsequently formed another company of one hundred enslaved men with a white commander in order to expand the role of enslaved Africans, not just as auxiliaries to the trained militiamen but also as soldiers themselves.[49]

Spanish military records from a decade later confirm that Gutiérrez, the captain of the thirteen enslaved men who led the successful raid from the Morro, had come to Cuba from the kingdom of the Kongo. The speed with which he distinguished himself by his military skill during the siege suggests he had been a soldier before he was captured and enslaved in Africa and brought to the Americas in chains. His expertise was no doubt the product

48. "Testimonio de los autos obrados sobre las livertades dadas a diferentes negros esclavos que sirvieron en el tiempo de la invasión de esta plaza," 1764, AGI, SD, 2209, 8v–9v. For accounts of prisoners, see "Diario del manuscrito de Madrid," in Rodríguez, ed., *Cinco diarios*, 31, 34; and lists compiled in AGI, SD, 1586.

49. Arriaga to the Conde de Ricla, May 13, 1763, AGI, SD, 1213; Olañeta, "Diario del sitio," July 26, 1762, Miscellaneous Manuscripts, MS 352, XV, box 83, folder 1662, Sterling Memorial Library. For their manumission, see Havana, Nov. ?, 1763, Prado to Arriaga, Nov. ?, 1763, AGI, SD, 1213. On the effect of the news, see Prado to Caro, June 27, 1762, AGI, Ultramar, 169; Prado to Arriaga, May 4, 1763, AGI, SD, 2209; Placer Cervera, *Inglaterra y la Habana*, 153–154; Placer Cervera, *Los defensores del Morro*, 42; García del Pino, *Toma de la Habana*, 94.

PLATE 1 Engraving of Havana. Derived from Arnoldus Montanus, *The New and Unknown World* . . . (Amsterdam, 1671). Courtesy of the John Carter Brown Library at Brown University

PLATE 2 A British Medal Minted in Anticipation of Admiral Vernon's Capture of Cartagena in 1741. On the back is printed "Vernon conquered Cartagena" (B) while the front identifies Vernon's next target as Havana (A). © National Maritime Museum, Greenwich, London

PLATE 3 *Watson and the Shark*. By John Singleton Copley. 1778. Oil on canvas.
Courtesy, National Gallery of Art, Washington, D.C. / Bridgeman Images

PLATE 4 *The Morro Castle and the Boom Defense Before the Attack.* By Dominic Serres. 1770. Oil on canvas. © National Maritime Museum, Greenwich, London

PLATE 5 *The Captured Spanish Fleet at Havana, August–September, 1762.* By Dominic Serres. 1768. © National Maritime Museum, Greenwich, London

PLATE 6 *The Capture of Havana, 1762: The English Battery before the Morro Castle.*
By Dominic Serres. 1770. Wikimedia Commons

PLATE 7 *General William Keppel, Storming the Morro Castle.* By Sir Joshua Reynolds. 1764 or
1765. Oil on canvas. Courtesy, Museu de Arte Antiga, Lisbon, Portugal / Bridgeman Images

PLATE 8 "The Breach of the Moro Castle, July 30, 1762." Engraving by Pierre Canot and Thomas Mason, based on a sketch by naval lieutenant Philip Orsbridge and a painting by Dominic Serres. Anne S.K. Brown Military History Collection, Brown University Library

PLATE 9 "His Majesty's Land Forces Going in Flat Boats to Take Possession of the North Gate of the City and Punto Castle, on the 14th of August." Engraving by Pierre Canot and Thomas Mason, based on an original sketch by Lieutenant Philip Orsbridge and a painting by Dominic Serres. Anne S.K. Brown Military History Collection, Brown University Library

PLATE 10 *The Piazza at Havana.* By Dominic Serres. Circa 1765–1770. Oil on canvas.
© National Maritime Museum, Greenwich, London

PLATE 11 *The Cathedral at Havana.* By Dominic Serres. Circa 1765–1770. Oil on canvas.
Wikimedia Commons

PLATE 12 *Defensa del Moro contra el ataque inglés.* By Rafael Monleón y Torres. 1873. Oil on canvas. Courtesy, Museo Naval de Madrid, Spain / Bridgeman Images

PLATE 13 Spanish Medal Commemorating the Commanders Don Luis Vicente de Velasco e Isla and Don Vicente González, Slain during the Loss of the Morro. Minted in 1763. © National Maritime Museum, Greenwich, London

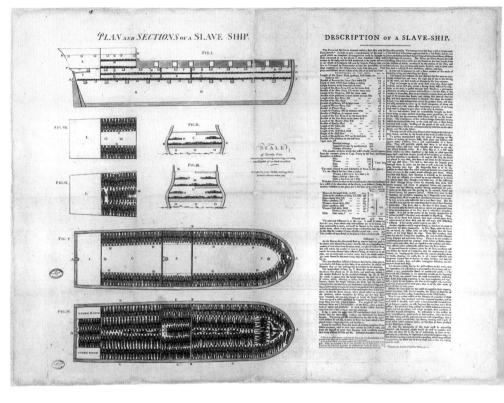

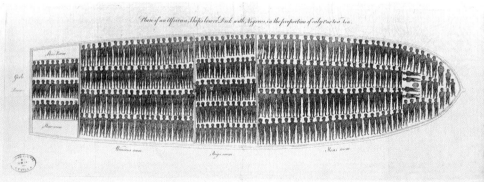

PLATE 14 "Plan and Sections of a Slave Ship" (A) and "Plan of an African Ship's Lower Deck . . ." (B). Courtesy, Archivo General de Indias, Seville, Spain

of military traditions developed over decades of civil war in the Kongo. In a matter of weeks, Gutiérrez was promoted from the position of an enslaved volunteer to commander of other slave soldiers, and then he was manumitted and made a newly minted captain in Havana's company of free blacks. That he had prior military experience is made particularly plausible by the success he had in raiding and capturing the enemy—a central practice in contemporary West African warfare, which would have given him an advantage against European troops accustomed to drilling and marching in formation. Perhaps because of the certainty and expertise with which Gutiérrez conducted himself, Prado later confessed he had not been sure whether the man was free or enslaved at the time.[50]

Given that they were fighting not only for their king but also to win their manumission, enslaved blacks might have been especially inclined to take risks. As previous experience had shown, wartime provided opportunities for men of African descent that they knew would not be available otherwise. A Spanish sailor defending the Morro commented on how "those of broken color did not cease to beg for another sally, promising to win from the enemy their batteries and maybe even take more prisoners." Perhaps Gutiérrez and others like him were also affected by memories—some quite recent—of a transatlantic passage on a British slaving ship that made taking British captives particularly sweet.[51]

Enslaved volunteers and free black militiamen had reasons to be less willing to surrender peaceably than their white counterparts. The knowledge that they were beyond the full protection of the rules of war and that if captured they would be particularly vulnerable to (re)enslavement at the war's end gave them a powerful incentive to do whatever it took to defeat the British enemy. Blacks in Cuba would have heard of or even experienced personally the harsh

---

50. Prado identifies Gutiérrez by name in Prado to Arriaga, May 4, 1763, AGI, SD, 1586, no. 391. His nation is listed as "Congo" in "Libro de servicios de los oficiales y sargentos del batallon de morenos libres de La Habana," 1773, AGI, Cuba, 1136A, fol. 695. Only because Gutiérrez went on to a distinguished military career was it possible to determine his probable origins, which were listed in later military records. Unfortunately, the other men in his company were not named in correspondence. Ethnic labels employed in the context of the slave trade are famously inexact; see, for example, Philip D. Morgan, "The Cultural Implications of the Atlantic Slave Trade: African Regional Origins, American Destinations, and New World Developments," in David Eltis and David Richardson, eds., *Routes to Slavery: Direction, Ethnicity, and Mortality in the Transatlantic Slave Trade* (London, 1997), 122–145. For further military records on Gutiérrez, see "Libro de servicios de los oficiales y sargentos del batallon de morenos libres de La Havana hasta fin de diciembre 1774," AGI, Cuba, 1136A, fol. 606. On the culture and practice of West African warfare, See John K. Thornton, *Warfare in Atlantic Africa, 1500–1800* (London, 1999); and Thornton, "African Soldiers in the Haitian Revoution," *Journal of Caribbean History*, XXV, nos 1–2 (1991), 58–80.

51. "Breve y puntual razon de la conquista de La Havana que fue del modo siguiente," AGI, SD, 1507.

treatment the enslaved received on the sugar plantations of neighboring Jamaica. This knowledge would have combined with the horrors many had experienced on the Middle Passage aboard British slaving ships. Even more, as a Spanish journal writer pointed out, the freedom of enslaved Africans fighting for the Spanish crown was understood to be contingent on Spain's victory in the fighting, as it had been promised to them by the Spanish monarch, not the British king they were fighting against. Men so motivated might well have been unwilling to put down their arms, and they might have seemed to their British combatants entirely unmanageable as prisoners of war. Although we cannot know for certain, these factors could have influenced events during the storming of the Morro.[52]

In addition to the goal of personal freedom, enslaved men who fought to defend Havana might have been driven by their feelings of connection to the Spanish king. Spanish imperialism had certainly exploited and oppressed them, but the Spanish king nonetheless inspired regular professions of loyalty and attachment among his subjects of African descent, in part because manumission, when it was offered, was extended in the name of this distant Spanish monarch. The king professed benevolence toward his diverse subjects, in contrast to the treatment they could receive from local officials and slaveowners. When enslaved Africans in Cuba were treated badly by a master, they had learned to petition for the king's protection or to invoke his name. Religious and political rituals affirmed this bond: on the feast day of the three kings each January, as well as on the coronation of a new Spanish king, people of African descent in Cuba celebrated. Kings were venerated in many African cultures, and the idea of serving a king in battle would likely have felt both righteous and familiar to many African men in Cuba. Thus, at least to some extent, their defense of the Spanish king in battle — even though it meant great risk to themselves — grew out of their own traditions as well as those of Spanish colonialism.[53]

52. In a report from 1740, during the War of Jenkins' Ear, prepared in advance of a prior attempt on Havana, a resident of Jamaica commented on the likely attitude of its residents to the idea of British annexation: "The negroes, who are well informed of the treatment the backs meet with from the English in Jamaica, will for that reason be frighted from changing their masters" ("An Account of the Havana and the Other Principal Places of the Spaniards in the West Indies," Add. MSS 32694, 72–100, BL). On the understanding that manumission was contingent upon Spanish victory in its defense of Havana, see "Diario del manuscrito de Madrid," June 13, 1762, in Rodríguez, ed., *Cinco diarios,* 25.

53. On royalism among populations of African descent during the Age of Revolutions, see, for example, John K. Thornton, "'I Am the Subject of the King of the Kongo': African Political Ideology and the Haitian Revolution," *Journal of World History,* IV (1993), 181–214; Marcela Echeverri, *Indian and Slave Royalists in the Age of Revolution: Reform, Revolution, and Royalism in the Northern Andes, 1780–1825* (New York, 2016); Gene E. Ogle, "The Trans-Atlantic King and Imperial Public Spheres:

Sustaining the Defense

As the battle wore on, militias and enslaved Africans helped make it possible for the Spanish defense to hold out far longer than the British war planners had calculated. They contributed to the prolonged defense of the city in three crucial ways. To begin with, they provided a constant stream of desperately needed new recruits to replace the sick and the dead. Especially as the siege wore on, Prado's letters to Juan Ignacio de Madariaga, his principal commander outside the plaza, became filled with pleas to send more "negros y paisanos" into the city, "the largest number that could be found . . . in order to put them to work on the infinite and most serious work of fortification, which is called for each and every day." Prado grew so desperate for laborers to help repair and build up the city's defenses, and to do similar work in the Morro under Velasco's command, that he was willing to use prisoners and anyone deemed "not fit for arms." That included *guachinangos* laborers who had run away at the outbreak of fighting and been rounded up in the countryside and returned to Havana, as well as both blacks and whites who had resisted service or been apprehended for allegedly committing crimes during the chaos of the siege. When 100 to 150 blacks were sent into Havana eleven days after the mining of the Morro, Prado thanked Madariaga and requested as many more as possible, "because of the many [blacks] maimed and killed, principally in the Morro."[54]

A second way in which people of African descent prolonged Havana's ability to hold out against the British was by providing food for the city during the siege, a critical service that determined the city's ability to survive the British attack. Concentrating his forces in the plaza of Havana while under blockade created a problem for Prado. His requests for more men to work in the city's defense were counterbalanced by his concern that there be enough people employed in the production of food to feed the reinforcements in the plaza. The food situation in the city was so bleak that the order was given to either kill all the dogs or throw them out of the city because they were so hungry they howled all night. As supplies of food ran low, the population inside Havana's walls had to feed itself from the hinterland, rather than rely on im-

---

Everyday Politics in Pre-Revolutionary Saint-Domingue," in David Patrick Geggus and Norman Fiering, eds., *The World of the Haitian Revolution* (Bloomington, Ind., 2009), 76–96; Peter Blanchard, *Under the Flags of Freedom: Slave Soldiers and the Wars of Independence in Spanish South America* (Pittsburgh, 2008); Landers, *Atlantic Creoles*; and David Sartorius, *Ever Faithful: Race, Loyalty, and the Ends of Empire in Spanish Cuba* (Durham, N.C., 2013).

54. Prado to Madariaga, Aug. 5, 1762, AGI, Ultramar, 169 ("negros y paisanos"); Prado to Caro, June 30, 1762, Aug. 4, 5, 1762, AGI, Ultramar, 169 ("not fit for arms"); Prado to Madariaga, Aug. 10, 1762, AGI, Ultramar, 169 ("maimed and killed").

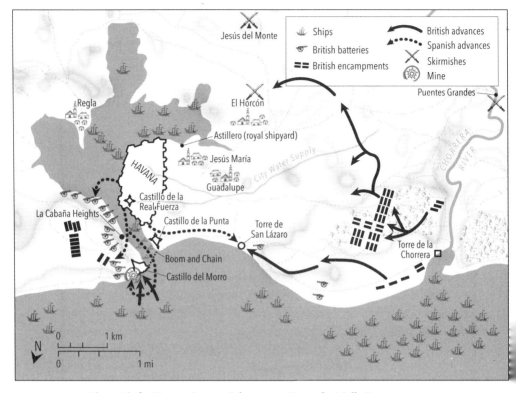

MAP 7 The Battle for Havana, June 16–July 30, 1762. Drawn by Molly Roy

ported food as it normally did. Without flour to make bread, the most viable starchy substitutes were cassava root, or *yuca*, sweet potatoes, plantains, and corn. Prado went to such great lengths to locate a black man named Miguel Nanciano, reportedly skilled in making cassava, and then to remand him to Madariaga to put him to work that Nanciano professed concern that he was being sent away for some punishment. Salt, too, already vital to imperial security in times of peace, became an especially crucial commodity during the siege for preserving meat for the troops and workers. To assuage Prado's concerns, a Havana resident outside the city walls assured him that he was putting "my intelligent slave" in charge of the critical task of salt procurement.[55]

The third and most crucial way in which people of African descent pro-

55. Prado to Madariaga, July 14, 1762, AGI, Ultramar, 169; Olañeta, "Diario del sitio," June 20, 1762, Miscellaneous Manuscripts, MS 352, XV, box 83, folder 1662, Sterling Memorial Library. Prado writes about the importance of "la fabrica de casave, cuyo renglon es aqui el mas considerable por ser un equivalente del pan" (Prado to the Marqués de Sobremonte, June 23, 1762, AGI, Ultramar, 169). On Miguel Nanciano, see Prado to Madariaga, July 2, 4, 1762, AGI, Ultramar, 169. On salt procurement, see Don Joseph de Ayala Matamoros to Prado, June 17, 1762, AGI, SD, 1585, no. 48.

longed the defense of Havana was by launching a series of counterattacks against the British advance (see Map 7). Outside the city walls, to the south and west of Havana, militia forces of pardos, morenos, and *blancos* kept British forces at bay and the roads open for materials and volunteers from the rest of the island. Without their protection, the supply lines would have been cut and the defense would have given out much sooner. Commanded by Don Luis Joseph de Aguiar and Don Carlos Caro and his cavalry, these militia forces engaged in skirmishes with British advance parties on the two fronts from which they approached the city. One Spanish account described one thousand cavalrymen and one thousand blacks protecting an area to the rear of the city. To the east, near Guanabacoa, militia harassed and captured British soldiers for many weeks during the siege. White militias from Havana and the surrounding areas made up a significant portion of these forces, and the white creole soldier, Pepe Antonio, has been held up as the hero on this front, but the militia of pardos libres was also there, mounting counterattacks at Guanabacoa and Cojímar.[56]

On Havana's western front, the island's militias executed a series of successful operations that repulsed the enemy and kept the defense alive. In mid-June, black militias featured prominently in several encounters with advancing British troops at Puentes Grandes, where bridges crossed the Chorrera River. On June 17, militia colonel Aguiar and a company of black troops turned back a British advance at the Chorrera River. They killed a British captain, took forty-five prisoners, and captured three regimental flags, while suffering only minimal deaths and injuries of their own. To protect the route through Jesús del Monte to Cuba's interior, Colonel Aguiar and his men burned down the five hundred houses in that hilltop village. They also defended a crucial crossroads at El Horcón, near the shipyard and on the edge of the extramuros neighborhood, where the two roads to the interior met. His men included not only whites but also four hundred armed black militiamen, and, during one of the skirmishes at El Horcón, they managed to kill six British soldiers, capture four, and gather twenty firearms left behind by those who fled running.[57]

---

56. "Diario del manuscrito de Madrid," July 5, 1762, in Rodríguez, ed., *Cinco diarios*, 32; "Libro de servicios del batallón de pardos libres de La Habana," 1771, AGI, Cuba, 1136A.

57. On the fighting at Puentes Grandes and La Chorrera, see Olañeta, "Diario del sitio," June 17, 1762, Miscellaneous Manuscripts, MS 352, XV, box 83, folder 1662, Sterling Memorial Library; "Diario del manuscrito de Madrid," June 29, 1762, in Rodríguez, ed., *Cinco diarios*, 29; Placer Cervera, *Inglaterra y la Habana*, 184; García del Pino, *Toma de la Habana*, 87, 93, 97. On El Horcón, see Olañeta, "Diario del sitio," June 24, 26, 1762, Miscellaneous Manuscripts, MS 352, XV, box 83, folder 1662, Sterling Memorial Library; "Diario del manuscrito de Madrid," June 26, July 6, 1762, in Rodríguez, ed., *Cinco diarios*, 28, 32, 39 nn. 16, 28; García del Pino, *Toma de la Habana*, 93; Placer Cervera,

Several weeks later, on July 18, the militia company of 100 enslaved Africans that was formed during the siege joined other companies in a surprise attack against the battery the British had constructed to cannonade the plaza at San Lázaro, also to the west of the city. The joint force of 60 whites and 150 blacks destroyed a mortar and three cannons and claimed to have killed 200 Englishmen and taken captive 18 men and the captain of artillery. Not content to wait until the end of hostilities, enslaved blacks who had distinguished themselves in the encounter at San Lázaro demanded their promised freedom in the midst of the fighting. The men went to Juan de Prado and the junta de guerra at San Isidro on the southern end of the walled city, where they were taking cover beyond the bombs' reach, to demand the freedom they had been promised. In the name of the king, Prado complied, ordering the production of *cartas de libertad* for 105 men and pledging to compensate their owners from the royal treasury.[58]

Finally, the actions of people of African descent were also crucial in the two main counterattacks Prado attempted against the Cabaña and the siege works threatening the Morro, on June 29 and July 22. These attacks were not as successful as other defensive measures, but they slowed the progress of the siege and took a toll on the British expedition. During the first of these two counterattacks, a party of six hundred men from Havana — "mostly Mulatos and Negroes, with some seaman," according to a British officer — sought to destroy the British batteries before the Morro but suffered the misfortune of having many of their numbers killed, wounded, and taken prisoner.[59]

Inglaterra y la Habana, 186; and Lourdes Ramos-Kuethe, ed., *Romance anónimo sobre el sitio y la toma de la Habana por los ingleses en 1762* (Prague, 2011), 58–59. On the skirmishes on Havana's western and southern flanks in general, see also Parcero Torre, *La pérdida de la Habana*, 102–107; Olañeta, "Diario del sitio," July 21, 1762, Miscellaneous Manuscripts, MS 352, XV, 83, folder 1662, Sterling Memorial Library; "Breve resumen de lo acaezido en el sitio de La Havana," Add. MSS 13974, BL; Prado to Arriaga, May 4, 1763, and Conde de Ricla to Arriaga, Nov. 20, 1763, both in AGI, SD, 2209; and Martínez-Valverde, "Operaciones de ataque y defensa de la Habana en 1762," *Revista general de Marina*, CLXIV (May 1963), 711–716.

58. "Diario del manuscrito de Madrid," July 18, 1762, in Rodríguez, ed., *Cinco diarios*, 34–35; Juan Miguel Palomino, "Copia de una carta escrita en la Habana a un correspondiente de la corte," Add. MSS 13976, BL; Olañeta, "Diario del sitio," July 21, 1762, Miscellaneous Manuscripts, MS 352, XV, 83, folder 1662, Sterling Memorial Library; "Breve resumen de lo acaezido en el sitio de La Havana," Add. MSS 13974, BL; Prado to Arriaga, May 4, 1763, Conde de Ricla to Arriaga, Nov. 20, 1763, both in AGI, SD, 2209.

59. *Authentic Journal of the Siege of the Havana*, June 29, 1762, 18–19 ("mostly Mulatos and Negroes"). On the counterattack of June 29, 1762, see Olañeta, "Diario del sitio," Miscellaneous Manuscripts, MS 352, XV, box 83, folder 1662, Sterling Memorial Library. See also *Archibald Robertson*, 55–56: "About four in the Morning the Enemy made a General sally upon all of our works. Their Numbers were nearly a Thousand 500 of which were Grenadiers who Embark'd about two in the Morning at the Havannah and landed between the Moro and Spanish Redoubt, the Rest mostly Negros and Mulatoes from the Moro."

During the second counterattack, launched at four o'clock in the morning just eight days before the mine at the Morro detonated, fifteen hundred men departed from the Morro and Havana simultaneously to attack the Cabaña and the British batteries before the Morro. The majority of the troops were white and black militiamen, including two companies of pardos libres and the company of one hundred enslaved blacks that had been formed during the fighting. The remainder of those who took part were blacks, guachinangos, and Spanish sailors who had been promised monetary rewards as recompense for volunteering for this dangerous enterprise. Although the Spanish attackers failed to seize or spike any of the large guns at the Cabaña or the Morro, they took British prisoners and injured Brigadier Guy Carleton. In another sign of a clash of cultures of warfare, a British officer complained that the enemy behaved with "great treachery, asking quarter, seeming to surrender themselves, and then stabbing our officers and men as they advanced to receive them." Afterward, the British called a truce to allow the recovery of the dead and injured, including eighty-five fallen British combatants. On the Spanish side, several hundred combatants were killed, including two officers of the pardos libres, and many others were taken prisoner or drowned while retreating. So many had fallen that a rumor circulated among the Spanish troops that these men had been sacrificed so that they would stop requesting that commanders send them out against the enemy. Sixty-one cadavers were recovered, "mostly blacks and *guachinangos,*" and buried by blacks in the cemetery at Regla. Undeterred, Prado proclaimed that the failed operation showed that "we have daring men capable of . . . defending hand to hand and drop of blood to drop of blood a plaza that is the key to both Americas and the theater of our reputation."[60]

"Passing" between Sides

Despite the buoyancy of Prado's claims and his ongoing reliance on local troops, the actions of men of African descent also triggered unease. For Prado, the rawest expression of that concern occurred during the outbreaks of violence in the chaotic first moments of the siege. Depending on people of African descent during this moment of imperial war activated anxieties, on

60. "MacKellar's Journal," 258, "Dundas's Memorandum on the Capture of Havana," 320–321, both in Syrett, ed., *Siege and Capture of Havana;* Diario de Juan de Casta, Sitio de la Ciudad de La Havana, 1762, July 22, 1762, Theodorus Bailey Meyers Collection, NYPL ("mostly blacks and *guachinangos"*); *Authentic Journal of the Siege of the Havana,* July 22, 1762, 30–31 ("treachery"); Carlos M. Trelles, *El sitio de la Habana y la dominación británica en Cuba* (Havana, 1925), 9; García del Pino, *Toma de la Habana,* 112–113; Placer Cervera, *Los defensores del Morro,* 49–50; Olañeta, "Diario del sitio," July 23, 1762, Miscellaneous Manuscripts, MS 352, XV, box 83, folder 1662, Sterling Memorial Library; Prado to Madariaga, July 22, 1762, AGI, Ultramar, 169, no. 2 ("we have daring men").

both sides of this conflict, about the ability of white authorities to harness the violence and loyalty of blacks who had been enslaved. While people of color managed to carve out an expanded role for themselves in the fighting on the Spanish side, Lord Albemarle's attitudes about the usefulness of black troops evolved from optimistic to somewhat less so.

People of African descent certainly were more than just loyal soldiers, stalwart workers, or unlucky victims of enemy fire on both sides of the battle. They also crossed between sides when they could to seek the best advantage for themselves. Given that the routes of the slave trade into eighteenth-century Cuba moved predominantly from and through Jamaica, during the invasion of Havana members of an interconnected African diaspora were aligned on opposite sides of this imperial conflict. Some of these individuals potentially knew one another or were relatives or even shipmates brought from Africa in the same British slaving ships. People of African descent were not the only individuals to move between sides during the siege and its aftermath, nor the only ones whose loyalty was questioned, but in many instances they seized opportunities for themselves as they arose. Their ability to "pass" as either with the British or the Spanish was an asset to them when British and Spanish forces were both vying for control of Havana and facilitated British war efforts. They could not be manipulated into rising up in rebellion as had been imagined, but they offered intelligence and worked behind enemy lines in ways that helped both sides of the campaign.

Because blacks from foreign colonies could pass as being Spanish blacks more easily than British whites could pass as Spanish whites, British officers used free blacks and enslaved men to obtain provisions across enemy lines. The British commanders knew Cuba had a lot of black people, thus making it easier for these men to move around clandestinely. British commanders could not have fed their troops without these black "pioneers." They would have missed gaining vital information as well, which the men often gathered during their reconnaissance efforts in and around Havana. Although they came with great risks, such assignments also provided opportunities for individuals to run away, either to the hills or to the Spanish enemy. If picked up by Spanish authorities, they could pretend to be African-born bozales and either hide or fake any indications attaching them to the British. Alternatively, they could offer military intelligence or profess a desire to convert to Catholicism, or both, in order to attempt to claim their freedom under Spanish rule.[61]

61. A Spanish account describes a "mulato" discovered with English documents on him who was hanged for being caught gathering provisions for the British (Diario de Juan de Casta, Sitio de la Ciudad de La Havana, 1762, July 15, 1762, Theodorus Bailey Meyers Collection, NYPL). According

Early modern imperial armies were plagued by desertion—especially a hastily assembled force like the British expedition—and yet Britain's black militiamen and enslaved laborers deserted at a much higher rate than its white soldiers and sailors. In early June, two enslaved blacks of the British deserted their camp and ran to the Morro, where they offered intelligence to Spanish officers in exchange for asylum. According to records of the British commander Lord Albemarle, by just over a month into the siege, twenty-five of the free troops of color from Jamaica had already deserted from the British side. Jamaica's free black troops constituted only five hundred in a force of twelve thousand soldiers, but they represented one of every five deserters from the British forces at that point. Even though Jamaica's free black militia members might have been reluctant to enlist in the first place and leave their families and livelihoods in Jamaica behind, a significant number of these men saw something to gain by deserting—an opportunity to escape the fighting or the yellow fever rampant among the troops—and running away into Cuba.[62]

So many enslaved Africans and free people of color deserted from the British forces over the course of the invasion and occupation that two years later colonial authorities in Cuba were still trying to figure out what to do with the sizable number of what they called *"negros ingleses"* who had run away from their commanders during the siege and occupation and either been captured or were still at large. As the battle wore on, the rate of blacks' desertion from British forces increased. One Spanish list of deserters who had come over to their side during the final stages of the fighting included almost as many individuals of African descent as of European descent. Predominant among them were people identified as bozales, but there were also those labeled "English" or "French" blacks, or freemen, even a sailor from Curaçao. Thirty-nine percent of the enslaved Africans from Jamaica, a total of 488 people, were never returned to their owners; instead, those that survived the fighting and the disease ran away or were captured and became a permanent part of Cuba's population of African descent.[63]

---

to a Spanish source, the British sent two hundred men to forage for food, particularly vegetables, from behind enemy lines (Prado to Madariaga, June 19, 1762, AGI, Ultramar, 169). For this British practice, see Bollettino, "Slavery, War, and Britain's Atlantic Empire," 124.

62. Olañeta, "Diario del sitio," July 7, 1762, Miscellaneous Manuscripts, MS 352, XV, box 83, folder 1662, Sterling Memorial Library; "Return of the Killed, Wounded, and Missing since the Army Landed on the Island of Cuba," CO 117.1, fols. 81–82, TNA; Thomas Agostini, "'Deserted His Majesty's Service': Military Runaways, the British-American Press, and the Problem of Desertion during the Seven Years' War," *Journal of Social History*, XL (2007), 957–985; Stephen Conway, "The Mobilization of Manpower for Britain's Mid-Eighteenth-Century Wars," *Historical Research*, LXXVII (2004), 377–404.

63. On "negros ingleses" in Cuba two years later, see Conde de Ricla to Arriaga, July 3, 1764, AGI,

There were many powerful incentives to flee the fighting or seek refuge on the Spanish side. Passing for free was potentially easier in Cuba than in a British colony like Jamaica, where there were far fewer individuals of that status. The Spanish crown's policy of offering manumission to enslaved Africans who ran away from British to Spanish colonies and professed a desire to convert to Catholicism was well known among people of African descent in Jamaica. At the time of the siege, there was already a long history of maritime marronage from the north coast of Jamaica to the south coast of Cuba. Enslaved Africans from Antigua and Saint Kitts would have been familiar with similar Spanish policies in the South American mainland.[64]

By no means, however, were all those people of African descent present at the siege of Havana running away *to* Cuba. In the mid-eighteenth century, Cuba might have been a better place to be a person of color—and particularly a free one—than Jamaica, but individuals in Cuba had a variety of motivations and loyalties framing their decisions about where to go and how to align themselves. Cuba's and Jamaica's populations of African origins were so closely linked that among those in Cuba were many men and women who had lived in British colonies before and now took the opportunity to desert to and even spy for the British side. Early in the siege, for example, one enslaved man, originally from a British colony but owned by an inhabitant of Guanabacoa, Cuba, was captured wearing British clothes and using British money. Reportedly, he had run away, joined the British forces, and was now scouting or working for them behind Spanish lines. If he had not been captured, the British would likely have manumitted him for this daring service.[65]

In several cases, enslaved men deserted from the Spanish to the British side in the hope of securing their manumission and getting back to Jamaica, where they had come from previously. Like María del Carmen, the woman discussed in the Introduction, they might have sought an opportunity to return to a place where they had family or greater cultural fluency and thus better social and economic prospects. Documents in the Jamaican National Archive mention several similar cases. One enslaved African from Jamaica named Cuffee had reportedly been captured by Spanish privateers in the Bay of Honduras in 1754 and taken to Cuba, where he was sold to a rancher. When the British

SD, 1213; "Relación de los desertores ingleses y franceses que se hallan el el castillo de la Real Fuerza," July 23, 1762, AGI, SD, 1586, no. 200; Jamaica Sessional Papers, Feb. 13, 1763, CO 140.42, TNA.

64. Linda M. Rupert, "Marronage, Manumission, and Maritime Trade in the Early Modern Caribbean," *Slavery and Abolition*, XXX (2009), 361–382; José Luis Belmonte Postigo, "'No siendo lo mismo echarse al mar, que es lugar de libertad plena': Cimarronajo marítimo y política transimperial en el Caribe español, 1687–1804," in Consuelo Naranjo Orovio, ed., *Esclavitud y diferencia racial en el Caribe hispano* (Madrid, 2017), 43–70.

65. Joseph Antonio Gomes to Prado, June 15, 1762, AGI, SD, 1585, no. 46.

ships arrived offshore, he deserted to their side and ended up fighting against the Spanish. As someone who knew the area intimately and spoke both English and Spanish, he was likely a great asset to British commanders, who later rewarded him with passage back to Jamaica and manumission for his service. Other cases include two young creoles of African descent from Jamaica who deserted Cuba by swimming to a British warship on August 1, just before Havana's surrender. That they waited to make their plunge until after the explosion at the Morro suggests that they were less interested in fighting than in securing their freedom and safe passage to Jamaica by changing sides before the siege was over and the opportunity slipped away.[66]

During the chaos of the fighting, enslaved Africans pretended to be someone they were not when it worked to their advantage. Because people of African descent were more likely than their European counterparts to speak multiple languages and to have familiarity with both British and Spanish cultures, they were sometimes able to find advantage by dissembling about who they were during the siege. These people are the least likely to show up in records, but there are a few suggestive examples of individuals who were caught trying this tactic. A Spanish royal slave is recorded as being punished for pretending to be a deserter from the British side in order to benefit from the Spanish policy of freeing the enemy's runaway slaves. One can only speculate about what measures he took to perform "Britishness" for Spanish officials in order to convince them he was from a British colony and desired to convert to Catholicism. If he knew English, this would have been a good opportunity to demonstrate that skill. If he had not been apprehended, of course, he would have left no record.[67]

Another letter provides a glimpse of the possibilities for double-dealing, as well as the eagerness to exploit them, among people of African descent who had literacy with both Spanish and British languages and cultures. A week before the mining of the Morro, a British prisoner of war, an officer who was being held in a convent outside Havana, wrote to the Havana governor that a "mulatto man" had entered the room where he was being held, spoken to him in English, and tried to befriend him and get him to go on a walk with him. Surprised and confused, the native Englishman, who had limited experience in the West Indies and consequently with black people, reported the incident

66. Saint Catherine Vestry Minutes, June 15, 1763, 1761–1769, JNA; Clinton V. Black, *The History of Jamaica* (London, 1983), 65; Marrero, *Cuba*, VI, 120; "Manumission of Slaves," 1760–1765, fol. 174v, JNA.

67. "Lista de los presos que ya juzgados se remiten a la plaza para que hagan el servicio," July 18, 1762, AGI, SD, 1586, no. 176. The man is listed after a number of slaves and referred to as "Sebastián Fuertes que se presentó como desertor agosar del indulto y ser de su Magestad."

to Spanish authorities. The Spanish official promptly had the stranger and his associate, also identified as "mulato," taken prisoner.[68]

Perhaps this man was one of the free black troops from Jamaica, spying on behalf of his commanders behind enemy lines. Or perhaps he was a Jamaican-born man living in Cuba and using his English to vie for some advantage to be gained from the officer. He might have been offering to spy on behalf of the British or trying to ingratiate himself with this officer in case his side was victorious. Or he might have had a simpler motivation, such as seeking to rob the officer of his money or watch. Spanish authorities apprehended and hanged another free black man who had been caught allegedly trying a similar tactic, going back and forth to the enemy's camp and providing them with intelligence. As intriguing as the possibilities may be, it is people like these two men who remain the most obscured by the fog of war.[69]

As the history of European colonialism has often shown, when ruling white populations are split by political or military conflict nonwhite groups gain room for maneuvering. Despite its extreme dangers, the siege of Havana might have been the greatest moment of openness and opportunity for people of African descent in Cuba. In contrast, the end of the fighting and the period of the occupation proved the most advantageous for whites, particularly for people of property, and in many instances it had dire consequences for black combatants. For both whites and blacks, the siege was a time of tremendous danger, but, given their ambiguous legal positioning in the codes of warfare, its end was particularly perilous for individuals of African descent.[70]

Surrendering

The explosion of the mine at the Morro and the British capture of the fort finally brought the Spanish defense of Havana to its effective end. On August 11, twelve days after the mine was detonated and six weeks after the commencement of the siege, Juan de Prado and the junta de guerra made the decision to surrender (see Figure 17). Since the loss of the Morro, the city had been subjected to relentless cannon fire, and they saw themselves as having no other option. In his announcement of the capitulation and the publication of its terms, Prado described his decision according to the laws of warfare

---

68. Edward Barron to Prado, July 23, 1762, AGI, SD, 1586, no. 198.

69. "Diario del Don Juan de Casta," 1762, July 8, 1762, Theodorus Bailey Meyers Collection, NYPL.

70. The chief example of this phenomenon is the Haitian Revolution. For examples of studies of the Haitian Revolution that discuss this dynamic, see Laurent Dubois, *Avengers of the New World: The Story of the Haitian Revolution* (Cambridge, Mass., 2004); and Franklin W. Knight, "The Haitian Revolution," *American Historical Review*, CV (2000), 103–115.

FIGURE 17 "The Grand Attack of That City and Punto Castle between the Hours of 5 and 10 in the Morning of August 13, 1762, When a Flag of Truce Was Hoisted on the Governor's Fort and on Board the Spanish Admiral." Engraving by Pierre Canot and Thomas Mason, based on an original sketch by Lieutenant Philip Orsbridge and a painting by Dominic Serres. Courtesy, Anne S.K. Brown Military History Collection, Brown University Library

and the "considerations of humanity." Like other articles of capitulation in the Seven Years' War, the negotiated terms were generally favorable to the newly surrendered population. As Albemarle's "Spanish Manifesto" had promised, the terms of capitulation protected Havana residents' freedom of religion and security of property. According to the articles of capitulation, the city council and the legal system would continue to operate, and traditional rights and privileges, or *fueros*, of Spain's subjects in Cuba would be protected. Should any residents of Havana wish to depart the British-occupied territory and relocate themselves and their families to another part of Spanish America or Spain, the capitulation guaranteed their right to purchase ships, sell their property, and receive safe passage elsewhere.[71]

71. Prado to Madariaga, Aug. 11, 1762, AGI, Ultramar, 169, no. 41; Prado to the City of Havana, Aug. 12, 1762, AGI, SD, 1585, no. 475 ("considerations of humanity"). For the articles of capitulation, see "Capitulación original representada por Don Juan de Prado," in *Proceso formado de orden*

When the military commanders leading the defense heard the news of the capitulation, many of them felt betrayed. According to one Spanish naval officer, "It's very certain that the Generals, city council, and wealthy men of this Plaza desired the capitulation in order to look after their riches." To them, the junta de guerra's decision seemed to be in keeping with its reluctance throughout the siege to prosecute the battle to its fullest extent, for Prado and the junta had repeatedly denied requests from soldiers and their commanders to authorize further counterattacks. Now, although the option had been discussed and they had ample time to carry it out, Prado and the members of the junta de guerra did not pursue the alternatives of evacuating the city, removing the king's treasure, or burning the fleet in Havana's harbor before surrendering.[72]

From outside Havana's city walls, Madariaga, who had led militia forces that provisioned the city and protected its flank, strongly advocated that they continue fighting. Why surrender? Why not instead retreat, remove the royal treasury, and regroup? They could abandon the plaza and, with or without gunpowder, continue to defend the island through hand-to-hand combat. According to Prado, the junta applauded the gallantry of this idea but pointed out the many complications in its execution. Instead, as they put it, they chose to abide by the regular rules of warfare governing the defenses and surrenders of plazas. When Madariaga received his first news of the official capitulation, he tore the letter to pieces. Meanwhile, inside the plaza, Prado and the junta were preparing for the formal handover of power.[73]

As part of the capitulation agreement for the entire jurisdiction of Havana, Prado ordered all the military men involved in the defense to come into the city and put down their arms. This order would later prove a sticking point in his treason trial upon his return to Madrid, as he had commanded Madariaga to march into the city rather than remove himself, his men, and munitions for a continuing defense of the rest of the island or a potential counterattack. By the terms of the capitulation, all those soldiers and sailors from Spain who were not too sick to travel would return there immediately on British transports. Militia troops were ordered to put down their guns and return home.

The capitulation accords left in limbo those enslaved men who had fought for their freedom on the Spanish side, as the sovereign in whose name they

---

del Rey Nuestro Señor por la Junta de Generales, I, BNE; Roig de Leuchsenring, ed., La dominación inglesa, 60–66.

72. Olañeta, "Diario del sitio," Aug. 11, 1762, Miscellaneous Manuscripts, MS 352, XV, box 83, folder 1662, Sterling Memorial Library.

73. "Cartas originales de Don Juan de Prado a Don Juan Ignacio Madariaga," Aug. 12, 1762, in Proceso formado de orden del Rey Nuestro Señor por la Junta de Generales, I, 21–22, BNE.

had been promised manumission no longer held jurisdiction over western Cuba. British seizure of Havana called into question whether the long-
standing rights of African subjects in a city where they constituted at least half
the population would continue there as before. There were no guarantees that
this was the case. In fact, all signs indicated otherwise. Albemarle had already
begun to court the propertied Havana vecinos, from the moment he began to
send his "Spanish manifestoes" into the city, but no overtures or accommodations were made to free people of color, let alone enslaved Africans. The
articles of capitulation made no mention of the rights or status of free people
of color on the island or enslaved Africans who had been promised their freedom in return for military service. In the articles of capitulation for the French
islands of Martinique and Guadeloupe, which were otherwise very similar to
those for Havana, enslaved individuals who had defended the islands in exchange for the promise of their freedom were to be set free, though required
to leave the island. A further proviso stated that no free blacks captured by
the British could be enslaved. Lord Albemarle, however, took a more hostile
stance to a population that had proven both difficult to control and Havana's
most dangerous defenders. For the blacks of Havana, after the extreme length
and bitterness of the siege and because so many black soldiers had captured
and killed British ones, there were no such guarantees.[74]

Once the siege was over, the British went to work accounting for the many
Spanish blacks whom they had taken prisoner or who had deserted to their
side during the hostilities. An orderly book describes how all those "Spanish negroes" in the possession of the British forces two weeks after the capitulation were to be sold back to Havana residents, with British officers to
be granted rights of first refusal on their purchase. Upon the signing of the
articles of capitulation, the Spanish king's large numbers of royal slaves were
immediately confiscated as part of the seizure of the king's property for the
division of booty.[75]

Along with white militiamen, some black veterans of the siege chose to retreat to other parts of the island, preparing for a potential defense against a
British advance or an offensive into British Havana that never materialized.
At the end of the siege, many people of African descent, both enslaved and
free, ran away from Havana to the island's interior, creating a second wave of

74. See Marshall Smelser, *The Campaign for the Sugar Islands, 1759: A Study of Amphibious Warfare* (Chapel Hill, N.C., 1955), 98, 139–141; "Articles of Capitulation between Their Excellencies and
the Inhabitants of Guadeloupe," in Thomas Mante, *The History of the Late War in North-America and
the Islands of the West-Indies . . .* (London, 1772), Article 9, 196.

75. "Orderly Book of the Havana Expedition," Sept. 1, 1762, in *The Two Putnams*, 66–67; 14th
Article of Capitulation, in Roig de Leuchsenring, ed., *La dominación inglesa*, 64.

refugees much like the one at the start of hostilities. Their flight was driven by fear, triggered by the murders of those at the Morro and rumors of reprisals as well as by the very real dangers—like rape and (re)enslavement by an enemy army—that they faced in the extralegal zone they now occupied.[76]

Conclusion

In fending off the occupation for sixty-five days, the defenders of Havana had performed extraordinarily well. Because of their resistance, Lord Albemarle had to blow up a sixteenth-century fort and lose half his army in order to emerge victorious. As evidenced by the state of Albemarle's troops when the siege was over, the Spanish could have defeated the British if they had had a few more days to do so. Disease and resistance had drastically reduced the British expeditionary forces by the time they set off the mine at the Morro, and, if they had not taken that extraordinary measure, they would not have won the battle. Even after British forces exploded the mine, they struggled to take the fort.

A British officer in Havana, sick with yellow fever, writing to his father two months after the surrender, provided a fitting summary of the campaign. Reflecting on how much the expedition had misjudged the strength of the prize they sought, he wrote, "We flattered ourselves we should have a most easy conquest . . . but in this we were not a little mistaken." The officer described the expedition's great losses from "the obstinate defense of the enemy, by which we had a great number killed and wounded, but likewise from the malignancy of the climate," by which he meant the disease. As he reasoned, the key to their success had been how little the Spanish commanders seemed to know of their desperate straits during the final stages of the siege and the surety that they would have had to withdraw if the Spanish had held on a few days longer. "Lucky for us," he concluded, "they did not know our situation."[77]

Because the siege went on so long, the effect of yellow fever on Albemarle's troops was staggering. More British forces had died in the Havana campaign than the entire Seven Years' War in North America. Even Spanish military officers commented on the ruin visited on the British forces by disease. When the

---

76. Roig de Leuchsenring, ed., *La dominación inglesa*, 114, 119; Olañeta, "Diario del sitio," July 31, 1762, Miscellaneous Manuscripts, MS 352, XV, box 83, folder 1662, Sterling Memorial Library. The town council of Santa Clara reported that one month after the surrender they were quartering 320 veterans from the fighting who had fled after the capitulation, half of whom are identified in their records as white and half as black; see "Acta de cabildo de la villa de Santa Clara para organizar la defensa de la invasión inglesa en el año de 1762," C.M. Pérez, BNJM.

77. Francis Browne ALS to Jeremiah Browne, Oct. 26, 1762, Richard and Francis Browne Papers, Clements Library.

fighting commenced, Albemarle had reported having 11,576 soldiers healthy and fit for duty. Directly after the capitulation, a British report counted 279 troops killed in battle, 601 wounded, 52 dead from wounds, and 657 dead from sickness, for a total of 988 dead and 601 wounded since the army had landed in Cuba. Even more dramatic, two months after the capitulation Albemarle had only 2,067 men still healthy and able to perform their duty. The latest British report we have from Havana, dated October 1762, lists 4,708 dead of disease.[78]

Without the late arrival of the North American troops, Albemarle's expedition would not have been able to hold out long enough to capture Havana or to hold it after its capitulation. The North Americans did not take part in the assault on the Morro, but their arrival extended the time window available to Lord Albemarle to prosecute the siege. Ironically, as soon as they arrived, they began to fall sick from yellow fever, and their losses were proportionally the greatest of all those there. On September 29, Albemarle wrote to the Duke of Newcastle, "My Army is so reduced by sickness, and the well so unfit for almost any service, that, if the governor had been firm, he might have named his own terms." For future attempts against Havana or other Spanish ports in the Caribbean, he advised calculating that "half your force" would fall sick. "It is not to be described," he wrote, "what we have all gone thro."[79]

Prior experiences at Cartagena and Guantánamo had warned the British to expect great losses to yellow fever, but they had underestimated the crucial role that Cuba's militias and enslaved Africans would play against them, prolonging the siege long enough for the disease to work its devastating course. They had made their careful calculations for battle plans and sufficient troop numbers to take Havana based on an understanding of how many soldiers and sailors were stationed there, failing to recognize the extra forces that would be mobilized against them. Although they likely no longer imagined that the enslaved Africans of the Spanish would rise in rebellion against their owners, they certainly did not foresee the skillful opposition blacks would pose on the front lines in the defense of Havana. As it turned out, Cuba's population of African descent represented a great strength, rather than a weakness, of Spanish colonialism.

78. McNeill, *Mosquito Empires*, 185; Auditor de Guerra Don Martín de Ulloa to Don Lorenzo Bregues, Aug. 29, 1762, AGI, SD, 1585, no. 503; "Abstract of the General Return of His Majesty's Forces under the Command of Lieutenant-General Lord Albemarle," May 23, 1762, in Syrett, ed., *Siege and Capture of Havana*, 126; "Return of the Killed, Wounded, and Missing since the Army Landed on the Island of Cuba" and "List of the Killed, Missing, and Wounded," CO 117.1, fols. 81, 107, TNA; Charters, "The Caring Fiscal-Military State," *Historical Journal*, LII (2009), 933; "General State of British Forces Fit for Duty on 7 June (total 11,576) and 18 October (total 2,067)," CO 117.1, fols. 157–158.

79. Albemarle to Newcastle, Sept. 29, 1762, in Blanck, ed., *Papeles sobre la toma de la Habana*, 195.

People of African descent were thus able to shape the outcome of this clash between Britain and Spain. They made the capture of Havana so difficult that the British almost failed, and their forces lost thousands more men to yellow fever than they might have otherwise. The responses of people of African descent in Cuba to the conditions of the siege were as diverse as the many different positions they occupied in the island's social worlds, and their actions were certainly not always taken in support of the Spanish king. Yet black resistance to the British attack made the victory a Pyrrhic one for Britain and severely restricted Albemarle's ability to gain a larger foothold on the island or to use Havana as a base for further expeditions.

Although the battle ended in defeat for Spain, through their actions people of African descent in Havana had made a powerful argument for their strategic military importance to the persistence of Spanish colonialism. In contrast to the white Havana elites, many enslaved and free people of color had proved themselves willing and proficient soldiers in the face of British attack. For commanders on both sides of the conflict, one of the most compelling lessons of the siege was the great strategic importance of people of African descent in Caribbean siege warfare. The Spanish, in particular, learned the need for more Africans and their descendants in Cuba and the danger of relying on their British enemies to supply them.

In the following days, weeks, and months, as Havana transitioned from siege to occupation, the military sectors retreated or left the island, and the commercial sectors came to the fore. Havana's elites had a different set of relationships with the British invaders from those of enslaved and free people of color, although they were also woven around the slave trade. The nature of these relations would become one of the most salient issues to emerge during Havana's occupation. The reactions of both groups to the outcome of the siege were quite different. The siege, despite its dangers, presented the greatest moment of opportunity for people of African descent in Cuba, while the occupation of Havana would strand them in a perilous extralegal zone either within the city or in other areas of the island where they had retreated. The occupation would prove most advantageous for Havana's commercial classes and wealthiest residents and would offer its own lessons for authorities in Spain.

4

• • •

"La dominación inglesa"

Eleven Months of British Rule

When the merchant, rancher, and slave trader Juan de Miralles first saw the massive British war fleet bearing down on his city in June 1762, he was already expecting it. Miralles was at sea, returning home to Havana after a year-long slave-trading mission, when a British frigate intercepted his vessel off the north coast of Cuba and brought him into the presence of Lord Albemarle on his warship offshore Havana. Miralles—born in Spain of a French family but long married and settled in Cuba—had been sent on a special commission by Governor Juan de Prado the year before to procure more shipments of enslaved Africans for the island from foreign colonies. The governor hoped to use these laborers to complete the urgent project, now rendered especially so, of repairing the fortifications at the Cabaña.[1]

On Miralles's travels, which had taken him to Jamaica, Barbados, Amsterdam, London, Saint Eustatius, and Martinique, he sought to purchase enough enslaved Africans to complete the governor's request and make a sizable profit in Havana's market. Before these journeys, he had lived in Kingston, Jamaica, for almost a year as a slave-trading agent for the Royal Havana Company. During his time in London, Miralles had heard word of the forces assembling for an attack against his city. On his way home to Havana, while sailing from Barbados to British-occupied Martinique, he had run across them preparing to depart for Cuba. When his captors delivered him to Lord Albemarle, British troops were beginning their landing at Cojímar.[2]

---

1. "No. 474: Relación simple de la comissión dada a Don Juan de Miralles para la negociación, y compra de negros en las colonias estrangeras" and "Carta de Don Juan de Miralles, escrita al gobernador de La Habana desde la isla de San Eustacio en 26 de abril de 1762," both in *Proceso formado por orden del Rey Nuestro Señor por la Junta de Generales que S.M. se ha dignado de nombrar a este fin sobre la conducta que tuvieron en la defensa, capitulación, pérdida, y rendición de la plaza de La Habana, y esquadra, que se hallaba en su puerto el Mariscal de Campo Juan de Prado . . . ," 2 vols. (Madrid, 1763–1764), I, BNE.

2. "No. 474: Relación simple de la comissión dada a Don Juan de Miralles," and "Carta de Don Juan de Miralles," both in *Proceso formado de orden del Rey Nuestro Señor por la Junta de Generales,*

Although the extent of Miralles's journey was exceptional among Havana's leading men of commerce, his complex positioning between British and Spanish colonies was not. Enslaved African men, women, and children moved between British and Spanish territories because smugglers, merchants, large landholders, and slave traders like Miralles did so, too, in pursuit of their purchase and sale. Officials in Spain would later deem the governor's decision to send Miralles abroad on this mission and his subsequent travels as "reprehensible conduct," but they reflected the frequency and eagerness with which the island's men of commerce engaged in transimperial trade, especially in slaves, often with the blessing of local authorities. A regular intermediary between Spanish and British territories, Miralles was a man whose very livelihood derived from connecting the commerce of Cuba with the British traders who then dominated the slave trade. Now that British forces had suddenly descended upon Havana and Miralles was meeting with Lord Albemarle on his warship offshore he would seem to be caught between sides.[3]

From what the sources tell us, though, Miralles successfully passed into Havana during the British siege and waited out the fighting safely like other men of his status. To do so, he leveraged his familiarity with both sides to play them off against each other, much like people of African descent who engaged in double-dealing during the siege. Miralles managed to persuade Lord Albemarle to allow him back into Havana in the midst of the fighting, on June 19 under a flag of truce, as a potential spy for the British. A Spanish naval captain inside the city witnessed the arrival of Miralles with suspicion, as he stepped ashore with his trunk of clothes, in his flashy suit and gold buckles. Governor Prado, nevertheless, trusted this prominent resident of Havana and agreed to imprison him on a boat in Havana's harbor, upon Miralles's own suggestion, so that he should have an excuse for not spying should the British invasion succeed and the enemy find him again in the plaza.[4]

Miralles was joined in his confinement by one of eight other merchants

I, BNE; Royal Havana Company Account Book, 1751–1758, Baker Business Library, Harvard University, Cambridge, Mass.; George Keppel to George Pocock, June 10, 1762, in David Syrett, ed., *The Siege and Capture of Havana, 1762* (London, 1970), 179–180.

3. "No. 474: Relación simple de la comissión dada a Don Juan de Miralles," and "Carta de Don Juan de Miralles," in *Proceso formado de orden del Rey Nuestro Señor por la Junta de Generales*, I, BNE; "Relación de los servicios de Don Juan de Miralles, vecino de la ciudad de La Habana," Dec. 4, 1763, AGI, SD, 1458.

4. Pedro Manuel de Olañeta, "Diario del sitio y rendición de la plaza de La Habana al Ingles," June 18, 1762, Miscellaneous Manuscripts, MS 352, XV, box 83, folder 1662, Sterling Memorial Library, Yale University; "Diario del Capitán Don Juan de Casta del sitio de la ciudad de Havana," 1762, Theodorus Bailey Meyers Collection, fol. 8, NYPL; "Diario del manuscrito de Madrid," July 17–18, 1762, in Amalia A. Rodríguez, ed., *Cinco diarios del sitio de La Habana* (Havana, 1963), 25; Juan de Prado to Juan Ignacio de Madariaga, June 19, 1762, AGI, Ultramar, 169.

who elicited suspicion during the siege: Pedro de Estrada, fellow rancher, slave trader, and former agent of the Royal Havana Company, who had also lived in Kingston. Accusations of spying are hard to verify, but these men's familiarity with the British enemy was undeniable. From the boat in the harbor, Miralles was able to inform the *junta de guerra* of the favorable terms of surrender on offer from Lord Albemarle as well as the commercial opportunities of British occupation, which he had witnessed firsthand in Martinique. As he waited out the siege, he must have been eager for it to end and to begin trading with the merchant ships that were already beginning to gather offshore.[5]

Once the danger and violence of the siege had ended, Havana's largest land- and slaveholders were poised to exploit the occupation as an opportunity to continue building ties to British Atlantic economies and expanding their access to enslaved Africans, just as they had in prior decades. From the point of view of those in Havana, the occupation presented, not a radical rupture, but instead the intensification of trading relations already in place. Compared to other British occupations of the Seven Years' War—such as Manila, Martinique, Guadeloupe, and Grenada—Havana stands out for the speed and surprising ease with which the city pivoted from a protracted and fiercely contested siege, the cause of tremendous loss of life and destruction, to a surprisingly smooth and harmonious occupation. What made the transition from Spanish to British rule run smoothly, despite the unmatched ravages of the British campaign for Havana, was a set of deep interimperial connections centered on the slave trade. These connections reflected the modus operandi of the island's elites developed over the previous decades and their commercial ambitions going forward. As the campaign ended, British warships returned Spain's military forces to Iberia, while Havana's wealthiest residents came back to the city from their rural estates or left their shipboard confinement in Havana's harbor to reclaim positions of prominence in social, political, and economic life. Free to pursue their commercial interests, many of these men betrayed not only their monarch but also their fellow subjects who had struggled the hardest—and lost their lives—defending the island from British attack.[6]

5. "Diario del manuscrito de Madrid," July 9–14, 1762, in Rodríguez, ed., *Cinco diarios*, 32–33. See also "Diario del Capitán Don Juan de Casta," July 10, 1762, Theodorus Bailey Meyers Collection, fol. 12, NYPL; Olañeta, "Diario del sitio," July 18, 1762, Miscellaneous Manuscripts, MS 352, XV, box 83, folder 1662, Sterling Memorial Library. On the fickleness of merchant "loyalty" during the Seven Years' War and generally during the eighteenth century in New York City, see Thomas M. Truxes, *Defying Empire: Trading with the Enemy in Colonial New York* (New Haven, Conn., 2008); and Cathy Matson, *Merchants and Empire: Trading in Colonial New York* (Baltimore, 1998).

6. On the invasions and occupations of Martinique and Guadeloupe, see Marshall Smelser, *The Campaign for the Sugar Islands, 1759: A Study of Amphibious Warfare* (Chapel Hill, N.C., 1955);

During the period when British forces exerted political control over Havana, the city continued as a hybrid space operating between empires, a zone of "layered sovereignty" that was in this regard similar to the period of Spanish rule over Havana. Tellingly, residents of Havana referred to the period of British rule as the time of "British dominion" (*"la dominación inglesa,"* or *"británica"*), a term they applied to contrast with the prelude and postlude to British rule, which they called *"la dominación española."* In British Havana, elites were willing to submit to British rule and even help enforce it themselves because they sought to maximize their economic opportunities in the space they occupied—and had for some time—between layers of British and Spanish sovereignty. Before the occupation, Havana's leading residents enjoyed the benefits of Spanish governance, even while they grew rich through slave trading, contraband, and privateering with the British commercial system. In British Havana, they sought to continue to exploit access to both British traders and Spanish American territories and markets. Essentially, they continued to want it both ways and, in many respects, got precisely that, gaining advantage through overlapping Spanish and British political, commercial, and legal systems.[7]

Like colonialism itself, an occupation is a "negotiated system" involving multiple actors both near and far from the territory in question and in pursuit of diverse and often opposing ends. Just as the expedition that made it possible represented a remarkable convergence of bodies and materials from all over the Atlantic world, the forces that shaped the occupation and the impacts and meanings it would have moved throughout this broader system. Havana's capture had unusually strong resonance throughout the Atlantic world and reactivated the imaginary of a British and British American public that had long desired its acquisition. Those farthest from Havana—the British, French, and Spanish negotiators seeking to hammer out a peace agreement that would

---

Anderson, *Crucible of War*, 308–309, 312–315, 490; and Richard Pares, *War and Trade in the West Indies, 1739–1763* (London, 1936), 186–226. For the literature on twentieth- and twenty-first-century occupations, which tend to be more authoritarian, see, for example, Adam Roberts, "Transformative Military Occupation: Applying the Laws of War and Human Rights," *American Journal of International Law*, C (2006), 580–622; David M. Edelstein, "Occupation Hazards: Why Military Occupations Succeed or Fail," *International Security*, XXIX, no. 1 (Summer 2004), 49–91; Robert O. Paxton, *Vichy France: Old Guard and New Order, 1940–1944* (New York, 1972); Paul A. Kramer, *The Blood of Government: Race, Empire, the United States, and the Philippines* (Chapel Hill, N.C., 2006); Mary A. Renda, *Taking Haiti: Military Occupation and the Culture of U.S. Imperialism, 1915–1940* (Chapel Hill, N.C., 2001); and Alan McPherson, *The Invaded: How Latin Americans and Their Allies Fought and Ended U.S. Occupations* (Oxford, 2014).

7. See, for example, AGI, SD, 1156, 1157, 1212, and 1213. On the concept of "layered sovereignty," see Lauren Benton, *A Search for Sovereignty: Law and Geography in European Empires, 1400–1900* (New York, 2010), 31–32.

end the Seven Years' War—would determine the ultimate disposition of territory. While the peace negotiators worked, though, British and British American merchants made their way to Havana, and ordinary Britons schemed and dreamed about its annexation. Meanwhile, those groups present in the occupied city—British Havana's governor Lord Albemarle, local residents, and the British and British American merchants they traded with—would vie with one another in their own competition to determine the possibilities the British occupation presented.[8]

Just eleven months long, the period of British occupation was far too short to have the transformative impact on Cuba's economy and society for which it has been given credit. As Lord Albemarle soon learned, retaining Havana and consolidating control over any territory outside its walls was more difficult than anticipated by all those who had plotted the island's easy capture. The siege had cost too much, and ongoing armed resistance from Cuba's multiracial militias and black veterans of the siege disturbed British rule, as did the fiery opposition of Havana's leading religious figure, Bishop Pedro Agustín Morell de Santa Cruz. If it had not been for the compliance of Havana's elites, Albemarle and his successor, his brother William Keppel, would never have been able to govern Havana for the brief time that it flew the Union Jack. To a remarkable degree, Albemarle and Keppel were able to rely on the Havana elite, who wanted more goods and enslaved Africans, just as the elites in neighboring colonies did. Not everything during the occupation went as Havana's most prominent residents might have liked. In terms of the sale of enslaved Africans, the self-aggrandizing policies of British governor Lord Albemarle made Havana a less freely trading zone than it had been before. Yet, like Juan de Miralles, Havana's most prominent residents successfully played two political and economic systems off against each other during the occupation of their city. Drawing upon existing commercial relationships, Havana's wealthiest residents were able to shape the occupation in pursuit of longer-term goals they imagined for themselves and the future of their island.[9]

8. Erik Hinderaker, *Elusive Empires: Constructing Colonialism in the Ohio Valley, 1673–1800* (Cambridge, 1997), xi. Mary Renda also argues for military occupation having broad-ranging impacts beyond the site where it takes place; see Renda, *Taking Haiti*, 11.

9. Historians of Britain and British America have argued for the large impact of the British occupation on Havana and, in particular, its economy. "British rule . . . served as an intellectual stimulus" toward commerce and freer trade; see Syrett, "Introduction," in Syrett, ed., *Siege and Capture of Havana*, xxxiv. "The occupation brought prosperity to Cuba"; see Fred Anderson, *Crucible of War: The Seven Years' War and the Fate of Empire in British North America, 1754–1766* (New York, 2000), 502. Havana "blossomed" under British rule; see Daniel Baugh, *The Global Seven Years' War, 1754–1763: Britain and France in a Great Power Contest* (Harlow, U.K., 2011), 648. An earlier generation of Cuban historians shared a similar interpretation. Herminio Portell Vilá, for example, argued that "la ocupación británica cambió el rumbo de la evolución de Cuba, y en especial de La Habana, por

A Great Prize at Last

The reaction to the news of Havana's capture in the British territories of the Atlantic world was jubilant — as though the frustration pent up since the failed attempts on Havana during the War of Jenkins' Ear had finally been released. Even after the capture of Quebec and French-controlled territories in the Mediterranean, West Africa, the West Indies, and India, this conquest stood out as a tremendous, long-desired achievement late in a wearying, drawn-out war. When word of the victory reached London on September 27, the Tower guns were discharged, fireworks and bonfires staged, and balls held. The flag captured from the Morro fortress was ceremonially presented to George III and remains in private hands in Britain to this day. Rapturous pronouncements in the press deemed the victory a mark of divine providence and perhaps the greatest achievement "in the British Annals." Many counties and cities in Britain delivered addresses of praise and thanksgiving to their king, doubly congratulating him on the conquest of Havana and the birth of his son the Prince of Wales, events which, providentially, occurred just one day apart. In the British West Indies as well, the governor and Assembly of Jamaica delivered speeches of praise upon receipt of the news, and the merchants of Jamaica wrote a letter of thanks to Admiral George Pocock.[10]

Newspapers had been following events in Cuba closely throughout the summer of 1762, and, when news of the surrender arrived in British and British American ports that fall, a profusion of accounts and memorabilia followed (see Figures 18, 19 [Plate 9], and 20). As had occurred after the capture of Portobelo during the War of Jenkins' Ear, ordinary Britons purchased artifacts that enabled them to participate in a shared political culture celebrating this

---

el camino del progreso"; see Portell Vilá, *Historia de Cuba en sus relaciones con los Estados Unidos y España*, I (*1515–1853*) (Havana, 1952), 59. Manuel Moreno Fraginals later argued that the British occupation was the impetus to Cuba's sugar boom; see Moreno Fraginals, *El ingenio: Complejo económico social cubano del azúcar* (Barcelona, 2001), 15–25. More recently, other historians of Cuba have argued for the lesser impact of this "ephemeral" occupation; see Celía María Parcero Torre, *La pérdida de La Habana y las reformas borbónicas en Cuba (1760–1773)* (Valladolid, Spain, 1998), 157–171 (quotation on 171).

10. Nelson Vance Russell, "The Reaction in England and America to the Capture of Havana, 1762," *HAHR*, IX (1929), 303–316, esp. 303–304; *Newport Mercury* (R.I.), Sept. 14, 1762, [1]; *London Evening-Post*, Sept. 30–Oct. 2, 1762, [4], Nov. 18–20, 1762, Nov. 27–30, 1762, and Dec., 7–9, 1762; *London Chronicle: or, Universal Advertiser*, Oct. 5–7, 1762, [3], [7]; *St. James's Chronicle, or, The British Evening-Post*, Oct. 19–21, 1762, Oct. 30–Nov. 2, 1762, Nov. 6–9, 1762; *London Gazette*, Nov. 2–6, 1762, Nov. 9–13, 1762, Nov. 16–20, 1762, and Nov. 23–27, 1762; *Lloyd's Evening Post, and British Chronicle* (London), Nov. 15–17, 1762; Announcement of the Victory at Havana and Response of the Assembly, House of Assembly Journals, Sept. 28, 30, 1763, JNA; Address of the Jamaican Council, Oct. 7, 1762, CO 137.32, fol. 218, TNA; Jamaica Merchants to Pocock, Sept. 17, 1762, in Russell, "The Reaction in England and America," *HAHR*, IX (1929), 315.

FIGURE 18 Havana Toasting Glass. A toasting glass adorned with a palm tree to commemorate the day of Havana's capitulation, August 12, which was declared a very good day to toast. © National Maritime Museum, Greenwich, London

successful imperial campaign. Within days of the news arriving in London, an officer's journal of the siege was published, followed by maps, descriptions of the island, and songs that were written and reproduced for sale. Magazines released special editions, and commemorative coins and prints were issued, prints that would soon be decorating homes in both Britain and its territories in the Atlantic world. Expectations were high about the windfall Havana's capture would provide plus the long-term benefits it would offer to the British empire.[11]

In British North America, the reaction was especially enthusiastic despite the tremendous loss of life sustained by provincial volunteers. The news was met with joyous celebration and religious sermons inspiring great expectations and providential interpretations about what Havana's capture, at long last, por-

11. Kathleen Wilson, "Empire, Trade, and Popular Politics in Mid-Hanoverian Britain: The Case of Admiral Vernon," *Past and Present*, no. 121 (November 1988), 74–109; J. M. Mancini, "Siege Mentalities: Objects in Motion, British Imperial Expansion, and the Pacific Turn," *Winterthur Portfolio*, XLV (2011), 125–140, esp. 135. For the journal of the siege, see classified advertisements, *London Chronicle; or, Universal Evening Post*, Oct. 2–5, 1762, [4]. For songs for sale, see classified advertisements, *Newport Mercury*, Sept. 14, 1762, [3]; and John Wignell, *A Collection of Original Pieces; Consisting of Poems, Prologues, Epilogues, Songs, Epistles, Epigrams, Epitaphs . . .* (London, 1762), including "A Song, Written on the Reduction of the Havannah; Intended to Be Sung in the Character of a Sailor," 165–167, and "An Ode, on the Same Glorious Occasion," 167–170; Philip Orsbridge, *These Historical Views of ye Glorious Expedition of His Britannick Majesty's Ships and Forces against Havana, under the Command of Sir George Pocock, the Rt. Honorable Lord Albemarle, and Rear Admiral Keppel; These Views Were Taken on the Spot by an Officer in His Majesty's Navy* (London, 1763). See also *Grabados de Dominique Serres sobre la toma de La Habana en 1762* (Havana, 1962).

FIGURE 19 "His Majesty's Land Forces Going in Flat Boats to Take Possession of the North Gate of the City and Punto Castle, on the 14th of August." Engraving by Pierre Canot and Thomas Mason, based on an original sketch by Lieutenant Philip Orsbridge and a painting by Dominic Serres. This engraving was part of a series of twelve sold as a full set in London in 1765 (see also Figures 13, 14, and 17). Note the British flag flying over the Morro. The Spanish flag captured at the fort is currently held by a private collector in Britain. Courtesy, Anne S.K. Brown Military History Collection, Brown University Library

tended. Benjamin Franklin in Philadelphia rued the tremendous costs of the campaign but also noted that it was "indeed a Conquest of great Importance." In the southernmost of the thirteen colonies, the capture of western Cuba meant release from the thrall of Havana's privateers and the threat of Spanish attack. Governor Arthur Dobbs of North Carolina, addressing the colony's upper house, declared the victory "a Manifestation of Divine Providence in favour of the Protestant Apostolick Religion and the cause of Liberty."[12]

12. J. R. McNeill, *Mosquito Empires: Ecology and War in the Greater Caribbean, 1620–1914* (New York, 2010), 186; Benjamin Franklin to William Strahan, Dec. 7, 1762, in Leonard W. Labaree et al., eds., *The Papers of Benjamin Franklin*, X (New Haven, Conn., 1966), 168 ("of great Importance"); William L. Saunders, ed., *The Colonial Records of North Carolina*, VI (Raleigh, N.C., 1888), 838; Russell, "The Reaction in England and America," *HAHR*, IX (1929), 313–314.

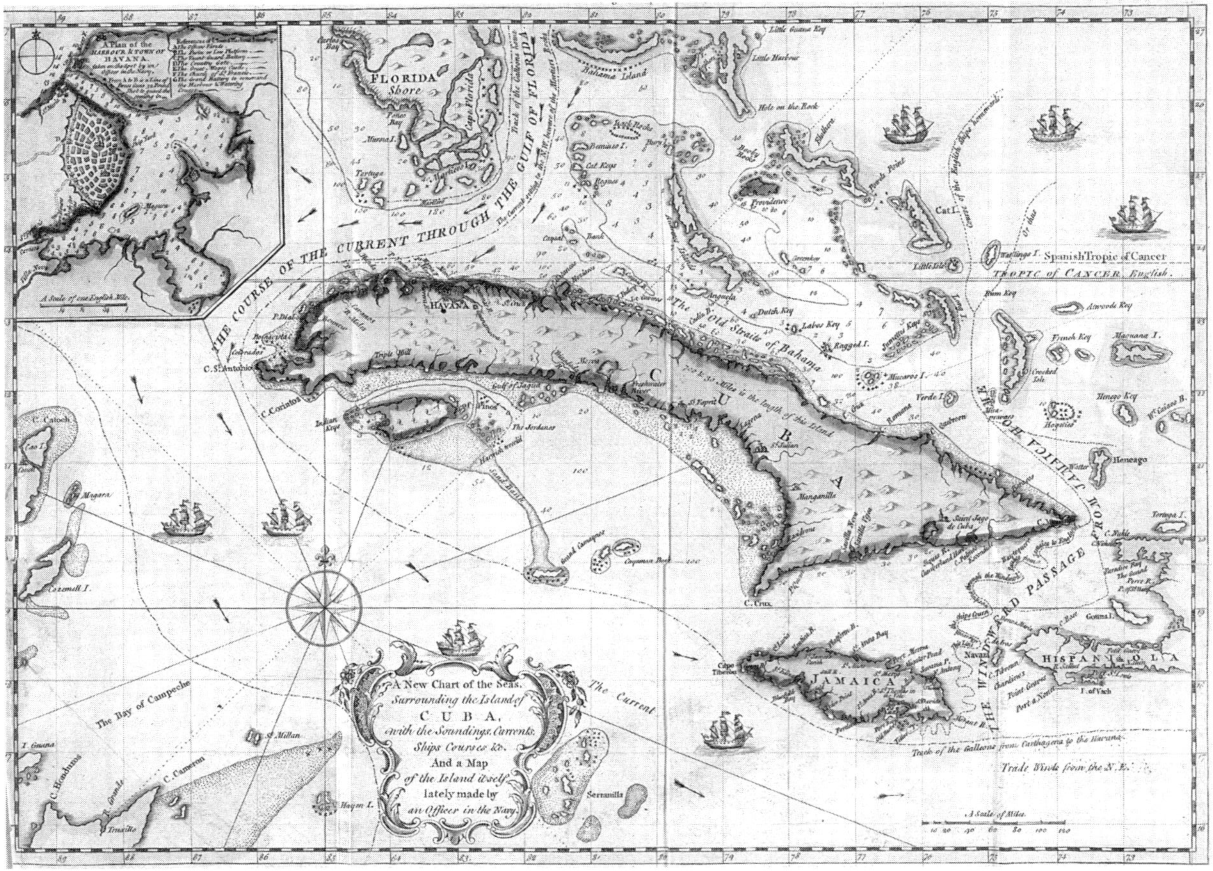

FIGURE 20
"A New Chart of the Seas Surrounding the Island of Cuba with the Surroundings, Currents, Ship Courses, etc. and a Map of the Island Itself Lately Made by an Officer in the Navy." From *London Magazine, or, Gentlemen's Monthly Intelligencer*, XXXI (1762), 520. Courtesy of the Bancroft Library, University of California, Berkeley

Protestant ministers in Boston and New York shared this interpretation. They touted victory as redemption for prior failed attempts and believed it was filled with providential meaning for the future of British imperial expansion—or, as they saw it, liberty's advance. In a sermon of thanksgiving in New York, Joseph Treat rejoiced that Havana's "gloomy sons" had been "subdued into liberty" and "become the chearful subjects of George the friend of man." Even more, "We have opened an avenue," he declared, "into the inexhaustible mines of Mexico and Peru." Rather than see Havana as a prize taken to hasten the peace, soon to be returned to Spain, Treat and his fellow men of the cloth declared its annexation as both a fait accompli and a stepping-stone to greater conquests, all part of God's plan for Britannia.[13]

In these celebrations, all the old tropes evident during the War of Jenkins' Ear were revived, as though no time had passed since the last plots against Havana. Indeed, the capture of the city reactivated a powerful strand of the British imaginary that had mostly lain dormant since the last war. In a sermon in Shrewsbury, Massachusetts, Samuel Frink evoked the old prophesy of Major Smith that Englishmen would walk Havana's streets one day. In Boston and London, George Cockings released a new and updated edition of his epic poem on the Seven Years' War, in which the seizure of the Morro was described as fitting retribution for Hernán Cortés's capture of Tenochtitlan. In an analogy casting the "dreadful, conq'ring troops of Britain" as triumphant conquistadors, the author described the Spanish soldiers diving into the water to escape the British storming of the Morro as vengeance for the Aztecs who were forced to throw themselves into Lake Tenochtitlan upon Cortés's bloody conquest. At long last, in this view, the British conqueror had redeemed the conquered.[14]

Historians have pointed out that the West India interest of absentee planters in British Parliament opposed turning Cuba into a British territory because they feared gaining a rival sugar producer. Commercial sectors in Britain, British North America, and the British West Indies, however, reacted enthusiastically to the possibilities opened up by Havana's capture. Mercan-

13. Joseph Treat, *A Thanksgiving Sermon, Occasion'd by the Glorious News of the Reduction of the Havannah* (New York, 1762), 9; Joseph Sewall, *A Sermon Preached at the Thursday-Lecture in Boston, September 16, 1762 before the Great and General Court of the Province of the Massachusetts-Bay, in New-England on the Joyful News of the Reduction of the Havannah* (Boston, 1762); Samuel Frink, *The Marvelous Works of Creation and Providence, Illustrated; Being the Substance of a Sermon Preached at the North Precinct in Shrewsbury on Thursday the 7th of October, 1762; a Day of Public Thanksgiving Occasioned by the Reduction of the Havannah* (Boston, 1763).

14. Frink, *Marvelous Works of Creation*, 38. George Cockings, *War: An Heroic Poem, from the Taking of Minorca, by the French; to the Reduction of the Havannah, by the Earl of Albemarle, Sir George Pocock*... (Boston, 1762), 187 n.

tile interests immediately began to lobby that the city be kept, both for its advantage in European balance-of-power politics and its strategic trade value as
a means of breaking British manufactured goods into Havana's market and
perhaps mainland Spanish America as well. At the same time, ordinary Britons
at home and in the Americas let their imaginations run wild with the many different things a British Havana might mean for their prospects. Some dreamed
of gaining a plantation in Cuba or claiming for themselves the fabled wealth of
this imagined El Dorado. In both the British West Indies and North America,
magical thinking predicted that the mines of Spanish America were next.[15]

British and British American merchants lost no time in seeking to capitalize on this attractive Caribbean market for their Atlantic commodities.
Under British occupation, Guadeloupe had provided a windfall to British
slave traders, who sold twenty thousand enslaved Africans there between 1759
and 1763. There was reason to think Havana's vast population and great silver reserves would lead to even greater gains. Havana's appeal as a market for
British and British American goods and enslaved persons was accentuated by
the prospect of inflated wartime prices and the presence of so many British
troops who had just been paid their prize winnings in Spanish silver. Henry
Laurens, Charleston's most prominent slave trader, speculated that the capture of Havana would be good for his business that year. Whether Havana's
seizure would be permanent or temporary, there were profits to be made.[16]

15. For the argument about the West India interest, see Peggy K. Liss, *Atlantic Empires: The Net-
work of Trade and Revolution, 1713–1826* (Baltimore, 1983), 18; Pares, *War and Trade in the West Indies*,
77–84, 185, 595; Levi Marrero, *Cuba: Economía y sociedad*, 15 vols. (Madrid, [1972]–1992), VI, 126;
Hugh Thomas, *Cuba; or, The Pursuit of Freedom* (New York, 1998), 55–56; Guillermo Calleja Leal and
Hugo O'Donnell y Duque de Estrada, *1762, La Habana inglesa: La toma de La Habana por los ingleses*
(Madrid, 1999), 207. For voices in Britain supporting Havana's acquisition, see *London Evening-Post*,
Oct. 5–7, 1762; *Gazetteer and London Daily Advertiser*, Oct. 12, 1762; *London Evening-Post*, Oct. 2–5,
1762; *St. James's Chronicle; or, the British Evening-Post*, Oct. 26–28, 1762; "Copy of a Petition to His
Majesty from the Merchants Trading to the Conquered Islands," Nov. 3, 1762, Additional Manuscripts 38373, fol. 89, BL. For mercantile interests in the British West Indies writing in support of
the conquest, see "Extract of a Letter from a Gentleman in Barbados; to Another in Boston," *New-
London Gazette* (Conn.), Feb. 17, 1764, [3]. For a Spanish spying report from Jamaica on speculation there that Mexico was next, see Antonio Raffelin to the Conde de Ricla, Dec. 5, 1763, AGI, SD,
1212. In 1763, outside Philadelphia, at the German community of Ephrata, Pennsylvania, a printer
published the first German translation in America of a Spanish mining manual from Potosí, Alvaro
Alonso Barba's *Arte de los metales* (1640), taken from the English translation, *The Art of Metals in
Which Is Declared the Manner of Their Generation and the Concomitants of Them . . . Translated in the
Year 1669 by the R. H. Edward, Earl of Sandwich* (London, 1674); see Harry Bernstein, *Making an
Inter-American Mind* (Gainesville, Fla., 1961), 14–15.

16. On the occupation of Guadeloupe, see Pares, *War and Trade in the West Indies*, 186–195; and
Anderson, *Crucible of War*, 312–316. For Henry Laurens, see Elizabeth Donnan, *Documents Illustrative
of the History of the Slave Trade to America*, IV, *The Border Colonies and the Southern Colonies* (New
York, 1965), 280; Thomas, *Cuba*, 49. Among those taking advantage of the influx of goods for sale in

Over the course of the occupation, more than seven hundred merchant ships made their way to Havana to trade. The speed and volume of merchants' response is a testament to the reactiveness and flexibility of the Atlantic commercial system and the long-standing appeal of Havana's market. For example, fewer than three weeks after British troops formally took possession of Havana, before official news of the capitulation had reached New York City or London, a merchant all the way up the Hudson River in Albany, New York, was already writing with excitement about the excellent prices that he had heard for flour and beaver pelts (popular for hats) in Havana. As the records of merchants and customhouses in London, New York, Dublin, Bridgetown, Philadelphia, and Kingston indicate, as soon as word spread of the imminent surrender of the city, trading vessels and slave ships were redirected to Havana from all over the Atlantic world.[17]

Among those more than seven hundred merchants who rushed into Havana after the city's surrender were many who had long-standing business relations there. These mostly British and British American merchants were both seeking further business and, in many cases, hoping to recoup money owed on prior debts with their Havana trading partners. Others had spent time there during the War of Jenkins' Ear as prisoners of war, during which they familiarized themselves with the port and its residents. A New York–based merchant and former prisoner of war in Havana, William Bedlow, provides a case in point. Bedlow established residence in British-occupied Havana to conduct business there and serve as an agent and liaison for other New York merchants. During the War of Jenkins' Ear, he had been a ship's captain often operating out of Jamaica; later he went on to become a prominent merchant and the first postmaster of New York City. Bedlow had been to Havana at least twice before 1762 — once when captured by a Spanish privateer in 1738 and then ten years later when he brought provisions under contract for the Royal

Havana was a Scottish soldier who noted in his commonplace book that he purchased sterling shoe buckles, a penknife, a mirror, and a gold ring with his prize money from the abundance of ships recently arrived in the city; see Commonplace Book of John Sinclair, 1762–1801, 14, 15, Special Collections, Perkins Library, Duke University, Durham, N.C.

17. Robert Sanders to John Sanders, Sept. 10, 1762, New York State 18th-Century Letters and Documents, Albany, N.Y., William L. Clements Library, Ann Arbor, Mich. There were no entry or exit logs for Havana's port under occupation, but in AGS, Hacienda, 2342, Havana, 1763, an anonymous report cites 742 ships in just eleven months of British occupation. Merchant papers from New York and customhouse records from Philadelphia track numerous ships departing to and returning from Havana in the period after the capitulation as well as some months after the return to Spanish rule. See, for example, Samuel Gilford Account Book, 1759–1763, and John Taylor Papers, 1762–1763, NYHS. Customs House Papers, II, HSP, records 17 ships from Philadelphia heading to Havana in the period from November 5, 1761, to October 5, 1764, esp. fol. 182.

Havana Company. The occupation provided an occasion for this man of commerce to return to a city he knew well.[18]

Ironically, the Britons least excited by the news from Cuba were those that had the most decision-making power over its political destiny. Lord Bute, the head of the British delegation and a leader of the domestic political faction that wanted to end the war, was dismayed by the news. Word of the victory arrived just as British, Spanish, and French negotiators at Paris had reached a preliminary peace agreement for the cessation of hostilities. By Bute's estimation, retaining Havana was diplomatically impossible. Charles III of Spain would never agree to its loss and would instead opt to keep fighting until his armies could make an analogous territorial acquisition in Portugal (which they were then invading) to trade for the so-called key to the Indies. For Bute and George III, the victory in Havana would mean unacceptably prolonging a wearying war with an exorbitant price tag. A British victory as overwhelming as this one might also prompt hostile maritime rivals to form a coalition to oppose Britain's naval power. The first deal had to be scrapped, and negotiators for all three monarchies went back to work brokering a new peace agreement. They hoped to do so before the British Parliament came back into session and the London public could potentially demand more conquests in Spanish America. The renewed peace negotiation would loom over the entire period of British rule in Havana and ultimately determine its fate.[19]

Despite the joyous celebration and rampant speculation set off by news of Britannia's triumph, for many British subjects the occupation of Havana would sorely disappoint. In this instance, as in so many others, the gap between imperial imaginings and realities on the ground was vast. While British merchants and other subjects far from Cuba imagined the possibilities of British Havana, and the peace negotiations wore on, in Havana Lord Albe-

18. Merchants seeking to collect debts included agents for New York merchant William Walton, who had been contracting with the Royal Havana Company to provision Florida since the early cycle of Anglo-Spanish wars in 1726, and London-based Wargeant Nicholson, the last South Sea Company factor in Havana; see "The Memorial of William Walton, of the City of New York, Merchant," *El escribano*, III, no. 3 (July 1966), 14–22; and William Fogo to Daniel Campbell, July 6, 1763, Campbell v. Orts, C 111.200, TNA. On William Bedlow, see Protocolos de La Habana, Escribanía de Salinas, tomo 1763, fol. 422, ANC; *The New York Genealogical and Biographical Record*, XXX (New York, 1899), 9; Los Oficiales reales al Consejo de Indias, Consejo de 27 de mayo de 1747, Mar. 18, 1747, AGI, SD, 412, no. 4; *The Political State of Great Britain . . .* , LVIII (London, 1739), 171; *Nuevos Papeles sobre la toma de La Habana por los ingleses en 1762* (Havana, 1951), 1–2, 160–164.

19. *The Correspondence of John, Fourth Duke of Bedford . . .* , III (London, 1846), 135–136; Francis Russell Hart, *The Siege of Havana, 1762* (Boston, 1931), 51; *War and Trade in the West Indies*, 604; Paul W. Mapp, *The Elusive West and the Contest for Empire, 1713–1763* (Williamsburg, Va., and Chapel Hill, N.C., 2011), 425.

marle faced the challenges of establishing British rule over this newly surrendered city. After all the losses suffered during the campaign, Lord Albemarle proved unable to establish the kind of occupation that was conducive to their commercial interests or to long-term British governance over the island. Albemarle had little desire to stay long in the city he had fought so hard to capture, at least once he had optimized his prize winnings and other profits available in British Havana. In a letter to British secretary of state for the southern section, Lord Egremont, he asked for permission to come home for "the recovery of my health" once he had "established the government upon a proper footing." To the Duke of Newcastle, he wrote, "Make a Peace as soon as you can, or send somebody here, That understands trade, and will not cheat the King. I have wrote to the Secretary of War, saying what is very true, that my constitution will not do for This climate." As it turned out, the person with the most power to shape British rule over Havana was perhaps the least interested in holding onto it. Within Havana's city walls, he behaved more like a pirate in search of spoils than the governor of a potential new British acquisition and node in its commercial system.[20]

Taking Possession

After the capitulation accords went into effect, the first order of business was the transfer of power and the taking of war booty, an activity both a weary Lord Albemarle and the whole British nation could revel in. As soon as the city was handed over, Albemarle promptly seized all the ships in harbor and ran up British flags on their masts. To the elation of the victors, the ships surrendered at Havana constituted nearly one-third of the entire Spanish navy. Without Havana, the treasure fleets could not make their way back to Europe, thus cutting off the funding to the war machines of both Spain and its ally France. Albemarle and Pocock had captured six warships of seventy guns, six of sixty guns or more, several merchant ships, and two ships-of-war on the stocks under construction (see Figure 21 [Plate 5]). The surrender of the shipyard and the ships in Havana's harbor, virtually all intact, represented one of the greatest coups for the British — and embarrassments for the Spanish — of Havana's loss. This battle fought predominantly on land by soldiers, sailors, local militia forces, and enslaved Africans was in fact a tremendous naval victory and defeat. As Richard Humphreys of the 28th Regiment of Foot wrote in

---

20. Albemarle to Egremont, Aug. 21, 1762, CO 117.1, fol. 138, TNA; Albemarle to Newcastle, Sept. 29, 1762, in Guillermo de Blanck, ed., *Papeles sobre la toma de La Habana por los ingleses en 1762* (Havana, 1948), 195–196.

FIGURE 21 *The Captured Spanish Fleet at Havana, August–September, 1762.* By Dominic Serres. 1768. © National Maritime Museum, Greenwich, London

his journal, "The Spaniards have not suffered such a sensible and humiliating loss since the defeat of their celebrated Armada."[21]

Once Pocock had raided the shipyard, Albemarle proceeded to seize the Spanish king's treasure to distribute to himself and his men. He had captured a windfall: 1.8 million pesos. Although not as much as the private holdings that had been removed by elite Havana residents who retreated from the city during the siege, 1.8 million pesos was still a vast treasure. The total seized included the king's treasury as well as trade goods from throughout the empire belonging to the crown and merchants in Spain, who were not protected by the capitulation accords. Havana residents' property rights were to be respected, but all property of the king and his subjects in Spain was up for grabs.

21. Journal of Richard Humphreys, Add. MSS 45662, fol. 62r, BL. The count of warships includes those sunk at the mouth of the harbor. For inventories of the ships seized, see "A List of the Ships-of-War That Were in the Harbor of the Havana . . . ," in Syrett, ed., *Siege and Capture of Havana,* 289; Henry Fletcher, "Seven Years' War Journal of the Proceedings of the 35th Regiment of Foot, by a British Officer, and Illustrated by a Military Engineer," Aug. 24, 1762, Codex Eng 41, JCBL; and "List of the Seamen and the Ships of War Taken at the Havana," Aug. 20, 1762, CO 117/2, fol. 34–35, TNA. Lord Egremont made an observation to the Spanish minister in London about the tremendous naval significance of the victory. Many of these vessels would soon be incorporated into the British navy or sold at auction in London. See Masserano to the Marquis de Grimaldi, Sept. 30, 1763, AGS, Estado, 6956/1, and Masserano to Grimaldi, Dec. 30, 1763, Feb. 21, 1764, AGS, Estado, 6956/12.

Albemarle immediately distributed these goods among Havana's captors according to customs established for pirate raids of the sixteenth and seventeenth centuries, which had enduring influence over this eighteenth century campaign.[22]

Even though the expedition was funded and organized by the state, the booty seized went directly into the pockets of participants, which had been a factor in recruitment. According to the agreement made before the beginning of the siege, 33 percent of the booty went to Lord Albemarle and Admiral Pocock, 7 percent to their seconds-in-command, with the remaining 60 percent to be split among the officers, sailors, soldiers, and volunteers. By the time accounts were finally settled in 1772, more than £737,000 had been distributed among the victorious members of the expedition. Lord Albemarle revived his family's fortunes with his winnings, using them to purchase a large estate in Norfolk, which — fittingly — was formerly owned by the director of the South Sea Company, who had also augmented his fortune with Spanish silver. Other officers made similar purchases, such as General George Eliott, who used his winnings to purchase an estate at Bailey Park, in Sussex (see Figures 22 and 23 [Plate 7]).[23]

The leaders of the expedition made their fortunes, but the outcome of the division of booty fostered a sense of disappointment among many of the lower-ranking men who served. Many participants were left feeling short-changed, and there were complaints of officers being cut out from the division of booty altogether or receiving far less than they deserved. As one common soldier complained, privates only received eleven Spanish dollars. Albemarle's secret instruction had stipulated that the free black troops from Jamaica be included in the division of prize winnings, along with British and American soldiers and sailors, but the commanders of the Havana expedition made no such provisions. Perhaps frustrated by being deprived of any war booty, two black auxiliaries serving on the British expedition were apprehended plundering a Spanish church. Some provincial volunteers from North America, in turn, later petitioned the British government for land grants elsewhere as their own form of delayed compensation.[24]

22. For the seizure of treasure worth 1,828,116 Spanish "dollars," or pesos, see Pocock to Clevland, Oct. 8, 1762, ADM 1.237, TNA. Francis Russell Hart cites treasure and goods worth 1.9 million pesos in his account (*Siege of Havana,* 49).

23. "Division of Booty or Prize Money between Army, and Navy, as Settled by Sir George Pocock, and the Earl of Albemarle, On Board the Namur," June 5, 1762, fols. 203–205, Petworth House Archives, HMC 164, 165, West Sussex Record Office, Chichester, U.K.; Thomas, *Cuba,* 56–57.

24. On the complaint about privates receiving only eleven Spanish dollars, see James Miller, "Memoirs of an Invalid," Transcripts of the Amherst Papers, Packet 54, fol. 45, Library and Archives of Canada; Syrett, "Introduction," *Siege and Capture of Havana,* xxiv. On the instructions to include

FIGURE 22 Bailey Park Mansion, East Sussex, England. By T. Malton. 1788. Ink on paper. General George Eliot bought and remodeled this country house with his share of the prize winnings from Havana. He was later granted the title Lord Heathfield after successfully leading the defense of Gibraltar from Spanish attack in 1779–1782. Courtesy, The British Library / Granger

Once the shipyard and the booty had been seized, the next order of business was removing Spanish armed forces and political leaders from the city. On August 24, Spanish soldiers and sailors were permitted to march out of the Punta gate with flags waving and drums playing, according to the honors of war, "in consideration of their vigorous and brave defense of the Morro castle." More than nine hundred of their numbers then boarded British transport ships bound for Spain, along with Governor Prado and the members of the junta de guerra, who were allowed to bring their personal possessions with them. Another thirteen hundred men that were too sick to travel were left behind in Havana to recover their health. All the multiracial militia forces, both inside and outside the city walls, were required to turn in their weapons, but they

the free black soldiers from Jamaica in the division of booty, see George Rex to the Earl of Albemarle, "Separate Instructions regarding Distribution of Booty," Feb. 18, 1762, CO 117.1, fols. 38–40, TNA. On the men accused of plundering a Spanish church, see William Starr Meyers, "Journal of William Starr of Connecticut Regiment at Havana, 1762," *Journal of American History*, IV (1909), 113–117, esp. 116. Regarding land petitions, see *The Two Putnams: Israel and Rufus in the Havana Expedition 1762 and in the Mississippi River Exploration 1772–73 with Some Account of the Company of Military Adventurers* (Hartford, Conn., 1931), 3–46, esp. 9, 15–17.

FIGURE 23 *General William Keppel, Storming the Morro Castle.* By Sir Joshua Reynolds. 1764 or 1765. Oil on canvas. Keppel commissioned this portrait from Reynolds, the first president of the Royal Academy of Arts in London, and posed for it at his London studio. This painting provides the inspiration for the cover of this book, which highlights the protagonism of other actors. Courtesy, Museu de Arte Antiga, Lisbon, Portugal / Bridgeman Images

were permitted to stay on the island. The day the Spanish soldiers departed for Europe, the remaining British army — except for one regiment stationed at Guanabacoa — marched into Havana to be quartered within the city.[25]

The length and intensity of the siege and the ongoing effects of yellow fever had devastated Albemarle's army, which was so depleted that holding onto Havana would be a precarious enterprise, especially if the population resisted its occupiers. In order to fulfill a prior obligation, Albemarle immediately sent

25. Albemarle to Egremont, Oct. 7, 1762, Lord Egremont Letter Books, West Indies, I, 1762, Petworth House Archives, HMC 164, 165, fols. 199–201, West Sussex Record Office; "Return that Don Nicolas Joseph Rapun, Knight of the Order of Santiago and Commissary of War of the Armies of His Catholic Majesty, Remits to His Excellency the Earl of Albemarle of the Troops . . . That Were Present in This Place the 12th of August and Those That Embarked for Spain . . . as Also of the Present Effectives, Dead and Deserted," Dec. 4, 1762, HA 67/973/A15, Suffolk Record Office; Fletcher, "Seven Years' War Journal," Aug. 30, 1762, Codex Eng 41, JCBL.

four battalions of Lieutenant General Eliott's corps to New York to recuperate. Without them, British numbers were reduced to just more than nine thousand men, two-thirds of whom were sick in Havana's hospitals, monasteries, and convents. Albemarle reported that his soldiers suffered so badly from the disease that shortly after the taking of the city there were only seven hundred men available to do duty and to guard the Spanish soldiers left behind for the recovery of their own health.[26]

The death toll from yellow fever continued to grow during the occupation and after these troops had departed Havana. North American troops experienced especially severe losses. One company from Connecticut that was hit especially hard had 76 mortalities, 11 deserters, and only 20 survivors. Of 1,050 men who composed the entire Connecticut regiment at Havana, 226 were dead before they could embark for the return voyage and 400 before the survivors were discharged from a military hospital at Staten Island early in February 1763. The Reverend John Graham, who accompanied this regiment, described their camp in Havana in September and October as "a constant Scene of Woe," where "fatal disease enters tent after Tent." Graham claimed men were moved to curse the day they enlisted in the service and met with joy the news that they were leaving "this Country that has proved so fatal to so many of our Troops." Like this Connecticut regiment, the death rate for North American volunteers might have been as high as 40 percent. These losses dampened enthusiasm for the victory, at least among the families of the deceased, and weakened the provincial army.[27]

The high mortality rate for Albemarle's troops undercut plans of using Havana as a stepping-stone to further conquests. Upon seizing the city, Albemarle had been ordered to use it as a launching pad for a rampage against Spanish America, similar to scenarios first imagined by British war planners and the public during the War of Jenkins' Ear. His initial secret instructions from the king had been to leave a garrison at Havana and to proceed directly to attacks on "Vera Cruz, St. Augustine, Santiago de la Cuba [sic], or any other part of the Spanish colonies, which from the state and condition of our forces

26. "Journal of the Siege of the Morro Castle and Havana, by Lord Albemarle," 1762, fols. 26–27, HA 67/973/A7, Suffolk Record Office; "General State of British Forces Fit for Duty on June 7th (Total 11,576) and October 18th (Total 2,067)," CO 117/1, fols. 157–158, TNA.

27. *Extracts from the Journal of the Reverend John Graham, Chaplain of the First Connecticut Regiment, Colonel Lyman, from September 25th to October 19th, 1762, at the Siege of Havana* (New York, 1896), 8, 10, 17; *The Two Putnams*, 5, 104–110; David Syrett, "American Provincials and the Havana Campaign of 1762," *New York History*, XLIX (1968), 375–390, esp. 389–390. Rhode Island provided 212 men of whom 2 were killed, 3 were wounded, 110 died of fever, and only 97 returned home unharmed; see Bruce Campbell MacGunnigle, "Introduction," in *Red Coats and Yellow Fever: Rhode Island Troops at the Siege of Havana, 1762* (Providence, R.I., 1991), 6.

under your command and from the circumstances of the climate and of the seasons, you shall judge to be most practicable and as shall appear to you most likely to be attended with success." As soon as the Havana expedition ended, Albemarle was also charged with lending men to Major General Jeffrey Amherst, who was preparing an attack on French Louisiana. Now that Spain had lost its Caribbean naval stronghold, its ability to protect its American dominions, or those of its ally France, was severely limited, and this next round of offensive warfare would meet diminished opposition. Yet both Albemarle and Pocock refused to mount any further attacks, citing the disease that ravaged their troops and the onset of hurricane season.[28]

Further troubling Albemarle and Pocock was the lack of clarity about what exactly they controlled in Cuba. British forces had captured the nearby ports of Mariel to the west of Havana and Matanzas to the east, but the territory that had been surrendered beyond that stretch of coastline was subject to dispute. Despite wishful thinking far from the Caribbean, Havana was not the entire island of Cuba; it was a city on Cuba's northwestern coast with Spanish political boundaries that determined the extent of its jurisdiction into its hinterland. Because there were no good roads running the course of this very large island, not land, but sea routes linked Havana to Santiago de Cuba, on the island's opposite end. Consequently, submitting the latter city to British rule would require another costly and difficult naval assault. Pocock hoped to capture Santiago de Cuba, and thus assert control over the entirety of Cuba, but he figured that the troops would not be in a condition to attempt a naval assault of that magnitude until the next year.[29]

As part of the debate over which territories should be retained at the end of the Seven Years' War, Lord Egremont sent Albemarle requests for a detailed report on Havana and all that Albemarle had managed to conquer on the island. He wanted to know Cuba's population, revenues, cost of government, defense, and fortification as well as "most especially . . . the disposition of the inhabitants on the change of their masters." The British governors of the other recent West Indian conquests, Martinique and Grenada, complied with this request and sent in extensive descriptions and census data, which fueled discussions over which acquisitions should be retained. However, Albemarle's

28. George Rex to Albemarle, "Secret Instructions," Feb. 15, 1762, CO 117.1, fols. 24–35, esp. 28, TNA; Pocock to Clevland, Aug. 10, 1762, ADM 1.237, fol. 65, TNA ("The sickly state of His Majesty's army renders them incapable of undertaking of any further operations this season"); Albemarle to Egremont, Aug. 21, 1762, CO 117.1, fols. 136–139, TNA. Recognizing that hurricanes strike the Caribbean in the fall, Pocock commented that "in November, December, and January, the north winds blow excessive strong, the other months fine weather and seldom rain"; see Pocock to Clevland, Oct. 9, 1762, ADM 1.237, fols. 74–78, TNA.

29. Pocock to Clevland, Oct. 9, 1762, ADM 1.237, fols. 74–78, TNA.

rule beyond the walled city was too tenuous to perform any such comprehensive accounting of the population or the island.[30]

Given the precarious state of British rule, it was abundantly clear that Albemarle would need to have the cooperation of Havana's inhabitants to make his governance over the city function. Just as the Spanish government required the cooperation of its elite population to govern, so did the occupying British one. Even after the fierceness of the military campaign, willing allies were not hard to find. The population shifts that occurred in British Havana meant that its elite residents and commercial sectors would have the opportunity to exert control over the city without the interference of Spanish colonial officials or naval and military interests, with which they sometimes clashed in normal times. Within city walls, only the city council and the bishop remained as local political and ecclesiastical authorities. After the departure of the Spanish army and navy and the governor and captain general, British forces were left occupying a civilian population that had a long history of trading with British territories and a desire to expand that commerce.

Brokering British Rule

The key to peaceful coexistence in British Havana was that Albemarle found willing brokers for his rule. After the violence of the conquest, Albemarle's instructions had been to foster the most positive relationship possible with the local inhabitants in order to soften them to British rule and convince them of its benefits. The relationship Albemarle was able to broker with Havana's elites was in marked contrast with the fraught relations that developed when British forces occupied Manila in 1762 and Buenos Aires in 1806. It also stood out in sharp relief against ongoing resistance from many of those militia soldiers and people of color who had played such a prominent role in the defense. In fact, the desire of Havana's commercial sectors to expand the slave trade, the sugar sector, and their own commercial relations made them embarrassingly complicit in British rule.[31]

30. Egremont to Albemarle, Oct. 2, 1762, Lord Egremont Letter Books, West Indies, I, 1762, Petworth House Archives, HMC 164, 165, fols. 191–192, West Sussex Record Office. No Spanish census had yet been performed of the island, so this task would have been especially difficult to fulfill.

31. On the Manila campaign, see Marqués de Ayerbe, *Sitio y conquista de Manila por los ingleses en 1762* (Zaragoza, Spain, 1897); Nicholas P. Cushner, ed., *Documents Illustrating the British Conquest of Manila, 1762–1763* (London, 1971); Nicholas Tracy, *Manila Ransomed: The British Assault on Manila in the Seven Years War* (Exeter, U.K., 1995); Tracy, "The British Expedition to Manila," in Mark H. Danley and Patrick J. Speelman, eds., *The Seven Years' War: Global Views* (Leiden, 2012), 461–486; and Kristie Flannery, "The Seven Years' War and the Globalization of Anglo-Iberian Imperial Entanglement," in Jorge Cañizares-Esguerra, ed., *Entangled Empires: The Anglo-Iberian Atlantic, 1500–1830* (Philadelphia, 2017), 236–254. On the invasion and occupation of Buenos Aires, see Carlos

The articles of capitulation gave Havana's propertied residents much to like. Almost none of them decided to leave even though they were permitted to do so. During the siege, the population had dropped by more than half, but now it began to grow again as Havana residents returned. Through rose-colored glasses, Albemarle reported that "numbers of people of all denominations are crowding into the town and if any judgment can be formed from their looks seem very happy." He continued, "I shall endeavor to make their government as easy to them as possible." Those that came back into Havana were less likely to have played a role in the defense of the city than those that fled at the end of the fighting. They were also more likely to be white—and thus safe from the fear of enslavement or sale—and to have commercial interest in access to British trade.[32]

Within Havana's city walls, Albemarle made superficial efforts to reconfigure the built environment of Havana as a British space. He surveyed the city and gave English names to the streets, which were affixed to the corners of intersections and on public squares. Plaza Nueva, where Havana's large market was held, was now supposed to be called "the Queen's Square" (see Figure 24 [Plate 10]), and Plaza San Francisco was renamed "Granby's Square." Other measures sought to assert British authority in the heart of Havana. On Plaza Nueva, Albemarle stationed the British guard and erected a gallows, which was used primarily to discipline his own army. British officials seized what was arguably Havana's most beautiful church, the Church of San Francisco de Asís, for their Protestant services (see Figures 25 [Plate 11] and 26). As his residence, Albemarle chose a brand-new home Juan de Prado had constructed for himself, "with very beautiful apartments and galleries decorated with stone columns," on the site of the former South Sea Company factory near Plaza Nueva and the Church of San Francisco. By choosing the same location occupied by the governor and British slave traders, he was inserting himself into a position of commercial monopoly and political privilege that accurately reflected his rule. Outside the city proper, Albemarle also began rebuilding Havana's fortifications to protect against Spanish attack.[33]

Roberts, *Las invasiones inglesas del Río de la Plata (1806–1807)* (Buenos Aires, 2000); Juan Carlos Luzuriaga, *Las invasiones inglesas en su bicentenario: Testimonios, revisiones, y perspectivas* (Montevideo, Uruguay, 2007); Alberto Mario Salas, *Crónica y diario de Buenos Aires, 1806–1807* (Buenos Aires, 2013); and Peter Blanchard, "An Institution Defended: Slavery and the English Invasions of Buenos Aires in 1806–1807," *Slavery and Abolition*, XXXV (2014), 253–272.

32. "Capitulación original presentada por Don Juan de Prado," in *Proceso formado de orden del Rey Nuestro Señor por la Junta de Generales*, I, BNE; *An Authentic Account of the Reduction of the Havanna . . .* (London, 1762); Albemarle to Egremont, Aug. 21, 1762, CO 117.1, fol. 136–139, TNA.

33. "Remarques sur la Havane," Pierre Eugene du Simitière Papers, West Indies No. 4, LCP; "Account of Expenses Incurred on Fortifications, Sept. 20, 1762, to Jan. 22, 1763," CO 117.1, fols. 275–276,

FIGURE 24 *The Piazza at Havana.* By Dominic Serres. Circa 1765–1770. Oil on canvas. Lord Albemarle renamed Havana's Plaza Nueva (depicted in this image) "the Queen's Square" and erected a gallows there (not depicted). In the foreground of this painting, note the British sailors gathered by the bench and the Jesuits in their black robes. In the mid-ground, a woman of African descent carries a basket on her head. In the background, British troops can be seen drilling, and one of Havana's distinctive carriages, known as a *calesa,* is portrayed. © National Maritime Museum, Greenwich, London

In contrast to what was done in occupied Manila, Martinique, and Guade-loupe, in Havana a civil government was established rather than a military one, and the city council and the judicial system continued to function. The decision to leave Havana's city council in place was likely owing to the challenges of governing such a populous city, especially given the reduced condition of Albemarle's army. In fact, the British government of Havana effectively took over but left intact the Spanish system of administration. In the wake of the victory, Albemarle pronounced himself the new governor of Havana and captain general of Cuba, in a sense seeking to insert himself into Cuba's political structure. Beneath his governorship, he established indirect rule. The

TNA. On the takeover of the Church of San Francisco, see Pedro Agustín Morel de Santa Cruz to the Council of the Indies, Dec. 31, 1762, AGI, SD, 1356.

FIGURE 25 *The Cathedral at Havana*. By Dominic Serres. Circa 1765–1770. Oil on canvas. This is not Havana's cathedral, but the convent church of San Francisco de Asís, which was used by the British occupiers for their Protestant services. Originally built in the seventeenth century but destroyed by hurricanes, the church was reconstructed and expanded in the 1730s. It was considered the most elegant church in Havana at the time of the occupation. Wikimedia Commons

very term used to refer to these new British subjects in Havana, *"los Españoles vasallos de su Mag[esta]d Británica,"* reflected the blended nature of this new political system. British officers collected Spanish taxes, customs, and duties already in place from Havana officials. As Pocock put it, "The civil administration of the city's affairs is carried on in the same manner as when in possession of the King of Spain, by *alcaldes, corregidores,* and inferior officers, and all things appear very quiet and easy."[34]

34. Emilio Roig de Leuchsenring, ed., *La dominación inglesa en La Habana: Libro de cabildos, 1762–1763,* 2d ed. (Havana, 1962), 113 (*"los Españoles vasallos"*), 179; Blanck, ed., *Papeles sobre la toma de La Habana,* 104–110; Pocock to Clevland, Oct. 9, 1762, ADM 1.237, TNA ("the civil administration"). Albemarle claimed that *he* was captain general of Cuba, not Lorenzo de Madariaga, governor of Santiago de Cuba, who was ceded the captain generalcy of the island by Prado during the siege. In a letter to Lorenzo de Madariaga, Albemarle wrote, "Know, Sir, that I am Governor and Captain General here and not your Excellency, and that I publish whatever I am directed by my royal master,

FIGURE 26 "A View of Havana Seen from Above." Circa 1762. Pen and grey ink and watercolor. This rendering was made by British officer William Harcourt, who served as Lord Albemarle's aide-de-camp. It appears that Harcourt sketched it from the bell tower of the Church of San Francisco de Asís looking north toward the mouth of Havana's bay. The Castillo de la Real Fuerza, on the Plaza de Armas, is visible in the mid-ground. © The Trustees of the British Museum

In order to rule over Havana, Albemarle relied on the cooperation of a local lieutenant governor to act as his liaison with the city's inhabitants. At the end of August, he announced the appointment to this role of Don Sebastián de Peñalver y Angulo, one of Havana's most prominent and wealthy residents. Peñalver was a member of the city council, an official in the Royal Havana Company, a royal officer, a vast landholder, and the proprietor of at least one sugar plantation. His most important task as lieutenant governor would be smoothing relations with the *cabildo,* where his son Gabriel replaced him when he accepted his new position. Alongside these men, Albemarle assembled an informal cabinet of local advisors, including Miralles and Estrada,

for the information of his new subjects in the island of Cuba." The letter was prompted by Madariaga's sending a communiqué to the Havana cabildo informing it of the preliminary articles of peace, which called for Havana's return to Spain. See Albemarle to Madariaga, Feb. 6, 1763, CO 117.1, fol. 216, TNA. On the expanding category of British subjecthood in the eighteenth century, see Hannah Weiss Muller, *Subjects and Sovereign: Bonds of Belonging in the Eighteenth-Century British Empire* (New York, 2017).

all men with extensive experience in the Royal Havana Company and the slave trade into Cuba.[35]

Aware of the importance of good relations with the city council to the success or failure of the occupation, Albemarle carefully courted its members. Rather than dictate terms from on high, on September 8 he appeared before a special meeting of the city council to introduce himself, making efforts to extend the proper courtesies and respects, as one noble reaching out to a group that included *condes, marqueses,* and other nobles as well. The city council minutes, which described Albemarle as the *"Ex[celentíssi]mo S[eñ]or Conde"* ["Most Excellent Mr. Earl"], noted that his first gesture upon entering their chambers for the oath-swearing ceremony was to "extend courtesies," or *"Urbanidad,"* to the council members. After some initial reluctance they responded favorably to him.[36]

Whatever Albemarle's intentions, during the rituals involved in this first meeting, the cabildo members maintained the kind of autonomy that would have been both familiar and desirable to them. The ensuing swearing of loyalty oaths guaranteed only that the city council members would "promise most faithfully and sincerely to pay due allegiance to serve and to be true to His Majesty George III of Great Britain, France, and Ireland, etc., etc. as long as they remain in this island." As amended in the Spanish version, which did not fully match the English oath, they stipulated that this allegiance was "according to our own law, and without having to take up arms in favor of or against either Majesty." This amendment would allow the cabildo members, in keeping with their behavior during the siege, to continue to occupy a space between the two crowns and avoid military engagement altogether.[37]

The cabildo members probably thought it unlikely that the Spanish king would allow his prized key to the Indies to slip from his fingers forever, but, in the meantime, they would make the most of the opportunities presented by the transfer of power. War was known in Havana as a boom time for lucrative interimperial trade, and the British occupation promised to be no exception. In expectation of the trading opportunities British rule would provide, many

---

35. Peñalver somehow alienated Albemarle and was replaced by fellow city council member Don Gonzalo Recio de Oquendo as lieutenant governor on September 14. By December, Peñalver had successfully lobbied for his reinstatement, and Recio de Oquendo stepped down. It was alleged that Peñalver's reinstatement was predicated on his offer to help Albemarle extract more silver from the city's wealthiest residents and the Church. See Roig de Leuchsenring, ed., *La dominación inglesa,* 90, 92, 113; "En La Habana año de 1763," AGS, Hacienda, 2342; "Nota de lo substancial que ha ocurrido en La Havana despues del 30 de agosto de 1762," Mar. 5, 1763 (unsigned), AGI, SD, 1584, no. 534.

36. Roig de Leuchsenring, ed., *La dominación inglesa,* 95.

37. Ibid. Ireland was translated in the city council minutes as "Islanda," similar to "Islandia," or Iceland.

members of the Havana elite reached out to Albemarle to extend a special welcome. Shortly after the end of hostilities, individuals hoping to inculcate good relations presented him with a number of gifts, including gold coins and a talking parrot. One city council member wrote a letter of introduction to Albemarle, lamenting that he had been ill during Albemarle's initial appearance at the city council and expressing his "pleasure" and "trust" in the new rulership.[38]

These men in Havana were not—as the British war planners had imagined—unhappy "creolios" bristling under Spanish rule; they were prominent merchants and ranchers, city council members, and high-ranking officials in the Royal Havana Company. They could be confident in their Spanish and Catholic affiliations—some even held titles of Castilian nobility. But, like Juan de Miralles and Pedro de Estrada, all of these men also had previous experience doing business with British subjects. Those who had prior commercial relations with British colonies from the slave trade or the Royal Havana Company were the first to step forward and the most able to profit from British rule.[39]

In occupied Havana, the city council became a willing agent of British rule. With so many British soldiers and sailors sick and with much of Cuba's militias having retreated inland, Albemarle was unable to gather enough provisions from Havana's hinterland to feed his army without the administrative, economic, and political cooperation of the cabildo. The cabildo proved so eager to bring in cattle to the city from beyond Havana's jurisdiction and even capture British deserters that had escaped inland that it overcame resistance from militia on the edge of its jurisdiction. By sending out commissions to complete these tasks in "Spanish Cuba," the cabildo was providing provisions and additional troops to an army that threatened to invade the rest of the island and other Spanish territories nearby.[40]

The cabildo's complicity with its occupiers brought it into conflict with the rest of the island, which raised an ongoing military campaign. Many of the militia soldiers who had defended Havana had withdrawn to five towns in central Cuba—Puerto Príncipe, Trinidad, Sancti Spíritus, San Juan de los Remedios, and Santa Clara—where they regrouped in defense against British advance and in preparation for a potential offensive into British Havana. Upon

---

38. Pedro Agustín Morel de Santa Cruz to Arriaga, Dec. 31, 1762, AGI, SD, 1356, nos. 2, 9; Simón Joseph Rodríguez to Albemarle, Nov. 4, 1762, in Blanck, ed., *Papeles sobre la toma de La Habana*, 24.

39. For the term *creolio* in British war plots during the War of Jenkins' Ear, see, for example, Hubert Fassell to Robert Walpole, Sept. 11, 1739, Add. MSS 32694, fol. 41, BL.

40. Roig de Leuchsenring, ed., *La dominación inglesa*, 163, 198. On "the war over cattle" between Spanish Cuba and British Havana, see Pablo J. Hernández González, *La otra guerra del inglés: Cabildos, milicianos, y casacas rojas en la Cuba de 1762* (San Juan, P.R., 2011), 383–468.

Prado's departure, the governor of Santiago de Cuba, Lorenzo de Madariaga, became the new captain general of "Spanish Cuba," and these militiamen now answered his command. Prado had technically surrendered all five of these towns, which had recently been attached to Havana's jurisdiction, but their cabildos refused to recognize Albemarle's rule or respond to his command to send delegates into the capital. In fact, Madariaga commanded them to set up a blockade in order to prevent the sending of cattle into Havana that might be used to feed the British army.[41]

Squads of local forces stole livestock from ranches that were supplying food to Havana and robbed and took prisoner agents commissioned by the cabildo to bring food supplies into the city. In their case, the battle for Havana had not ended. In protest, the Havana cabildo wrote to Lorenzo de Madariaga in Santiago de Cuba to get them to stop. In the words of two of these agents, the majority of these squads were composed of "the many blacks" and *"guachinangos"* who had escaped to the interior. The agents of the cabildo might have pinned this opposition on blacks and guachinangos in order to belittle it or to justify their capture, but, as we have seen, many of those who had fought in the siege and retreated were nonwhite volunteer soldiers from inland areas or refugees from the city who had refused to surrender. Many of the enslaved and people of color had fled what was for them a perilous extralegal zone of British occupation and articles of capitulation that did not protect their rights. Outside Havana, the military struggle between Britain and Spain wore on, but inside its walls the occupation had moved into a very different phase of elite commerce, sociability, and exchange.[42]

Havana Elites' Commercial Ambitions

Signs of Havana elites' commercial ambitions had already made themselves visible during the siege itself, beginning with Juan de Miralles's appearance on the scene and double-dealings with Lord Albemarle. During the negotiation over the terms of capitulation, Prado and the junta de guerra — perhaps influenced by Miralles — had proposed that Havana be made a neutral port and that ships of many flags be allowed to dock there, similar to the arrangement

41. Roig de Leuchsenring, ed., *La dominación inglesa,* 191–199; Albemarle to Egremont, Oct. 7, 1762, Lord Egremont Letter Books, West Indies, I, 1762, Petworth House Archives, HMC 164, 165, fols. 199–201, West Sussex Record Office. The bases of operation for the inland military opposition to British Havana were in Santiago de Cuba, Santa Clara, Jagua, and Bayamo. For a comprehensive account of their efforts, see Hernández González, *La otra guerra del inglés,* 221–468.

42. Roig de Leuchsenring, ed., *La dominación inglesa,* 193–194, 198–199; Pablo J. Hernández González, "Indios y negros prófugos en la jurisdicción de La Habana, 1762," *Revista del Centro de Estudios Avanzados de Puerto Rico y el Caribe,* XIII (1994), 98–122.

with Portobelo after its seizure by Admiral Edward Vernon during the War of Jenkins' Ear. Prado also requested that even Spanish ships be allowed to enter Havana at will and that the tobacco harvest then in port awaiting shipment to Spain be permitted to continue on its way to the Royal Tobacco Factory of Seville. Although these requests were denied, they reveal how Havana's decision makers were reimagining their city under occupation: like a Dutch free port, still trading with the Spanish empire but also transcending its limits. This kind of arrangement was similar to what occurred naturally during times of war, but in this case Prado and the junta de guerra hoped to establish this custom as part of the rights protected in the articles of capitulation.[43]

After the initial expressions of sorrow and trepidation in the weeks after the surrender, the prevailing mood in the city changed into calm and even business as usual. Within two weeks of the capitulation, busy Havana notaries were stamping out the seal of Charles III of Spain on their official paper and replacing it with that of George III, *"Su Magestad Británica."* Already Havana's notaries were back at work: writing receipts for sales of enslaved Africans and homes, loans and mortgages, *cartas de libertad,* powers of attorney, and last wills and testaments. They were kept busy by the influx of British and British American merchants arriving in port with goods and people for sale.[44]

A mere month after the surrender, Havana's residents were lining up to buy enslaved Africans from John Kennion, Albemarle's chief commissary for British Havana who was granted a slave-trading monopoly over the city. Juan de Miralles became the chief local agent for the sale of enslaved Africans for Kennion. Among the buyers was even one of the few leaders of the military campaign who was still in Havana—Laureano Chacón, a city council member, ordinary mayor of Havana, and militia coronel, who secretly corresponded

43. At the time of Havana's surrender, there were three Dutch ships in harbor that had brought munitions and passengers before the declaration of war; Prado asked that they be allowed to embark freely. On the Dutch ships, see Enclosure to Albemarle's of Aug. 21, 1762, Articles of Capitulation, CO 117.1, fols. 122–127, TNA. See also *Proceso formado de orden del Rey Nuestro Señor por la Junta de Generales,* I, BNE; "Artículos preliminares de capitulación," Aug. 12, 1762, AGS, Marina, 426; "Mackellar's Journal," Aug. 13, 1762, in Syrett, ed., *Siege and Capture of Havana,* 290. See also Journal of Richard Humphreys, Add. MSS 45662, fol. 62r, BL.

44. For expressions of sorrow over Havana's loss, see "Documento Numero III: Memorial dirigido á Cárlos III por las señoras de La Habana . . . ," Aug. 25, 1762, in Roig de Leuchsenring, ed., *La dominación inglesa,* 243; and "Dolorosa métrica del sitio y entrega de La Habana," MS 12980/19, BNE. For Havana notarial records on paper with the crossed-out stamp of Charles III of Spain alongside the new stamp of George III of Britain, see, for example, Protocolos de La Habana, Escribanía de Salinas, 1763, tomo I, fol. 375v, ANC. By 1763, several notaries had transferred their record keeping to new paper bearing the stamp of George III alone; see, for example, Protocolos de La Habana, Escribanía de Galetti, 1763, ANC. The town council ordered all magistrates of justice and public scribes back to work on August 26, but, by that time, Havana's self-employed notaries had already complied; see Roig de Leuchsenring, ed., *La dominación inglesa,* 84.

with the governor of Spanish Cuba about the possibility of a counterattack. Other leaders of the defense joined him in purchasing enslaved Africans and trade goods from the flood of merchants coming into port from Britain, British North America, the Caribbean, and West Africa. The possibilities of this trade served as a powerful force binding Havana residents to their British occupiers.[45]

It was not so much free trade that Havana men of commerce were pursuing, however, but the continuation of their own privileged access to both British trade and protected Spanish American markets. Access to British trade goods and connections in other American and Spanish ports afforded them an opportunity to try to set themselves up as middlemen for both an internal trade with other parts of Cuba and an external trade to places such as New Spain. Direct access to British goods in an American port also enabled ambitious Havana merchants to gain advantages over Cádiz merchants, who held a monopoly on American trade. In fact, Cádiz shareholders of the Royal Havana Company would later sue Havana shareholders for allegedly colluding with the British to dispossess them of their property in Havana at the time of the capitulation. The accusations by Cádiz shareholders can be traced to the initial months of British rule, to a chain of events that began when several wealthy landowners sought to ingratiate themselves by offering a gift of sugar to Lord Albemarle worth thirty thousand pesos. The sugar harvest had been gathered recently, and those most invested in this nascent industry in Cuba had the most to gain from close relations with Lord Albemarle and access to the British slave trade. Enslaved Africans were needed in greater numbers on *ingenios* than other kinds of agricultural properties, and many enslaved Africans from Havana's hinterland had been killed or escaped during the siege.[46]

Albemarle liked the idea of a gift, though he was less interested in sugar than silver pesos. In response to this offer, he charged Peñalver and Gonzalo Recio de Oquendo with gathering one hundred thousand pesos in cash as a

45. Juan Miguel Palomino, "Carta a Nicolas de Ribera sobre la toma de La Habana por los ingleses," Aug. 28, 1762, C.M. Pérez, no. 24, Sala Cubana, BNJM; "Recopilación compendiada de los servicios hechos a SM y a la ciudad de La Havana por Don Juan de Miralles," May 10, 1765, AGI, IG, 2820A. On Miralles's role as an agent for John Kennion, see House of Lords, *John Kennion, Esq., Appellant; Samuel Gardner, John Turner, Samuel Hucks, John Bindley, William Wright, and William Maskall, Respondents; The Case of the Respondents* [London, 1773]. For Kennion's slave sales in occupied Havana, see Protocolos de La Habana, Escribanía de Fornari, 1762–1763, ANC. Fred Anderson discusses trade and loyalty as the "integuments of empire" in *Crucible of War*, 517.

46. "Representación de los accionistas de España contra los isleños de la Compañía de La Habana sobre convenio con los ingleses a la pérdida de aquella plaza," 1770, Colección Mata Linares, LXXV, fols. 408–439, Real Academia de la Historia, Madrid. On the original idea for a gift to Albemarle, or *donativo*, see Consejo de las Indias, Jan. 15, 1765, AGI, SD, 1134; Carlos M. Trelles, *El sitio de La Habana y la dominación británica en Cuba* (Havana, 1925), 24. Trelles credits Don Joseph Gelabert with the original idea.

"donation" from Havana's secular residents and religious orders. Albemarle's idea of a cash donation was likely suggested by Peñalver in his eagerness to build good will, as it mimicked a Spanish custom during wartime. According to the practice of giving *donativos*, dating from a time before modern banking systems, subjects of means would make emergency loans, or essentially donate money to the crown, with the expectation of either repayment with interest or forgiveness of the loan in return for titles or other favors granted after the war. In order to gather this amount, Peñalver announced he would be collecting two thousand pesos from each of Havana's wealthiest households. In this case, Peñalver was taking advantage of his privileged position close to Albemarle to seek advantage for himself and his closest associates. He was also tapping the extensive silver reserves of the Havana elite to help them gain advantages. Although there would later be many complaints about the forced donativo, all of Havana's investors in the Royal Havana Company benefited from Peñalver's cultivation of Albemarle.[47]

When Albemarle tried to seize the assets of the Royal Havana Company (based on the word "royal" in its name), Peñalver blocked him by arguing that the largest number of shareholders were Havana residents. Together with other investors, including Don Pedro de Estrada, Peñalver persuaded Albemarle to sell all the company's assets and the several warehouses of goods it stockpiled by the wharf back to its Havana residents at a negotiated, discounted price. For $170,000, all the company's enslaved Africans, goods, lumber, ships, properties, and credits would fall to them and not, importantly, to those shareholders who lived outside the port and were not protected by the articles of capitulation.[48]

In essence, the Havana shareholders had managed, with a flat payment to the British governor, to seize the Cádiz shareholders' property without com-

47. Consejo de las Indias, Jan. 15, 1765, AGI, SD, 1134; Trelles, *El sitio de La Habana y la dominación británica en Cuba*, 24. On the practice of wealthy subjects making emergency loans to the crown before the advent of a modern banking system in Spain in 1782, see Allan J. Kuethe and Kenneth J. Andrien, *The Spanish Atlantic World in the Eighteenth Century: War and the Bourbon Reforms, 1713–1796* (New York, 2014), 39; and Viviana Grieco, "Politics and Public Credit: The Limits of Absolutism in late Colonial Buenos Aires" (Ph.D. diss., Emory University, 2005).

48. "The Case, as Submitted by the Humble Mr. Yorke," Mar. 12, 1765, and "Copy of the Instrument of Sale," Oct. 25, 1762, both in AGI, Estado, 7, no. 11. Havana shareholders ended up paying another $322,000 for the ships *Asunción* (loaded with sugar in the harbor) and *La Perla* (sunk). Under William Keppel's governorship of Havana, British authorities tried to seize another new warehouse, located outside city walls, that they learned belonged to the Royal Havana Company. Havana shareholders also appealed through Spanish-British diplomatic channels for the restitution of goods worth 71,283 *pesos fuertes* in that storehouse that were never returned to them by William Keppel. See Marqués de Grimaldi to Príncipe Masserano, Nov. 19, 1764, and Masserano to Grimaldi, Dec. 7, 1764, both in AGS, Estado, 6956.

pensating them. As the British occupying government became more aware
of the extent of the Royal Havana Company's possessions, which included
naval stores and warehouses both inside and outside city walls, it extracted
a higher sum from the Havana shareholders. Still, the Havana investors involved had achieved a considerable coup against the Iberian shareholders,
with whom they bore a historical grudge. After the end of the War of Jenkins'
Ear, Peñalver, a former director of the company, had been jailed and taken to
Spain, along with the other Havana-based directors, in an investigation into
the Royal Havana Company's commercial activities during the war. Exoner-
ated, they returned from Madrid to Havana. But now, given the opening the
British occupation presented, Peñalver and other members of the company
seized the moment to wrest power back from the Cádiz stakeholders who had
tried to remove Havana merchants from the company's control. Albemarle
profited from this transaction, but it is likely he did not realize its ramifications. Thanks to Peñalver, Havana shareholders suddenly had more economic
power over the company under British than Spanish rule and had gained a
large warehouse of goods they could now consider trading across broader geographic horizons.[49]

During the British occupation, merchants in Havana began to set themselves up as middlemen in prohibited trade between British and Spanish territories. Peñalver sent a boatload of British goods to Veracruz, along with "some
slaves as gifts" *("unos negros de regalo"),* to a major trading house at that port.
It was rumored in Havana that Pedro de Estrada, the British commissary John
Kennion, and even William Keppel had an interest in this shipment. Not only
did this voyage defy the Spanish ban on intercolonial trade but it also provided the enemy inroads into New Spain. Yet the possibility of displacing the
Cádiz merchants' monopoly on trade between Britain and Spanish America
was too attractive to resist. In order to send a message to Veracruz merchants,
the "negros de regalo" signaled the benefits to be accrued by those who traded
with Peñalver, given his privileged access to British slave traders. It was by exploiting these kinds of openings that Havana's city council members and merchants sought to make British rule more advantageous to the city's commerce
than Spanish rule.[50]

49. Montserrat Garate Ojanguren, *Comercio ultramarino e ilustración: La Real Compañía de La
Habana* (Donostia-San Sebastián, Spain, 1993), 119–142. After the occupation, this transfer of property was locked up in lawsuits with Cádiz merchants for more than a decade. See "Representación
de los accionistas de España," 1770, Colección Mata Linares, LXXV, fols. 408–439, Real Academia
de la Historia.

50. "Expediente contra Don Sebastián de Peñalver y otros reos en la rendición de la plaza de La
Habana a los ingleses," 1771, AGI, SD, 1590; Trelles, *El sitio de La Habana,* 30.

The Havana elite eagerly purchased boats that could be used in regional commerce and abundant, cheap goods that British merchants brought them. Essentially, they were doing as they did during prior wars, when Spanish privateers brought a plethora of British ships and goods into port for auction. Don Juan de Miralles purchased the *Duke of York,* a warship of thirty cannons, from a merchant from Barbados, where he had traveled that winter. In an arrangement negotiated with two British merchants who established themselves in Havana, he sent a shipload of thirty-two hundred boxes of sugar to Cádiz, contracted to a British commercial house and insured by London backers. Though it did not turn out well for him in the end—he claimed he was shorted money he was owed—the aspirations behind Miralles's voyage mirrored those of Peñalver's to Veracruz.[51]

Miralles and Peñalver might have been exceptional, but many Havana residents also purchased sloops, frigates, and schooners and stockpiled goods they purchased from British merchants in their homes. Doing so would enable them to sidestep the Cádiz merchant monopoly and reap profits from a prohibited intra-American trade. A year after the British occupation, the Council of the Indies in Spain asked for an inventory of the 333 *vecinos* of Havana, Matanzas, and Guanabacoa self-identified as having bought significant quantities of goods from the British. The inventories, which were made for tax purposes, do not survive. Julián de Arriaga of the Council of the Indies, however, did not hesitate to opine that likely they planned to traffic those goods to New Spain, given that such a large quantity would take several years to be consumed on the island of Cuba. The British occupation allowed hundreds of local residents access to British trade goods and the chance to pursue long-standing commercial goals.[52]

Sociability and Its Limits

Through the mechanisms of commerce and sociability, Albemarle successfully curried favor with those leading residents without whom his rule could not function. Precisely because so many Havana residents were culturally confident in their Spanish and Catholic identifications and had prior con-

51. For bills of sale showing boat purchases by Havana residents, see, all in ANC: Protocolos de La Habana, Escribanía de Ortega, 1762, fols. 986, 987, 1763, fols. 188–189, Escribanía de Salinas, 1762, fol. 1008, 1763, fol. 64, Escribanía de Galetti, 1763, fol. 40, Escribanía de Ponton, 1763, fols. 31, 45, 149–150. For Juan de Miralles, see Protocolos de La Habana, Escribanía de Fornari, 1763, fols. 243–244; Resumen sobre Don Juan de Miralles, Mar. 27, 1765, AGI, IG, 2820A.

52. Conde de Ricla to Arriaga, Nov. 20, 30, 1763, and Arriaga to Conde de Ricla, Mar. 23, 1764, all in AGS, Hacienda, 2342; Testamentaría del Conde de Ricla, 1748–1781, AGI, SD, 1212 and 1213.

nections to their occupiers, the occupation showed evidence of processes by which English-speakers and Spanish-speakers, Protestants and Catholics operated in a fluid, shared world. Cosmopolitanism had been prevalent in elite circles before, among those with trading ties abroad, but it became more pronounced during the occupation and smoothed the transfer of power. Before the invasion, the city's white population already included numerous foreigners from Britain, Ireland, and other British territories who now helped provide the glue of British rule. A man who served as one of Albemarle's translators, for example, was Eduardo Hamlin, a London-born doctor married in Havana and resident there since the War of Jenkins' Ear. Men like Hamlin and the cabildo members provided a necessary glue that enabled Albemarle to establish what was in general a peaceful rule within city walls.[53]

In theory, an occupying army might overwhelm a city's infrastructure, but Havana had a long history of receiving thousands of sailors at a time during *tiempo de flota,* when the Spanish treasure fleet came into port. Despite the destruction, the city had homes for rent and space to put up this army, as well as taverns, brothels, and gambling houses to entertain them and lighten their pockets of prize winnings. British officers rented out homes befitting their station, while many of the soldiers slept in the emptied convents and monasteries or the Castillo de la Real Fuerza, where they used piles of Spanish government papers as mattresses. Lord Albemarle tried to restrict the sale of alcohol to his soldiers and sailors in order to keep his men in check, but they were eager to avail themselves of the city's many diversions for sailors on furlough.[54]

The volatile mix of blacks and whites, British and Spanish, and men and women on the streets of occupied Havana and in its taverns sometimes led to tense relations. Altercations occasionally broke out between the occupying army and ordinary Havana residents, including men of color. For example, one *negro* reportedly stole a gold watch from a British man and tried to avoid capture by seeking refuge in the convent of Saint Augustine and appealing to religious personnel there for immunity. This was a clever stratagem, exploiting the overlapping legal and religious codes of the occupied zone. Perhaps inspired by this example, another black man named Joseph de Leon sought refuge in a church after allegedly killing an Englishman. Several individuals of

53. Consejo de Indias, Apr. 7, 1766, AGI, SD, 1135, no. 4. After a visit in 1746, M. Villiet d'Arignon remarked that "strangers land [in Havana] from many parts"; see *Voyage du Sr. Villiet d'Arignon, a la Havane, la Vera-Cruz, et le Mexique,* in [Nicolas Louis Bourgeois and P. J. B. Nougaret, eds.], *Voyages intéressans dans différentes colonies françaises, espagnoles, anglaises, etc. . . .* (London and Paris, 1788), 301.

54. John J. Clune, Jr., *Cuban Convents in the Age of Enlightened Reform, 1761–1807* (Gainesville, Fla., 2008), 28; ? to Julián de Arriaga, Apr. 6, 1763, AGI, SD, 2082; El comisario de Guerra Don Nicolás Joseph Rapun to Arriaga, Apr. 25, 1763, AGS, Hacienda, 2342.

African descent were implicated in the murders of British subjects during the period of British occupation.[55]

Within city walls, several men of color returned violence with violence, disturbing what was otherwise an easy British rule. Though the surviving archival trail is scant, in at least one instance the violence might have spilled over from confrontations during the siege. In the month after the capitulation, a man described as pardo allegedly murdered a sergeant of the Royal American forces. This individual was likely a veteran of the siege: the majority of pardos in Havana were free rather than enslaved, and many were members of the militia. The Royal Americans were in the first wave of those storming the Morro and might have been involved in the moment of reprisal at the tower and the murder of black soldiers. Doing Albemarle's bidding, the cabildo hanged this man on the gallows in Plaza Nueva. Its members' desire to preserve good relations with the British governor won out over their loyalty to the city's defenders, and Albemarle did his part to return the favor. Indeed, in occupied Havana the social worlds of blacks and wealthy whites operated on different axes.[56]

Shortly after the capitulation, Albemarle began hosting weekly soirees, or *"saraos,"* at his quarters on Thursday nights, which worked in tandem with the cabildo's oath swearing and other rituals to build mutually beneficial political and social relations with the city's elite. These events were designed to mitigate the uninvited nature of the British presence and signal the transition from war to peace. According to Havana's leading religious figure, Bishop Morell—Albemarle's most committed critic and adversary—"He wisely introduced them in order to celebrate his triumph and ease the yoke of his command with diversions." Dancing, which was a central feature of these events, facilitated interaction between British officers and Havana's leading families, particularly their daughters. At first, these events were not well attended, but they soon became so, as Albemarle continued to lavish the city's leading residents with courtly pleasantries.[57]

55. For the two men who sought refuge from Havana's religious institutions, see Bishop Pedro Agustín Morel de Santa Cruz to the Council of the Indies, Aug. 23–26, 1762, paras. 15, 17–18, AGI, SD, 1356. A "negro" was also accused of being involved in the robbery and murder of two Philadelphia merchants named William Read and H. Boyd in occupied Havana, as reported in North American newspapers; see *Providence Gazette; and Country Journal* (R.I.), Apr. 9, 1763 (quotation); and *Pennsylvania Gazette* (Philadelphia), May 26, 1763.

56. Roig de Leuchsenring, ed., *La dominación inglesa,* 188–189; "Orderly Book of the Havana Expedition," Sept. 17, 1762, in *The Two Putnams,* 85.

57. "Remarques sur la Havane," Pierre Eugene du Simitière Papers, West Indies No. 4, LCP; Thomas Milton, *A Plan of the City and Harbor of Havana, Situated on the Island of Cuba . . .* (London, 1739); Morell de Santa Cruz to Arriaga, Dec. 31, 1762, AGI, SD, 1356; "Documento Numero IV: Carta que en 12 de diciembre de 1763 escribió un padre Jesuita de La Habana al Prefecto Javier Bonilla,

British officers' journals from the period of the occupation describe ami-
cable relations with Havana's most powerful families. Many officers were put
up in private homes, in some cases with the owners present. Although some
Havana residents later complained that British officers treated their homes
poorly and did not pay their rent, Henry Fletcher, a British officer, commented
that "the Spaniards in general were polite and very obliging, the better sort
treated the English Officers with very great Civility." British officers converted
a Spanish outdoor theater for their own use and reportedly "invited people
with tickets" to their productions. Theater would have served to socialize new
subjects to British culture and language and also provide a place to meet, flirt,
interact, and display the latest fashions, like Albemarle's soirees. To celebrate
the birth of the Prince of Wales in early December, the theater put on a special
production of Nicholas Rowe's *Fair Penitent*. Subsequently, the British officers
continued to put on weekly performances for some time after.[58]

During the occupation, British and British American merchants and the
goods they brought to sale helped enhance a shared transimperial culture of
elite consumption and exchange, accelerating processes already in motion for
men like Juan de Miralles. British fashions in clothing and leisure activities
became popular in Havana during the occupation; residents noted that Peñalver's wife dressed "English-style." Items that were normally difficult to obtain
in Havana, like Chinese silks and hats of beaver skin, came into vogue. Playing
cards from Genoa, normally prohibited, became popular in the city's many
card games. The practice of freemasonry also arrived in occupied Havana and
became another forum for elites to engage in the cosmopolitan currents of
Atlantic society.[59]

---

de Sevilla, dándole cuenta circunstanciada de la toma de esta plaza por los ingleses . . . ," in Roig
de Leuchsenring, ed., *La dominación inglesa*, 275. This analysis of "sociability" under occupation is
in part inspired by the work of Paul Kramer, who refers to a similar phenomenon, which he terms
"fiesta politics," during the U.S. occupation of the Philippines in 1899. On the whole, he attributes
more coercive violence and ultimate authority to the occupiers than I do for eighteenth-century
British Havana. See Kramer, *The Blood of Government*, 185–191.

58. Hernández González, *La otra guerra del inglés*, 41–94; "Vecinos de La Habana sobre veja-
ciones sobre generales ingleses," 1762, AGI, Estado, 7, no. 9; Fletcher, "Seven Years' War Journal," Jan.
22, 1763, Codex Eng 31, JCBL. As Fletcher wrote, "The English Officers . . . Amus'd themselves, and
entertained the Town with some excellent Theatrical performances." For references to weekly theatrical performances in occupied Havana, see "Extract of a Letter from a Gentleman at the Havannah, to Another in This City, Dated Nov. 27, 1762," *New-York Mercury*, Jan. 3, 1763, [2]; "Charlestown,
South-Carolina, January 12: "Extract of a Letter from the Havannah, Dec. 13," *Newport Mercury*,
Feb. 14, 1763, [1]. For an examination of the global history of *The Fair Penitent* and the relationship between English theater and imperialism, see Kathleen Wilson, "Rowe's *Fair Penitent* as Global
History; or, A Diversionary Voyage to New South Wales," *Eighteenth-Century Studies*, XLI (2008),
231–251.

59. Olañeta, "Diario del sitio," Jan. 3, 1763, Miscellaneous Manuscripts, MS 352, XV, box 83, folder

Like the South Sea Company factors before him, a group of British merchants set up shop in Havana and cultivated relationships with the city's leading commercial families. Inventories of the well-stocked warehouses of twelve firms, performed in the summer of 1763 — during the grace period extended to British merchants for their removal from Cuba — suggest these merchants assumed they would be there for some time and perhaps would trade to New Spain as well. Even British and British American merchants that did not stay behind in Havana were willing to extend credit until the final moments of British rule, which would have provided them a pretext to sail back into harbor in search of payment, with additional cargo to sell, even if the port should return to Spain.[60]

Just as they did before the British occupation, some merchants sought to marry into the upper echelons of Havana society. As was always the case, Catholicism helped to pave the way. An Irish Catholic slave trader who had a commercial house in Alicante, Spain, moved to Havana during the occupation and followed the local custom of marrying into an elite family. He then went into business with Juan de Miralles, whose wife was now a relative of his. It is likely that this man, Cornelio Coppinger, and Miralles had prior connections, as Miralles was born in Alicante and spent the first twenty-five years of his life there. Once established in Havana, Coppinger went into the slave trade with Miralles, tapping into merchant networks in British America, Britain, Spain, and Africa. He was among the handful of British and British American merchants who stayed in Havana after its restitution to Spanish rule, and who

1662, Sterling Memorial Library; "Don Julián de Arriaga avisa el Rey aprueba lo que se informó sobre el desordenado abuso de sarasas de China," Jan. 31, 1767, AGI, SD, 1194. By December 1762, 414 dozen beaver hats and 135 dozen felt hats had been exported from London to Havana (Add. MSS 38373, fol. 134v–135r, BL). More than ten years after the end of British rule, Spanish authorities were still lamenting the popularity of playing cards from Genoa in Havana, which they attributed to the great number imported to the island during the occupation; see "Apuntaciones de La Habana sobre distintos ramos y utilidades que podrían resultar a la Real Hacienda," Nov. 21, 1776, AGI, SD, 1157, fols. 268–293. The practice of freemasonry, which had been expressly forbidden by Spanish colonial authorities, gained adherents in Havana during the occupation; see Roig de Leuchsenring, ed., *La dominación inglesa*, 281; María del Carmen Barcia, *Cuba: Acciones populares en tiempos de la independencia americana* (Matanzas, Cuba, 2011), 23–24; Manuel de Paz Sánchez, "Aspectos generales y principales características de la implantación sistemática de la francmasonería en la Gran Antilla, durante la segunda mitad de XIX," *Anuario de estudios americanos*, XXXVI (1979), 531–568, esp. 531. For an individual identified as a *"fraemason,"* who arrived at the time of the British occupation, see Consejo de Indias, Dec. 7, 1769, AGI, SD, 1136. The first freemason lodges were established in Jamaica in the 1740s; see James Robertson, *Gone Is the Ancient Glory: Spanish Town, Jamaica, 1534–2000* (Kingston, Jamaica, 2005).

60. Ricla to Arriaga, Nov. 25, 1763, sobre géneros de comerciantes extranjeros con 16 inventarios, Gobierno Superior Civil, 451, no. 18574, ANC. For examples of merchants returning in 1767, see Phelipe Durell [*sic*] to Antonio María Bucareli, June 20, 1767, no. 9, and Bucareli to Don Phelipe Durell, June 22, 1767, no. 11, both in AGS, Estado, 6966.

would go on to play a prominent role in the economic life of the island in the decades that followed.[61]

Letters sent from the occupied city to Spain warned that loyalty to the Spanish crown and Catholic ritual practice was decreasing over time. A Spanish Jesuit, writing to his superior in Spain, reported that, in general, most Catholics maintained their commitment to the faith, but housing British officers in their homes had "reprehensible" effects on the Havana elite. It brought "familiarity," and in some cases the officer class received "treatment with distinction." Marrying foreigners, which was a long-standing custom in Havana, now became a cause for religious authorities' alarm in the altered religious and political climate of British Havana. Another Jesuit in Havana complained of the "disorder of some women who have abandoned their religion, their honor, and their children and *patria* and have left with them [the British], and contracted marriage according to Protestant rites." A foreigner present during the occupation described how three women who had "stayed with Englishmen" were caught and confined in the San Francisco de Paula hospital for women but noted that they "escaped shortly after."[62]

In a sense, these accounts of diminishing loyalties warned of an identity process similar to what scholars have described for borderland communities. The concern was that, after a while, a series of everyday choices to adhere to, obey, or affiliate with British rule would have a cumulative effect, a contagion, or a tendency of "sticking to the skin." Havana was already a cosmopolitan space, but the pace of exchange with its neighbors intensified with increased contact with the goods, culture, and practices of the British occupiers. Too brief to radically alter the dynamics of the city, the occupation nonetheless raised alarm bells about the behavior of Havana's elite denizens. What Bishop Morell saw, through his partisan eyes, was a drop in Catholic worship and the reduction of the city to "an extreme confusion . . . so disfigured from what it was previously that nobody would recognize it."[63]

61. "Relación de méritos y servicios de Cornelio Coppinger," Sept. 9, 1776, AGI, IG, 2821; Francisco Xavier de Santa Cruz y Mallén, *Historia de familias cubanas,* VII (Havana, 1985), 109.

62. "Documento Numero IV: Carta que en 12 de diciembre de 1763," in Roig de Leuchsenring, ed., *La dominación inglesa,* 274; "Remarques sur la Havane," Pierre Eugene du Simitière Papers, West Indies No. 4, LCP; Sherry Johnson, "'Señoras en sus clases no ordinarias': Enemy Collaborators or Courageous Defenders of the Family?" *Cuban Studies,* XXXIV (2003), 11–37, esp. 12.

63. Pedro Agustin Morell to Arriaga, Dec. 31, 1762, AGI, SD, 1356; Andrés Reséndez, *Changing National Identities at the Frontier: Texas and New Mexico, 1800–1850* (Cambridge, 2005), 1–14; Peter Sahlins, *Boundaries: The Making of France and Spain in the Pyrenees* (Berkeley, Calif., 1989), 87. Writing to the Spanish king to encourage him to retake Havana by force, Lorenzo de Montalvo warned of a law of diminishing loyalty among Havana residents; see Pedro Azerace to the King, Aug. 28, 1762, AGI, Ultramar, 169.

"La dominación anglicana"

As Morell's comment indicates, religion produced a point of friction during the occupation, a telling exception to the harmonious climate among whites within city walls. Other than what went on many leagues from Havana, and black resistance within city walls, the only attempts to oppose British rule came from the Spanish officer Lorenzo de Montalvo and Bishop Morell. In a way, their efforts to resist only accentuate by contrast the otherwise smooth functioning of the occupation and the willing complicity of the cabildo and other prominent Havana residents. An official and commissary for the army and navy, stationed in Havana at the time of the attack, Montalvo kept up a secret correspondence with Madariaga about the possibility of a counterattack, though nothing came to concrete planning stages. Bishop Morell, already seventy-two years old by the time of the British occupation and famous for his strong and obstreperous personality, mounted the only sustained opposition to Lord Albemarle from elite society.[64]

Morell saw himself as a defender of his Catholic flock and duty-bound to make Albemarle's rule as trying as possible. A creole born in Santo Domingo, who had also served in Bolivia and Nicaragua, Morell had a character that had been forged in other fires, far from Havana. He had been in Santiago de Cuba during the British occupation of Guántanamo in 1741, and, during that invasion, he donated Church funds to the defense. Afterward, he wrote a book (sadly lost) that was a history of British attacks on Spanish America, a text that prefigured the siege of Havana as much as any English prophesies. During Havana's occupation, he waged a campaign of drafting letters, deemed "long" and "tedious" by Albemarle, in which he mocked the British governor's poorly translated Spanish and characterized his rule over Havana as *"un imperio absoluto."* At one point, Morell gloated that one of his letters had enraged Albemarle so much that the British commander, according to one witness, became "absolutely frenetic," like "a furious lion."[65]

Morell's defiance was so exceptional and dogged that allegations arose that he was the chief conspirator in an island-wide anti-British insurgency. A rumor even took hold in Havana—reported in North American newspapers as well—that the bishop was the ringleader of a rebellion that sought to rise up and murder all the British occupiers. Such a scenario was improbable, invented by a suggestible British imaginary activated by the specter of

64. Thomas, *Cuba,* 48. The letters of Lorenzo de Montalvo during the occupation are mostly in AGS, Marina, 426.

65. Pedro Agustin Morell de Santa Cruz to Council of the Indies, Dec. 31, 1762, AGI, SD, 1356; César García del Pino, *Vida de Pedro Agustín Morell de Santa Cruz* (Havana, 1985), 13.

armed Spanish Catholic priests. Outside the city walls, military opposition to the British occupation continued, but in Havana and its immediate vicinity, Morell found few allies.[66]

Predictably, the main point of contention between the British commander and the Spanish bishop was Church property. Shortly after the capitulation, Lieutenant Colonel Samuel Cleaveland, Pocock's commander of artillery, insisted on the conqueror's prerogative of seizing all the church and monastery bells in Havana. Albemarle's covetousness had even led him to produce a list of Havana's many monasteries, convents, and other religious institutions, categorizing them as "rich," "very rich," and "very, very rich." Morell staunchly opposed his demands, based upon the protections extended to Church property in the articles of capitulation. As a compromise, Albemarle demanded the payment of ten thousand pesos and a detailed list of all personnel and property for each church, monastery, and convent in the city. Morell paid the initial ten thousand pesos, but, when Albemarle demanded an additional one hundred thousand pesos, he refused, countering that the two sovereigns should decide on the propriety of said payment. This statement accurately reflected the nature of the articles of capitulation and the space between sovereigns that British Havana occupied; however, it could be interpreted as seditious in a territory where technically only the British monarch reigned. For that reason, it provided the opportunity Albemarle had been waiting for to eliminate the bishop.[67]

At six o'clock in the morning on November 3, Albemarle sent two officials and fifty soldiers to surprise Morell in his home before breakfast and forcibly carry him on his bishop's chair into the street. These men then transported him to the docks and placed him on a boat headed to exile in Saint Augus-

66. "We had a report that the Spaniards intended to rise and put us all to Death, as our Garrison was now much Weaken'd by Sickness having scarcely 700 Men that could do Duty. The Bishop was the Chief incendiary, who Endeavor'd to spirit up the People to this Massacre; Lord Albemarle had him Seized and Sent immediately off in one of our Frigates, to St. Augustine." See Fletcher, "Seven Years' War Journal," Nov. 4, 1762, Codex English 41, JCBL. See also *Pennsylvania Gazette,* Dec. 16, 1762.

67. Morell to Arriaga, Dec. 31, 1762, AGI, SD, 1356; García del Pino, *Vida de Pedro Agustín Morell de Santa Cruz,* 26–32; "Lista de conventos y colegios," in Blanck, ed., *Papeles sobre la toma de La Habana,* 41 ("rich"). On the impulse to loot religious institutions in occupied Havana, see also Mancini, "Siege Mentalities," *Winterthur Portfolio,* XLV (2011), 139. In the capitulation accords, the British commander had insisted that all promotions within religious orders be sent to him for approval, but Church property was supposed to be respected. Regarding the payment to Albemarle, see "Papel sobre la expulsión del Obispo por el Sr. Don Lorenzo Montalvo," n.d., Colección Mata Linares, LXXIX, fol. 224, Real Academia de la Historia; Provisor y Vicario General Doctor Don Santiago de Echaverría to King Carlos III, Nov. 3, 1762, and Morell to Arriaga, Dec. 31, 1762, both in AGI, SD, 1356; César García del Pino, *Toma de La Habana por los ingleses y sus antecedentes* (Havana, 2002), 136–143.

tine, Florida. Even though the articles of capitulation had guaranteed that the bishop should remain in place and Church property be protected, Albemarle felt justified in his actions. In his communiqué describing events to Lord Egremont, Albemarle referenced Morell's planned appeal to the king of Spain and described his behavior as "troublesome and impertinently litigious." "The bishop of Cuba," he wrote, "has at last given me a good pretense for removing him from this island, and the government of the church, an event I have long wished for as I considered him a very dangerous man here."[68]

Despite this spectacular breach of the articles of capitulation, Morell found little support from the Havana population. The cabildo did not rally to Morell's defense or oppose the religious donativo; they only briefly protested his exile. In fact, one Havana clergy member seemed not the least surprised that Morell was sent abroad. In a reference to prior conflicts between Morell and Governor Prado, he wrote that it took only the briefest amount of time for the Englishman "to recognize the character of the diocesan Bishop." It seems that the clash was mostly one of personalities between Albemarle and Morell, as William Keppel restored Morell to Cuba around the time of the announcement of the island's ultimate return to Spain, perhaps as a conciliatory gesture.[69]

One might have expected hostility from other priests or members of the religious orders in occupied Havana, but Morell was the exception. The religious orders in Havana owned many enslaved Africans and agricultural properties, which gave them incentive to stay in British Havana and pursue financial advantage in the trade fair taking place there. In contrast with Morell, a prominent Jesuit father, Thomas Ignacio Butler, of Irish origin and London-educated but resident many years in Havana, served, not as an opponent to Albemarle's rule, but rather as a commercial liaison between British merchants and Havana residents. On behalf of the Jesuit order, Butler was running one of the largest and most efficient sugar plantations of the day, and he had close ties to Peñalver and Miralles, who sold the order's sugar abroad. He also had been an associate of the South Sea Company factor Wargeant Nicholson,

---

68. Lord Albemarle to Lord Egremont, Nov. 4, 1762, Lord Egremont Letter Books, West Indies, I, 1762, Petworth House Archives, HMC 165, fol. 224, West Sussex Record Office; Bishop Morell to Albemarle, Nov. 2, 1762, CO 117.1, fols. 182–183, TNA; Roig de Leuchsenring, ed., *La dominación inglesa*, 41; Morell to Arriaga, Dec. 31, 1762, AGI, SD: 1356; "Documento Numero IV: Carta que en 12 de diciembre de 1763," in Roig de Leuchsenring, ed., *La dominación inglesa*, 254–255.

69. Pedro Diego[?] de Adromite, Auxiliador de Cuba, y efecto de Quito, to Juan de Prado, Mar. 3, 1763, AGI, SD, 1585. The cabildo did not support Morell on matters such as his opposition to paying one hundred thousand pesos to Albemarle, on behalf of the Church, and his complaints about the use of monasteries as hospitals for sick British soldiers; see Morell to Arriaga, Dec. 31, 1762, AGI, SD, 1356; Roig de Leuchsenring, ed., *La dominación inglesa*, 37–42.

who relied on him to mediate on the factory's behalf. During the occupation, Butler offered to collect debts on behalf of the former South Sea Company factors in Havana.[70]

Unlike Morell, Butler portrayed British rule as lenient. Four months after the city's surrender, he wrote to his superiors in Seville that the British occupiers "did not behave that badly with us, but better than we could have expected." After all the violence of the campaign and the surrender of the city, "we began to live with a foreign nation, mixed together the one with the other. ... They behaved not with the tyranny that we read about in the history of victors, but with the greatest humanity and subjection." Direct British rule provided considerable commercial opportunities. Butler marveled at the "incredible" number of ships that arrived in port and the abundance of provisions, clothing, and other goods.[71]

As the administrator of the Jesuit order's properties in western Cuba (the Jesuits were one of the largest slaveholders of the time), Butler seized the commercial opportunities presented by the occupation. In 1762, the Jesuits operated three sugar plantations outside Havana, along with three *estancias* (small farms), three houses inside city walls, and more than ten cattle ranches. The Jesuits had been precocious investors in sugar, drawing from their experience with the crop in Brazil and New Spain to found some of its most important and valuable early ingenios of the mid-eighteenth century.[72]

During the occupation, Butler made out the best of anyone who purchased enslaved Africans in occupied Havana. In total, he purchased 395 forced laborers, many at discounted prices, and resold some of them on the local

70. Mercedes García Rodríguez, *Misticismo y capitales: La Compañía de Jesús en la economía habanera del siglo XVIII* (Havana, 2000), 106–107, 157; William Fogo to David Hodge, July 13, 1763, and Fogo to Campbell, July 31, 1763, both in C 111.200, TNA. Butler served as a character witness for Sebastián de Peñalver during his treason trial; see "Rendición de la plaza de La Habana a los ingleses," AGI, SD, 1590, no. 4. Butler also testified on behalf of a fellow Catholic and native of Cork, Cornelio Coppinger, who stayed on after the British occupation to continue trading enslaved Africans to the island; see "Informe sobre el antiguo catolicismo de Coppinger por Padre Butler de la Compañía de Jesus," 1766, AGI, SD, 2210, no. 5. On Jesuit holdings in and around Havana in 1767, at the time of the order's expulsion, see "Documentación sobre la expulsion de las jesuítas y la administración de sus bienes," 1767–1768, AGI, Cuba, 1098.

71. "Documento Numero IV: Carta que en 12 de diciembre de 1763," in Roig de Leuchsenring, ed., *La dominación inglesa*, 272; "Carta del Jesuíta Thomas Butler," Dec. 12, 1763, C.M. Pérez, no. 26, Sala Cubana, BNJM.

72. The largest Jesuit plantation at the time was worked by 242 enslaved Africans; see García Rodríguez, *Misticismo y capitales*, 55, 60, 99. For an economic history of Jesuits in the sugar industry of Bahía, Brazil, see Stuart B. Schwartz, *Sugar Plantations in the Formation of Brazilian Society: Bahia, 1550–1835* (Cambridge, 1985). For Jesuits' producing sugar in New Spain, see Fernando B. Sandoval, *La industria de azúcar en Nueva España* (Mexico City, 1951); and James Denson Riley, *Hacendados jesuítas en México: La administración de los bienes inmuebles del Colegio Máximo de San Pedro y San Pablo de la Ciudad de México, 1685–1767* (Mexico City, 1976).

market. Always interested in improving efficiency and maximizing production, Butler took advantage of the opportunity to acquire enslaved Africans
the British expedition brought with it for the Havana campaign. These Africans and creoles from Antigua, Jamaica, and Martinique had technical experience in sugar production learned in the British and French West Indies
that Butler would have found desirable. Because many of these individuals
were sick or injured, Butler purchased them at discounted prices. He sent
many of the men he purchased to recover, ostensibly, while working on the
Jesuits' largest ingenio. The purchase helped the Jesuits to replace enslaved
Africans lost during the siege and recover from the loss of their sugar harvest
of that year, destroyed during the fighting. Though this Jesuit found a way
to use the connection with Albemarle to profit, it was not until the return of
Spanish rule that the slave trade opened up further and began to expand the
industry.[73]

Monopolizing the Slave Trade

Despite overall commercial gains for local residents in British Havana, the
one branch of trade that did not grow during the occupation was the trade in
enslaved Africans. In this regard, both residents of Havana and British slave
traders had their expectations disappointed. There is no better example of
Albemarle's profiteering and restrictions on trade in British Havana than the
slave trading that went on there. Slave sales in British Havana formed part of
the raiding and gifting economy of Albemarle's governance. Establishing a system that mimicked the Spanish asiento, the British governor restricted slave
sales in British Havana under a monopoly system, with high duties imposed,
to enrich himself and deprive the island of the enslaved Africans its consumers
demanded. Many of Havana's elites cozied up to their British occupiers with
the hope of expanding access to the African slave trade, but their ambitions
were largely thwarted by Albemarle's greed. Those with the closest relations to
Albemarle did manage to gain more enslaved Africans, but in general the slave
trade during the British occupation, unlike during the occupation of Guadeloupe, defied those hoping to expand it dramatically.

Historians have traditionally argued that British Havana, like the French
sugar islands, saw a vast influx of enslaved Africans for sale during its occupation. The British occupation was once credited with catalyzing Cuba's transition to sugar monoculture, following the model of its neighbors Jamaica

73. García Rodríguez, *Misticismo y capitales*, 130–147, 155–156; Ricla to Arriaga, Nov. 24, 1763, AGI,
SD, 1213; Protocolos de La Habana, Escibanía de Fornari, 1763, fols. 566, 568, 615v, ANC; Protocolos
Junco, 1763, fols. 360, 427v, ANC; C.M. Bachiller, no. 308, BNJM.

and Saint Domingue. This interpretation assumed similar commercial outcomes of the British occupations of Havana and Guadeloupe. It also aligned
with the view that Havana had a stagnant, inward-facing economy before
its British occupiers broke open Spanish trade monopolies. The narrative of
the occupation as the precipitant of Cuba's sugar boom persists, especially
in English-language scholarship, despite its debunking some time ago by
Spanish-language scholars. As a result of a historian's copying error in a book
published in 1907, the period of the occupation has been credited with the
importation of 10,700 enslaved Africans—and continues to be credited in
some cases. A more accurate figure for the number of enslaved Africans sold
under British occupation, including those sold illegally outside Albemarle's
monopoly, however, would be approximately 3,200 enslaved Africans. This
number would not have appreciably increased the rate of growth for Cuba's
population of African descent once one accounts for the many enslaved Africans who died in the fighting.[74]

In comparison with Havana's many mechanisms for human trafficking
throughout the earlier decades of the eighteenth century, the slave trade was
actually more restricted under British than Spanish rule. Albemarle gave the
Liverpool merchant John Kennion a monopoly on slave sales in Havana in return for a two-thirds to one-third revenue split in favor of himself. Enslaved
Africans were priced at the same level or higher than they were by the Royal
Havana Company in the period before the invasion, and they were sold under

74. For the original estimate of 10,700 imported enslaved Africans during the occupation, see
Hubert H. S. Aimes, *A History of Slavery in Cuba: 1511 to 1868* (New York, 1907), 33. Eric Williams
repeated the estimate of 10,000 slaves in *Capitalism and Slavery* (1944; rpt. Chapel Hill, NC, 1994)
33. Hugh Thomas discovered the copying error of Aimes and recalculated that number at 4,000 enslaved Africans (Thomas, *Cuba, or the Pursuit of Freedom*, 49–50). The majority of subsequent histories of Cuba and its slave trade either used Thomas's estimate or more or less agreed with it; see, for
example, Juan Pérez de la Riva, "¿Cuántos africanos fueron traídos a Cuba?" *Economía y desarrollo*,
no. 3 (July–September 1970), 141–142; Marrero, *Cuba*, VI, 29–30; Moreno Fraginals, *El ingenio*, 24;
Laird W. Bergad, Fe Iglesias García, and María del Carmen Barcia, *The Cuban Slave Market, 1790–
1880* (New York, 1995), 25; John Robert McNeill, *Atlantic Empires of France and Spain: Louisbourg
and Havana, 1700–1763* (Chapel Hill, N.C., 1985), 167. For the most thorough analysis of slave sales
in the notarial protocols in the Archivo Nacional de Cuba during the British occupation and an
overview of this controversy, see Enrique López Mesa, "Acerca de la introducción de esclavos en La
Habana durante la ocupación británica (1762–1763)," *Rábida*, XIX (2000), 29–40. López Mesa estimates 3,200 enslaved Africans sold, which I have followed here. His estimate includes those enslaved
Africans sold by Kennion and others sold clandestinely by members of the expedition or other merchants. Scholars of Cuban slavery who agree with López Mesa's estimate include Pablo Tornero
Tinajero, *Crecimiento económico y transformaciones sociales: Esclavos, hacendados, y comerciantes en
la Cuba colonial (1760–1840)* (Madrid, 1996), 35. English-language histories that still use the 10,000
estimate include Louis A. Pérez, Jr., *Cuba: Between Reform and Revolution*, 5th ed. (New York, 2015),
45; Herbert S. Klein and Ben Vinson III, *African Slavery in the Caribbean and Latin America*, 2d ed.
(New York, 2007), 82.

the same high customs duties exacted by the Spanish crown. Albemarle limited the total number allowed to be imported to two thousand (fifteen hundred men, five hundred women) and duplicated the system of duties under Spanish rule (forty dollars on adults, twenty on youths). The persistence of contraband with British merchants, even under British rule, meant that about 50 percent more enslaved Africans were sold than the two thousand stipulated by Albemarle.[75]

Albemarle claimed to be restricting the number of enslaved Africans for sale in occupied Havana in order to protect the interests of neighboring British West Indian sugar islands. He asserted that he was thinking strategically about a branch of trade that had always played a crucial role in imperial rivalry. As he explained after the fact to superiors in London, "It is surely not in the interest of Great Britain to drain their old colonies of slaves in order to supply the wants of their new conquests." He continued, "Nothing could have been more detrimental to our lands or more advantageous to that of Cuba in particular[,] a fertile country of which a great part remain uncultivated for want of a sufficient number of negroe slaves." According to this rationale, Albemarle suspected there was little chance of Havana's retention and sought to avoid granting a rival colony economic advantages that would extend into the postwar period.[76]

Just as likely, though, Albemarle was seeking to defend his profiteering in occupied Havana. By setting up a personal monopoly and justifying it according to Spanish practices, he kept prices artificially high and reserved maximum revenues for himself and his business associate Kennion. In so doing, he was mimicking the practice of the Spanish government and instating an import tax that would later be deemed illegal by parliamentary authorities in London. Ironically for residents of occupied Havana, these monopolies were more easily avoided under Spanish than British governance. By holding the slave trade close and channeling it through himself, Albemarle wielded it as an effective tool to enrich himself and build loyalty among the city's elites. Slaves were, after all, the highest priced "goods" on offer in British Havana, and Havana residents had a reputation for their insatiable demand for enslaved Africans.[77]

Despite the constraints on slave trading in British-occupied Havana, the city's leading residents found ways to get their hands on enslaved Africans

75. Suits Involving the Earl of Albemarle, Manuscripts Relating to the Siege of Havana, no. 1, May 21, 1776, Boston Public Library; López Mesa, "Acerca de la introducción," *Rábida*, XIX (2000), 29–40; Report received from the Earl of Albemarle, May 6, 1763, PRO 30/47/18, TNA.

76. "Papers relating to an Expedition Sent against Havana," PRO 30/47/18, TNA.

77. House of Lords, *John Kennion, Esq., Appellant; Samuel Gardner, John Turner . . . Respondents.*

and either keep them for their agricultural estates or make a profit in Havana's busy resale market. Several of those with close ties to Albemarle and John Kennion—such as Peñalver, Miralles, and cabildo members Don Laureano Chacón and Don Pedro Beltrán de Santa Cruz—were able to purchase enslaved Africans from Kennion in large lots and resell many of them at a profit using Albemarle's artificially high prices. Juan O'Farrill, the son of the former South Sea Company factor Ricardo O'Farrill and the proprietor of the largest sugar plantation in the area, was also able to purchase sixty-two enslaved Africans from Kennion. Perhaps surprisingly, some of those individuals buying enslaved Africans in occupied Havana were free men and women of color, which was a sign of both their ongoing importance in the urban economy and the city's large and diversified market for enslaved Africans. On the whole, though, the city's population of African descent suffered from the bonds Albemarle forged with the Havana cabildo over their shared interest in enriching themselves through interimperial slave trading.[78]

In fact, the Havana cabildo conspired with Lord Albemarle to capture and resell enslaved Africans who had run away to the interior during the course of the siege and its immediate aftermath. In so doing, its members violated the promises and guarantees made to enslaved Africans who had fought against the British invasion in exchange for their freedom. Many of these individuals captured had been combatants who had elected to withdraw to Spanish-controlled lands rather than surrender and were now finding themselves apprehended by fellow Havana residents acting as Lord Albemarle's proxies. Recognizing their value as commodities, Albemarle promised rewards (ten pesos for an enslaved African, five pesos for a guachinango) to anyone who captured "runaways" and brought them to him in Havana. During the British occupation, the cabildo issued as many as nineteen commissions to agents, for the same fee, to go into the rest of the island, including areas of "Spanish Cuba," and recapture and return blacks and guachinangos who allegedly had escaped inland.[79]

78. Protocolos de La Habana, Escribanía de Fornari, 1762–1763, ANC. Of 1,060 enslaved Africans sold by John Kennion and identified in the Havana notarial protocols, the largest lot sold (342 enslaved Africans) went to Sebastián de Peñalver Angulo, Laureano Chacón, and Pedro de Santa Cruz. The next largest group was purchased by Don Juan O'Farrill, followed by the Marqués de Villa Alta, María de Miralles, Don Pedro de Santa Cruz, Condesa de Casa Bayona, the regidor Don Mateo Pedroso, and Don Feliz de Acosta. Ten free black and mulatto men and women also appear in Havana's notarial protocols as purchasers of one enslaved African each from the British commercial agent; see Protocolos Fornari, 1762, fols. 490, 503, 506, 507, 1763, fols. 52, 81, 83, 100, 218, 475, ANC. They might have been purchasing these individuals to help run their inns, taverns, workshops, small businesses, and households.

79. Roig de Leuchsenring, ed., *La dominación inglesa*, 73–75, 81. On August 19, 1762, the city council initially commissioned two men, whom it stipulated had to be *"personas blancas y honrradas,"* for

The cabildo's agents gained notoriety for roaming through the countryside taking blacks they encountered prisoner for British authorities in Havana. By February 1763, forces loyal to Spanish Cuba in the interior of the island apprehended several of these slave hunters to prevent sending the enslaved Africans to Havana, which in their eyes constituted aiding and abetting the enemy. In response, the Havana cabildo insisted that they were only "gathering" their own runaway blacks, though they were really doing so on commission for the British governor. Whether these individuals had been free or enslaved before the siege, royal slaves or privately owned, upon their capture they were pressed into work rebuilding the fortifications, or they were sold.[80]

Through the recapture and resale of these so-called runaways, the Havana cabildo colluded with the British governor to turn black subjects of the Spanish king into war booty and commodities to be bought and sold. For Peñalver and members of the cabildo, cooperating with Lord Albemarle paid dividends beyond the nominal monetary rewards. Toward the end of the occupation, in April 1763, Kennion gifted Peñalver ten enslaved Africans that had been captured. They would have fetched a good price along with the many that Peñalver bought from Kennion and sold to his fellow residents of occupied Havana. Given the extent of Albemarle's profiteering, he was also likely willing to share some of these profits as long as these men helped him govern.[81]

The resale market for captured Africans in occupied Havana was one of many reasons people of African descent remained largely outside the practices knitting Havana's commercial classes to its British occupiers. Many blacks who had fled the aftermath of the siege became victims of a shared, transimperial elite culture that collaborated in their enslavement and sale. In his report to the Spanish crown about the transition of power from the British to the Spanish, the new governor of Havana, the Conde de Ricla, reported that everything went smoothly except that "there was no remedy for some murders Spanish blacks had committed against Englishmen they encountered in the streets." The moment of British withdrawal would have presented a moment of political and legal transition, during which those who wished to settle scores potentially had an opportunity to do so without recourse. As we have seen, relations ran much more smoothly between the occupying army and the city's elite residents.[82]

---

this task: Don Gabriel de Alberoo and Don Cristobal de Sayas Basan. They were also provided with travel allowances to help finance their efforts.

80. Roig de Leuchsenring, ed., *La dominación inglesa*, 136–139, 198–199.

81. Protocolos de La Habana, Escribanía de Fornari, 1763, fol. 177, ANC; López Mesa, "Acerca de la introducción," *Rábida*, XIX (2000), 29–40.

82. Miscelánea de Libros, no. 1435, ANC, cited in José Luciano Franco, *Comercio clandestino de esclavos* (Havana, 1996), 46.

Imperial Reckonings

By February 1763, word reached Havana that the city would be returned to Spain in the peace treaty at the end of the war. This news came crashing into the world that the occupiers and the occupied had made. British rule over Havana did not provide sufficient time to secure control over much of the western part of the island, let alone Havana's jurisdiction, which never came to recognize the capitulation. Moreover, the nature of Lord Albemarle's patchwork and arbitrary rule was not conducive to facilitating more permanent British governance. Despite the joyous celebration and geopolitical dreaming Havana's capture inspired, the peace negotiations were too far along by the time of Havana's seizure for it to be retained. The favorable climate in London supporting the idea of more conquests had shifted.

The deal to return Havana, initially agreed on in November 1762, had required extensive diplomatic negotiations and Spain's agreement to give up Florida. Knowing somewhere important would have to be offered to compensate for Havana's loss, the French delegate, the Duke of Choiseul, asked Spain if it would be willing to cede Florida to the British if France gave Spain the Louisiana Territory, which included the port of New Orleans and nonexclusive access to the Mississippi River basin. Although this trade would remove the French presence from North America, French authorities thought so little of Louisiana that the Duke of Choiseul had made an earlier proposal to sell it to the Spanish. This time, France had made Spain a compelling offer. Florida was considered a poor fringe land, controlled by Native peoples and difficult for Spain to protect and provision adequately, whereas New Orleans was seen as a more desirable port. The Spanish negotiator, the Marquis de Grimaldi, agreed to the deal, and, on November 3, 1762, preliminaries of peace were signed. Although William Pitt made a famously long, three-hour speech in the House of Commons in protest of peace preliminaries, both houses of the British Parliament voted in favor of them. Mercantile interests still saw Havana as a desirable market and advantageous stepping-stone for British trade akin to Gibraltar, and they briefly protested the return of Havana when news of its fate in the peace treaty was revealed. Their arguments, however, were not so impassioned as those voiced in the protracted pamphlet war about whether Britain should retain the French sugar islands of Martinique and Guadeloupe or snowy Canada.[83]

83. Vicente Palacio Atard, *El tercer pacto de familia* (Madrid, 1945), 261, 263; Julian S. Corbett, *England in the Seven Years' War: A Study in Combined Strategy*, II (1907; rpt. London, 1992), 285–365; Pares, *War and Trade in the West Indies*, 596–612; Anderson, *Crucible of War*, 503–517; Linda Colley, *Britons: Forging the Nation, 1707–1837* (New Haven, Conn., 1992), 101; S. Max Edelson, *The New*

Economically, the occupation of Havana had provided considerable trade revenues to Britain, but the greatest boon from Havana's capture was the prize booty that went directly into the pockets of the expedition's commanders. After the enormously expensive, state-funded campaign to capture Havana, its occupation was too short and corrupt to provide the revenue windfall that had been imagined. Records in London indicate that the volume of trade between Britain and occupied Havana made up nearly 20 percent of all Great Britain's commerce with South America and the Caribbean for 1762 and 1763. The export with the highest value sent from Cuba in 1763 and 1764 was Havana's famous snuff, which was twice as much in value as the next item, brown (unprocessed) sugar, followed by a variety of lumbers, cacao, hides, tortoiseshell, and rum. Not insignificant, this volume reflected Havana's large and diversified economy, and yet it fell far short of the trade with occupied Guadeloupe and Martinique, which were held by Britain for a longer period of time.[84]

Though British and British American merchants profited from Havana's occupation, some of those merchants more experienced in Anglo-Spanish trade considered the occupation a letdown, especially in light of their expectations on learning of Havana's capture. A merchant from Jamaica practiced in the Havana trade reported to a correspondent in London that by late spring of 1763 he found the trade in Havana not as brisk as he had expected. From the point of view of British American merchants, it might have been more desirable, in the end, to transact with Spanish subjects in the ports of their own colonies or through the mechanisms of contraband.[85]

Albemarle's economic restrictions made trade in British Havana less lucrative than normal contraband trade. Lord Albemarle imposed import duties on British merchants' goods, which he claimed was in accordance with the laws of Havana and negligible in comparison with the high prices for goods in the city. An additional 2.5 percent tax was placed on all goods exported from Cuba to other Spanish American colonies, which was a tax entirely of Albemarle's own design, as this trade was prohibited under prior Spanish gover-

---

Map of Empire: How Britain Imagined America before Independence (Cambridge, Mass., 2017), 21–47; Mapp, *The Elusive West*, 413–428; Russell, "The Reaction in England and America to the Capture of Havana," *HAHR*, IX (1929), 303–316; Colin G. Calloway, *The Scratch of a Pen: 1763 and the Transformation of North America* (Oxford, 2006), 8.

84. "Imports from Havannah in the Underwritten Years of 1763 and 1764," T 38363, fol. 190, TNA; Marrero, *Cuba*, VI, 121. See also "Valor de importaciones e exportaciones de Inglaterra," 1761–1765, AGS, Estado, 6968. Trade returns from Jamaica during 1762 and 1763 suggest that some of the clandestine, inter-island trade—for example, in hides—that usually traveled onward from Jamaica to London was exported directly from Havana during the occupation, leading to a dip in Jamaica's exports to Britain; see McNeill, *Atlantic Empires*, 172–173.

85. Fogo to Campbell, July 6, 1763, C 111.200, TNA.

nance. To many merchants from British North America, in particular, Albemarle's meddling and double taxation left them disappointed with how they fared in Havana. A number of them sued him for double taxing in a case that would drag on with his estate for more than a decade. In general, British and British American merchants felt thwarted by Albemarle's policies, which were irregular and centered on his own enrichment at the expense of others; he even reinstated "Spanish" monopolies and taxes for his own personal gain.[86]

On a local level, British Havana became a commercial space more advantageous to Havana residents than Spanish rule had been. Tracking this interstitial commerce through British Havana, as opposed to Spanish Havana or British Kingston, provided advantages to Havana residents. Trade with British merchants was entirely legal, and it flowed through their own Spanish notaries and legal system, rather than through the illicit fringes of Spanish rule. The notarial protocols and other local records document as many as fifty British merchants who integrated their trading practices into Spanish customs and protocols. This integration was not entirely a comfortable process for them, as they lost leverage to their trading partners.[87]

The frustrations British merchants experienced are visible in Havana's notarial protocols and reveal the limits of the cosmopolitan atmosphere that prevailed in occupied Havana. Havana's notaries continued their customary practices, which were, of course, not transparent to British merchants and definitely not in English. In one bill of sale for an enslaved African, an Englishman's name is written as "Don Memorandum Thomas Jeffrey." One can imagine Thomas Jeffrey standing before the notary, little understanding, insisting on the writing of a "memorandum" when asked for his name. Next to the seller's signature was scrawled, "The above agreement is just if it amounts to 300 dollars." This was the amount he wanted to be paid for a boy of twelve, a *bozal* from the Kongo perhaps brought from the Lesser Antilles or captured in Cuba whom he was now selling to a Havana resident. In this instance, the bill of sale did indeed record a price of 300 pesos, but he would not have been able to do much about it in the opposite case.[88]

The greatest frustration for British merchants and advantage for Spanish ones in Havana was the continuing operation of Havana's legal system. As

86. Suits Involving the Earl of Albemarle, Manuscripts Relating to the Siege of Havana, 1776, fol. 34, Boston Public Library; "Copy of Minutes of the Treasury about Duties Levied at the Havana," May 15, 1764, Add. MSS 35916, fol. 93, BL; "Papers Relating to an Expedition Sent against Havana," PRO 30/47/18/5, TNA.

87. Protocolos de La Habana, tomos 1762–1763, ANC. Many sales of these British merchants show up in notarial records.

88. Protocolos de La Habana, Escribanía de Ponton, 1763, fol. 45 ("Don Memorandum"), Regueira, 1763, fol. 639 ("300 dollars"), both in ANC.

outsiders, British merchants struggled to obtain favorable judgments when they took debtors to court. The only "reforming" measure that Albemarle put into place in Havana—in response to Lord Egremont's injunction to set an example of the benefits of British rule—was to prohibit the longtime custom of giving gifts to judges, lawyers, or the governor with the intent to influence their decisions in pending judicial cases. Albemarle claimed to be abolishing this practice in the interest of "impartiality of justice," but, in fact, it had been a complaint of South Sea Company factors, and banning it would give leverage to outsiders in pursuit of favorable judgments and the repayment of debts. Yet this measure did not substantially improve the experience of British merchants operating in Havana.[89]

In British-occupied Havana, merchants continued to experience problems confronting the Spanish legal system as they pursued their trade, just as the South Sea Company factors before them. A London merchant and creditor of former South Sea Company factor Wargeant Nicholson, who sought repayment in Havana of long-standing debts from the 1730s, was frustrated to find that Havana residents under occupation were not required to abide by British law. He sent a letter to British Havana begging its governor to force the Havana residents to abide by British laws, "as they are now English subjects. . . . for the Spanish forms, by way of *autos* [Spanish judicial decrees], are not only tedious, but perplexing with their chicanery." In the end, though, it was precisely this kind of chicanery that made Anglo-Spanish commerce in a British-occupied city, operating under Spanish law with a corrupt British governor, potentially more advantageous for Havana's leading citizens and less so for its British visitors.[90]

Within seven days of the confirmation that Havana would be given up as part of the peace accords, Albemarle departed the island. His brother, Major General William Keppel, who took over the governorship from him, immediately ransacked the shipyard. Once word arrived of the impending return of Havana, what had been a policy of profiteering transformed into one of pillage and looting. Despite the explicit prohibitions in the peace accord against destroying Spanish naval property, the departing occupiers removed all naval stores as quickly as possible. Keppel even acknowledged in a letter to Lord Egremont that he had hoped to destroy the forests near the city for shipbuilding but could not figure out how to do so in time. Instead, his men set a large

89. Blanck, ed., *Papeles sobre la toma de La Habana*, 69.

90. John Cathcart to "His Excellency Major General Lafausville, Governor of the Havannah, or the Governor for the Time Being," Nov. 10, 1762, C 111.200, TNA. The letter was addressed to Major General Laufasuille, as opposed to William Keppel, because Laufasville was rumored to be taking over the governorship of Havana after Lord Albemarle.

bonfire to incinerate a remaining ship and naval stores at the shipyard and prepared to evacuate the city.[91]

When the British forces withdrew, they left behind in Cuba many of the enslaved Africans brought from Jamaica for the campaign. Many had run away and couldn't be located or had been sold to local residents. Keppel, as well as their Jamaican owners, might have no longer wanted them after their experiences in Cuba. Instead they took with them an English Protestant who had been resident in Cuba, Nathaniel Watts, who had worked as a mechanic for the Spanish constructing "various machines" for the dockyard and the snuff mills. In so doing, they sought to deprive Havana of "such an ingenious man" and reclaim for the British empire the shared knowledge built in this interstitial space.[92]

Conclusion

From the point of view of many British subjects, the occupation of Havana ended up a disappointment. After more than a century of buildup and a siege that decimated a massive army, the city was occupied only briefly, just eleven months. The toll of the campaign and Lord Albemarle's thirst for the spoils of war did not give him much patience for establishing the kind of systematic governance over the island that authorities in Westminster had asked of him. Albemarle, Keppel, the other army and naval commanders, and certain well-placed merchants like John Kennion prospered handsomely from their trading and raiding in Havana. The capture of the city, however, had cost so much, occurred so late in the war, and borne so many outsized expectations accrued over many decades of prior attempts that it could only have been experienced, more broadly, as anticlimactic.

Merchants invested in trading with the island had faced fewer taxes, restrictions, and headaches before the British capture of the city in the extralegal economy, which was also more profitable. It should come as no surprise that contraband trade between Cuba and Jamaica continued while Cuba was under British occupation. The returns from Havana were unsatisfying—at

---

91. Fletcher, "Seven Years' War Journal," Jan. 15, 22, 1763, Codex English 41, JCBL; "Remarques sur la Havane," Pierre Eugene du Simitière Papers, West Indies No. 4, LCP; CO 117.1 and 117.2, TNA; AGS Marina, 426; AGS, Superintendencia de Hacienda, 1056; "Copy of Instructions Issued by the Lords of the Admiralty to Rear Admiral Augustus Keppel Sent to Albemarle," Feb. 9, 1763, CO 117.1, fols. 194–196, TNA.

92. William Keppel to Egremont, June 6, 1763, CO 117.1, fols. 223–224, TNA. Seven hundred enslaved Africans were returned to Jamaica, but 486 people, or 39 percent, of those who had embarked for Cuba were declared dead or to have run away or been taken by the enemy; see Jamaica Sessional Papers, Feb. 13, 1763, CO 140.42, TNA.

least compared with the human and material expense of its capture and the commercial possibilities of this populous, sprawling Caribbean island. Those with an interest in the Cuba trade were less vehement in their protest of Havana's return in the rush of territorial decisions that marked the end of the Seven Years' War. The occupation had intensified trading relations already in place, relations that did not need British political rule over Havana to flourish, and in fact might have worked more smoothly without it.

Because of Havana's geostrategic and symbolic importance, British subjects and their government had relentlessly coveted the city for over a century. By the time they finally had the skills and luck to obtain their prize, they were too late, the moment had passed, the battle was too hard, and Albemarle's economic restrictions made occupying Havana less lucrative than normal contraband trade. The perceived value that had once made Havana so desirable to the British now made it too diplomatically troublesome to hold. Even more, the peace treaty at the end of the war and the postwar period saw a change in British imperial priorities. At the end of the war, Britain's political emphasis began to shift from the acquisition of new territories to the protection of those the crown already possessed. A more sober attitude toward the possibilities of territorial conquest followed the euphoria of earlier eras. In particular, the focus became shielding Britain's North American colonies from external threats, producing revenue to help pay the staggering war debt, and centralizing Britain's increasingly sprawling empire.

After 1763, Britain finally abandoned the quest to capture Havana. The cold, hard lessons of the difficulties of trying to invade and annex Havana and its tremendous price tag dissuaded further attempts. When news of Manila's successful seizure finally made it back to Britain six months after the peace accord, the Spanish colonial city was immediately and unceremoniously returned to Spain, which evinced public outcry that the Peace of Paris had sold Britain short, like the Treaty of Utrecht before it. Rather, by the time both of these conquests could be completed, they had become relics of a past war.[93]

Back in Havana, during its occupation by British forces, the city's most powerful commercial classes had managed to shape the occupation to their own advantage, despite Keppel and Albemarle's destruction and profiteering. Like Juan de Miralles, Cuban elites got the best of both empires. They gained more ships, trade goods, and enslaved Africans; performed an end run around their Cádiz rivals; made some money; and brokered further relations with the

---

93. P. J. Marshall, *The Making and Unmaking of Empires: Britain, India, and America, c. 1750–1783* (Oxford, 2005), 82; Anderson, *Crucible of War*, 487–517; Mapp, *The Elusive West*, 420–425. Manila capitulated on October 5, 1762. On the effect of the Manila news, see Anderson, *Crucible of War*, 515–516. The news of Manila's fall reached Spain on May 7, 1763; see AGS, Marina, 426, no. 124.

British Atlantic commercial system. Investors in Havana's sugar sector sought favor with Albemarle, yet the strongest ties connecting the elite to their occupiers were those forged through the British slave trade to Havana. Havana's elites exploited opportunities during the occupation to sell out the people of African descent who had so recently defended their city.

As evident here, the British occupation had a mixed and only limited impact on Cuba's economy. Ultimately, it was the Spanish reoccupation of Havana, not the British occupation beforehand, that had the most transformative impact on the island and throughout the Atlantic world. Because of Havana's tremendous geopolitical importance, the actions of individuals in Cuba during Havana's sudden and disastrous loss influenced the subsequent course of political, economic, and military reform in Cuba and other Spanish territories. By drawing attention to what had become the modus operandi of the island's elite, the occupation inspired accusations of treason directed at several of the city's leading citizens. Elite disloyalty to Spain in British Havana opened the eyes of the government in Madrid to the alarming degree of local autonomy and integration into a regional system that had developed in Cuba. The way the Havana elite shaped the occupation of their city would lead, in the occupation's aftermath, to new realizations in Spanish political circles and new departures in the social, political, and economic life of the island and the empire.

Ironically, just as Britain gave up its quest to capture Havana, Spain became obsessed with ensuring the city was never conquered again. Over the next several decades, the Spanish crown and its councillors would fixate on the British challenge to its American possessions and the need to strengthen itself against it. To do so, Spain would launch a series of new political and economic initiatives designed to reconstitute its empire and retaliate against its British rival.

PART III Aftermaths

5

. . .

Spanish Reoccupation
New Beginnings upon Havana's Return

During the final months of the British occupation of Havana, in April 1763, a man of African descent from the island of Cuba paid a visit to the official chosen to repossess Havana for Spain. The future governor of Havana and captain general of Cuba, a nobleman from Aragon known as the Conde de Ricla, was in Cádiz, preparing to sail to Cuba for his new post. The Seven Years' War was not yet over, but the peace treaty ensuring the restitution of western Cuba to Spain in return for Florida had been signed. At that moment, this man from Cuba, named Santiago de Sotolongo, presented himself before Ricla. Sotolongo claimed to have fought in the defense of Havana the year before. Somehow he had journeyed to Cádiz, either via a British merchant ship or in a transport carrying Spanish troops home after their surrender in Havana. Now he was making an appeal to the incoming governor for his promised freedom.[1]

According to Sotolongo's account, which he had documentation to verify, he had been among those fighting to defend the Morro and was taken prisoner after the British mine blew it open. As he pointed out, Juan de Prado, then governor and captain general, had promised freedom to all enslaved Africans who fought for the Spanish crown. Because of that promise, he, an enslaved man owned by a royal officer in Trinidad, Cuba, had made the mountainous overland journey to Havana to join the defense. After the surrender, when Havana was lost to the British, Sotolongo had been taken prisoner, even though both his owner and the town of Trinidad refused to submit to the rule of the British commander Lord Albemarle. In essence, Prado's call to enslaved Africans had brought him into Havana and led to his capture. With British forces occupying Havana and his status in limbo, he had escaped to Spain to request the formal *carta de libertad* he was owed.[2]

1. Conde de Ricla to Julián de Arriaga, Apr. 26, 1763, AGI, SD, 1212.

2. King to Conde de Ricla (regarding Santiago de Sotolongo, slave of Don Manuel Antonio de

Ricla was not yet aware of the role played by enslaved Africans in the defense of Havana, nor had Charles III learned of the promise that had been made in his name. It was Sotolongo's forceful appeal that first drew the attention of the king and his ministers to the matter. In response, Ricla wrote a letter of inquiry to the Council of the Indies, which in turn asked former governor Prado, now under house arrest in Madrid awaiting trial for treason, to explain. Prado confirmed in a letter that he had promised manumission in the king's name in order to preempt any such promise made by the British enemy. The king promptly instructed Ricla to manumit Sotolongo and reimburse his owner from the royal treasury. Ricla was further instructed that on his arrival in Cuba he should reconcile Prado's outstanding promise of freedom to other enslaved Africans "as reward for their fidelity and honor." The Spanish court forwarded to Ricla Prado's letter, outlining which officials and military commanders would be most informed on this matter and could help him in manumitting all those enslaved Africans who could be "verified as having distinguished themselves with equal valor."[3]

Sotolongo's appearance in Spain and his entreaty to the future governor of Havana and captain general of Cuba triggered an inquiry into the recent dramatic events in Havana. The return of Havana to Spanish rule catalyzed a reckoning with the events of the year before and a clash of interpretations about the lessons to be taken from Britain's successful capture of the city and the proper course of action to be followed going forward. Sotolongo was not only making a case for his own freedom when he appeared before the king's representative; he was also presenting himself as a narrator, with corroborating documents, of the events of the siege and the heroism of enslaved Africans. In this way, he was a participant in the process of ascribing meaning to recent events in Havana—reconstructing what had happened and directing future actions—a process in which soldiers, priests, preachers, widows, and political figures throughout the Atlantic world took part in the aftermath of Havana's seizure and return.[4]

The appearance of Sotolongo in Cádiz, the letters of inquiry, and the reaction of the king illustrate the charged nature of Havana's return for Spain

Sotolongo), May 10, 1763, AGI, SD, 2209. Don Manuel Antonio de Sotolongo was the *alferez mayor* and a town council member in Trinidad; see "Descripción del Governador de la ciudad de la Habana dispuesta al año de 1759 por Don Francisco Cagigal de la Vega, Governador y capitan general de ella," AGI, SD, 1157, fol. 12v.

3. Ricla to Arriaga, Apr. 26, 1763, Juan de Prado to Arriaga, May 4, 1763, and Arriaga to Ricla, May 13, 1763, all in AGI, SD, 2209.

4. On the discourse surrounding an event and the ascription of meaning to it, see, for example, Shahid Amin, *Event, Metaphor, Memory: Chauri Chaura, 1922–1992* (Berkeley, Calif., 1995); and Michel-Rolph Trouillot, *Silencing the Past: Power and the Production of History* (Boston, 1995).

and its subjects. In the wake of the occupation, repairing relations with Spanish subjects in Cuba took on great urgency for administrators in Spain. The Spanish monarchy had always relied on compacts with local populations in claiming sovereignty over territory. Now it would have to rebuild those ties that had been so dramatically sundered in Havana. Successfully reoccupying Havana would necessitate soliciting accurate information about what had transpired, rewarding loyal subjects, punishing treasonous ones, and forging stronger, less breakable bonds with the local population. When Spain reclaimed her so-called key to the Indies, Charles III sent the Conde de Ricla to conduct an exhaustive inquiry into the state of the island, rebuild all that had been destroyed, and begin reforming its military and economy. Upon the island's restitution, Spain desperately needed to strengthen the defenses of the island, broker stronger ties with its local ruling class, and set its economy on a new and more productive path.

The reoccupation of Havana and reconstitution of Spanish rule would unfold on multiple levels, in both Havana and Madrid, and in conversation with the various constituencies on whom the government intimately relied. Authorities pursued these ends through a four-step process: the staging of treason trials in Madrid to expedite healing and clear the path for new beginnings; a reunion with the monarchy's elite subjects in Cuba, who perhaps had betrayed it; a reunion with its subjects of African descent, who had outstanding promises owed by the crown; and implementation of a comprehensive plan of reform and renewal that would inaugurate a new era for the Spanish crown in its rivalry with Britain. The enormity of Havana's capture and its calamitousness for both Spain and, by association, France meant that many eyes in America and Europe were on Madrid. The king and the Council of the Indies felt acutely the need to find a redemptive path, one that would ensure such a disaster could never happen again.

Historians have long recognized the occupation of Havana as a catalyst to extensive reforms in the Spanish empire, paralleled by similar measures in virtually all European empires in the wake of the Seven Years' War. In part, these reforms reflected governments' attempts to generate sufficient revenue to pay for the war debt accrued in the conflict, and in part they grew out of the relentless, ongoing nature of late-eighteenth-century imperial competition. Spain had begun to enact reforms before the Seven Years' War, but, given its disastrous entry into the war, the postwar period took on heightened urgency. The shock of the loss of Havana drew the attention of reformers at the Spanish court to Cuba, highlighted its strategic importance as never before, and placed tremendous pressure on officials to better develop the island's economy and military or risk losing it for good. Thus, they gained the leverage to pursue new ideas that had been germinating during prior decades of imperial war and rivalry.[5]

Cuba subsequently became the site of a trial run for a series of commercial, political, and military reforms that were later exported to other parts of Spanish America. These included the expansion of the military and the introduction of freer trade between the Americas and Spanish ports. Historians of colonial Latin America and Spanish empire more broadly have written extensively about these reforms undertaken by the Bourbon monarchy, drawing attention to the active, collaborative role of Havana's elites in these so-called absolutist measures. Yet, as frequently as scholars refer to these Bourbon reforms, they do not often connect them to slavery, the slave trade, or populations of African descent. Cuba's dramatic events of 1762–1763, however, highlighted as never before the importance of free and enslaved people of African descent to the security of the island and the empire.[6]

5. Sophus A. Reinert and Pernille Røge, eds., *The Political Economy of Empire in the Early Modern World* (New York, 2013); J. H. Elliott, *Empires of the Atlantic World: Britain and Spain in America, 1492–1830* (New Haven, Conn., 2006), 292–324; Elena Schneider, "African Slavery and Spanish Empire: Imperial Imaginings and Bourbon Reform in Eighteenth-Century Cuba and Beyond," *Journal of Early American History,* V (2015), 3–29. On the symbiotic relationship between war and reform in the Spanish empire, see Allan J. Kuethe and Kenneth J. Andrien, *The Spanish Atlantic World in the Eighteenth Century: War and the Bourbon Reforms, 1713–1796* (New York, 2014), 231–345.

6. The general consensus of the vast literature on the Bourbon reforms is that the invasions of Havana and Manila acted as catalysts for fiscal, military, and political reorganizations directly afterward, even though projects of reform had started before. For studies that focus on Cuba's role in the reforms, see Allan J. Kuethe, *Cuba, 1753–1815: Crown, Military, and Society* (Knoxville, Tenn., 1986); Kuethe, "'Los llorones cubanos': The Socio-Military Basis of Commercial Privilege in the American Trade under Charles IV," in Jacques A. Barbier and Kuethe, eds., *The North American Role in the Spanish Imperial Economy* (London, 1984), 142–156; Kuethe and Andrien, *The Spanish Atlantic World;* Kuethe and G. Douglas Inglis, "Absolutism and Enlightened Reform: Charles III, the Establishment of the Alcabala, and Commercial Reorganization in Cuba," *Past and Present,* no. 109 (November 1985), 118–143; Francisco Pérez Guzmán, *La Habana: Clave de un imperio* (Havana, 1997); Celía María Parcero Torre, *La pérdida de la Habana y las reformas borbónicas en Cuba (1760–1773)* (Madrid, 1998); Sherry Johnson, *The Social Transformation of Eighteenth-Century Cuba* (Gainesville, Fla., 2001); Juan B. Amores [Carredano], *Cuba en la época de Ezpeleta (1785–1790)* (Pamplona, Spain, 2000); María Dolores González-Ripoll Navarro, *Cuba, la isla de los ensayos: Cultura y sociedad (1790–1815)* (Madrid, 1999); Evelyn Powell Jennings, "War as the 'Forcing House of Change': State Slavery in Late Eighteenth-Century Cuba," *William and Mary Quarterly,* 3d. Ser., LXII (2005), 411–440; and Gabriel B. Paquette, *Enlightenment, Governance, and Reform in Spain and Its Empire, 1759–1808* (New York, 2008).

For the literature on the Bourbon reforms in general, see, for example, Josep M. Fradera, *Colonias para después de un imperio* (Barcelona, 2005); Stanley J. Stein and Barbara H. Stein, *Apogee of Empire: Spain and New Spain in the Age of Charles III, 1759–1789* (Baltimore, 2003); Paquette, *Enlightenment, Governance, and Reform in Spain;* Gabriel Paquette, "Introduction: Enlightened Reform in Southern Europe and Its Atlantic Colonies in the Long Eighteenth Century," and Jorge Cañizares-Esguerra, "'Enlightened Reform' in the Spanish Empire: An Overview," in Paquette, ed., *Enlightened Reform in Southern Europe and Its Atlantic Colonies, c. 1750–1830* (Burlington, Vt., 2009), 1–22, 33–36; John Fisher, *Bourbon Peru, 1750–1824* (Liverpool, 2003); Anthony MacFarlane, *Colombia Before Independence: Economy, Society, and Politics under Bourbon Rule* (New York, 1993); MacFarlane, *Reform and*

The slave trade and populations of African origins played a crucial role in the way Spain sought to reconstitute its authority in Havana and modernize its imperial policies in response to British competition and threats. Havana's capture had illustrated for the government in Spain the perils of relying on the merchants of foreign powers, especially its British rival, for an ongoing supply of Africans, increasingly understood to be critical to Spanish state building and military and economic security. Developing the island's economy, subsidizing its defense, protecting it against foreign attack, and rebuilding relations with a powerful elite that demanded greater access to enslaved Africans — all these factors required an expanded African slave trade. Coupled with British dominance of the slave trade at the time, slavery and the slave trade became the most urgent and pressing problems Spain faced on its reoccupation of western Cuba. In its dialogue with Havana elites, the Spanish monarchy would begin to embrace the necessity of more Africans and their descendants for the island's defense and economy.

This and the next chapter will trace the process by which the Spanish government came to this new understanding, its multifaceted response to the problem, and the variety of effects its efforts would have both near and far from Cuba. Sotolongo's appearance in Spain marked the beginning of a new consensus at the Spanish court about the importance of African slavery, black soldiers, and the transatlantic slave trade to imperial rivalry. Despite their differences, the conflicting accounts about what had transpired in Havana mostly agreed on one point: free and enslaved blacks had played a critical role in the events of the siege and were essential to the future security and economic growth of the island. Not only Sotolongo but also slaveowners who bought and sold men like him conveyed this message to officials in Madrid.

Reactions in Spain

When Charles III of Spain first received word of Havana's surrender, he was, as one royal official put it, "disgusted" by the news. According to the French consul in Madrid, "News of the taking of Havana has gravely upset the Spanish nation. . . . There is no consolation for the irreparable loss of one-third of Spain's naval forces, surrendered without a cannon-shot." The Spanish public

Insurrection in Bourbon New Granada and Peru (Baton Rouge, La., 1990); Jacques A. Barbier, *Reform and Politics in Bourbon Chile, 1755–1796* (Ottawa, 1980); John Lynch, "The Institutional Framework of Colonial Spanish America," *Journal of Latin American Studies*, XXIV (1992), 69–81; John R. Fisher, *The Economic Aspects of Spanish Imperialism in America, 1492–1810* (Liverpool, 1997); Jaime E. Rodríguez O., *The Independence of Spanish America* (Cambridge, 1998); and D. A. Brading, "Bourbon Spain and Its American Empire," in Leslie Bethell, ed., *The Cambridge History of Latin America*, I, *Colonial Latin America* (Cambridge, 1984), 389–440.

was indignant over Havana's surrender and satirized the seemingly incompetent officials who had directed the defense. After the embarrassing loss, the king's councillor Ricardo Wall was forced to resign, and the Council of the Indies's Julián de Arriaga lost clout. Each was in turn usurped and replaced by the Italian reformers, the Marqués de Esquilache and the Marqués Grimaldi.[7]

It was not so much the attack on Havana but its capture that shocked Spain. The siege had been foreshadowed by many prior attacks on the city, as well as by the campaigns against Cartagena and Guantánamo during the War of Jenkins' Ear, but Havana was thought too well defended to fall. Adding insult to injury was the news reaching Spain in May 1763 that Britain had also captured Manila and one of Spain's transpacific treasure galleons as well. Because the peace treaty had already been signed several months before, Manila was returned in the spring of 1764 without any accompanying territorial transfer, but the twinned losses hit Spain hard, and the capture of Havana especially so. Unlike Manila, a trade entrepôt comparatively poorly defended at the farthest reach of Spanish territories, Havana was the center of Spain's naval and military power in the Americas and the defense of the Gulf of Mexico. Both its surrender and the potential consequences were unthinkable. As Queen María Amalia wrote in a letter to a Spanish official in Naples, after the loss of Havana the fear was that all of New Spain was in danger of British usurpation.[8]

The territorial transfers in the Treaty of Paris at the end of the war only accentuated Cuba's strategic geopolitical value and drew the monarchy's attention to the island as never before. In order to recover Havana, Spain had been willing not only to hand over Florida to the British but also to recognize effective British control of the Miskito Coast and its supply of valuable dyewoods and to relinquish any claim to fishing rights off Newfoundland. With the loss of Florida and the cession of the Miskito Coast, Cuba took on heightened

7. Marqués de Esquilace to Prado, Nov. 2, 1762, AGI, SD, 1586, no. 387 ("disgusted"); Béliardi to Choiseul, Oct. 13, 1762, MS Fonds Français, fol. 297v, Bibliothèque Nationale, Paris ("News"), cited in Stein and Stein, *Apogee of Empire*, 51; Ricardo Wall to Bernardo Tanucci, Dec. 21, 1762, AGS, Estado, 6093; Vicente Palacio Atard, *El tercer pacto de familia* (Madrid, 1945), 246. On the political shifts between Spanish ministers, see Kuethe and Inglis, "Absolutism and Enlightened Reform," *Past and Present*, no. 109 (November 1985), 121–122; Parcero Torre, *La pérdida de la Habana*, 192–194; Vicente Rodríguez Casado, *La política y los políticos en el reinado de Carlos III* (Madrid, 1962), 86–94; Juan B. Amores Carredano, "La elite cubana y el reformismo borbónico," in Pilar Latasa, ed., *Reformismo y sociedad en la América borbónica* (Pamplona, Spain, 2003), 133–154.

8. AGS, Marina, 426, no. 124; Nicholas Tracy, "The British Expedition to Manila," in Mark H. Danley and Patrick J. Speelman, eds., *The Seven Years' War: Global Views* (New York, 2012), 461–486, esp. 484; Kristie Flannery, "The Seven Years' War and the Globalization of Anglo-Iberian Imperial Entanglement: The View from Manila," in Jorge Cañizares-Esguerra, ed., *Entangled Empires: The Anglo-Iberian Atlantic, 1500–1830* (Philadelphia, 2018), 236–254. On the correspondence between Queen María Amália of Spain and Justice Bernardo Tanucci, see Manuel Danvila y Collado, *Reinado de Carlos III*, II (Madrid, 1893–1896), 38–39; Stein and Stein, *Apogee of Empire*, 353.

value as a first and last stand against British North America and an important outer bulwark of New Spain's defense. The acquisition of Louisiana from the French had provided some compensation for the Spanish monarchy's losses, but it also accentuated the military necessity of Havana as the base without which it could not administer this new territory to its north.[9]

Initially, the king and his officials did not assign blame for the military defeat but instead commemorated its noble but ill-fated defense. Havana had held out against the siege for six weeks, and Britain's unanticipated use of the mine at the Morro, executed without any warning, might even have been against the rules of war. Spain held public displays of mourning centered on its naval captain killed at the Morro, Don Luis Vicente de Velasco e Isla, and his deputy, Don Vicente González. Spanish poems lamented Velasco's loss, medals were produced to commemorate his last stand at the Morro, and paintings and sculptures were commissioned to honor him, channeling all the pathos of Spain's defeat (see Figure 27 [Plate 13]).[10]

But, even as the Spanish public mourned Velasco's loss, letters began to filter back from Havana pointing fingers at those deemed culpable for the city's capture. Bishop Pedro Agustín Morell de Santa Cruz sent his secretary to the court in Madrid with a letter reporting on the events of the siege that characterized Prado's capitulation as overly hasty. Offering a different narrative, a detailed account by Juan de Castro Palomino, written to his friend at court, Nicolás de Ribera, and circulated there, made a strong case for the valor of local troops — including those of African descent — refuting any Spanish commanders who would criticize their performance.[11]

Elite women in Havana represented some of the most prominent voices influencing opinion at the Spanish court. The wives of Havana's *cabildo* members jointly sent a carefully constructed, highly political letter to the king that expressed their unremitting sorrow at Havana's loss, which they blamed on the unfit leadership of Prado and the other members of the *junta de guerra*. Specifically, they faulted Prado for failing to fortify the Cabaña fortress dur-

9. Stein and Stein, *Apogee of Empire*, 56; Hugh Thomas, *Cuba, or the Pursuit of Freedom* (New York, 1998), 53; Manuel Moreno Fraginals, *El ingenio: Complejo económico social cubano del azúcar* (Barcelona, 2001), 4–5.

10. Prado claimed that the explosion of the mine at the Morro without warning was "against the laws of humanity" and "good war"; see Prado to Juan Ignacio de Madariaga, July 30, 1762, AGI, Ultramar, 169, no. 28. For commemoration of Velasco in Spain, see Nicolás Fernández de Moratín, *Égloga a Velasco y González, famosos españoles, con motivo de haberse hecho sus efigies en la Real Academia de San Fernando* (Madrid, [1763]); *Gazeta de Madrid*, Feb. 1, 1763, 39–40; Miguel Carabias Orgaz, "Dolorosa métrica expresión del sitio y entrega de la Habana: Edición crítica," *Nueva revista de filología hispánica*, LXIV (2016), 91–115, esp. 93.

11. Pedro Agustín Morell to the King, Aug. 26, 1762, AGI, SD, 1356; Juan Miguel Palomino, "Noticias de la Habana que refieren como la ganaron los Ingleses el año de 1762," MS 10818/33, BNE.

FIGURE 27 Spanish Medal Commemorating the Commanders Don Luis Vicente de Velasco e Isla and Don Vicente González, Slain during the Loss of the Morro. Minted in 1763. The medal's dramatic depiction of the moment the mine exploded accentuates the extraordinary and shocking measures the British took to capture the city, beyond what their commanders could have foreseen or withstood. Charles III made the brother and heir of Velasco a grandee of Spain with the title Viconde del Morro, gave him a pension, and erected a statue in Velasco's honor near his birthplace. A royal decree ordered that there would always be a ship named for Velasco in the Spanish Armada. Velasco even earned the respect of his British enemies, who ceased their assault on the Morro to allow the mortally wounded captain to be taken into Havana for medical attention. © National Maritime Museum, Greenwich, London

ing his first sixteen months in office. (This charge was ironic given that their own households had refused to lend out their enslaved Africans for that very project.) In their letter, they extolled the *"fidelidad"* and *"lealtad"* (loyalty) of the cabildo members as well as the bravery of the militias, Bishop Morell, and the local populace. By contrast, the women criticized Prado and the leaders of the defense for abandoning the Cabaña early in the siege and surrendering without consulting the bishop or the city council after only nine hours of direct fire on the city.[12]

With the specificity of their letter, these elite women were furnishing the

12. "Diferentes señoras de aquella ciudad" to the King, Aug. 29, 1762, AGI, SD, 1356, also published as "Memorial dirigido a Carlos III por las señoras de la Habana," Aug. 25, 1762, in Emilio Roig de Leuchsenring, ed., *La dominación inglesa en la Habana: Libro de cabildos, 1762–1763*, 2d ed. (Havana, 1962), 243–280. The signatories included Doña Isabel Josepha de Arrate, Doña María Santa Cruz, Doña Luisa Ana y Castellón, Doña Ana de Sayas, Doña María Luisa de Cárdenas, Doña María Antonia Navarrete, Doña Cathalina Santa Cruz, Doña Manuela Coca, and Doña Theresa Santa Cruz. The authors claimed Prado tried to make the pardo militias work on the construction of the Cabaña, but without offering these poor men, who lived by day labor, rations or pay. In fact, he had asked prominent Havana residents, including cabildo members, to loan out their enslaved Africans, and they refused.

king and other government figures in Madrid with the material they would need to level charges against Prado and absolve their husbands of blame. Also circulating at the Spanish court was an unsigned poem attributed to a learned female author in Havana that made similar claims. Comparing the sufferings of Havana residents to those of the Israelites, Job, Noah, and Daniel, the poem enumerated the many errors of the defense, including the sinking of ships in the mouth of the harbor. Sophisticated rhetorical documents like these carried all the weight of shame that only women could bring to bear as the safeguards of nobility and honor in a patriarchal, martial culture. These women also made accusations that would have been more difficult for their husbands to level, given that the men could be criticized for not having taken a more active role in the fighting. Together the jointly authored letter, the anonymous poem, and other communiqués from Havana helped to precipitate Prado's treason trial and formed the basis of the charges against him. The seriousness with which Charles III and his councillors took such communications from Havana demonstrated the urgency with which they sought to repair the good esteem and reputation of the king's rule.[13]

In February 1763, Charles III organized a junta of generals to try Prado and others responsible for Havana's loss on charges of treason. In addition to the accusations coming from residents of Havana and Madrid, Charles III felt pressure from France, which had suffered tremendous losses at the negotiating table as a result of Spain's entry into the war. Throughout the Seven Years' War, the French government had established a precedent in staging treason trials for military commanders seen as responsible for pivotal losses, such as those in Pondicherry (India), Martinique, Guadeloupe, and Canada. These trials followed the example of the trial and execution in London of Admiral Byng, who had lost Menorca at the beginning of the war. Madrid, too, would join in this European practice of staging treason trials for officials and commanders responsible for embarrassing territorial losses.[14]

The prolonged, public treason trial for Juan de Prado and eleven other military and civil officials identified as most responsible for the failures of Havana's

13. "Dolorosa métrica expresión del sitio y entrega de la Havana, dirigida a Nuestro católico Rey y Señor Don Carlos Tercero por una poética de la misma ciudad," MS 12980/19, BNE; Orgaz, "*Dolorosa métrica expresión del sitio y entrega de La Habana,*" *Nueva revista de filología hispánica*, LXIV (2016), 91–115; Parcero Torre, *La pérdida de Habana*, 196–197. Scholars disagree about the authorship, attributing it to one of two women: Doña Beatriz de Jústiz y Zayas, the Marquesa de Jústiz de Santa Ana, or Doña Teresa Beltrán de Santa Cruz y Calvo de la Puerta, la Condesa de San Juan de Jaruco, who also signed the letter from the wives of cabildo members.

14. Christian Ayne Crouch, *Nobility Lost: French and Canadian Martial Cultures, Indians, and the End of New France* (Ithaca, N.Y., 2014), 128–129; Marshall Smelser, *The Campaign for the Sugar Islands, 1759: A Study of Amphibious Warfare* (Chapel Hill, N.C., 1955), viii, 200.

defense began in June. The charges were shaped by the reports from Havana residents, but the trial was orchestrated to appease audiences in Madrid and Paris. In a sign of the high profile of the proceedings, seen as an inquest into the Spanish empire more broadly, the presiding junta included the most renowned lieutenant generals, the king's closest advisers, and Jorge Juan, the famous Enlightenment-era explorer, naval officer, mathematician, and scientist. To determine what happened during the siege, the leader of the junta of generals, the Conde de Aranda, studied the diaries of Prado and the chief of the naval squadron, the Marqués del Real Transporte, alongside the minutes of the juntas de guerra called in Havana during the siege. He also reviewed all the royal orders sent to Prado throughout his governorship and the letters that had reached the Council of the Indies from Havana.[15]

Two one-thousand-page tomes of testimony were published to ensure the transparency of the proceedings, with the first appearing while the verdict was still under deliberation. Making public all the testimony and evidence was designed to restore the people's faith in the Spanish military and government and appease local and international critics, who would have the opportunity to pour over the details of the failed Spanish defense. The presiding junta was aware of this broader interest in the trials, especially given the impact that events in Havana had on the peace negotiations in Paris. As the members of the junta wrote in their decision, "All of Europe desired to see the royal determination" (see Figure 28).[16]

Charles III was anxious to find someone responsible for the defeat to deflect the criticism from his own leadership. There was no precedent for such a trial in Spain, and the king did not even clarify until three months into the trial that it was a court-martial and not some other specialized legal tribunal. The charges against Prado took into account his performance as captain general and governor of Havana as well as the tactical decisions he made during the British attack. The tribunal's charges echoed those of the elite women of Havana and also blamed Prado for failing to destroy the naval squadron, protect the king's treasury, or evacuate the city rather than hand it over. Indeed, many flawed tactical decisions were made, but, as Prado pointed out in his de-

15. Juan José Morón García, "El juicio por la pérdida de La Habana en 1762," *Baluarte: Estudios Gaditano-Cubanos*, I (1994), 19–48, esp. 24–25. These documents, which may be found in AGI, SD, 1588, included the letters from Morell, Havana's cabildo members and their wives, various militia commanders, and others.

16. *Proceso formado de orden del Rey Nuestro Señor por la Junta de Generales que S.M. se ha dignado de nombrar a este fin sobre la conducta que tuvieron en la defensa, capitulación, pérdida, y rendición de la plaza de la Habana, y esquadra, que se hallaba en su puerto el Mariscal de Campo Juan de Prado . . .*, 2 vols. (Madrid, 1763–1764), BNE; "Proceso y sentencia dada al Gobernador de la Habana, Don Juan de Prado," 1765, MS 10421, BNE.

FIGURE 28 *Vue de la prise des forts et ville de Havane par les Anglois en 1762*. 1763, Paris. Hand-colored engraving. This heavily stylized scene of the final stage of the bombardment of Havana is a *vue d'optique,* a type of popular print meant to be viewed through an optical device that provided an illusion of depth. Its production in Paris testifies to the great interest there in events in Cuba. Courtesy, Library of Congress, Washington, D.C.

fense, it was perhaps unreasonable to expect that a governor would take the extraordinary measure of evacuating and destroying his own city, particularly such a populous one.[17]

17. Morón García, "El juicio por la pérdida de La Habana en 1762," *Baluarte,* I (1994), 31. The charges against Prado were: he failed properly to fortify the Cabaña fortress and abandoned it too easily; he ignored the news of the impending British expedition and failed to notify the court of local conditions; he chose to sink three ships in the mouth of the harbor in order to block entry to British ships and left the largest Spanish naval base in the Americas and a crippling percentage of its entire naval fleet there useless during the siege; he launched no counterattacks during the entire course of the fighting; he surrendered Havana to the British rather than evacuate to the rest of the island and destroy the city's fortifications; he erred in handing over the naval squadron intact, rather than burning the ships before surrender; and he failed to evacuate the royal treasury from the city before capitulation. See "Defensa del Mariscal de Campo Don Juan de Prado," in *Proceso formado de orden del Rey Nuestro Señor por la Junta de Generales,* II, 79–94, BNE.

Nonetheless, the junta placed the majority of the blame on Prado and the Marqués del Real Transporte, the admiral of the Spanish fleet in the Americas. Faced with an unusual situation for a court-martial, in that Prado was not a military commander and yet had handed over to the enemy royal ships and a crucial fort, the members of the commission were told to render a ruling based on both military law and the civil code, the Siete Partidas. The latter considered treasonous and punishable by death any mayor who failed to fortify a castle or gave it up. Riven by factionalism, the ruling junta came to sharply divergent decisions about the proper punishment, and Charles III ended up meting out a far more lenient punishment than the death penalty most of the junta recommended. All except Prado were eventually pardoned, and even Prado was assigned a secret pension before he died in prison in 1770.[18]

The treason trial was just one element of a larger process of soul-searching among Spanish officials about the fate of the monarchy. The loss of Havana was a severe blow to Spanish honor. It undermined Spain's confidence in its old way of doing things and made it consider new and more British approaches. In November 1762, the royal counselor Francisco de Craywinckel presented a report to the crown comparing Britain and Spain and emphasizing the need "to make the most of this disgrace." Although the loss of Havana had demonstrated Britain to be at that time "much more powerful than Spain," he did not find the differences between the two realms insurmountable. Britain surpassed Spain in the arts of navigation, commerce, and agriculture, but, given some time to remake itself, Craywinckel predicted, Spain would catch up with its rival and throw off its "dependence on other states." What Spain needed was a new formula for managing war, trade, and slavery, at home and abroad. Losing Havana and then regaining it at the cost of Florida would provide the impetus for large-scale commercial, political, and military reforms in Cuba and other Spanish overseas territories. But first Spain needed to reestablish its government in Havana, rebuild relations with its subjects there, and determine the right remedy for what exactly had gone wrong.[19]

18. *Proceso formado de orden del Rey Nuestro Señor por la Junta de Generales,* I, II, BNE; "Proceso y sentencia dada al gobernador de la Habana, Don Juan de Prado," 1765, MS 10421, BNE; Morón García, "El juicio por la pérdida de la Habana en 1762," *Baluarte,* I (1994), 40–46; Parcero Torre, *La pérdida de la Habana,* 194–202.

19. "Discurso que con motivo de la pérdida de la Habana formó Don Francisco Craywinkel," Madrid, 1762, II/2869, fols. 289–300, esp. 290r, 291v, 295v, BRP; Craywinckel to Wall, "Discurso sobre la utilidad que España pudiera sacar de su desgracia en la pérdida de La Habana," Nov. 12, 1762, AHN, Estado, 2927, no. 271; Eduardo Torres-Cuevas, "El grupo de Aranda en Cuba y los inicios de una nueva época," in José Antonio Ferrer Benimeli et al., eds., *El Conde de Aranda y su tiempo,* II (Zaragoza, Spain, 2000), 323–348.

Reuniting with Spanish Subjects in Cuba

When the Conde de Ricla arrived in Havana on June 29 to reconstitute Spanish rule, the moment was laden with symbolic meaning. Ricla stayed in a house outside the city walls until the evacuation of British troops and the formal handover of authority on July 7. His entourage included Dublin-born Alejandro O'Reilly as his field marshal (whose English-language skills would be useful while meeting with Keppel), Captain Conde de Freylin, and Agustín Crame, who would follow Ricla and take part in a review of the island. These reformers, all born in northern Europe, represented a new way of thinking that was sweeping the Spanish court.[20]

Now it was time for crowds in Havana, not Britain or British America, to celebrate. Spontaneous festivities in honor of the restoration of Spanish rule began even before the British evacuation, during the three days that British troops were boarding ships in the harbor for their departure from the city. As a British officer remarked in his journal, the city was "in a blaze" with fireworks and celebratory gunfire. After the interruption of British rule, individuals in Cuba sought a fresh start with the Spanish sovereign. British invasion and occupation had caused great loss of life, dislocation, and uncertainty. Ricla commented on the joy with which Havana residents greeted his arrival, with the singing of the "Te Deum," the pealing of church bells, and the shouts of "¡Viva el Rey!"[21]

On Ricla's arrival, the religious orders and Bishop Morell also expressed their joy at the city's return to their beloved religion and monarchy in what was for them a hopeful moment of restoration and renewal. In general, Havana's men and women of God depicted *"la dominación anglicana"* as a time of persecution, during which they persevered in their loyal service to the Catholic king. In ceremonies marking the return of Spanish rule, the bishop, recently returned from exile in Florida, organized a procession to the convent of the Bethlehemite order, where many hundreds who had been ill since the time of the siege continued to convalesce. With this act, he highlighted the service of the religious orders in offering consolation and care to Havana's population during the upheaval of the invasion and occupation.[22]

20. Ricla to Esquilache, [June 1763], AGI, SD, 2082.

21. Henry Fletcher, "Seven Years' War Journal of the Proceedings of the 35th Regiment of Foot, by a British Officer, and Illustrated by a Military Engineer," July 9, 1763, Codex English 41, JCBL ("in a blaze"); Ricla to Arriaga, Sept. 22, 1763, AGI, SD, 1506 ("Viva"). One anonymous letter alleged that a small group of the population visibly suffered the pain of return; see "Nota de lo substancial que ha ocurrido en la Habana desués del 30 de agosto en 1762," Mar. 5, 1763, AGI, SD, 1584.

22. For the religious orders' accounts of the damages and suffering they endured during the occupation, see Thomas López de Aguirre to Arriaga, Apr. 22, 1763, and "Las monjas de Santa Clara dan

Official religious commemorations throughout western Cuba venerated Velasco as a Catholic martyr and a symbol of Havana's suffering and Bishop Morell as the city's stalwart champion. In an elegy for Velasco— "that Catholic hero, who along with Hercules, has made his name with his invincible valor"—a Havana priest lamented the loss of the Morro. He avowed that, during the assault on the fortress, "those who fled should not have fled," referring to the soldiers serving under Velasco. They should have held their ground, he declared, and faced the Anglican onslaught as their brave commander did. In paying tribute to the Spanish naval captain, these men of the Church were echoing the message emanating from Madrid and reaffirming the city's ties with its Spanish sovereign. Their disparagement of the local militia forces and Spanish sailors who had abandoned their commander reflected their sense that defenders of their city had betrayed them.[23]

At least one member of Havana's religious community honored not only Velasco, however, but also soldiers of African descent for their sacrifice during the siege. Another sermon delivered on the restoration of Spanish rule gave credit to the *pardo* volunteers for their bravery in defending the city. In his "Sermon of the Flags," delivered on July 30, Rafael Castillo y Sucre invoked the memory of "so many spirited pardos whose desire for immortality was equaled by their valor." Free blacks had founded the church in which he gave this sermon, Havana's oldest standing church, the Iglesia del Espíritu Santo, in 1638. Within its walls, Castillo y Sucre avowed that those pardo men were surely headed to heaven and that they were of a blood that he himself "would not disdain to mix in [his] own veins." His sentiment about African blood was uncommon for this era. It reflected both the presence of an elite class of pardos who patronized the religious life of the city and the ennobling and "whitening" effect of their achievements during its defense.[24]

---

gracias por haverselas restituido a su amada patria y religión," July 18, 1763, both in AGI, SD, 1506; El Obispo de Cuba, Mar. 1, 1766, AGI, SD, 1458, no. 24; "La comunidad del convento Hospital de Nuestra Sra. de Bethlen de aquella ciudad," Aug. 17, 1762, and the King to the Bishop of Cuba, Sept. 28, 1763, both in AGI, SD, 1506.

23. "Funebre y melancólica historia sobre la toma y azedio que padeció la gran ciudad de la Havana el año del señor de 1762 . . . perifrazada en treinta y tres décimas por el Ben.do Don Blas de Bonora sacristán mayor por S.M. de la Villa de Santa María del Puerto del Príncipe tierra adentro de dicha isla," AGI, SD, 1357; "Sermón que en la Iglesia de S.S.P.S. Francisco de al ciudad de La Habana predicó el día 10 de agosto de 1763 el R.P. Andrés Menéndez," MS 18701/11, BNE.

24. On the Iglesia del Espíritu Santo, see José Martín Félix de Arrate, *Llave del Nuevo Mundo: Antemural de las Indias Occidentales* (Havana, 1964), 175; and Joaquín E. Weiss, *La arquitectura colonial cubana*, I (Havana, 1979), 121–122. The sermon, as given on July 30, 1763, is cited in Antonio Bachiller y Morales, *Cuba: Monografía histórica que comprende desde la pérdida de la Habana hasta la restauración española* (Havana, 1883), 84–86. See also María Carmen del Barcía, *Los ilustres apellidos: Negros en la Habana colonial* (Havana, 2009), 245; Roig de Leuchsenring, ed., *La dominación inglesa*, 272. On black blood in the early modern Hispanic world, see María Elena Martínez, *Genealogical*

Ricla's encounter with Havana's secular elites was much more ambivalent. The reunion between Spain and its most powerful subjects in Cuba was a delicate affair. Along with complaints about Prado's missteps, word of alarming conduct among elites conducting business in occupied Havana had reached the crown before Ricla's departure from Cádiz. During the British occupation, priests had written the Spanish king to alert him to the behavior of Sebastián de Peñalver y Angulo, for example. Their letters described in detail the *donativo* he had expropriated from religious institutions on Albemarle's behalf. In the following months, other Havana residents described how both Peñalver and Gonzalo Recio de Oquendo had extracted funds from private individuals. Correspondents alleged that Peñalver had invented the donativo himself and that he, or he and Oquendo, had pocketed a substantial portion of it.[25]

The public's resentment of those who capitulated and collaborated with the British was voiced in popular, unsigned poems called *décimas,* which circulated in Havana during and after the occupation. The décimas offered Havana residents a way to criticize and satirize those who had betrayed them and their sovereign. For example, décimas decried that the poor had defended the city on behalf of the rich, who had stayed out of the fighting. One verse speculated that the principal members of the city, left unnamed "out of respect," had been prompted to hand over Havana to the enemy for fear of losing their property. From the safety of anonymity, other writers of these verses lampooned "Milor" Albemarle, Prado, Peñalver, and even the women in Havana who had married British troops and tried to depart with them. Prado bore the brunt of these verses for his botched defense and precipitous surrender, but the décimas often targeted Peñalver as well. Depicted as a Lutheran, a Freemason, and a traitor, Peñalver, these verses claimed, had at least symbolically renounced Catholicism for Protestantism and governed by greed.[26]

Fictions: Limpieza de Sangre, Religion, and Gender in Colonial Mexico (Stanford, Calif., 2008); and Ann Twinam, *Purchasing Whiteness: Pardos, Mulattos, and the Quest for Social Mobility in the Spanish Indies* (Stanford, Calif., 2015).

25. El provisor Don Santiago de Echevarría, Mar. 3, 1763, and Don Diego de Campos, Presbitero, teniente de Cuba de la parroquial mayor de San Cristóbal, Mar. 8, 1763, both in AGI, SD, 1357. For accusations that Peñalver and Oquendo had invented the donativo, see AGS, Hacienda, 2342, 763; Lorenzo Montalvo to Arriaga, AGS, Marina, 426; Parcero Torre, *La pérdida de la Habana*, 164.

26. Décima copied in Pedro Manuel de Olañeta, "Diario del sitio y rendición de la plaza de la Habana al Ingles," 1762, Miscellaneous Manuscripts, MS 352, XV, box 83, folder 1662, Sterling Memorial Library, Yale University ("out of respect"). Other verses can be found in Bachiller y Morales, *Cuba*, 198–206; and Sherry Johnson, "'Señoras en sus clases no ordinarias': Enemy collaborators or Courageous Defenders of the Family?" *Cuba Studies / Estudios cubanos*, XXXIV (2003), 11–37, esp. 12. As Johnson has pointed out, the famous décima about women's disloyal behavior in occupied Havana was written down in the late nineteenth century, and thus its eighteenth-century authorship is in some doubt: "Las muchachas de la Habana / no tienen temor de Dios / pues se van con los ingleses / en los bocoyes de arroz."

Accusations of treason and disloyalty spread far beyond Prado, Peñalver, and Oquendo to include a larger group of wealthy Havana families perceived as having collaborated with and profited from Albemarle's rule. Allegations involved price gouging and profiteering. The priest Don Diego de Campos complained that Peñalver, together with the other wealthy *regidores* Don Laureano Chacón and Don Pedro Beltrán de Santa Cruz, for example, had bought 450 enslaved Africans from the British commissioner John Kennion and resold them at prices "so elevated they had never been seen before on the island." An anonymous writer lower down on Havana's social scale implicated Don Pedro de Estrada and four of the city's other wealthiest residents for their complicity with Albemarle. With the restoration of Spanish rule, they continued to enjoy immunity, the writer alleged; "Knowing that the governors need their silver," he complained, "powerful men do whatever they feel like."[27]

Much like the British government before it, the renewed Spanish government in Havana could not function without the compliance and financial assistance of its wealthiest subjects. Establishing good relations with the city council members was a first priority for the new captain general of Cuba and governor of Havana. The king had prepared Ricla for the swirl of recriminations he would likely encounter and had given instructions on how to control their impact. On his first day in newly restored Spanish Havana, Ricla met with the city council in a special session just as Albemarle had before him. In accordance with his directives from Charles III, Ricla first thanked them for their service during the invasion and occupation. Then he announced that all cases of infidelity to the Spanish crown would be handled privately, and directly, by him.[28]

The members of the Havana city council greeted Ricla's statement with protestations of their undying loyalty. Like the priest who criticized the retreating soldiers in the Morro, they blamed Havana's loss on the few individuals — chiefly, Prado — who had failed them. After the city council meeting on Ricla's arrival in Havana, members of western Cuba's landowning class informed the new captain general of their economic contributions during the siege, much as the cabildo members' wives had done in their letter to the crown. In these testimonials and petitions, they highlighted their willingness

---

27. Marqués de Jústiz de Santa Ana to Prado, Feb. 28, 1763, AGI, SD, 1584; Don Diego de Campos, Presbitero, teniente de Cuba de la parroquial mayor de San Cristóbal, Mar. 8, 1763, AGI, SD, 1357 ("so elevated"); Anonymous, 1763, AGI, Hacienda, 2342 ("knowing"). The other individuals named were Don Augustín de Cardenas, Don Joseph Cipriano de la Luz, Don Laureano Chacón, and Don Joseph Gelabert.

28. Ricla to Arriaga, "Testimonio de las diligencias practicadas por el Conde de Ricla," Aug. 9, 1763, AGI, SD, 1357; Ricla to Arriaga, July 22, 1763, AGI, Santo Domingo, 1212. For Ricla's instructions, see Arriaga to Ricla, Apr. 16, 1763, AGI, SD, 1213.

to send their enslaved Africans to the city to aid in the defense. They also enumerated other ways in which their households had made economic contributions to the defense, such as by loaning money to the war effort, provisioning
cattle, allowing the military the use of their houses and *haciendas,* and providing aid to the sick and infirm. Elites hastened to point out, as well, the destruction the British siege had wrought on their homes and their finances. To
establish good faith with the returning Spanish government, several Havana
residents, including the wealthy Marqués de Jústiz de Santa Ana, offered to
the Conde de Ricla and their king the use of their funds, haciendas, and enslaved Africans for the work of repairing and expanding the fortifications of
Matanzas and Havana. Men like the marqués had refused to lend former governor Prado laborers to build the defenses of the Cabaña before the British
attack, and this offer bore the signs of a sense of guilt for their earlier refusal.[29]

Ricla had initially intended to investigate Sebastián de Peñalver and
Gonzalo Recio de Oquendo quietly, but the volume of verse pasquines and
other anonymous accusations circulating about the two men prompted him
to form a commission to scrutinize their behavior on the charge of treason.
Additionally, he began an inquiry, on the same charge, into members of their
immediate circle, including two of their sons, along with a pardo scribe accused of falsifying documents for Peñalver and other individuals accused of
collaborating with Peñalver and misappropriating royal funds during the siege.
Despite Ricla and the king's desire to contain the inquiry, it quickly spread.[30]

Privately, Ricla expressed his concerns about the loyalty of the entire class
of Havana elites. In a letter to his supervisor on the Council of the Indies,
Ricla complained that many of the city's leading citizens refused to testify
against Peñalver or Oquendo, despite all the damning anonymous accusations. In a moment of candor, Ricla groused that Havana elites "care more for
their own private interest than for the King himself, or the good of the *patria.*"
But, with Ricla's focus on Peñalver, Oquendo, and their associates, the cases of
the other men who had been accused of disloyalty were dropped. Even though

29. "Don Luís de Guereña Mendoza Theniente a guerra y de justicia mayor de la ciudad de San
Felipe y Santiago y su jurisdicción," Aug. 13, 1762, AGI, SD, 1357; "Informes dados por Don Juan de
Prado sobre los servicios que durante el sitio de la plaza de La Havana hicieron los sugetos que aquí
se mencionan," Oct. 29, 1763, Pedro Alonso to Arriaga, Apr. 18, 1763, Marqués de Jústiz de Santa
Ana and Don Geronimo de Contreras to Ricla, July 18, 1763, Ricla to Arriaga, July 25, 1763, Ricla to
Arriaga, Sept. 28, 1763, Marqués de Jústiz de Santa Ana to Arriaga, Dec. 17, 1763, all in AGI, SD, 1506.
See also, for example, the mérito of Don Joseph Antonio de La Guardia describing the actions of his
father Don Joseph de La Guardia during the siege; after the occupation, his father loaned Ricla thirty
thousand pesos for the fortifications; see Oct. 17, 1769, AGI, SD, 1460, no. 14.

30. Ricla to Arriaga, Nov. 25, 1763, AGI, SD, 1212. The Marqués de Jústiz de Santa Ana served as
judge; see "Servicio de Don Manuel Manzano Parques Justiz de Santa Ana," Dec. 10, 1763, AGI, SD,
1506; Don Sebastián Peñalver y otro, 1763, AHN, Comisiones, 20,872.

Juan de Miralles, for example, had actively offered to spy for Lord Albemarle, a point that came up at Prado's treason trial, O'Reilly considered Miralles too "useful" for Havana's commerce to investigate further. Instead Peñalver and Oquendo were the ones scapegoated.[31]

Despite Ricla and the king's desire to contain the commission's inquiry, accusations of treason against Peñalver and Oquendo mounted. That fall, Julián de Arriaga of the Council of the Indies wrote to Ricla inquiring about accusations against Peñalver and Oquendo made by the Intendente de Marina Lorenzo de Montalvo. He ordered Ricla to send these two men to Spain and embargo their possessions if these charges appeared to be true. A month later, in response to many further complaints, the king ordered Ricla to place them under arrest. Ricla seized both men's possessions and imprisoned Peñalver in the Morro fortress and Oquendo in the Castillo de la Real Fuerza for the duration of the investigation.[32]

When Ricla sent Peñalver and Oquendo to Cádiz in October 1764, he recommended their imprisonment and exile from any location in the Indies, given the dangerous example their behavior had set. The Spanish government had always preferred to handle cases like these, not in the Americas, but back in Spain. Ricla said he found Peñalver, in particular, afflicted with "excessive ambition, preoccupied with greed, and with an audaciousness rarely seen in an individual subject." At the same time, Ricla also lamented the considerable support the two men still received from their many family members and associates in Havana.[33]

In Spain, Peñalver and Oquendo faced charges of treason for their collaboration with their British occupiers when they served as lieutenant governors of British Havana. Dragging on until 1771, the trial ended up focusing on the donativo and Peñalver's financial interest in the merchant vessel carrying British goods that was sent to Veracruz in the spring of 1763. As part of his defense, Peñalver depicted the occupation of Havana as a time of terror, inflicted by "conquistadors who lacked the piety of religion." This astute strategy aimed to play to Spanish preconceptions. Peñalver argued that he had intervened in many situations to lessen the abuses and extractions Albemarle sought to inflict on the local population. Nevertheless, he was condemned to death for

31. Ricla to Arriaga, Nov. 25, 1763, AGI, SD, 1212: "Estiman su interés más que al Rey mismo, y al bien de la Patria." On Miralles, see Informe reservado de Alejandro O'Reilly, Sept. 27, 1765, AGI, IG, 2820A.

32. Arriaga to Ricla, Sept. 28, 1763, AHN, Diversos Collecciones, 28, no. 26; Arriaga to Ricla, Oct. 3, 1763, AGS, Hacienda, 2342.

33. On the restitution of Spanish rule, for example, Peñalver sent a gift of tobacco to the crown and a request for a title of Castile; see Esquilache to Ricla, July 16, 1763, AHN, Diversos Colecciones, 28, no. 25; Ricla to Arriaga, Oct. 30, 1764, AGI, SD, 1590.

treason by the Spanish court, like Prado, although he later had his sentence commuted. Peñalver lived out his final days in a prison in Ceuta, in North Africa, but his family and their descendants in Havana remained among the most prominent and decorated elites in the city. Oquendo, however, was absolved by the Council of the Indies and died of natural causes back in Havana in 1773.[34]

The prosecution of Peñalver and Oquendo was one of the crown's scapegoating strategies, part of the protracted legal fallout from the British occupation in Cuba, Spain, and Britain. In addition, in the final years of Peñalver's treason trial, those proceedings merged with a suit against his estate brought by Havana-based investors in the Royal Havana Company for the donativo extracted from them during the British occupation. In another courtroom, Cádiz merchants invested in the Royal Havana Company accused their Havana counterparts of colluding with the British and sued them for failing to protect their property in the city. Their suit implicated the leading men of Havana commerce, whose ambitions, they alleged, led them to collaborate with their British occupiers and illegally seize their property. A favorable resolution eluded the Cádiz claimants, however, despite the many years they spent pursuing their case and documenting the appropriation of their goods.[35]

Initiating the prosecutions of Prado and the members of the junta de guerra along with those of Peñalver and Oquendo allowed the Spanish king to pin disloyalty on a few individuals and downplay a broader and more ambiguous phenomenon in the Havana population. Irrespective of final sentences, the ritual of scapegoating performed an important function by affirming the bonds between subjects and sovereign during the crucial restoration of Spanish rule. In reality, however, in spite of the actions that came to light during those trials, many Havana elites, including members of the Peñalver family, received titles of nobility over the next decade, and at a more accelerated rate than elites in any other locale in Spanish America at the time. In essence, the logic was that loyalty could be bought, and disloyalty was very danger-

34. Expediente contra Don Sebastián de Peñalver y otros reos en la rendición de la plaza de la Habana a los ingleses, 1771, AGI, SD, 1590; "Escrito de descargos de Don Sebastián Peñalver Angulo," [1765?], AGI, SD, 1590, no. 1; Carlos M. Trelles, *El sitio de la Habana y la dominación brtánica en Cuba: Trabajo de ingreso en la Academia de la Historia (jueves 3 de julio de 1919)* (Havana, 1925), 10–36, esp. 15, 21.

35. "Expediente y testimonio de autos que los accionistas de la compañía han seguido contra Sebastián Peñalver," 1770–1772, AGI, Ultramar, 988, no. 3. For the Havana resident shareholders' defense of their actions, see "Carta del apoderado general de los vecinos interesados en la Real Compañía de la Habana al Excmo. Sr. B. Fr. Don Julián de Arriaga," Feb. 3, 1763, Real Academia de la Historia, Madrid. For the suit by Cádiz shareholders, see "Expediente y testimonio de autos que los accionistas de la compañía han seguido contra Sebastián Peñalver sobre cantidad de pesos, 1770–1772," Nov. 23, 1772, AGI, Ultramar, 988.

ous to root out and punish. The crown understood that pulling too hard on any thread risked unraveling the very fabric of Havana's elite society, given its close commercial ties with its British occupiers.[36]

Rewarding Spain's Black Subjects

The reunion between the Spanish sovereign and his subjects of African descent in Cuba was an entirely different sort of affair. As conveyed by letters and the arrival in Spain of Santiago de Sotolongo, reports of the heroism of Cuba's blacks reached the king and his councillors before the end of the occupation. These reports reflected both a reality of events as they had unfolded and the narratives people of African descent presented to Spanish authorities in their petitions and testimonials during the occupation and after the restoration of Spanish rule.

Since the start of the siege, people of African descent had depicted themselves as protagonists in a valiant defense of the city against great odds. To these men of color, their defense of Havana was to be celebrated as a victory achieved for their king. In addition to Santiago de Sotolongo's in-person petition in Cádiz, Pedro Martínez González, lieutenant of one of the pardo militia companies of Havana, had written to Charles III in March 1763 to solicit a promotion, a small salary, and a gold medal "that would bring respect to people of his color." During the siege he had led an assault from the Morro on the enemy's batteries, in which his men had killed a British soldier and taken seven prisoners (verified by documentation signed by Don Luis de Velasco and another Spanish commander who was there). He was wounded twice while in the Morro, and, after his recovery, he served in the Castillo de la Punta as a soldier and builder repairing the fortifications. In addition to these achievements, he explained that he had paid out of his own pocket to help arm and uniform members of his company. Convinced of Martínez González's valor and great personal and economic sacrifices, the king sent Ricla to Havana with medals to be conferred on him and other heroic defenders of Havana among the militias of pardos and *morenos libres*.[37]

---

36. Kuethe and Inglis, "Absolutism and Enlightened Reform," *Past and Present*, no. 109 (November 1985), 123. Although the Peñalver family had already received one title of Castile, Sebastián's son Gabriel petitioned for another title over many years; see Consejo de Indias, Aug. 31, 1785, AGI, SD, 1140, no. 18. On Spain's many political accommodations in favor of Havana elites, see also Jorge Domínguez, *Insurrection or Loyalty: The Breakdown of the Spanish American Empire* (Cambridge, Mass., 1980).

37. Before the Seven Years' War, Martínez González had thirty years of experience fighting for the Spanish king, including service against the British in Florida and shipboard in the Spanish navy during the War of Jenkins' Ear; see "Resumen: Pedro Martínez González, Theniente de una de las

People of African descent in Cuba had fewer opportunities than their European counterparts to write down their version of events. Yet, in the eighteenth-century record, produced primarily by people of European descent, enslaved blacks and militias of free people of color were described as willing and proficient soldiers in the face of the British attack, in contrast with the Havana elites. In general, very few individuals from Cuba, as opposed to military men from Spain, were singled out for their active role in the fighting. But, within that group, men of African descent figured prominently. Ricla arrived in Havana with a short list provided by Prado of individuals who merited recognition for their courageous actions during the siege. Of the three individuals cited, one was a soldier of African descent and another a leader of enslaved soldiers.[38]

On the list, Prado deemed worthy of a salary and a medal "a *mulato* or *pardo*" whose last name he could not remember. According to Prado's testimony, the man had led a number of scouting missions against the British encampments and engaged in several dangerous skirmishes. Other documentation from the siege confirms that this man was Dionisio Pérez, a captain in the company of free pardos who had led forty men in reconnaissance after the loss of the Cabaña and had taken two British sergeants prisoner during the attacks on San Lázaro. Prado also wrote of Juan de Cabrera, a white *vecino* who demonstrated "extraordinary valor" on multiple occasions as the commander of an ad hoc company of enslaved Africans that formed during the fighting. Gravely injured and taken prisoner during the sortie that Prado ordered against the Cabaña and the British siege works on July 22, Cabrera deserved a promotion, a salary, and a medal, in Prado's mind. The company he led of enslaved Africans had shown "the greatest bravery" in turning back British advances, ambushing their positions on multiple fronts, and taking many prisoners, including sentinels.[39]

White residents of Havana echoed this praise for black soldiers who fought on behalf of the Catholic sovereign. For whites, the achievements of troops of African descent represented one of the few bright spots to be celebrated

---

compañías de milizias de morenos de La Havana," AGI, SD, 2117; César García del Pino, *Toma de la Habana por los ingleses y sus antecedentes* (Havana, 2002), 105.

38. "Informe dado por el Mariscal de Campo Don Juan de Prado particularizando los oficiales que más se distinguieron durante el sitio de la Plaza de la Havana," Dec. 9, 1762, AGI, SD, 2117.

39. "Informes dados por Don Juan de Prado sobre los servicios que durante el sitio de la Plaza de la Havana hicieron los sugetos que aqui se mencionan," AGI, SD, 1506 ("extraordinary valor"). On Dionisio Pérez, see "Libro de servicios del batallón de pardos libres de La Havana," June 1765, AGI, SD, 2093, fol. 74; "Libro de servicios de oficiales y sargento de el batallón de pardos de esta plaza, hasta fin de diciembre de 1762," AGI, SD, 2117, fol. 11; Cuentas de la Real Hacienda de La Habana, 1761–1762, AGI, SD, 1842, no. 51; García del Pino, *Toma de La Habana*, 91.

in what was a deeply troubling event for Spain. Embracing them as Havana's own made the white population look better by association. One Havana resident of European descent commented in a letter to the king from occupied Havana on the extraordinary loyalty the city's population had exhibited, "up to the most humble blacks." An anonymous letter writer in Havana, in the fall of 1763, mentioned "the unbelievable loyalty that blacks showed to their King and Señor during the siege," adding that, "even after the capitulation, they were a scourge to English blacks and whites." Although there is no evidence that Havana's blacks acted violently toward English blacks, making that claim certainly would have accentuated the depths of their allegiance to the Spanish king.[40]

These assertions must be read carefully. To laud the role of blacks in the defense of Havana was a way of shaming whites for not taking a more active role and for being complicit in the occupation. Praising the ardor of blacks' commitment to the Spanish king was also a self-satisfying way to contrast British and Spanish colonial rule. It perpetuated a reverse Black Legend that criticized Britain and praised Spain for its more benevolent, reciprocal relationship with its African subjects. Indeed, over many generations, colonial subjects in Cuba had regarded people of color as fundamentally loyal and interpreted their loyalty as confirmation of the civilizing mission of Spanish colonialism. In their view, this idea had been validated by the events during the British invasion of Havana.

White Havana residents' accounts of the siege drew on historical analogies from the greater Mediterranean world to make the case to Madrid for the courageous actions of Cuba's population of African descent. One of the décimas circulating in Havana praised the white commander of the company of enslaved soldiers Prado had singled out, Juan de Cabrera, along with his "Ethiopian squad." With this reference, this anonymous author elevated Havana's enslaved Africans into a noble and recognizable Old Christian tradition. A lengthy poem titled *Romance anónimo,* written directly after the siege, likely by the *regidor* and chronicler José Martín Félix de Arrate, described the actions of black militias and enslaved African volunteers in the tradition of an epic ballad. The author commented on *bozales,* who, by their opposition to the British

---

40. Olañeta, "Diario del sitio," July 22, 23, 1762, Miscellaneous Manuscripts, MS 352, XV, box 83, folder 1662, Sterling Memorial Library; Pedro Azerace [Lorenzo de Montalvo] to the King, Aug. 28, 1762, AGI, Ultramar, 169: "El fervor y lealtad sin exemplo que respiran y han manifestado hasta los más humildes negros"; Anonymous letter, Havana, circa fall 1763, AGS, Hacienda, 2342 ("scourge"): "la lealtad no crehida, que manifestaron de su rey y Señor pues durante el sitio, es constante, del modo que se portaron, y aun despues de capitulado se fueron asote de ingleses blancos y negros."

attacker, showed deep commitment to Catholicism, even though they were New Christians or even unbaptized. The poem also commended the pivotal moment when the sortie of thirteen enslaved Africans from the Morro, led by native of the Kongo Andres Gutiérrez, had killed a British soldier and taken seven prisoners. The men came down upon their British targets with such "audacity" and "furor," the author wrote, "that they were able to apply to them / the sentence of Alexander [,] / I came and saw and conquered."[41]

It may be surprising that a Havana slaveowner like Arrate would laud enslaved Africans with an analogy to Alexander the Great (even if he meant Julius Caesar) for their killing and imprisoning of whites. As the author also noted, the soldiers themselves had proposed the sneak attack against the enemy. But, at the same time, the praise for black troops in the letters and poems of white Havana residents had roots in a long military tradition in Havana. When white writers highlighted the sacrifices of enslaved Africans, they were drawing attention not just to these men's exploits but also to their own largesse as owners who had, as they portrayed it, made them available to the defense. Along with its praise of the heroism of enslaved Africans, the *Romance anónimo* lamented that slaveowners were left without workers or compensation when their men headed out to fight.[42]

Not only did these stories of blacks' military exploits during the siege ring true but they also appealed to the new Spanish government, which eagerly sought positive examples of attachment to the sovereign that could be celebrated and thus inculcate further loyalty. Shortly after his arrival in reoccupied Havana, Ricla began seeking out officers of color to reward for their roles in the defense of Havana. While Ricla acknowledged white elites for loaning financial resources to the crown, blacks in Cuba were the ones he recognized for their military contributions. As directed by the Council of the Indies, Ricla inquired about the moreno Pedro Martín González—who had petitioned the crown for rewards for his service—in order to bestow on him a gold medal. Ricla found, however, that González had died a few days after his arrival in Havana, likely because of complications from injuries he sustained during the siege. After consultation with local military personnel, Ricla instead sent two

41. Olañeta, "Diario del sitio," Feb. 21, 1762, Miscellaneous Manuscripts, MS 352, XV, box 83, folder 1662, Sterling Memorial Library ("*etiopicia cuadrilla* [sic]"); Lourdes Ramos-Kuethe, ed., *Romance anónimo sobre el sitio y la toma de la Habana por los ingleses en 1762* (Prague, 2011), 52, 82 ("audacity" and "furor"), 99. For accounts of Ethiopians in early modern Iberia, see Pedro Páez, *História da Etiópia* (Porto, Portugal, 1945–1946), I–III. Whites used the label "Ethiopian" to cast aspersions on black soldiers during the time of the Haitian Revolution; see Ada Ferrer, *Freedom's Mirror: Cuba and Haiti in the Age of Revolution* (New York, 2014), 303–311.

42. Ramos-Kuethe, ed., *Romance anónimo*, 74.

members of the battalion of free morenos of Havana to the Spanish court to be decorated for their brave service.[43]

On Christmas Eve in 1763, Captain Antonio de Soledad and his sublieutenant Ignacio Albarado, veterans of the siege and leaders of the battalion of morenos libres of Havana, performed a display of arms before Charles III and his court in Madrid. The message Havana's white population and its subjects of African descent had been conveying — of the great value of Havana's black militias to the Spanish crown — could not have been more powerfully communicated to the king and his councillors than by this display. These two morenos from Havana, one a mason and the other a carpenter, had the honor of kissing the king's hand and receiving a medal with his effigy for their service in the siege. According to the certificate of merit that recognized the occasion, they had been sent to provide an example to the king of the "care and dedication" with which "people of their color" performed the important task of defending the territories of the Spanish king. This was an honor these two men and Havana's population of morenos would not soon forget. It also sent a clear message to all those present at the Spanish court. As Sotolongo had before them, Soledad and Albarado made physically manifest for the Spanish court the importance of men of African descent in protecting one of Spain's most valuable and vulnerable overseas possessions.[44]

Although the Spanish monarchy might generally have preferred to forget its embarrassment in Havana, these black soldiers from Cuba were celebrated as heroes. The only other participants in the defense to be so honored were Velasco and his fellow captain, who were acknowledged in memoriam. The contrast between the veneration of Soledad and Albarado, on the one hand, and the accusations brought against the Havana leadership, on the other, was stark. At the time of this Christmas ceremony at court, Prado and his eleven co-defendants were on trial in Madrid, and Peñalver and Oquendo were being investigated in Havana.

In newly restored Spanish Cuba, members of the pardo and moreno militias hoped to parlay the recognition they were receiving into an expansion of their role serving His Majesty. In addition to sending these two moreno officers to Spain, Ricla also extended salaries and further institutional recognition to the battalion of pardos libres of Havana. In a letter of thanks to the king, nine of the men affirmed their desire to continue to serve their sovereign as vassals, "within or beyond the island" and "to emulate the veteran [Span-

43. Ricla to Arriaga, Nov. 26, 1763, AGI, SD, 1506.

44. "Libro de servicios de batallón de morenos de La Havana," 1765, AGI, SD, 2093; "Libro de servicios de batallón de morenos libres de La Havana," 1770, AGI, Cuba, 1136A, fols. 614, 631. For the text of the certificates of merit they received at court, see Barcia, *Los ilustres apellidos*, 245.

ish] troops and overcome any enemy whatsoever." Among the signatories of this letter was Pedro de Menéndez, a veteran of the attack on Georgia during the War of Jenkins' Ear who had taken over the command of the battalion of pardos in place of Antonio de Flores when he had fallen ill. In reward for his service, Menéndez later received his own medal as he continued to fight on behalf of his Spanish king.[45]

Reconciling with Spain's Enslaved Subjects

Ricla also sought to recognize enslaved Africans for their role in recent events, in response to both the king's instructions and their own appeals. As soon as he arrived in Havana, enslaved men who had fought in the siege began to approach him to ask for their promised manumission, just as Sotolongo had done before them in Cádiz. Thus, in the fall of 1763, Ricla began reconciling outstanding promises of freedom extended during the siege. Drawing upon what he had learned from Prado's letter on the topic, Ricla issued a general call of assembly for all enslaved Africans Prado had declared free during the defense of the city, almost all of whom had not yet received their promised manumission. They were to report to the *casa capitular,* or city hall, where the city council met in the Plaza de Armas, along with their owners, at ten o'clock in the morning on September 30.[46]

So many men showed up seeking manumission, accompanied by their owners, that Ricla had to keep reconvening them over the course of two weeks to get through all their cases. Assisted by a notary and Domingo de Cabrera and Don Luis de Aguiar, the two most recognized white commanders of enslaved Africans during the siege, Ricla's officials labored to verify the men's claims. In total, Ricla manumitted 156 men in those first weeks and compensated their owners, with all the liberated men's names posted publicly in Plaza Nueva, the market square, so that there could be no question about their newfound status.[47]

The symbolism of these manumissions was poignant. Enslaved Africans

45. Batallion of pardos libres of Havana to the King, Dec. 7, 1763, AGI, SD, 2117; "Libro de Servicios de los Oficiales y Sargentos del Batallón de Pardos Libres de La Habana," 1771, AGI, Cuba, 1136A, fol. 452; Royal order to the governor of Havana, July 16, 1771, AGI, Cuba, 1140.

46. Ricla to Arriaga, Nov. 20, 1763, AGI, SD, 1212; Ricla to Arriaga, November 1763, AGI, SD, 1213; "Testimonio de los autos observados sobre las libertades dadas a diferentes negros esclavos que sirvieron en el tiempo de la invasión de esta plaza," 1764, AGI, SD, 2209. Prado also liberated two other enslaved Africans for their actions during the siege, which never came up in these discussions but were recorded in Havana's notarial protocols; see Protocolos de La Habana, 1762, fols. 639, 640, ANC. The first was identified as a twenty-seven-year-old mulato named Francisco Manuel Sánchez and the second as a twenty-six-year-old caravalí named Luis de Cardenas.

47. "Testimonio de los autos observados sobre las libertades dadas," 1764, AGI, SD, 2209.

had made great sacrifices on behalf of their crown, and now Spanish authorities were publicly recognizing their efforts. During this bureaucratic ritual of reward and recompense, giving oral reports of their actions to colonial officials allowed these men to convey personal accounts of valor and suffering that would otherwise not have been heard in Havana's corridors of power or preserved in historical records. By their very numbers, these enslaved veterans of the siege broadcast to Spanish authorities the crucial role that not just free men of color but also the enslaved had played in the defense of Havana.[48]

In one public ceremony, the king rewarded not only enslaved Africans for risking life and limb in the name of their king but also their owners for ostensibly loaning out their human property to the war effort. Enslaved Africans emphasized their own volition in the decision to join in the fighting, but their owners stressed that they had volunteered these men of their own accord. Repaying these slaveowners for their contribution, like any wartime loan to the royal treasury, affirmed and renewed the compact between sovereign and subject. With this ritual, the crown was performing both its obligation to its enslaved subjects and its financial commitment to respect the property of its slaveowning subjects.

The first to be manumitted were the 13 participants in the famous raid from the Morro, the moment lauded in Arrate's poem. Their manumission had been decreed but never certified, and their owners had not been compensated. The second group included the company of enslaved Africans that Prado had formed in the midst of the fighting, led by the white commander Juan de Cabrera. Although 105 men were on the list created at the time of the fighting, 115 men presented themselves before Ricla to be set free. Cabrera identified the 10 additional individuals as having rightfully earned their freedom during that military action as well, and their names were added to the manumission list. By the time payment to their owners had been completed and all the cartas de libertad had been issued, it was a year later and the total

48. On manumission rituals for black veterans in the independence wars, see Peter Blanchard, "The Slave Soldiers of Spanish South America: From Independence to Abolition," in Christopher Leslie Brown and Philip D. Morgan, eds., *Arming Slaves: From Classical Times to the Modern Age* (New Haven, Conn., 2006), 255–273; and Blanchard, *Under the Flags of Freedom: Slave Soldiers and the Wars of Independence in Spanish South America* (Pittsburgh, 2008). On popular royalism among enslaved soldiers of the Spanish king during the independence wars, see Marcela Echeverrí, *Indian and Slave Royalists in the Age of Revolution: Reform, Revolution, and Royalism in the Northern Andes, 1780–1825* (New York, 2016). On enslaved soldiers in colonial Latin America more generally, see Jane Landers, "Transforming Bondsmen into Vassals: Arming Slaves in Colonial Spanish America," 120–145, and Hendrik Kraay, "Arming Slaves in Brazil from the Seventeenth Century to the Nineteenth Century," 146–179, in Brown and Morgan, eds., *Arming Slaves*; and Kraay, *Race, State, and Armed Forces in Independence-Era Brazil: Bahia, 1790s–1840s* (Stanford, Calif., 2001).

number freed had climbed to 175, pushed upward by additional enslaved Africans who lobbied for inclusion.[49]

Ricla wished to follow through on the king's promise, but he was also concerned about limiting the number of claims enslaved Africans could make. Far more enslaved Africans had played a role in the defense than Ricla or the king had imagined. Completing this task risked draining the royal treasury and potentially alienating Havana's largest slaveholders, without whom he could not govern. If all those enslaved Africans who had joined the defense were set free—a number as high as three thousand, according to Palomino's letter—Havana's slave society could be thrown into crisis, and its slaveowners might turn against the crown. Even if many of Havana's largest slaveholders had been disloyal during the occupation, the Spanish king could not govern without the cooperation of that sector, and the demand for more enslaved Africans was great. Taking all these factors into account, Ricla's solution was to protect the interests of slaveowners against the petitions of the enslaved.[50]

After the first public accounting, Ricla issued a proclamation directing the remaining men who had shown up at the city council building but had not received manumission to go home and return to "subordination under their owners." A large number of men had presented themselves with debilitating injuries they claimed they had sustained while fighting for their king, however, and Ricla resigned himself to assessing those cases. Appointing his military deputy Alejandro O'Reilly and two surgeons to the task, Ricla agreed to review the men's injuries and select for manumission only those who had been rendered *"inútil"* (useless), or unable to work, by wounds sustained during the siege. Slaveowners appreciated Ricla's decision to liberate only injured veterans of the siege because it allowed them to retain their most productive laborers and off-load those who could not work. Thus, they avoided paying for their food and maintenance.[51]

In the early days of the British siege, Prado's offer of freedom had often been understood as having no limitation—all enslaved Africans who volunteered to fight would earn it. But in this effort at a compromise between the numbers of enslaved claimants and the slaveowners whose support he needed, Ricla decided to grant manumission only to those Prado had declared free in the midst of the fighting for feats of great daring and those who had been in-

49. "Testimonio de los autos observados sobre las libertades dadas," 1764, AGI, SD, 2209.

50. "Carta de Don Juan Miguel Palomino a Don Nicolás de Ribera, vecino de Madrid, fecha en la Havana a 28 de agosto de 1762 sobre la toma de aquella plaza por los ingleses," C.M. Pérez, BNJM; "Testimonio de los autos observados sobre las libertades dadas," 1764, AGI, SD, 2209, fol. 2.

51. Ricla to Arriaga, Nov. 20, 1763, AGI, SD, 1212 ("subordination"); "Testimonio de los autos observados sobre las libertades dadas," 1764, AGI, SD, 2209.

jured beyond the ability to work. In essence, the crown was more interested in honoring a few heroic examples than systematically following through on Prado's pronouncement and liberating such a large portion of Havana's enslaved population.

Nearly three hundred injured enslaved Africans presented themselves to have their wounds inspected and stories heard, most of whom would be turned away. Overwhelmed by the number of injured, the officials chose only twenty-three more individuals whom they deemed both veterans of the siege and injured beyond the capacity for work. In their careful accounting, they partially liberated four of these men, according to the local practice of *coartación*, or self-purchase, for injuries they judged had reduced their capacity to work by half. Ricla's men granted three individuals a prize of thirty pesos each in addition to their manumission; he granted another three men, "rendered so useless, by lost limbs, that they are unable to solicit for themselves support," pensions of one real a day. Because their injuries had come "in the service of the King and the *patria*," Ricla explained, they received freedom and a pension "for the greater stimulus to others, and their own reward."[52]

To compensate the owners, Ricla appraised all the enslaved Africans who were to be manumitted to determine the price their owners would be paid. Their decisions were generous to the owners, often 350 pesos or even 400 pesos a man, which was quite high for prices in Havana at the time. Some owners chose to cede to the crown the value of the enslaved African, some requested repayment in silver, but the majority (eighty owners) asked for another enslaved worker instead. To meet the demands of those who wanted another slave, Ricla agreed to distribute replacements among them. To be fair, as he saw it, he assigned each enslaved African to his or her new owner by pulling the recipient's name out of a hat, as though awarding a prize in a raffle. In miniature, this raffle captured Ricla's dawning realization that the way to keep Havana's more powerful residents loyal was to give them more enslaved Africans.[53]

This manumission process was glaringly incomplete. For anyone walking by Havana's city hall that day, the wounded men must have presented a striking sight—as they stood there displaying signs of grave injuries sustained on the front lines of the siege, crowded together with their owners anxiously awaiting a decision on their fate. Given what enslaved veterans had been through during the siege of Havana, and in the subsequent limbo of British rule, many

52. "Testimonio de los autos obrados sobre las livertades dadas," 1764, AGI, SD, 2209. Some slaveowners chose freely to waive the compensation out of good will to the crown. In total, the Real Hacienda paid 14,270 pesos to these slaveowners in Cuba. See Ricla to Arriaga, Oct. 30, Nov. 20, 1764, AGI, SD, 2209.

53. "Testimonio de los autos obrados sobre las livertades dadas," 1764, AGI, SD, 2209.

at the city hall that day must have felt relief at the raising again of the Spanish flag. For most, however, that relief quickly changed into frustration with the new governor. Far more enslaved Africans had participated in the siege than Ricla manumitted, and the majority found themselves turned away. Freedom had been promised to them in the king's name, they had answered his call, and now the new governor had snatched away their long-awaited reward. With few exceptions, enslaved Africans' status as property of the king's subjects took precedence over their identity as subjects of the king themselves.

Some enslaved Africans got into conflicts, not with Ricla, but with their owners, who thwarted their efforts to claim manumission for service during the siege. During Ricla's accounting and manumission, a Jesuit priest claimed that his enslaved African, Juan de Dios, had been injured, not in the siege, but afterward, on the sugar plantation, by "carelessly" catching his left arm in the sugar mill. Diego de Peñalver, Sebastian's son, insisted that his enslaved African Francisco Antonio had not been injured by a bomb during the siege, as he claimed. Instead, Peñalver maintained that Antonio had fled inland at the onset of the attack and been returned, uninjured, by a paid slave catcher, only to run away again three days later. These owners easily could have fabricated stories to avoid losing their property. On the other hand, among those who turned up in answer to Ricla's call, there were also men who had not been involved in the siege and were trying to take advantage of the circumstances to secure their freedom. Whether their accounts were true or not, and it is important to leave open both possibilities, the word of the owners carried the day.[54]

After the public accounting was concluded, enslaved Africans who claimed to have served in the siege continued to petition Ricla. When Ricla denied them, on the grounds that it would allow untold numbers of others to make similar claims, petitioners appealed to his successor as governor of Havana or directly to the crown, sometimes even in person. One manumission claim denied by Ricla, but granted by the crown under the next captain general's watch, involved an enslaved creole from Havana who had been injured by British gunfire and captured in the Cabaña. Taken to Jamaica by General William Keppel at the end of the siege, he later fled to Cartagena and then returned to Havana, where he appealed for his freedom as his just reward.[55]

Several enslaved Africans who subsequently traveled with their owners to Spain also seized the opportunity to appeal directly to the king for their release from bondage. At least in one case, their claims were expressly against the wishes of their owners. Joseph Antonio Moreno, an enslaved African from

54. Ibid., fols. 62v–67r.

55. El Rey to the Governador y capitán general de la Isla de Cuba y ciudad de San Cristóbal de La Habana, Sept. 6, 1768, AGI, SD, 1215, no. 84.

Puerto Príncipe, complained in person in Spain that Ricla had unfairly denied him manumission. He argued that just "by the very act" of journeying the 150 leagues across the island to Havana to offer himself for the defense he had already earned his freedom. He claimed he had fought in the company that launched the raid on San Lázaro, battled alongside Dionisio Pérez, and then retreated to Villa Clara instead of surrendering after the capitulation. Eager to reward this loyal subject, and not facing a sea of angry slaveowners, as Ricla was in Havana, the king released Moreno from his bondage, as he did for others in similar cases presented at the Council of the Indies. Yet Havana slaveowners' acute demand for more enslaved Africans, combined with the urgency to secure their loyalty, meant that decisions in Cuba often went in the owners' favor.[56]

Despite their varying levels of success with Ricla, people of African descent also sought rewards for service outside the military realm and used their actions during the siege to appeal to the Spanish king for other advantages. This practice was in keeping with a long tradition of free blacks and pardos using their wartime service to carve out more rights and privileges in postwar peacetime. Their claims reflected the myriad roles that people of African descent played in Havana's social worlds and during the siege itself. The free pardo Miguel Joseph de Aviles, for example, petitioned the Council of the Indies in the fall of 1763 for compensation for medical services he had provided while treating the sick and wounded during the invasion and occupation. As Aviles recounted, he had spent more than a year caring for the sick among members of his militia company of pardos and the lower orders of Havana society in the Hospital de San Juan de Dios. Despite these signs of his honorable character and his experience in the surgeon's arts, which he had learned on the job, Aviles complained that he had been subsequently barred by Havana's medical board (*protomedicato*) from practicing surgery "solely for the reason" that he was pardo. Overruling the Conde de Ricla and the protomedicato, the Council of the Indies approved his petition, once again demonstrating that royal authorities could choose to affirm the bonds with their pardo libre subjects, in spite of opposition from local authorities.[57]

In general, the reoccupation did strengthen the bond between the sovereign and Cuba's population of African descent and gave them leverage against

56. Letter of Joseph Antonio Moreno, AGI, SD, 2208; Consejo de Indias, Sept. 6, 1768, AGI, SD, 1215, no. 84; Barcia, *Los ilustres apellidos,* 242–243.

57. Aviles made the case that he should be certified just like another pardo libre, Joseph Francisco Baez Llerena, who had been licensed in 1760. He also argued that, if his sons showed aptitude for medical practice, they, too, should be permitted to practice medicine throughout the island. See AGI, SD, 1455, no. 10; AGI, SD, 1457, no. 7; and AGI, SD, 1458, no. 15.

slaveowners and local authorities. The aura of honor and gratitude for their performance during the siege gave them a vehicle for making claims in peacetime and created heroes among them who were perceived to have special access to and status with the sovereign. People of African descent in Havana thus persisted in petitioning their sovereign for rights and privileges based upon service rendered and losses sustained during the siege. For example, widows in the free population of African descent appealed directly to the king to ask for pensions after losing their husbands in the fighting. During troop reviews, members of the militias of pardos and morenos continued to describe their valiant service to military officials over the decades that followed. A small percentage of these men who made claims might have exaggerated their exploits or made them up altogether. But the memory of black heroism during the siege buttressed their cases and made a powerful argument to Spanish officials and the crown for the military value of their African subjects. That military value would come into conflict with the many other roles reformers were imagining for people of African descent in Cuba.[58]

Rebuilding and Reform

During the period of Ricla's rule, from 1763 to 1765, he and his field marshal O'Reilly launched a number of ambitious reform projects designed to strengthen Spanish sovereignty over the island and enhance its economic development, royal revenue production, and military preparedness. The circle of government and military officials who arrived in Havana with Ricla wrote several reports about plans for developing the economy of Cuba. These reports were meant to provide suggestions for policy reform to the Council of the Indies and a more general response to Francisco de Craywinckel's call to meet the British challenge. Across the board, a central point often repeated was that trade restrictions needed to be relaxed and the supply of enslaved Africans to the island needed to be expanded. Ricla and O'Reilly argued that the best way to rebuild the island and stimulate its economy was by doing as they did during their time there—further opening its commerce to its neighbors, West Africa, and the Atlantic system.

As Ricla acknowledged, "the first difficulty" that arose upon Havana's resti-

---

58. María Francisca Solano, a free *morena* widow with three children, submitted multiple requests for a pension. She accompanied them with testimonials about her former husband, a free moreno militia member who had been killed in the Morro by a bullet from a British gun. She submitted petitions beginning in the 1760s, but, as of 1771, she had not yet had a response. See María Francisca Solano to Arriaga, Jan. 10, 1771, AGI, Cuba, 1140; Pasqual de Cisneros to Arriaga, Mar. 31, 1770, AGI, SD, 2093.

tution to Spanish rule was "the lack of blacks." Slaveowners were eager to replace those enslaved Africans killed, lost to the interior, or manumitted, and
Ricla needed laborers to rebuild the city's fortifications and initiate a new
round of construction at the royal shipyard. He had been advised to look first
to New Spain, but not enough *guachinangos,* convicts, or other forced laborers
from there were available. Ricla found that Cuba could not satisfy elites' demand for more enslaved Africans without reliance on British slave traders.
After holding an open bidding war between British, Irish, and Swiss merchants, as well as Juan de Miralles, Ricla awarded a new asiento to Cornelio
Coppinger, the Irish merchant newly arrived and immediately well married in
Cuba to a relative of Miralles. In 1763, Ricla contracted for a large importation
of enslaved Africans, more than the British had brought in during the occupation. At least three thousand men from this group were put to work rebuilding and expanding the city's fortifications. In total, during his short tenure in
Cuba, the captain general, Conde de Ricla, sanctioned the importation of up
to seven thousand royal slaves to rebuild the city's fortifications.[59]

In the period directly after the occupation, Ricla extended the popular
commercial practices that were brought to light by the city's loss. In spite of
the promise of a new beginning and the urgent cry from Madrid for reform,
Ricla's governorship in fact extended Havana's trading relationships with
British and British American merchants. Ricla even bought the forty thousand
bricks necessary to rebuild the Morro from his British enemies, contracting
with a French merchant to procure them in the port of New York. Although
he was charged with coming up with a new formula for the workings of war,
trade, and slavery on the island, he and O'Reilly ended up co-opting the old
local practices. As they both found, exchange with foreign — and, in particular, British and British American — merchants was an integral and unavoid-
able way the city engaged in the Atlantic economy. Despite the Spanish king's
interest in cutting off exchanges with British merchants, Ricla and O'Reilly
saw officially opening Cuba to commerce with its neighbors as the best way
to rebuild Havana and stimulate its economy.[60]

Ricla and a number of officials sent to survey the situation in Cuba were
also charged with figuring out how to make the island produce enough royal

59. For attempts to find laborers in New Spain, see Ricla to Arriaga, July 22, 1763, and the King to
Ricla, Sept. 22, 1763, both in AGI, SD, 2117. On the importation of royal slaves to work on the fortifi-
cations, see Pérez Guzmán, *La Habana*, 63; Powell Jennings, "War as the 'Forcing House of Change,'"
WMQ, 3d. Ser., LXII (2005), 424.

60. For the purchase of bricks for the Morro in New York, see License Issued by Miguel de Altarriba, Mar. 19, 1765, AGI, SD, 1213. The bricks were brought from New York on a Spanish ship by a
French ship's captain named Francisco Salvator.

revenue to pay for the troops, fortifications, naval protection, and administration the island required. Their reform measures were based on extensive consultation with Havana elites, who were able to persuade them to continue their modus operandi for the island, which had enriched it up to that time. After trying out initial reform measures, O'Reilly convoked a junta of the leading vecinos a year later. He even shared with them the royal account books for the city and asked for their help devising new solutions to cover shortfalls between royal expenses and revenues on the island. The annual situado from New Spain of five hundred thousand pesos was an expedient solution, not a permanent one.[61]

In a sign of their increasing ambitions, Havana elites provided a long list of recommendations, including a request for "one or two" permanent representatives from Havana at the court in Spain, something no other Spanish territory had. Their other suggestions for improving revenue included measures that would reduce duties, eliminate monopolies, and free up Cuba's trade with Spanish America and other Iberian ports beyond the Cádiz merchant monopoly. Because these men were some of the leading investors in sugar, they also asked for concessions for that industry. Realizing that he was perhaps opening up Pandora's box by soliciting a wish list from Havana residents, Ricla canceled a second junta and consulted a few leading citizens in private. Yet he forwarded the Havana residents' petition to the Council of the Indies with his own enthusiastic endorsement.[62]

A great number of these commercial suggestions emanating from Havana would make their way into the *comercio libre* policy issued in 1765 by the Council of the Indies. It raised the taxes on brandy, rum, and the sales tax *(alcabala)* while simultaneously liberalizing trade. As a concession to induce residents of Cuba to willingly accept a heavier tax burden, metropolitan authorities freed the island to trade with all the major ports of Spain as well as the Caribbean re-

61. Initially, in December 1763, Ricla worked through the well-connected Jesuit Father Butler to ask Havana patricians how they would recommend developing the island's commerce and attendant ability to pay a greater quantity of taxes to the crown. See Alejandro O'Reilly to Arriaga, Apr. 1, 1764, AGS, Hacienda, 2342, fol. 330r; Bibiano Torres Ramírez, *Alejandro O'Reilly en las Indias* (Seville, 1969); Kuethe and Inglis, "Absolutism and Enlightened Reform," *Past and Present*, no. 109 (November 1985), 124.

62. Ricla to Arriaga, Oct. 30, 1764, AGS, Hacienda, 1056; Ricla to Arriaga, Oct. 30, 1764, AGI, SD, 2188. These juntas are described at length in Kuethe and Inglis, "Absolutism and Enlightened Reform," *Past and Present*, no. 109 (November 1985), 122–134. The Havana junta's demands included open trade for Cuba with all ports of Spain, an end to duties on goods exported to Iberia, the termination of all monopoly contracts (for enslaved Africans or goods), an open slave trade to the island, support for the sugar industry, the right to trade tobacco to other Spanish American ports, the right to trade in *aguardiente de caña* (unprocessed rum) with Yucatán and the new colony of Louisiana, and open passage to Cuba for all skilled laborers and artisans.

gion — Santo Domingo, Trinidad, Puerto Rico, and the island of Margarita. This new policy was moving closer to the aspirations of Havana residents evident during the occupation. After its initial success, the Cuban model of comercio libre and alcabala was extended to the rest of the empire in 1778 and Caracas and New Spain in 1789. The ban on intercolonial trade was abolished, and more Spanish ports were made legally accessible to colonial merchants. This increased availability of enslaved laborers, combined with new Spanish investments in the island and the policy of comercio libre, made the postwar period a time of growth in many industries. Freer commerce, along the lines of the British imperial model, would be the key to rejuvenating the Spanish empire.[63]

The Havana elites and the captain general and governor also made specific demands to the Council of the Indies for new policies governing the slave trade to the island. The Havana city council suggested that residents of Cuba be permitted to trade in slaves directly with British colonies and to exchange Cuban produce for enslaved Africans. Gaining formal permission would make legal what was already common practice on the island. Though not immediately successful, their lobbying influenced the captain general and began to reframe the council's thinking about the trade in enslaved Africans. Spanish political thought had traditionally been more focused on developing policies for the mining economies of Mexico and Peru, the core sites of royal revenue production in the empire, and the indigenous peoples who predominated in those regions. Now events in Cuba had drawn their attention to the Caribbean and its populations of African descent.[64]

All the reports coming to the Council of the Indies from Ricla and the government and military officials that accompanied him advocated opening the slave trade to the island. The consensus was that enslaved Africans and free people of color were essential as both engines of the island's development and loyal manpower for its defense. Their recommendations echoed those in 1750 from city council lawyer Bernardo Joseph de Urrutia y Matos, who put it succinctly: "Nothing is undertaken on the island that doesn't need slaves, and making them available would help everything usable." At the time, Urrutia had

63. Stein and Stein, *Apogee of Empire*, 61; Brading, "Bourbon Spain and Its American Empire," in Bethell, ed., *Cambridge History of Latin America*, I, *Colonial Latin America*, 389–440; Lynch, "The Institutional Framework of Colonial Spanish America," *Journal of Latin American Studies*, XXIV (1992), 69–81; Antonio García-Baquero González, *El comercio colonial en la época de absolutismo ilustrado: Problemas y debates* (Granada, 2003); Paquette, *Enlightenment, Governance, and Reform*, 100–105; Elliott, *Empires of the Atlantic World*, 307; Amores, *Cuba en la época de Ezpeleta*, 179–182.

64. Pablo Tornero Tinajero, *Crecimiento económio y transformaciones sociales: Esclavos, hacendados, y comerciantes en la Cuba colonial (1760–1840)* (Madrid, 1996), 22–27; Schneider, "African Slavery and Spanish Empire," *Journal of Early American History*, V (2015), 17–27; Ricla to Arriaga, Oct. 30, 1764, AGS, Hacienda, 1056; Ricla to Arriaga, Oct. 30, 1764, AGI, SD, 2188; Kuethe and Inglis, "Absolutism and Enlightened Reform," *Past and Present*, no. 109 (November 1985), 134.

gained little traction, but now a new consensus about the utility of people of African descent to the Spanish empire had coalesced in the wake of the siege and occupation of Havana.[65]

As Ricla and his circle of reformers saw it, people of African descent and the slave trade were a panacea for virtually all of Cuba's most pressing problems. To begin with, they were crucial to the militarization and defense of the Spanish empire. Ricla and O'Reilly's inquiry into Havana's experience during the invasion and occupation convinced them of the strategic utility of black militias for both offensive and defensive action on a broader imperial scale. Ricla wrote to Arriaga in October 1764 that the island's "excellent militia, when necessary, will be able to provide prompt relief to any part of these dominions." O'Reilly's reorganization of the island's militia defenses led to one of the most well-known and influential reforms carried out in Cuba in the period 1763–1765. The military *reglamentos* O'Reilly established for Cuba would become models for those adopted in Mexico, Venezuela, and Peru in 1769. The further militarization of both African- and European-descent creole populations would play a pivotal role in the independence wars and their legacies throughout many areas of Spanish America. Often depicted as a top-down imperial decision, in this instance it was pursued after people of African descent had taken it upon themselves to fight in this critical battle in Cuba (see Figure 29).[66]

Influenced by evidence from the siege, these reformers perceived great military potential not just in the free black militias but also in enslaved Africans. Alejandro O'Reilly proposed a special artillery regiment of royal slaves that could be employed in combat and would reproduce itself through natural increase. The very idea to form this artillery regiment showed the eupho-

65. "Informe de Bernardo José de Urrutia y Matos, catedrático de la Universidad de la Habana, sobre los intereses y posibles aumentos del comercio en la isla de Cuba," 1750, AGI, Ultramar, 986.

66. Ricla to Arriaga, Oct. 30, 1764, AGI, SD, 2188. For the military reglamentos developed by Alejandro O'Reilly, see, all in the Escoto Cuban History and Literature Collection, Houghton Library, Harvard University: "Reglamento del pie, servicio, gobierno, y disciplina de cadetes de la Havana, aprobada por S.M., y mandado su observancia por real orden, expedida en San Ildefonso a 24 de octubre de 1764"; "Reglamento para el govierno militar, político, y económico de la compañía de artillería compuesta de negros de Su Magestad y sus familias," 1768; "Reglamento para las milicias de infantería, y caballería de la Isla de Cuba y mandando que se observen inviolablemente todos sus artículos, por real cedula expedida en el Pardo a 19 de enero de 1769." On the military reglamentos, see also Pedro Deschamps Chapeaux, *Los batallones de pardos y morenos libres* (Havana, 1976), 40; and Juan Marchena Fernández, *Ejército y milicias en el mundo colonial Americano* (Madrid, 1992), 135–138. Ironically, Ben Vinson III has found that these Bourbon military reforms signaled a period of "crisis and decay" for the free-colored militias of colonial Mexico, when they were introduced there. As a result, they lost some of their previous autonomy, and the militia leadership in many regions of Mexico was whitened. See Vinson, *Bearing Arms for His Majesty: The Free-Colored Militia in Colonial Mexico* (Stanford, Calif., 2001), 2, 37–45.

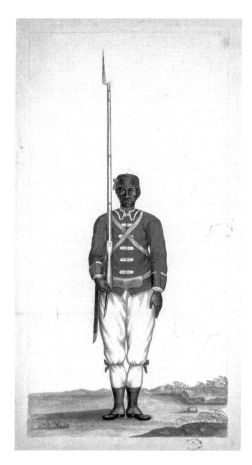

FIGURE 29 Design of the Uniform of the Battalion of Morenos of Havana. By the *mulato* painter José Nicolás de la Escalera. From a letter sent back from Havana by Alejandro O'Reilly to Julián de Arriaga, on December 21, 1763. Permission, Spain, Ministerio de Educación, Cultura y Deporte, Archivo General de Indias, Mapas y Planos-Uniformes, 25

ria for enslaved Africans—and all they could do for the island economically and militarily—in the period after Havana's restitution. Modeled after both the royal slaves of the mines of El Cobre in eastern Cuba and Juan Cabrera's enslaved soldiers active during the British siege, this regiment of one hundred men would all be married and live in special family quarters. Their wives' labor and reproduction would by design be harnessed for the military state. Women would do cleaning and washing for the army and navy, and both husband and wife would be rewarded with their freedom if they managed to raise twelve live children. Male sons would be apprenticed as carpenters and artisans, learning trades that would be useful for the royal shipyards and fortifications, or they would train in the military arts.[67]

67. "Reglamento para el govierno militar, político, y económico de la compañía de artillería compuesta de negros de Su Magestad y sus familias," 1768, Escoto Cuban History and Literature Collection. See also Deschamps Chapeaux, *Los batallones de pardos y morenos libres*, 63–69; and John-

Despite the large gap between prescription and realities, there are letters corroborating that initial steps were taken to create this artillery regiment of royal slaves. The one hundred male artillerymen were selected from the influx of royal slaves under Coppinger's contract, and uniforms were designed for them. Officials also designated one hundred enslaved women to be their spouses and placed them, on their arrival from Africa, in the homes of Havana's elite for acculturation, Christianization, and further training. At the time, in March 1765, Ricla estimated it would take two months to build the proper living quarters and marry the slaves off to each other.[68]

Enslaving African bozales chosen at random and forcing them into military service had never been a tradition on the island or anywhere else in the Americas. The militia units of free and enslaved Africans that had proved so useful during the defense of Havana had all been made up of volunteers — self-selected individuals who either had experience or a vital interest in military combat. The Jesuits claimed to have experimented with socially engineering families of the enslaved on their plantations, but Ricla no doubt would not have found such an endeavor as easy as he imagined. After the expulsion of the Jesuits in 1767, though, the Spanish state became the largest single slaveholding body in Spanish America. Other experiments arose to keep its population of bonded laborers sufficient, if possible, without relying on foreign slave traders.[69]

These reformers responded to conditions in Cuba with new ways of thinking and talking about the productive economic value of enslaved Africans to Spanish imperial projects. In addition to enthusiastic and expansive ways of imagining the military potential of enslaved Africans, they also began to ar-

son, "'Señoras en sus clases no ordinarias,'" in Johnson and Stoner, eds., *Trespassing Historic Gender Boundaries in Cuba*, 27–28. On the royal slaves of El Cobre, see María Elena Díaz, *The Virgin, the King, and the Royal Slaves of El Cobre: Negotiating Freedom in Colonial Cuba, 1670–1780* (Stanford, Calif., 2000); and Levi Marrero, *Los esclavos y la Virgen del Cobre: Dos siglos de lucha por la libertad de Cuba* (Miami, Fla., 1980).

68. Ricla to Don Miguel de Altarriba, Mar. 18, 1765, and Ricla to Arriaga, Mar. 27, 1765, both in AGI, SD, 1213; "Reglamento para el govierno military, político, y económico de la compañía de artillería compuesta de negros esclavos del rey y sus familias," 1768, AGI, Cuba, 1098, fol. 539. Johnson has found records that the wives were still being paid in 1772 for their labor sewing uniforms for the state; see Johnson, "'Señoras en sus clases no ordinarias,'" in Johnson and Stoner, eds., *Trespassing Historic Gender Boundaries in Cuba*, 27.

69. Ricla's interim successor, the intendente Miguel de Altarriba, also advocated for promoting slave marriage to reduce the demand for more imported enslaved Africans; see Altarriba to Arriaga, Apr. 24, 1765, AGI, SD, 2210. Thinking along similar lines, in 1778, the Marqués de Enrile was writing to the crown about the need to bring more enslaved Africans to Cuba in order to foster natural increase in the island's enslaved population. See Don Gerónimo Enrile, director general del asiento, "Consideraciones sobre el comercio de negros y harinas," 1778, AGI, IG, 2820A; Manuel Lucena Salmoral, *Los códigos negros de la América española* (Alcalá de Henares, Spain, 1996), 17.

ticulate new political economies and modes of thought that came into conflict with older understandings of black subjecthood in Cuba, though their authors did not see it that way. In his general report of 1764, O'Reilly considered the scarcity and high cost of enslaved Africans as one of the principal causes of Cuba's economic underdevelopment. Because African slaves were the only workforce for the island's logging, ranching, and agricultural industries — particularly sugar and tobacco — O'Reilly considered them "the most indispensable merchandise in order to make this interesting colony flourish." More enslaved Africans would not only produce more revenue for the king but also make Spain's slaveowning vassals there more loyal to him; as O'Reilly put it: "And when a vassal is rich, what can he fault his Sovereign?"[70]

Not only did O'Reilly use the explicitly commercial language of "merchandise" to describe enslaved Africans but he also looked for models in the slave-trading patterns of Spain's European competitors. He pointed out that the Spanish policy of monopoly contracts had impeded, not aided, the supplying of Cuba with enslaved laborers. "The French, English, and Dutch," he wrote, "whose establishments on the coast of Africa assure them that they obtain blacks with great convenience, know how greatly the happiness of their colonies depends on them, and far from imposing tributes, or measures that make it difficult, they have encouraged it, and always protect the trade through as many means as the government can." Indeed, O'Reilly was aware of Albemarle's restrictions on slave imports in occupied Havana, which he saw as the outgrowth of rivalry between British and Spanish Caribbean isles. In his mind, the way to develop the island of Cuba and bind its elites to Spain was simple: the expansion of the slave trade, state support of slave purchase, and the removal of duties on imported Africans.[71]

Writing from Havana in 1768, the Belgian-born military engineer Agustín Crame, who took part with O'Reilly in the military review of the island, took his colleague's conclusions even further — to unprecedented levels. Crame's writings reveal a new departure for Spanish political and economic thought, one that foreshadowed developments in the nineteenth-century Spanish Caribbean during the ascendance of large-scale sugar plantation agriculture. As Crame saw it, agricultural zones reliant upon enslaved labor required a different political economy than mining regions devoted to the extraction of rich metals. According to his prescription for this new type of "agricultural colony" in Cuba, abundant numbers of Africans were needed because no European migrants would willingly submit to the rigors of labor in the field, and forcing

70. O'Reilly to Arriaga, Apr. 1, 1764, AGS, Hacienda, 2342, fol. 331v.
71. Ibid., fol. 333.

indigenous families to migrate from Mexico for this work would be against the spirit of Spanish laws. In order to meet the island's need for enslaved Africans, there was no option but to cast aside prohibitions against trade with foreigners. In essence, Crame's writings reveal a new mode of thinking about Spanish empire that was coalescing around the slave trade (see Figure 30).[72]

Borrowing modern, mechanistic metaphors from manufacturing and from Spain's rival Britain, Crame described "blacks" as "the most useful machines for agriculture." As both "machines" and "prime material" for colonial economies, he said, once "put into motion cultivating the land, they take on a value much greater than they cost initially." He optimistically calculated that bringing just one hundred slaves to Havana would generate two hundred thousand pesos in sugar production. Just as Britain needed to acquire wool for its cloth industry, Crame argued, Spain needed to buy slaves for its expanding tobacco and sugar industries.[73]

Even as Crame used new, dehumanizing language referencing machinery and raw materials, he also grappled with the paradoxes of this unprecedented way of thinking about Africans in Spain's overseas territories. This was the crux of the problem: to see enslaved Africans as machines broke from several centuries of precedent in which the Spanish crown and the Church recognized the personhood of enslaved Africans and in fact justified the African slave trade with the logic that it was better to live as a slave in Catholic lands than be free in pagan ones. Black loyalty was a pillar of the Spanish empire, crucial to its defense, and different forms of slavery might imperil it. Yet Crame saw no cause for concern, even in light of Jamaican slave rebellions — most recently, the large-scale revolt of 1760–1761 — because of what he considered the unique and superior modes of Spanish slavery. "In our constitution," he wrote, "obedience is more certain than the English one." In essence, Crame justified the radical transformation of the slave trade and expansion of agricultural slavery based on the fallacy that the black loyalty so evident in Cuba was a given.[74]

72. "Discurso político sobre necesidades de la isla de Cuba, escrito en el año 1768 por el ingeniero en jefe, Don Agustín Crame," II/2827, fols. 240v, 254r, BRP; Leida Fernández Prieto, "Crónica anunciada de una Cuba azucarera," in María Dolores González-Ripoll and Izaskun Álvarez Cuartero, eds., *Francisco Arango y la invención de la Cuba azucarera* (Salamanca, Spain, 2009), 55–65.

73. "Discurso político sobre necesidades de la isla de Cuba," II/2827, fols. 243v, 244r, 254v, BRP.

74. Vincent Brown, "Slave Revolt in Jamaica, 1760–1761: A Cartographic Narrative" (2012), http://revolt.axismaps.com; "Discurso político sobre necesidades de la isla de Cuba," II/2827, fol. 242v, BRP. The classic justification for African slavery in Spanish America can be found in Alonso de Sandoval, *Un tratado sobre la esclavitud*, trans. Enriqueta Vila Vilar (Madrid, 1987), 415. The contradiction of arming slaves and, in fact, all people of African descent is explored in Brown and Morgan, eds., *Arming Slaves*.

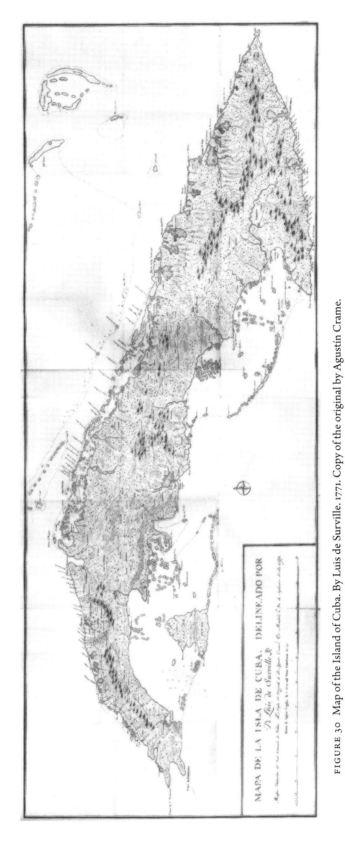

FIGURE 30 Map of the Island of Cuba. By Luis de Surville. 1771. Copy of the original by Agustín Crame. This map, which accompanied Agustín Crame's report, was the most detailed yet produced of the island. Biblioteca del Real Palacio, Madrid, II-2827

In the influx of reports from Cuba in the 1760s, a central point often repeated was that the supply of slaves to the island of Cuba, and the Spanish empire more broadly, needed to be expanded. In these reports, Africans were seen as necessary labor to grow and develop virtually every aspect of the diversified economies of the Spanish Caribbean. Because free and enslaved blacks composed "almost all the artisans, workers, and day laborers," in addition to militia soldiers and field hands, ultimately, claimed one report, "upon them depends entirely the greater or lesser happiness the island achieves, and in the case of their lacking in number, they would reduce everything here to a pitiful embryo." The reasons for expanding the slave trade were political (ensuring the satisfaction and hence loyalty of the island's elite), military (populating the island and providing manpower for its defense), and economic (curbing contraband, supplying laborers in all facets of the economy, and developing the agricultural sector, which would drive further settlement and provide revenue for the crown). Inhabitants of Cuba were well aware of the development their island lacked and the freedom of commerce it needed. Striking an ominous tone, several of these authors shared the concern that the Havana elites' desire for more slaves was so acute it might even trump their loyalty to Spain. Elites in Havana demanded more enslaved Africans and would build ties with Spain's British enemies and even abandon their loyalty to the fatherland in order to get them.[75]

Proposals coming back to Madrid from Havana reinforced the sense that, if Spain were to compete with Britain and France, it would have to secure its own direct supply of enslaved laborers from Africa. Imperial rivalry put Spain's supply for its own colonies in constant jeopardy, which was extremely detrimental to both its economy and security. Though some of the language advocating more enslaved Africans for the island of Cuba was new—with its emphasis on agriculture and mechanization—the overall case being made also relied on older notions of Africans as loyal and necessary subjects that could protect Spanish territories and fight on behalf of the king.

Not as immediately successful as their lobbying for freer commerce, their

75. "Dictamen sobre las ventajas que pueden sacarse para el mejor fomento de la isla de Cuba," n.d. [late 1760s], AGI, SD, 1156, no. 4, fols. 34v–35r; "Prospecto del proyecto para el establecimiento del abasto de negros de la Isla de Cuba," II/2855, no. 2, fols. 19–31, BRP. Crame made a similar point about how economic growth could curb disloyalty: "Jamas se ha visto que un pueblo que se está fomentando se rebele"; see "Discurso político sobre necesidades de la isla de Cuba," II/2827, 237r–237v, BRP. In a representation to the king, a group of Havana cabildo members threatened that, without the commercial reforms they needed, they would be forced to abandon the fatherland; see "Copia de la representación que puso en manos de SM Don Antonio Ventura Montenegro, Apoderado General del cabildo secular de la Habana, solicitando la remisión del impuesto de alcabalas establecido por el Conde de Ricla," 1766, Colección Mata Linares, LXXVIII, fols. 351–357, Real Academia de la Historia.

reports nonetheless began to reframe the Council of the Indies' thinking about the trade in slaves. In a request that would make common practices on the island legal, the Havana city council suggested that residents of Cuba be permitted to trade in slaves directly with British colonies and to exchange Cuban products of the land for enslaved Africans. In deliberations on the issue in January 1768, the Council determined that the ideas were contrary to fundamental laws of good government. It pointed out the "prejudice" caused by "frequent communication and commerce with foreigners" and the dangers of letting the interests and convenience of one or another vecino, region, or province override the well-being and security of the monarchy and royal treasury. At the same time, the council raised the idea with the king that there could be benefits to erecting "plantations and factories" in Africa, either in the name of the king or under the provenance of private subjects, to facilitate the slave trade. As the Council of the Indies pointed out, there still existed ports and other regions of Guinea where Africans could be found to trade with and other nations had not yet established fortifications or entrepôts.[76]

The events of 1762 placed new pressure on metropolitan reformers finally to resolve the problem of the slave trade to Spanish America, which had been a source of conflict and attempted reform across a longer period. Ever since 1713, concerns had grown about sovereignty and governance in Spain's overseas territories, given reliance on a British slave trade, and they had contributed to the outbreak of wars. The idea to attempt to re-route or regain control over the slave trade had been moving through policy circles in Madrid for several decades by the time 1762 forced action. Owing to both his intense sense of rivalry with the British and advice from his circle of Enlightened absolutist reformers, Charles III had already set in motion changes to the mechanics of commerce and the slave trade before British warships arrived offshore of Havana. The early 1760s had also seen increasing calls in Charles III's administration for the liberalization of American trade. In 1760, Charles III began seeking out a Spanish merchant to take on the asiento contract, the first Spanish merchant to be singled out for the privilege in the long history of the importation of Africans into Spain and Spanish America. Don Miguel de Uriarte of El Puerto de Santa María, next to Cádiz, petitioned for a new asiento de negros for the province of Caracas and the island of Cuba under consideration by the crown in August 1760. His newly formed Compañía gaditana de negros was granted the asiento, but, owing to the interruption of the Seven Years' War, he did not take it on until it could be reconstituted five years later.[77]

---

76. Consejo de Indias, Jan. 8, 1768, AGI, SD, 2515.
77. Arriaga to the King, Aug. 22, 1760, AGS, Hacienda, 973; Pedro Rodríguez Campomanes,

Havana's capture by the British hastened the sense of urgency for these planned reforms. The mechanics of the slave trade and the relationships it had created between Havana residents and British merchants were central to the accusations of Cuban disloyalty that swirled in Cádiz, Seville, and Madrid after the British siege. Study of the occupation had revealed the extent of local autonomy on the island and its dependence on an integrated regional economy. These factors were what had made Havana so rich in the first place and such an object of British fascination. But, as Spanish officials were just learning, for some time Spain had failed to govern, defend, and effectively supply labor to its "key to the Indies." New Spain had proven unable to provide either sufficient flour to feed the island or enough guachinango laborers to maintain its defenses. Smugglers and British slave traders, during their term as asiento holders from 1713 until its curtailment in 1750, had done a better job meeting those demands in Cuba. Reports from Havana affirmed this. The consequence of failing to meet Cuba's commercial and labor needs had been the undermining of Spanish loyalty in the colonial capital.

Historians have depicted the British occupation of Havana as a moment of massive slave importation that tipped the island's fate toward sugar monoculture on a British West Indian model. What it showed Havana's elites and the bureaucrats whose ears they captured, however, was that Cuba could not solely rely on its British competitors for its enslaved Africans, an essential labor supply that met a myriad of the island's needs, including but by no means limited to sugar plantation agriculture. After all, to protect the interests of powerful British subjects, Albemarle had placed restrictions on slave importation during the occupation of Havana, capping the total number to be sold and setting a higher price than had been the norm under the Royal Havana Company monopoly. The slave trade was a strategic branch of trade vital to imperial competition, and Spanish officials were finally beginning to embrace its importance as such.[78]

Conde de Campomanes, *Reflexiones sobre el comercio español a Indias (1762)*, ed. Vicente Llombart Rosa (Madrid, 1988); Pablo Tornero Tinajero, "El suministro de mano de obra esclava en Cuba: Estado español y oligarquía criolla (1765–1820)," in Consuelo Naranjo Orovio and Tomás Mallo Gutiérrez, eds., *Cuba la perla de las Antillas: Actas de las I Jornadas sobre "Cuba y su historia"* (Madrid, 1994), 313–324; and Tornero Tinajero, *Crecimiento económico y transformaciones sociales*, 38; José A. Piqueras, "Los amigos de Arango en la corte de Carlos IV," in González-Ripoll and Cuartero, *Francisco Arango*, 151–166; Bibiano Torres Ramírez, *La compañía gaditana de negros* (Seville, 1973); Schneider, "African Slavery and Spanish Empire," *Journal of Early American History*, V (2015), 1–17; and Elena Andrea Schneider, "The Occupation of Havana: War, Trade, and Slavery in Eighteenth-Century Cuba" (Ph.D. diss., Princeton University, 2011), 356–364, 372–377.

78. Crame, O'Reilly, and Ricla all wrote to the Council of the Indies about Albemarle's restrictive slave-trading policy in the occupied city. For Crame, see "Discurso político sobre necesidades de la isla de Cuba," II/2827, fol. 256v, BRP. For classic accounts that use 1762–1763 as a turning point

The influx of reports from Cuba in 1763–1765 added new perspectives on the potentially vital role enslaved Africans and free people of color could play expanding the imperial economy and protecting against foreign military threat. A Spanish proposal for the supply of blacks to Cuba put it in no uncertain terms: Cuba needed to establish a Spanish factory off the coast of Guinea, which would give it "direct commerce" with Africa, "without the dependence" that the island then had on foreign merchants. The British occupation of Havana, combined with these reports and recommendations that flowed from Cuba in its aftermath, broke through a policy logjam and brought to fruition ideas that had been incubating about the slave trade. After Ricla's short tenure ended, the Spanish administration took into its own hands the project of reforming the slave trade into Cuba. The realization had set in that, if Spain were to satisfy the demands of the inhabitants of Cuba and consolidate its hold over the island, against both internal and external threats, it would have to secure its own direct supply of Africans, as did the French, British, and Portuguese.[79]

Conclusion

In the wake of the loss of Havana and subsequent restitution to Spanish rule, the crown sought to tie its subjects better to the Spanish empire. A flurry of demands for reform in Cuba were made, moving from Havana to Madrid and producing various competing road maps for instituting changes. A unifying, central point often repeated was that the island needed freer trade and a larger supply of enslaved Africans. One of the responses was the initiation of comercio libre in 1765. After 1763, the Spanish crown also began more actively supporting the slave trade, both for state economic interests and in order to create allegiances with a creole oligarchy in Cuba who demanded greater access to markets in enslaved African laborers.[80]

---

in Cuban history, opening up the pathway to sugar's ascendance, see, among others, Levi Marrero, *Cuba: Economía y sociedad*, VI (Madrid, 1978); Moreno Fraginals, *El ingenio;* Thomas, *Cuba;* Fernando Portuondo del Prado, *Historia de Cuba, 1492–1898* (Havana, 1957).

79. "Prospecto del proyecto para el establecimiento del abasto de negros de la Isla de Cuba," II/2855, no. 2, fols. 19–31 (quotation on 31r), BRP.

80. I agree with Pablo Tornero Tinajero on this point but argue that, in the period before the Haitian Revolution, Spanish pro–slave trade reformers also saw people of African descent, both enslaved and free, as critical to the defense of the island and imperial competition in both economic and military terms; see Tornero Tinajero, *Crecimiento económico y tranformaciones sociales,* 24. Other regions of Spanish America were also continuing to raise their own arguments for expanding the slave trade in the late eighteenth century. On the case for Peru, see Miguel [de] Gijon [y León], *Memoria que Don Miguel Gijón escribía para la Real Sociedad de Madrid, relativa al comercio de Indias, presentada en la junta general de 7 de marzo de 1778,* in *Memorias de la Sociedad económica de Amigos*

Ultimately, the great windfall for the island was not the British occupation itself; it was the investment that the Spanish crown made after the island returned to its control as a result of new policies put into place beginning in 1763. During this time, Havana was strengthened as a military launching pad against its hostile neighbors in Jamaica, the Bahamas, and British North America. Government officials imported a large number of royal slaves in order to construct on the grounds of the Cabaña the largest fortress complex in all of the Americas. (Havana was never directly attacked again, not even in the twentieth century.) They continued to enforce new measures to open the slave trafficking and commerce for the island in order better to develop and protect it from foreign encroachment. And they persisted in their reliance on the military service of free and enslaved subjects of African descent to protect Havana and project Spanish military power abroad.

In the aftermath of the loss and return of Havana, matters became starkly clear. Reports and fact-finding missions from Cuba confirmed and reasserted that people of African descent and the slave trade were and would continue to be critical to the development and defense of the island. On this point, black veterans of the siege, Havana elites, the Conde de Ricla, Ricla's field marshal Alejandro O'Reilly, and, ultimately, the Council of the Indies and Charles III would soon agree. Post-1763, the Spanish empire would see a new convergence of opinions between Cuban elites and the Spanish court around finding a better solution to the problem of the British-dominated slave trade into Cuba. The slave trade would become a new bonding agent between center and peripheries, as Spanish authorities committed themselves to experimenting with ways to expand access in Cuba to enslaved Africans. Cuba's elites, in turn, continued to assert the primacy of the population of African descent in their unique island society and to pursue their own improvisational and often extralegal methods for meeting local demands for enslaved Africans. In the wake of western Cuba's loss and restitution, these elites became more insistent and assertive to Spanish policymakers about the commercial reforms they desired and would seek to implement, even if it meant breaking the ties of imperial loyalty.

Through the occupation of Havana, Spain awoke to the power of people of African descent and the slave trade to modernize its empire in the face of British threats. The implications of this new understanding would make Spain's process of reform after the Seven Years' War stand out from that of

---

del Pais de Madrid, III (Madrid, 1787), 262–281: "Los negros transportados de Africa al Perú, son unos colonos infinitamente más útiles al Rey y al Estado, que los que se convidan voluntarios y pagados" (277).

its rivals. The uniqueness of this moment was striking: Spanish practices per-petuated a corporatist colonial model for its African subjects, even as it em-braced a new mechanized language of slave production. The Council of the Indies prepared to launch a newly expanded transatlantic slave trade similar to its rivals even as thinkers, officials, and jurists continued to function accord-ing to a model of compact building with loyal African-descended subjects that was quite distinct. Dehumanizing language like Crame's could be uttered on an island that sent accomplished black soldiers to display their prowess before the Spanish king, a king who still had a policy offering freedom to es-caped enslaved Africans from the colonies of its foreign rivals who expressed the desire to convert to Catholicism. This policy made a striking contrast be-tween the worlds of slavery in Cuba and its neighbor Jamaica, where enslaved recruits for the siege of Havana had been appraised only as property and never offered their freedom or rewarded for their service. This difference did not go unnoticed. In the years immediately after the siege, enslaved Africans in Jamaica, perhaps informed by rumors carried by those of their number who had been to Havana and returned, fled to Cuba in search of their freedom in ever greater numbers.[81]

Although African slavery, the slave trade, and populations of African de-scent have tended to be discussed separately, or not at all, they cannot be iso-lated from questions of imperial reform, which included a dramatic escalation in the number of royal slaves and the creation and expansion of black mili-tia regiments. Because people of African descent played a particularly criti-cal role in both the economy and military of Cuba, which in turn played an outsized role in the Spanish empire's process of reform, African slavery, the slave trade, and populations of African descent were pertinent to all discus-sions of changes in the political, economic, and military life of the island and the rest of Spanish America. This new attention to the African slave trade was intertwined with Madrid's concerns about sovereignty in its own empire. This move to prioritize and—to use an anachronistic term—"nationalize" slaving was both related to Havana's shocking loss in 1762 and located at the heart of Spain's program of "rival modernization" across the late eighteenth century.[82]

The following discussion will show how these resolutions were put into practice, as Spain made reforms near and far from Cuba in order to mod-

81. As Jeremy Adelman has argued, a logic of liberal economics emerged in the Spanish empire on the backs of bound labor. See Adelman, *Sovereignty and Revolution in the Iberian Atlantic* (Prince-ton, N.J., 2006), 73–90; Hubert H. S. Aimes, *A History of Slavery in Cuba, 1511–1868* (1907; rpt. New York, 1967), 20. For cases of maritime marronage from Jamaica to Cuba, see AGI, Cuba, 1077.

82. Stanley J. Stein and Barbara H. Stein called this "defensive modernization," but it was pursued alongside parallel processes in rival European courts. See Stein and Stein, *Apogee of Empire*, 88.

ernize its empire and fight a war of retaliation against Britain. Findings from Cuba catalyzed programmatic political, economic, and military reform first tried out on the island and later exported to other areas of the Spanish empire. Collectively, these new departures would set the stage for the tremendous expansion of slavery in Cuba that would occur in the nineteenth century, the century of slavery's apogee. As it turned out, people of African descent, who by their actions directly inspired these new Spanish policies, would suffer the most, along with their descendants, from their implementation.[83]

83. On "the 'second slavery,'" or "modern" / ninteenth-century slavery, see Dale W. Tomich, "The Wealth of Empire: Francisco Arrango y Parreño, Political Economy, and the Second Slavery in Cuba," *Comparative Studies in Society and History*, XLV (2003), 4–28; Tomich, *Through the Prism of Slavery: Labor, Capital, and World Economy* (New York, 2004), 56–94; and Tomich, ed., *New Frontiers of Slavery* (Albany, N.Y., 2016).

6

· · ·

Consequences

Memories of the Siege on an Island Transformed

Fifty years after the invasion and occupation of Havana, in March 1812, José Antonio Aponte, a former member of the free black militia of Havana, was accused of leading the first major rebellion against slavery and colonial rule in Cuba. This movement has been described as one of "the most ambitious and important" in the history of the Black Atlantic. Two months before Aponte's trial, a series of coordinated slave rebellions had fanned out across the island east to west. Sugar plantations burned, and thirteen whites were killed before colonial authorities regained the upper hand. Aponte — not only a soldier but also an artist, carpenter, and perhaps also an African *cabildo* member and Santería priest — was accused of being the architect of the rebellions. This was the first time that someone who had served in the free black militia in Havana is known to have conspired in, let alone to have led, a slave rebellion in Cuba. It marked a radical reversal from an era when black militias had willingly defended the colony, as opposed to attacking it. Coming just a generation or two later, how had such an about-face become possible?[1]

The Aponte Rebellion is often associated with the Haitian Revolution (1791–1804) and the rumors of the abolition of slavery inspired by the debates then occurring at the meeting of the Cortes de Cádiz in Spain. In Aponte's home, investigators found portraits of the Haitian revolutionary leaders Toussaint Louverture, Jean François, Jean-Jacques Dessalines, and Henri

---

1. Ada Ferrer, *Freedom's Mirror: Cuba and Haiti in the Age of Revolutions* (New York, 2014), 274. For the events of the rebellion, see ibid., 271–328; José L. Franco, *La conspiracion de Aponte* (Havana, 1963); Franco, *Las conspiraciones de 1810 y 1812* (Havana, 1977), 133–134; and Matt D. Childs, *The 1812 Aponte Rebellion in Cuba and the Struggle against Atlantic Slavery* (Chapel Hill, N.C., 2006). The anti-French riots of 1809 and the conspiracy of Don Román de la Luz, also known as the conspiracy of Infante, in 1810 were important precursors to the Aponte Rebellion that did not reach the same scale; see María del Carmen Barcia, *Cuba: Acciones populares en tiempos de la independencia americana* (Matanzas, Cuba, 2011), 59–107; Franco, *Las conspiraciones*, 7–13; Matt D. Childs, "The Revolt against the French": Race and Patriotism in the 1809 Riot in Havana," in Christopher Belaubre, Jordana Dym, and John Savage, eds., *Napoleon's Atlantic: The Impact of Napoleonic Empire in the Atlantic World* (Boston, 2010), 137.

Christophe. Just a year before, on June 12, 1811, Christophe had crowned himself Henri I and had Haiti declared a kingdom, which caused both conversation and celebration throughout the slaveholding societies of the Americas. The recent visit to Cuba of a famous black general from Saint Domingue, Jean François, who had fought alongside the Spanish in their intervention in the Haitian Revolution, had electrified the black population in and around Havana. On the eve of the Aponte Rebellion, Spain was caught in the grip of a constitutional crisis, rumors of the end of slavery and the slave trade swirled, and revolts were spreading across the Spanish American mainland in Mexico and Venezuela. Meanwhile, Cuba was in the throes of its sugar boom, transforming itself into a plantation society where race was becoming an ever more important marker of social status. Amid all this revolutionary change, these powerful black generals and political figures from Haiti must have provided an inspiring example to Aponte. They would have represented all that could be achieved by enslaved Africans and free people of color uniting in an insurgency against colonialism, slavery, and racial hierarchy.[2]

As much as it was a product of all these revolutionary ruptures, the Aponte Rebellion also looked backward to the defense of Havana against British attack. The links are direct and even familial. Aponte was a third-generation soldier whose grandfather had fought against the British in 1762. His co-conspirators in Havana included other members of the *moreno* militia whose fathers, grandfathers, and uncles had in many cases fought alongside Aponte's grandfather during the siege. Their multigenerational network of relationships and elevated social status as militia members made coordinating the rebellion possible. Several leaders of the rebellion had joined the militias during their expansion after the Spanish reoccupation of Havana. Their coordinated plan to attack the city's arsenal and steal its weapons relied on knowledge and expertise gained from their military careers. Even more, according to evidence and testimony during his trial, Aponte explicitly invoked the events of the siege of Havana during meetings with his co-conspirators at his house. The memory of the achievements of black soldiers defending the city from British attack was very much alive in Cuba fifty years later, although in Cuba's altered racial and political landscape it had acquired radical new meanings for the descendants of those who had taken part.[3]

The Aponte Rebellion was inspired by the Age of Revolutions but also the struggles of black veterans of the siege of Havana and their descendants during the decades of reform and transformation that followed the Spanish re-

2. Ferrer, *Freedom's Mirror*, 279; Childs, *The 1812 Aponte Rebellion*, 79, 92.
3. For the most thorough treatment of the relationship between the black militias and the rebellion, see Childs, *The 1812 Aponte Rebellion*, 78–100, esp. 94–95.

occupation of Havana. The connections between the siege of Havana and the Aponte Rebellion remind us that the compacts between the sovereign and his diverse colonial subjects normally associated with an earlier colonial history in the Atlantic world survived into the nineteenth century of global capitalism, export commodity agriculture, and (predominantly but not exclusively) nation-states. Indeed, both the memory and the reality of this earlier corporate society endured, even if there were attempts on the local level to revoke traditional rights and privileges from the king's African and indigenous subjects. In fact, in Cuba in the wake of the Seven Years' War, the Spanish king's efforts to strengthen political compacts with his wealthiest white subjects propelled a new set of economic policies that would ultimately end up undoing them for his subjects of African descent.[4]

The siege of Havana was a proud memory giving Havana's population of African descent political expectations dashed during the decades that followed. At first, the British invasion and Spanish reoccupation had seemed a moment of promise for blacks in Cuba, when they proved their value to the Spanish king and were recognized and rewarded for doing so. Over the course of the ensuing decades, even before the outbreak of the Haitian Revolution, however, that promise had begun to dissolve around them. Members of the free militias of color in Cuba did not necessarily change their patterns of behavior during this time. They continued to demonstrate their skill and dedication serving the Spanish king when given the opportunity and petitioning him to make good on his promises. Yet the world in which they did so had altered. For no group did this occur as swiftly and painfully as for the city's population of free morenos (even more, as we shall see, than for *pardos*).

Cuba's rapid socioeconomic transformation in the period after 1763 stemmed from new Spanish policies adopted in the wake of the island's return in the Treaty of Paris. These policies saw Spain remaking its imperial project in response to rivalry with Britain, much as England had shaped its initial imperial expansion in the sixteenth and seventeenth centuries in competition

---

4. Historians often separate the study of the Cuba of sugar plantations and agricultural slavery that arose in the final decade of the eighteenth century from the precapitalist Cuba that came before and was patriarchal but less exploitative. Famously, one Cuban historian described this divide as that between "Cuba A" and "Cuba B." By this logic, on the side of Cuba A belongs the siege of Havana, and on the side of Cuba B belongs the Aponte Rebellion. See Juan Pérez de la Riva, "Una isla con dos historias," in Pérez de la Riva, *El barracón: esclavitud y capitalismo en Cuba* (Barcelona, 1978), 175. For scholarship on the endurance of corporate society, popular royalism, and black loyalty to the Spanish monarch into the nineteenth century, see, for example, Jane G. Landers, *Atlantic Creoles in the Age of Revolutions* (Cambridge, Mass., 2010); Marcela Echeverri, *Indian and Slave Loyalists in the Age of Revolution: Reform, Revolution, and Royalism in the Northern Andes, 1780–1825* (New York, 2016); and David Sartorius, *Ever Faithful: Race, Loyalty, and the Ends of Empire in Spanish Cuba* (Durham, N.C., 2013).

with Spain. In the period of soul-searching catalyzed by the British seizure of Havana, Spanish insecurity in the face of British competition led to two offensives against its rival that had enduring consequences for the island of Cuba. One entailed ostensibly borrowing from British and French political economy by promoting the expansion of the African slave trade and agricultural slavery within its territories. With renewed fervor in the aftermath of the Seven Years' War, Spain pursued a host of pro–slave-trading policies that had been in part inspired by the events of the siege and occupation of Havana. For the first time in the long history of the presence of people of African descent in the Americas, Spain began actively and programmatically to promote and prioritize its own transatlantic trade in Africans. From a position one royal official in 1752 had described as "with our eyes closed as to the manner of this traffic," the crown and the Council of the Indies made a number of reforms both to expand the traffic in slaves under the Spanish flag and to govern the growth of African slavery and the populations of African descent in its overseas territories.[5]

The other Spanish initiative entailed making more war against Britain, an offensive war of retaliation, for which it continued to rely on black soldiers to help execute. Surprisingly, given the increasingly apparent danger in arming slaves or indeed all people of African descent, these two new plans — expanding the slave trade and the military role of people of African descent — went hand in hand. The Bourbon monarchy's efforts to break into the slave trade and promote plantation agriculture were coordinated with attempts to build up the military and strike back against Britain. In the postwar period, Spain was bristling for another fight with Britain wherever in the world it could find one and building up its state military apparatus to ensure that the results would be better than last time. Its best opportunity arose, improbably, during the American Revolution, when Spain assisted the thirteen colonies in their anticolonial rebellion and won back Florida. These two components of Spain's response to the British capture of Havana — an escalation of both militarization and slave trading — had impacts near and very far from Cuba. But both were felt especially profoundly on the island, a center of agricultural slavery and military operations in Spanish America.

As they had during prior wars, during the American Revolution Spanish subjects in Cuba seized upon the opportunities of wartime to pursue proven

5. Julián de Arriaga to the Marqués de la Ensenada, Mar. 18, 1752, AGI, SD, 2209. Spanish territories benefited from Portuguese transatlantic slave traders during the union of the two Iberian crowns, 1580–1640. On the ties between West and west central Africa and the Spanish Caribbean during that time, see David Wheat, *Atlantic Africa and the Spanish Caribbean, 1570–1640* (Williamsburg, Va., and Chapel Hill, N.C., 2016).

strategies to defend the *patria* and further their own economic interests. These goals had been in tension during the British occupation of Havana, but the successful military intervention in the American Revolution and the wealth it generated locally in Cuba presented an instance when they coincided. Collectively, Spain's new policies supporting the slave trade and its entry into the American Revolution made possible a tremendous expansion of wealth and slavery in Cuba by the 1780s and 1790s. Spain's postwar reforms set in motion a cascading set of changes that remade the economy and racial landscape of Cuba, laying the foundation for the rise of an industrial mode of plantation slavery — that is, slavery with railroads — that occurred simultaneously in the Spanish Caribbean, Brazil, and the U.S. South during the nineteenth century, the century of slavery's apogee. By their actions, people of African descent had proven their necessity to empire in a climate of intensifying military rivalry and economic competition. However, they would be betrayed in the end by the long-term impacts of the reforms they had directly inspired.[6]

A Slaving Fever

The British occupation of Havana changed the way that Spain looked at Africa. After the Seven Years' War, the Spanish king and his councillors began to think differently about Spain's presence in West Africa and the need for a transatlantic slave trade under a Spanish flag. For the first time, African slavery and the transatlantic slave trade became a priority of Spanish imperial geopolitics. From the mid- to late eighteenth century, the Spanish government came to see the slave trade as a kind of imperial arms race and competition for resources in which it had a tremendous amount of catching up to do with its rivals. Slave trading was suddenly seen to be a strategic branch of trade that Spain had to wrest from foreign control, as a matter of what one might call national security. Relying on the British slave traders who dominated the trade in the Greater Caribbean, or the Portuguese, Brazilian, French, Dutch, or Danish traders active there and elsewhere, was no longer tenable. Gaining a transatlantic slave trade under Spain's own control and no longer depending on the slave traders of its British enemy would constitute a form of revenge. Triggered by rivalry with Britain and recent events in Cuba, a "slaving fever" overcame Spanish politics in the final years of the reign of Charles III and his successor Charles IV.[7]

6. On the rise of industrial nineteenth-century slavery, or "the second slavery," see Dale W. Tomich, *Through the Prism of Slavery: Labor, Capital, and the World Economy* (Lanham, Md., 2004).

7. For the phrase "slaving fever," see Manuel Lucena Salmoral, *La esclavitud en la América Española* (Warsaw, 2002), 220. Charles IV began his reign in 1788, upon Charles III's death, and remained

The expansion of the slave trade into Spanish America is normally dated to the declaration of "free trade in slaves" of 1789, which ended the era of the asientos for the Spanish Caribbean. The 1789 declaration came just two years before the outbreak of the Haitian Revolution, which destroyed the sugar industry in the world's then largest producer and drove up global prices. Together these two developments helped launch Cuba's boom of sugar and slavery in the final decade of the eighteenth century, which remade the island into what was for all intents and purposes a plantation colony. Historians often see "free trade in slaves" as an inevitable concession to the forces of global capitalism and the burgeoning sugar boom in the Spanish Caribbean, which grew out of *comercio libre* and other fiscal reforms. However, the Spanish crown began this shift toward promoting the slave trade earlier and much more consciously in an attempt to modernize its empire in a shifting climate of imperial competition. The famous 1789 declaration was in fact part of a concert of changes and reforms in slave-trading policies, some experimental and short-lived and others more lasting, starting earlier, in the mid-eighteenth century, just after the British occupation of Havana.[8]

Beginning in the 1760s, the Spanish king and his councillors began to experiment with a number of reforms both to expand the traffic in slaves under the Spanish flag and to govern the growth of African slavery and the populations of African descent in its overseas territories. In the period between 1763 and 1789, multiple measures were put into place. They included the establishment of a Spanish slave-trading monopoly company, the Compañía gaditana de negros; the dramatic escalation of the number of royal slaves in Cuba; the acquisition of territory meant to serve as Spain's first slave-trading entrepôt in West Africa; the establishment of the Royal Philippine Company with a West African slave-trading asiento; and the attempt to codify laws for the first time

king until 1808. In the South Atlantic during this period, the Portuguese and Brazilians dominated transatlantic trafficking. See, for example, Joseph C. Miller, *Way of Death: Merchant Capitalism and the Angolan Slave Trade, 1730–1830* (Madison, Wis., 1988); Jeremy Adelman, *Sovereignty and Revolution in the Iberian Atlantic* (Princeton, N.J., 2006), 56–100; Alex Borucki, *From Shipmates to Soldiers: Emerging Black Identities in the Río de la Plata* (Albuquerque, N.M., 2015), 25–56, esp. 47–48; and Fabrício Prado, *Edge of Empire: Atlantic Networks and Revolution in Bourbon Río de la Plata* (Oakland, Calif., 2015).

8. The 1789 declaration of "free trade in slaves" applied to the islands of Cuba, Santo Domingo, Puerto Rico, and the province of Caracas. In 1795, the monarchy extended this privilege to New Granada, Cartagena, the Río de la Plata, and Peru, and in 1804 to Guayaquil and Panama. See "Real cédula de Su Magestad concediendo libertad para el comercio de negros con las islas de Cuba, Santo Domingo, Puerto Rico, y provincia de Caracas, a españoles y extrangeros, bajo las reglas que se expresan," 1789, AGI, IG, 2821; James Ferguson King, "Evolution of the Free Slave Trade Principle in Spanish Colonial Administration," *HAHR*, XXII (1942), 34–56; Dale Tomich, "World Slavery and Caribbean Capitalism: The Cuban Sugar Industry, 1760–1868," *Theory and Society*, XX (1991), 297–319; and Tomich, *Through the Prism of Slavery*.

in the long history of Spanish slaveholding with regard to not only enslaved Africans but also people of African descent in its American possessions. Spanish authorities were so eager to promote this realm of commerce that not only did they remove import duties on slaves but also, as early as 1780, they began introducing tax exemptions and even bounties as rewards for each enslaved African that a Spanish subject brought to Spanish American territories. Collectively these new initiatives constituted a crucial component of Madrid's efforts to respond to the British capture of Havana and shore up the Spanish imperial system economically, politically, and militarily through the Bourbon reforms.[9]

This new thinking emerging in Spain — that African slavery and the slave trade were essential to the wealth of nations — was unique. In virtually all European empires, the mid-eighteenth century and especially the aftermath of the Seven Years' War were times of reform. Not only the Spanish but also the British, French, Portuguese, Dutch, and Danish reconfigured political philosophies and their concrete applications during this time. But, while Spain was seeking to expand the institution of slavery, French physiocrats were denouncing it as economically backward, and Adam Smith was at least failing to endorse it. Only in Spain did this particular view of slavery and the slave trade take such powerful hold. In part, Spanish attitudes were a product of new modes of thought at court that emphasized the benefits of commerce and agriculture, rather than Spain's age-old model of conquest and mining. Slave-based agricultural economies were producing tremendous revenues for Spain's rivals; however, they required a different, less restrictive political economy than Madrid had pursued until then. As they rethought these fundamental principles of political economy, Spanish reformers began to see the necessity of reevaluating how the monarchy managed the African slave trade.

---

9. "Real cédula de Su Magestad concediendo libertad para el comercio de negros," AGI, IG, 2821; Ferguson King, "Evolution of the Free Slave Trade Principle," *HAHR*, XXII (1942), 51–52; Josep M. Delgado Ribas, "The Slave Trade in the Spanish Empire (1501–1808): The Shift from Periphery to Center," in Josep M. Fradera and Christopher Schmidt-Nowara, eds., *Slavery and Antislavery in Spain's Atlantic Empire* (New York, 2013), chap. 1 (13–42); Pablo Tornero Tinajero, *Crecimiento económico y transformaciones sociales: Esclavos, hacendados y comerciantes en la Cuba colonial (1760–1840)* (Madrid, 1996), 22–76; Tornero Tinajero, "El suministro de mano de obra esclava en Cuba, estado español y oligarquía criolla (1765–1820)," in Consuelo Naranjo Orovio and Tomás Mallo Gutiérrez, eds., *Cuba la perla de las Antillas: Actas de las I Jornadas sobre "Cuba y su historia"* (Madrid, 1994), 313–324. On the first introduction of bounties in 1780, see Lucena Salmoral, *La esclavitud en la América española*, 220. On "the Bourbon reform of slavery," see Elena Andrea Schneider, "The Occupation of Havana: War, Trade, and Slavery in Eighteenth-Century Cuba" (Ph.D. diss., Princeton University, 2011), 341–418; and Schneider, "African Slavery and Spanish Empire: Imperial Imaginings and Bourbon Reform in Eighteenth-Century Cuba and Beyond," *Journal of Early American History*, V (2015), 3–29.

The influential reformer Count of Campomanes, writing in 1762, called the British asiento of 1713 both "the most intolerable yoke the Spanish nation had ever suffered" and "the worst error" Spanish politics had ever made. In the minds of Campomanes and a widening circle of officials, freer trade in both goods and persons along the model of its rivals was the answer Spain sought. After the pain of the loss of Havana, a heightened sense of urgency put these reforms into action.[10]

In the wake of Havana's restitution, the Spanish crown chose to actively support the slave trade both for state economic interests and in order to create allegiances with creole oligarchies who demanded greater access to markets in enslaved African laborers. This new attention to the African slave trade was a product of Madrid's concerns about sovereignty in its own empire and its efforts to forge a renewed compact with its wealthiest subjects in Cuba investing in agricultural slavery. The new logic guiding Spanish political and economic thought was that the potential revenues from productive colonial economies, well supplied with African labor, exceeded the value of im-

---

10. Pedro Rodríguez de Campomanes, Conde de Campomanes, *Reflexiones sobre el comercio español a Indias (1762)*, ed. Vicente Llombart Rosa (Madrid, 1988), 93–95, 279, 316, 332, 334–335, 457; José A. Piqueras, "Los amigos de Arango en la corte de Carlos IV," in María Dolores González-Ripoll and Izaskun Álvarez Cuartero, eds., *Francisco Arango y la invención de la Cuba azucarera* (Salamanca, Spain), 157; Pernille Røge, "A Natural Order of Empire: The Physiocratic Vision of Colonial France after the Seven Years' War," 32–52, esp. 35–36, 42, and Thomas Hopkins, "Adam Smith on American Economic Development and the Future of European Atlantic Empires," 53–75, esp. 66, both in Sophus A. Reinert and Røge, eds., *The Political Economy of Empire in the Early Modern World* (Basingstoke, U.K., 2013); John Shovlin, "War and Peace: Trade, International Competition, and Political Economy," 307–348, in Philip J. Stern and Carl Wennerlind, eds., *Mercantilism Reimagined: Political Economy in Early Modern Britain and Its Empire* (Oxford, 2014). On this reform process across multiple European empires, see Reinert and Røge, eds., *Political Economy of Empire*; Sophus A. Reinert, *Translating Empire: Emulation and the Origins of Political Economy* (Cambridge, 2011); and Reinert, "Rivalry: Greatness in Early Modern Political Economy," in Stern and Wennerlind, eds., *Mercantilism Reimagined*, 348–370, esp. 350.

On Spanish reform processes at this time and their relationship to those of Britain and France, see Allan J. Kuethe and Kenneth J. Andrien, *The Spanish Atlantic World in the Eighteenth Century: War and the Bourbon Reforms, 1713–1796* (New York, 2014); Gabriel B. Paquette, *Enlightenment, Governance, and Reform in Spain and Its Empire, 1759–1808* (New York, 2008); and Paquette, "Introduction: Enlightened Reform in Southern Europe and Its Atlantic Colonies in the Long Eighteenth Century," 1–22, and Jorge Cañizares-Esguerra, "'Enlightened Reform' in the Spanish Empire: An Overview," 33–36, in Paquette, *Enlightened Reform in Southern Europe and Its Atlantic Colonies, c. 1750–1830* (Farnham, Eng., and Burlington, Vt., 2009); Stanley J. Stein and Barbara H. Stein, *Apogee of Empire: Spain and New Spain in the Age of Charles III, 1759–1789* (Baltimore, 2003); J. H. Elliott, *Empires of the Atlantic World: Britain and Spain in America, 1492–1830* (New Haven, Conn., 2006), chap. 10 (292–324). In several studies of Spain's Bourbon reforms, Paquette has described the process of adapting British and French political and economic models as one of "creative emulation"; see, for example, Paquette, "Views from the South: Images of Britain and Its Empire in Portuguese and Spanish Political Economic Discourse, ca. 1740–1810," in Reinert and Røge, eds., *Political Economy of Empire*, 76.

port duties. Through this battery of new measures, Spanish royal authorities sought not only to promote Spanish and Spanish American traders' role in the slave trade but also to liberalize the trade, seemingly contradictory goals that were interlinked. Together these two initiatives would expand both the trade in enslaved Africans to Spanish America and the role of Spanish and Spanish American merchants in the traffic.[11]

To the minds of Spanish administrators, enslaved Africans became similar to what silver had been to British war planners and expansionists in the sixteenth and seventeenth centuries: the precious commodity that was the key to strengthening its empire in a climate of intensive imperial rivalry. Like English interlopers in prior centuries trying to find their way to American silver mines, Spanish subjects had very little direct experience of the West African trade in humans. Since the era of the union of the two Iberian crowns (1580–1640), when Portuguese slave traders flew the Spanish flag, its vessels had scarcely appeared on the West African coast. Consequently, Spanish sailors and ship's captains had little knowledge of how to navigate the eastern shores of the Atlantic and participate in this trade. On its first voyage in 1765, the Compañía gaditana de negros, Spain's new asiento monopoly company, optimistically fleeted out a warship called *La Venganza (Revenge)* to sail to West Africa and purchase 600 or 700 enslaved Africans for the transatlantic voyage, yet it was handicapped by the lack of a Spanish way station in the region. After many stops at trading posts along the coast of Guinea and a longer stay than the company had prepared for, the *Venganza* only managed to purchase 250 enslaved Africans at inflated prices. The company's first expedition turned out to be a total financial loss.[12]

Secretly, a Spanish duke with knowledge of the West African slave trade had tried to warn the Council of the Indies of its complexities and the disadvantages the Spanish faced as a late entrant. Spain produced only a small portion of the trade goods demanded by African slave traders. Its merchants lacked the experience of previous voyages and networks for news about the shifting and distinctive demands of African consumers. The goal of reformers in Madrid was to build a Spanish slave trade that operated independently of the British and French; the voyage of the *Venganza* had shown, though, that the Spanish duke was right. Spanish merchants didn't yet have the resources

11. Tornero Tinajero, *Crecimiento económico y transformaciones sociales*, 24.

12. The asiento granted to the Compañía gaditana de negros in 1765 extended to Caracas, Puerto Rico, and Cuba. This measure was part of the package of fiscal reforms introduced that year, including increasing the *alcabala* tax in Cuba, opening up trade with the Spanish Caribbean and with all Spanish ports (no longer just Cádiz), and switching from an import tax on slaves to a head tax. See Bibiano Torres Ramírez, *La compañía gaditana de negros* (Seville, 1973), 167–170.

to make the trade profitable. They would have to learn from these rivals in order to break into this trade.[13]

After this first unsuccessful expedition, the Compañía gaditana received royal permission to carry out all its ensuing transatlantic voyages from London, Liverpool, or Nantes under the flag of its ally France or, more frequently, Britain with crews from those nations. The crown also agreed to allow the Compañía gaditana to contract with British merchants in the West Indies to bring enslaved Africans to Puerto Rico directly and then the company would redistribute them to other Spanish American ports. With this arrangement, authorities in Madrid hoped Spanish merchants would eventually acquire the knowledge to make their own transatlantic slave-trading voyages. They also hoped to increase the pace of African arrivals in its Spanish Caribbean ports while protecting such strategic cities as Havana from the intrusions of foreign slaving ships.[14]

Clearly the next step for Spain was to acquire an enclave for Spanish slaving in West Africa. As the crown's councillors put it, their objective was to gain something "only we don't have, and thus need more than any other nation." In the Treaty of Pardo of 1778, Spain ceded to Portugal the colony of Sacramento, on the contested borderlands of the Río de la Plata and Brazil, in order to gain two West African islands in the Bight of Biafra — Annobón and Fernando Po, now Bioko — as well as claims along the adjacent coast (see Map 8). According to the treaty, Spanish officials intended the accession "to promote the advantages of commerce to their respective subjects, who may carry out the buying and selling of blacks, without the burden of prejudicial agreements and contracts, as were made in other times with Portuguese, French, and English companies." Seizing on Britain's distraction with the rebellion of its thirteen North American colonies, Spanish diplomats sent a secret expedition from Montevideo to formally possess these West African islands for Spain. As the Council of the Indies acknowledged, without Portuguese cooperation and the utmost secrecy, "all the nations would have resisted Spanish entry, having spoken against our navigation in those seas."[15]

---

13. "Forma de perpetuar y establecer el comercio de negros entre los españoles," n.d. [late 1760s or early 1770s], MS 12966/30, BNE.

14. Torres Ramírez, *La compañía gaditana de negros,* 53–56, 167.

15. Resumen, El Pardo, Jan. 9, 1779, AGI, Buenos Aires, 41 ("only we don't have" and "all the nations"); I. K. Sundiata, "A Note on an Abortive Slave Trade: Fernando Po, 1778–1781," *Bulletin de l'Institut Fondamental d'Afrique Noire, Serie B,* XXXV, no. 4 (1973), 793–804 ("to promote" on 798; the words "blacks" or "negros" were often used synonymously with "slaves," as in this instance); Mariano L. de Castro and María Luisa de la Calle, *Origen de la colonización española en Guinea Ecuatorial (1777–1860)* (Valladolid, Spain, 1992), 28–49; Manuel Cencillo de Pineda, *El brigadier Conde de Argelejo y su expedicion militar a Fernando Poo en 1778* (Madrid, 1948); Paquette, *Enlightenment, Governance, and Reform,* 106–109, 117, 119–122.

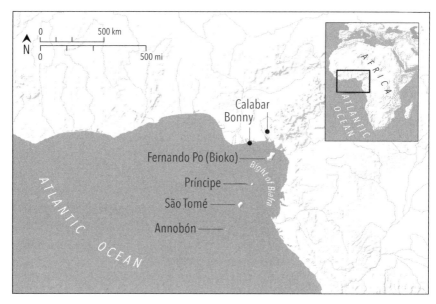

MAP 8 The Bight of Biafra in West Africa. Drawn by Molly Roy

As the acquisition of Fernando Po demonstrated, recent events in Cuba had given its inhabitants the leverage to transform the nature and even geographic shape of Spain's imperial projects. In the fall of 1778, three Spanish ships under the command of the Conde de Argelejo and 150 men sailed from Buenos Aires to Annobón and Fernando Po. On board the ships were 127 soldiers and an assortment of chaplains, carpenters, and merchants; in their holds were one hundred thousand *pesos fuertes* and enough food for fifteen months — all that was thought necessary to establish a Spanish slaving station on one or both of the islands. This expedition was not as massive as the one that had descended upon Havana, but it, too, was engendered by centuries of imperial rivalry in the Caribbean.[16]

Before Argelejo had even arrived at the islands, a royal order about the acquisition of Fernando Po and Annobón was promulgated throughout Cuba. The Spanish king presented the news of the acquisition of Fernando Po and Annobón to residents of Cuba as an answer to their supplications. The king promised that these new Spanish African islands would at long last extend to Spain's subjects in Cuba what they had repeatedly clamored for: "the freedom for slavery." The crown would soon permit the leading agricultural men

16. Resumen, El Pardo, Jan. 12, 1779, AGI, Buenos Aires, 41.

of the island to sail to Fernando Po and Annobón to provision themselves "firsthand" with "a copious abundance of blacks." Echoing the language of the Conde de Ricla and other reformers sent to Cuba in 1763, the king insisted that the acquisition of these new islands would meet a multiplicity of needs in Cuba. It was designed not only to provide more enslaved Africans to creole oligarchs but also to expand the population of African descent in the king's territories. According to this royal announcement, greater availability of en-slaved Africans would enhance the overall population, defense, and indeed "happiness" of the island. In response, eager investors across Cuba began to mobilize their resources and capital to launch joint slave-trading ventures to these new Spanish African islands.[17]

As we have often seen, though, there was an appreciable gap between the imaginings of a king and his administrators and their capacities to bring these plans to fruition. As one historian has put it, empire states across the ages have had long arms but weak fingers. English exploits in the Caribbean in earlier eras demonstrated the difficulty of breaking into new continents and seas without stepping-stones for navigation or trade. Spain's calamitous ini-tial foray into West Africa was no different. Several ships sailing between the Bight of Biafra and Spain to coordinate with the expedition were captured by the British. Disease, mutiny, and a failure of full cooperation from Portuguese authorities at São Tomé and Príncipe all conspired against the expedition's success. Even more critically, the inhabitants of Fernando Po and Annobón launched incessant raids that drove away their Spanish interlopers, who re-ferred to them in surprise as *"negros bravos,"* or "wild blacks." Despite their proximity to the major British slaving ports of Old and New Calabar and the rest of the Slave and Gold Coasts, the peoples who inhabited Fernando Po did not participate in the slave trade. Their islands were not the generalized African site for buying generic "blacks" that the expedition thought it was.[18]

17. King to the Governor of Havana, May 18, 1778, AGI, SD, 1525 ("freedom for slavery"); Real orden, May 18, 1778, AGI, Cuba, 1258 ("firsthand" and "a copious abundance"). Hundreds of the wealthiest landholders in Cuba pledged numerous boats to the planned African voyages as well as significantly more capital than the Spanish crown had invested in the expedition in the first place: 289,900 pesos; see King to the Governor of Havana, May 18, 1778, AGI, SD, 1525; Gamba to Navarro, Dec. 20, 1778, AGI, Cuba, 1230, no. 213; Circular, Nov. 3, 1778, AGI, Cuba, 1265, no. 62, fol. 177–178.

18. On the long arms but weak fingers of empire states, see Frederick Cooper, *Colonialism in Question: Theory, Knowledge, History* (Berkeley, Calif., 2005), 197. For an account of the expedition, see AGI, Buenos Aires, 41; Antolín and Muñoz, *Origen de la colonización española*, 47–48; Arlindo Manuel Caldeira, "Uma ilha quase desconhecida: Notas para a história de Ano Bom," *Studia Afri-cana—Revista interuniversitària d'estudis Africans*, no. 17 (October 2006), 99–109; and Manuel Cal-deira, "Organizing Freedom: *De Facto* Independence on the Island of Ano Bom (Annobón) during the Eighteenth and Nieteenth Centuries," *Afro-Hispanic Review*, XXVIII, no. 2 (Fall 2009), 293–310;

Despite its initial failures, the Fernando Po expedition of 1778 signaled a turning point in Bourbon imperial re-imaginings. The plans for Fernando Po reveal the flexibility of the Spanish government and its willingness to adapt new and foreign models in its high-priority effort to enter into the transatlantic slave trade. Because the slave trade was a global operation, participating in West African trade also necessitated strengthening commercial ties to Asia, the source of cloth coveted by African traders. As part of the Fernando Po expedition, the king also sent orders to the governor of the Spanish Philippines to gather cloth samples produced there and in China and Bengal and to forward them in haste to West Africa to rendezvous with the expedition. In 1785, after the first expeditions to Fernando Po had failed, Charles III would commission a new Royal Philippine Company, modeled on the British West India Company, to develop a hoped-for slave-trading station at Fernando Po and connections between Atlantic and Asian commerce.[19]

In fits and starts, the crown and its councillors were pursuing multiple avenues in their effort to acquire the necessary tools to participate in the slave trade. Whereas in 1762 Campomanes had complained that the slave trade in Spain was "a subject almost wholly ignored," Spanish authorities had now become careful students of the technology of the slave trade as developed by foreign merchants. From the 1760s, the Spanish king and his officials had begun actively soliciting knowledge about how to go about this essential aspect of its "modernization" project. On one front, they encouraged Spanish merchants to purchase foreign-made slave ships, usually in Britain, and form joint slave-trading ventures to learn the techniques of their rivals. On another front, the king and his councillors directly solicited intelligence about the slave trade from French, Portuguese, British, and other European merchants, who inundated the court with their clandestine reports and recommendations (see

---

Sundiata, "A Note on the Abortive Slave Trade," *Bulletin de l'Institut Fondamental d'Afrique Noire, Serie B*, XXXV, no. 4 (1973), 801.

19. King to Governor of the Philippines, Sept. 18, 1779, and Joseph Barco y Vargas to Joseph de Galvez, Dec. 23, 1778, both in AGI, Buenos Aires, 41; AGI, Mapas y Planos, Tejidos, 34 (1–15). The samples did not arrive in time to meet up with the Argelejo expedition and instead went directly to Cádiz. See also William Lytle Schurz, "The Royal Philippine Company," *HAHR*, III (1920), 491–508; María Lourdes Díaz-Trechuelo Spínola, *La real compañía de Filipinas* (Seville, 1965); *Real cédula de erección de la Compañía de Filipinas de 10 de Marzo de 1785* (Madrid, [1785]). Gabriel Paquette has shown how the Bourbon reformers were inspired by study of the British East India Company; see Paquette, "Enlightened Narratives and Imperial Rivalry in Bourbon Spain: The Case of Almodóvar's *Historia Política de los Establecimientos Ultramarinos de las Naciones Europeas* (1784–1790)," *Eighteenth Century*, XLVIII (2007), 61–80. The new Royal Philippine Company also was part of the response to Spain's loss to the British during the Seven Years' War, similar to commercial reforms enacted in Havana. See Carlos Martínez Shaw, *El sistema comercial español del pacífico (1765–1820): Discurso leído el día 11 de noviembre de 2007* (Madrid, 2007), 22.

Figure 31). All these slave-trading proposals sought to help Spain catch up with its European rivals by acquiring the knowledge and practices to displace their dominance in the trade to Spanish America.[20]

Slavery was considered so crucial to the development of the Americas that it was the first free trade of any kind proclaimed in all of the Spanish empire. When the new policy of "free trade in slaves" was announced in 1789, it marked the first time Spanish merchants could legally trade with any foreigners anywhere they wished, as long as it was only in slaves. The new policy also continued to give incentives to Spanish and Spanish American slave traders in the form of tax exemptions and bounties as a reward for each enslaved African imported. This policy was a dramatic departure from the restrictive monopoly contracts with foreign slave traders that had been in place since the sixteenth century. Cuba would not receive similar concessions for other branches of its trade for another thirty years.[21]

Ironically, Spain's euphoric entry into transatlantic slave trading coincided with the rise of British and French abolitionism. One might think that this climate put a damper on this Spanish project, but, to the contrary, it gave it momentum. Looming British abolition of the slave trade freed up many slaving vessels for purchase by aspiring Spanish and Spanish American slave traders. Even more, the effort to ameliorate the conditions of the trade circulated a great deal of useful information about the technologies of violence used to attempt to control and transport African bodies. The forces of international abolitionism made public technical details of the trade usually kept secret in the competitive arena of African slave trading. Spanish envoys in London and Paris had a unique opportunity to gather information about the way the

20. Campomanes, *Reflexiones sobre el comercio español a Indias (1762)*, 307. Both the Compañía gaditana de negros and the Royal Philippine Company received permission to purchase and charter foreign slave ships and crews. For the Royal Philippine Company, see Ferguson King, "Evolution of the Free Slave Trade Principle," *HAHR*, XXII (1942), 48. Of the many reports and proposals submitted to the Spanish crown, see, for example, Miguel de Lucca, "Descripción de la costa donde se hace comercio de negros," Sept. 8, 1778, and "Sucincta descripción de la costa de África," 1780, both in AGI, Buenos Aires, 41; El Marqués de Branciforte to the Conde de Floridablanca, Dec. 3, 1784, AHN, Estado, 550; "Oferta hecha al Secretario del Despacho Universal de Indias por un extrangero residente en Burdeos de facilitar el establecimiento de una factoría de negros en Guinea, en el paraje llamado Costa de Oro," Feb. 16, 1782, II/2855/8, BRP; "Proyecto anónimo relativo a formar un establecimiento en la isla de Bouam [sic] en Guinea," II/2870, BRP. Manuel Moreno Fraginals discusses this technology transfer of slave-trading know-how from British and U.S. slave traders to those in Cuba and Spain, but he dates that process to after the British abolition of the slave trade in 1807 and the parallel transfer of sugar cultivation technology; see Manuel Moreno Fraginals, *El ingenio: Complejo económico social cubano de azúcar*, I (Havana, 1978), 262–263.

21. "Real cédula de Su Magestad concediendo libertad para el comercio de negros," 1789, AGI, IG, 2821; Ferguson King, "Evolution of the Free Slave Trade Principle," *HAHR*, XXII (1942), 34–56, esp. 51–52. Cuba was granted free trade in 1818.

FIGURE 31 Spanish Map of European Slave-Trading Forts in West Africa, from Modern-Day Ghana (at the top) to Nigeria (at the bottom). 1778. Hand-drawn. Miguel de Luca, a merchant envoy on the Argelejo expedition to Fernando Po and Annobón, sent this map back to the Council of the Indies from São Tomé. Accompanying it were detailed instructions on how Spanish merchants might break into the slave trade conducted by other Europeans in the region. Note that it contains no information about African populations or towns. Permission, Spain, Ministerio de Educación, Cultura y Deporte, Archivo General de Indias, Mapas y Planos-Europa y Àfrica, 109

trade was carried out. A suggestive example of this technology transfer, as well as Spain's eagerness to emulate its rivals, is this copy of the iconic rendering of the method of "tight packing" on the slave ship the *Brooks* (see Figure 32 [Plate 14]). The document, dated to 1789, is in the Archive of the Indies in Seville, tucked into a bundle of slave-trading contracts from the 1780s. The textual description of how a slaving ship is packed that accompanies the image is carefully translated into Spanish. It seems likely that the document was sent back to Spain from London or Paris less as a warning of the moral dangers of the trade, or of the growth of abolitionism, than as a "how-to" manual for efficiently loading African bodies into a slave ship, essential knowledge for a burgeoning slaving power.[22]

As this image attests, the Spanish government was clearly seeking to imitate the brutal practices of its rivals, and yet it also took pains to distinguish what it considered the uniquely benevolent nature of Spanish slavery. The relentless need to reflect and self-justify was a long-running trait of the Spanish monarchy, from the first moment of its transatlantic expansion and the controversy that ensued over the treatment of Amerindians. In this instance, the Spanish crown was indisputably buying into Cuban elites' deeply cynical pro-slave-trading vision. At the same time, it still saw itself as protecting its black subjects and fostering a softer, gentler form of slavery than its rivals. In order to affirm that this new departure was in keeping with the professed values of Spanish colonialism, in the 1780s Spanish royal authorities sought for the first time to codify laws for its populations of African descent. The goal of these Spanish slave codes was to establish norms for the management of the enslaved, their basic rights and obligations, as well as limits for their owners' exploitation of their bodies, reproduction, and souls. According to the language of the first of these codes, written in 1784 in Santo Domingo, blacks should not be treated as "pure automatons, only useful for the ignominious work of agricultural labor, nor be directed along the path of oppression." Instead, Hispanicization and Christianization would redeem their passage into servitude in the territories of the Spanish king, unlike in those of its rivals.[23]

22. "Descripción del navío Brooks, harto conocido en el comercio de esclavos, hecha por el capitan Parrey [sic] enviado expresamente por la camara de los Comunes a Liverpool para tomar las dimensiones de los bastimientos empleados en dicho tráfico," AGI, IG, 2821. On the *Brooks,* see Marcus Rediker, *The Slave Ship: A Human History* (New York, 2007), 308–342; and Jacqueline Francis, "The *Brooks* Slave Ship Icon: A 'Universal Symbol'?" *Slavery and Abolition,* XXX (2009), 327–338. On Spanish antislavery, see Christopher Schmidt-Nowara, *Empire and Antislavery: Spain, Cuba, and Puerto Rico, 1833–1874* (Pittsburgh, 1999); Schmidt-Nowara, *Slavery, Freedom, and Abolition in Latin America and the Atlantic World* (Albuquerque, N.M., 2011), 90–116; Fradera and Schmidt-Nowara, eds., *Slavery and Antislavery in Spain's Atlantic Empire;* and Emily Berquist, "Early Anti-Slavery Sentiment in the Spanish Atlantic World, 1765–1817," *Slavery and Abolition,* XXXI (2010), 181–205.

23. Javier Malagón Barceló, *Código negro carolino (1784)* (Santo Domingo, 1974); "Extracto del

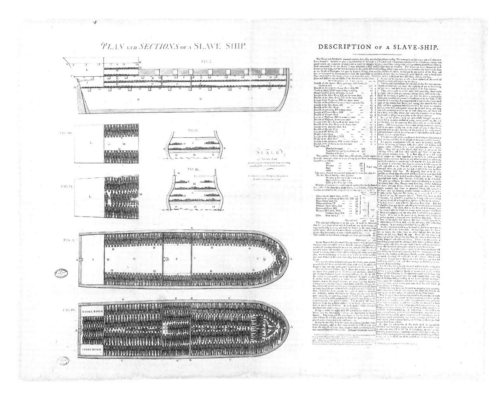

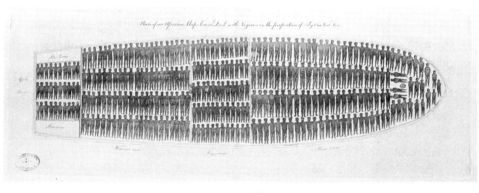

FIGURE 32 "Plan and Sections of a Slave Ship" (A) and "Plan of an African Ship's Lower Deck . . ." (B). In 1788, William Wilberforce and Thomas Clarkson produced this pamphlet as part of the first successful effort to ameliorate the conditions of the slave trade. It was printed and circulated widely by the Society for Effecting the Abolition of the Slave Trade. In Britain, the United States, and France, it would come to play a ubiquitous part in abolitionist movements. In the Archive of the Indies, it is bundled into a pile of slaving contracts from the 1780s, with no explanation of the context of its production and the text that accompanies the image carefully translated into Spanish. Contextual materials suggest that it might have been collected in Paris from the Société des Amis de Noirs. Permission, Spain, Ministerio de Educación, Cultura y Deporte, Archivo General de Indias, Mapas y Planos-Ingenios, 66 and 67

Written to coincide with the declaration of free trade in slaves in 1789, the second of these two codes, the Guide to the Education, Treatment, and Occupations of Slaves, or the Cédula of Aranjuez, went even further. It was an attempt to claim the moral high ground during Spain's descent into new practices of transatlantic slavery. Developed from the Código negro carolino and other ordinances and codes, it was meant to apply to all overseas Spanish possessions, from America to the Philippines. Its prologue cited the declaration of free trade in slaves as the reason "the number of slaves in both Americas will rise considerably, meriting attention to this class of human beings." The code established basic rights for the enslaved to Sundays as a day of rest, religious instruction, adequate food and housing, the right to marriage, and limits to the master's rights of physical punishment. According to its dictates, the enslaved ought to be educated in Christianity, baptized within their first year in America, and given access to priests on the agricultural estates where they lived and worked. Like Agustín Crame when he visited the island of Cuba in the 1760s, Spanish reformers were trying to have it both ways. On the one hand, the monarchy was trying to keep slavery aligned with its larger political and religious mission, and, on the other hand, it was radically expanding its highest-revenue, most repressive agricultural iteration.[24]

The Cédula de Aranjuez reveals the unique way Spain was reconfiguring itself as a slaving power. As a window to the lived experiences of the enslaved, it is not particularly useful; however, it demonstrates that, at least in the initial years of the takeoff of the slave trade to the Spanish Caribbean, the Spanish king continued to issue decrees and pronouncements guaranteeing the rights of its African subjects. The way authorities were imagining the categories of race and slavery marked a major difference from its rivals, but, in many respects, it would prove to be fleeting. As the sugar boom increased demand for the labor of enslaved Africans in Cuba, these rights would begin to be eroded and curtailed locally. As a result of freer trade and slave trading, times had changed in the Spanish territories of the Greater Caribbean region. The supposedly kinder, softer form of slavery that the Spanish monarchy sought to re-

---

código negro carolino," AGI, Estado, 7, no. 3. On the Spanish tendency toward self-doubt and self-reflection, see Anthony Pagden, "Heeding Heraclides: Empire and Its Discontents, 1619–1812," in Richard L. Kagan and Geoffrey Parker, eds., *Spain, Europe, and the Atlantic World: Essays in Honour of John H. Elliott* (Cambridge, 1995), 316–333, esp. 316.

24. "Real cédula sobre la educación, trato, y ocupaciones de los esclavos en todos sus dominios de Indias e islas Filipinas," 1789, AGI, SD, 2588; Manuel Lucena Salmoral, *Los códigos negros de la América española* (Alcalá de Henares, Spain, 1996), 95–123 (quotation on 96); Lucena Salmoral, ed., *Regulación de la esclavitud negra en las colonias de América española (1503–1886): Documentos para su estudio* (Alcalá de Henares, Spain, 2005); and Lucena Salmoral, *La esclavitud en la América española*, chap. 10.

inforce had become imperiled by other reforms it had set in motion. The new pro-slave-trading policies of the Spanish crown, combined with the manipulations and redirections of those policies achieved by Cuba's elites, meant that the world Spanish officials sought to govern had changed.

Socioeconomic Transformation in Cuba, 1763–1790s

Spanish commercial reforms and military investment led to dramatic socioeconomic transformation in Cuba. During his reoccupation of Havana, the Conde de Ricla had set the tone for what was to follow. Driven by an ambition to make up for its losses during the Seven Years' War, the Spanish monarchy's intensive military investment in Havana facilitated economic growth. Military expenditures, combined with the increased availability of enslaved laborers, made the postwar period a time of population growth and economic expansion, especially in the sugar industry. Cuba's full-fledged boom of sugar plantation slavery did not begin until the 1790s, but the industry's expansion during the postwar period made that later takeoff possible. With more enslaved workers available, the island's sugar plantations grew in both size and number. Whereas in the first half of the eighteenth century the average number of enslaved workers on Cuba's sugar plantations was between sixteen and eighteen, between 1750 and 1780 that number rose to fifty. In 1759, the island had just 200 sugar plantations, but by 1778 it had 480.[25]

25. Mercedes García Rodríguez, *La aventura de fundar ingenios: La refacción azucarera en La Habana del siglo XVIII* (Havana, 2004), 12; "Proyectos para que toman los azucares de cuenta en la Real Hacienda," MS 20,144, BNE; Padrón general de Navarro, 1778, AGI, IG, 1525; Juan B. Amores, *Cuba en la época de Ezpeleta (1785–1790)* (Pamplona, Spain, 2000), 182; Alejandro de la Fuente, "Esclavitud, 1510–1886," in Consuelo Naranjo Orovio, ed., *Historia de Cuba* (Madrid, 2009), 144–145.

Historians of Cuba debate the exact timing of Cuba's sugar boom. Scholars see multiple, overlapping points of origin for the rise of Cuba's export-oriented sugar plantation complex. Most agree that the industry took root before the British siege, grew in response to Spanish reforms, and took off in earnest in the 1790s. See García Rodríguez, *La aventura de fundar ingenios*; and Mercedes García Rodríguez, *Entre haciendas y plantaciones: Orígenes de la manufactura azucarera en la Habana* (Havana, 2007); José A. Piqueras, *Las antillas en la era de las luces y la revolución* (Madrid, 2005); Tornero Tinajero, *Crecimiento económico y transformaciones sociales*; Franklin W. Knight, "Origins of Wealth and the Sugar Revolution in Cuba, 1750–1850," *HAHR*, LVII (1977), 231–253; and Knight, *Slave Society in Cuba during the Nineteenth Century* (Madison, Wis., 1970), 3–24. John Robert McNeill argued that the growth of sugar plantations occurred somewhat earlier than the conventional wisdom, from the 1740s (McNeill, *Atlantic Empires of France and Spain: Louisbourg and Havana, 1700–1763* [Chapel Hill, N.C., 1985], 166). In an older, classic view, Manuel Moreno Fraginals interpreted the rise of Cuba's sugar plantation complex as more or less inevitable, advanced rapidly after the economic stimulus of the British occupation of Havana (Moreno Franginals, *El ingenio*, I, 15–38). Cuba also had a more artisanal sugar industry in the long seventeenth century, which went into decline by the start of the eighteenth century; see Alejandro de la Fuente, "Sugar and

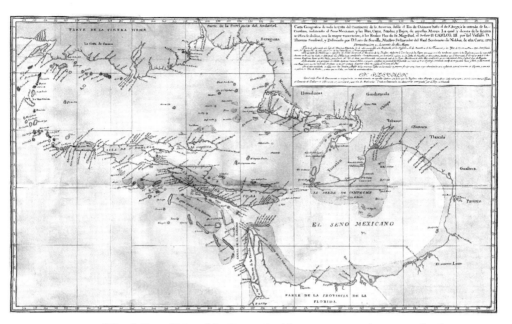

FIGURE 33 "Upside Down" Map of the Greater Caribbean Region. By Thomas Southwel. 1770. This map accompanied a proposal for expelling British smugglers and logwooders from the region. British territories are colored pink, French are yellow, and Dutch are red. It accurately reflects the Spanish obsession with revenge against Britain after the Seven Years' War and the heightened sense of the strategic value of both Havana and Cuba to Spanish geopolitics. Biblioteca del Real Palacio, Madrid, II-2831

Spain's quest to further militarize its empire and strike back against Britain inspired extensive military buildup in Havana (Figure 33). As in the past, military and commercial sectors had a synergistic relationship. Thousands of royal slaves, for example, were resold to plantation owners after their work on the fortifications was completed. A new burst of activity at the royal shipyard in Havana led to the construction of eleven ships by 1790, including the famous *Santíssima Trinidad* in 1769, which mounted a staggering 140 cannons and would go on to participate in the Battle of Trafalgar. Logging, cannon making at the foundry, and the skilled artisanship of many individuals employed at the shipyard circulated royal investment back into the local economy. Thousands of peninsular migrants also arrived in Havana to serve in newly deployed companies of professional soldiers meant to defend the city

---

Slavery in Early Colonial Cuba," in Stuart B. Schwartz, ed., *Tropical Babylons: Sugar and the Making of the Atlantic World, 1450–1680* (Chapel Hill, N.C., 2004), 115–157.

alongside the expanded militias. The buildup of troops in Havana necessitated large outlays into the local economy to feed them. Although these migrants were often European born, many married and made their lives in Cuba, thus contributing to rapid population growth.[26]

The slave trade to Cuba also grew in volume throughout the postwar period, but in ways that defied Spanish administrators' carefully laid plans. Between 1766 and 1770, the short-lived Compañía gaditana brought more than seven thousand enslaved Africans to Havana. Between Africans arriving in both Havana and Santiago de Cuba, that was 79 percent of all the men, women, and children the company purchased and resold. Before its finances completely unraveled, local slave buyers had enough leverage to compel the relocation of its American base from San Juan to Havana. At that point, however, enslaved Africans could be had much more cheaply through regional trade.[27]

Instead of the ill-fated Compañía gaditana, Cuba's slave markets continued to rely on slave-trading asientos with British merchant houses, combined with the growth of its own residents' intra-American trafficking and the arrival of U.S. slave traders in its waters. As they had before, residents of the island depended on contraband and wartime exceptions to open the slave trade and commerce to the island. Wealthier Cuba residents also petitioned the governor and the Council of the Indies to be granted small-scale, ad hoc slave-trading asientos. Plantation owners would band together in groups of six or seven to send regular ships to Jamaica, Bermuda, Barbados, and Saint Eustatius to purchase several hundred enslaved Africans at a time — all with the permission of local authorities. These Spanish policies dovetailed with the British Free Port Act of 1766, enacted at the end of the Seven Years' War to give Span-

---

26. Francisco Pérez Guzmán, *La Habana: Clave de un imperio* (Havana, 1997); Evelyn Powell Jennings, "War as the 'Forcing House of Change': State Slavery in Late-Eighteenth-Century Cuba," *William and Mary Quarterly*, 3d Ser., LXII (2005), 411–440; César García del Pino, *La Habana a través de los siglos* (Havana, 2012), 171; Allan J. Kuethe, "Havana in the Eighteenth Century," in Franklin W. Knight and Peggy K. Liss, eds., *Atlantic Port Cities: Economy, Culture, and Society in the Atlantic World, 1650–1850* (Knoxville, Tenn., 1991), 13–39, esp. 22–26. Sherry Johnson makes the argument that these Spanish migrants, by marrying and settling in Cuba and interacting in the military and society with creoles, helped to bind Cuba to Spain in the decades after 1763; see Johnson, *The Social Transformation of Eighteenth-Century Cuba* (Gainesville, Fla., 2001). For a study of this same period of reform in Cuba focused on similar themes, but with somewhat more attention to military and commercial policy, see Kuethe, *Cuba, 1753–1815: Crown, Military, and Society* (Knoxville, Tenn., 1986). During this period, there was growing tension over logging between the royal shipyard and Havana *ingenio* owners, who needed wood for sugar crates and tinder for their boiling houses; see Reinaldo Funes Monzote, *From Rainforest to Cane Field in Cuba: An Environmental History since 1492* (Chapel Hill, N.C., 2008).

27. Torres Ramírez, *La compañía gaditana de negros*, 39, 135, 176.

ish American merchants incentive to sail into British American ports and trade in goods and persons.[28]

Like other wars before it, the American Revolution was a boom time in Havana, which served as Spain's American staging ground in the war. The Havana commercial elite exploited the opportunity it presented, like so many other wars beforehand, to expand trade within the hemisphere. Even before Spain agreed to align itself with France and the rebelling thirteen North American colonies against Britain, Juan de Miralles and an associate had already petitioned to sail to North America to establish commercial and political relations with the Continental Congress. By now an old hand at Anglo-Spanish commerce, Miralles used contacts to facilitate his mission in Charleston and Philadelphia: Henry Laurens, the foremost slave trader in Charleston and a signer of the Declaration of Independence, and Robert Morris, chairman of the Continental Congress's Committee on Finance, known as the "financier of the Revolution." During the two years he spent as a secret informant and later official Spanish emissary to the Continental Congress, Miralles helped coordinate Spanish aid to the thirteen colonies and open up avenues of trade.[29]

Unlike during the British occupation of Havana, in this war the commercial interests of Havana elites dovetailed with the political aims of the Spanish monarchy. Spain had been looking for a chance for revenge in war against Britain, and the American Revolution provided a suitable enough occasion. There was some dissent about this choice of war in that the Spanish monarchy found itself aiding a rebellion of thirteen American colonies against their king.

28. On the growth of the slave trade to Havana and Santiago de Cuba at the end of the century, see Herbert S. Klein, "North American Competition and the Characteristics of the African Slave Trade to Cuba, 1790 to 1794," *WMQ*, 3d Ser., XVIII (1971), 86–102; and José Luis Belmonte Postigo, "'Brazos para el azúcar': Esclavos para vender: Estrategias de comercialización en la trata negrera en Santiago de Cuba, 1789–1794," *Revista de Indias*, LXX, no. 249 (2010), 445–467; and Manuel Barcia, "'Un coloso sobre la arena': El camino hacia la plantación en Cuba, 1792–1825," *Revista de Indias*, LXXI, no. 251 (2011), 53–76. On plantation owners' slave trading, see "Apuntaciones de la Habana sobre diferentes ramos y utilidades que podrían resultar a la Real Hacienda," Nov. 21, 1776, AGI, SD, 1157, fols. 265–267; Arriaga to Miguel de Altarriba, Aug. 16, 1765, AGI, SD, 2210. On the British Free Port Act of 1767, see Gregory E. O'Malley, *Final Passages: The Intercolonial Slave Trade of British America, 1619–1807* (Williamsburg, Va., and Chapel Hill, N.C., 2014), 302–307; Allan Christelow "Contraband Trade between Jamaica and the Spanish Main, and the Free Port Act of 1766," *HAHR*, XXII (1942), 309–343.

29. For Miralles's letters from Charleston and Philadelphia to Havana, see AGI, Cuba, 1281, and AGI, SD, 1233. On Miralles, see also María E. Rodríguez Vicente, "El comercio cubano y la guerra de emancipación norteamericana," *Anuario de Estudios Americanos*, XI (1954), 61–106; Helen Matzke McCadden, "Juan de Miralles and the American Revolution," *Americas*, XXIX (1973), 359–375 (quotation on 361); Nikolaus Böttcher, "Juan de Miralles: Un comerciante cubano en la guerra de independencia norteamericana," *Anuario de estudios americanos*, LVII (2000), 171–194; and Vicente Ribas, *Don Juan de Miralles y la independencia de los Estados Unidos* (Valencia, Spain, 2003).

Even before the conflict had ended, concerns arose about the threat posed by the new nation that had just been created to the north and the commercial inroads it had made into Havana and New Orleans during the war. Yet, despite these worries, the American Revolution presented a cathartic moment for Spain of opportunism and retribution. Although Spanish armies failed to win back Gibraltar during the war, the successful reconquest of Florida and victories along the Mississippi and the Gulf Coast demonstrated how quickly and effectively reformers had rebuilt its American military apparatus after its losses at the end of the Seven Years' War.[30]

In Cuba, the American Revolution was another "happy time" for the island's commerce, much like the War of Jenkins' Ear had been before. Overall, it had three major effects on the island. The war led to more military investment in Havana, a staggering thirty million pesos during the three years that Spain was officially involved in the war. It allowed Cuba to participate in neutral trade, or what was effectively free trade with France, North America, and other European powers aside from Britain, which brought a massive entry of trade goods and enslaved Africans. And, finally, it spurred the further development of the sugar industry, more than the brief and vexed British occupation of Havana had. During the war and its immediate aftermath, the production of British West Indian sugar dropped, which raised prices and gave openings to Cuba's producers in European and American markets. Even more fatefully, during the American Revolution Cuba developed powerful economic relations with North America that would fill the void left by the loss of the British West Indies in U.S. trade patterns. Soon these newly strengthened relations would contribute to the further social and economic transformation of Cuba toward the slave-based, export-oriented plantation complex.[31]

30. Spain nearly started a war with Britain over the Malvinas / Falkland Islands in 1770, but France was not yet ready to ally with Spain in another war; see Vera Lee Brown, "The Falkland Islands," *HAHR*, V (1922), 387–447, esp. 413, 438; Kuethe, *Cuba*, 93, 128. On the debate about Spain's entry into the American Revolution and war aims, see Thomas E. Chávez, *Spain and the Independence of the United States: An Intrinsic Gift* (Albuquerque, N.M., 2002), 55–64, 126–127; Paul W. Mapp, "The Revolutionary War and Europe's Great Powers," in Edward G. Gray and Jane Kamensky, eds., *The Oxford Handbook of the American Revolution* (Oxford, 2013), 311–326. As early as 1775, the Spanish ambassador in Paris, the Conde de Aranda, was referring to the thirteen colonies as "a great power in the making." See Aranda to Marquis de Grimaldi, July 24, 1775, AGS, Estado, 4599; Eric Beerman, *España y la independencia de Estados Unidos* (Madrid, 1992), 19.

31. As noted earlier, Nicolas Joseph de Ribera had called the War of Jenkins' Ear "the happiest time" ("la época más feliz"); see Ribera, *Descripción de la isla de Cuba*, ed. Hortensia Pichardo Viñals (Havana, [1975]), 115. On Spanish military investment in Havana during the American Revolution, see Amores, *Cuba en la época de Ezpeleta*, 146; see also 183, 202–214. Intra-American slave-trading voyages from French, Danish, British, and North American ports accelerated during the war and the immediate postwar period, bringing approximately fifty-seven thousand enslaved people to Cuba in the period 1775–1792; see David Eltis and Jorge Felipe González, "The Rise and Fall of the Cuban

Greater availability of enslaved Africans and the opening of new markets in the United States caused Cuba to climb rapidly up the list of the world's largest sugar producers. In 1760, it was the eleventh-largest producer, but, by 1787, four years after the end of the American Revolution, it had already become the fourth-largest. By other measures, the industry made large gains. Between 1774 and 1792, the number of enslaved Africans in Cuba doubled, and between 1760 and 1800 sugar plantations in Cuba doubled and almost tripled in size. As the economy moved toward the monoculture of sugar plantation agriculture, western Cuba's sugar zones began to look more like its British and French Caribbean rivals Jamaica and Saint Domingue at their peaks. At no time would Cuba reach their population levels—when whites dropped to as low as 15 percent of the population—but the area around Havana already looked quite different by the last decade or so of the eighteenth century. That meant a rising population of enslaved Africans toiling in cane fields and boiling houses.[32]

By the time the colonial authorities sought to enact the Cédula de Aranjuez in 1789, slaveholding elites in Cuba and elsewhere in Spanish America had enough wealth and clout to block its imposition locally altogether. Although the Spanish monarchy maintained its rhetoric and policies across this time emphasizing the rights and privileges of its African subjects, local interests in the Spanish Caribbean's newly evolving plantation zones refused to maintain these ancient customs for a population group whose labor was crucial to new economies. Powerful slaveholders in Caracas, Louisiana, Puerto Rico, and Cuba (both Havana and Santiago) rejected this legal code. Times had changed. When Cuba's buyers of enslaved Africans had refused to comply with the Spanish asiento funneled through San Juan, they did so less directly, through evasion and co-option. By contrast, the dismissal of this proposed Spanish law was so swift and unequivocal, the crown ended up suspending it in March 1794, retreating with the request that it be honored in spirit. The

---

Slave Trade: New Data, New Paradigms," *From the Galleons to the Highlands: The Slave Trade into Spanish America* (Albuquerque, N.M., 2019).

32. Kuethe, *Cuba*, 132. The American Revolution is still somewhat underacknowledged as a cause of growth in the Cuban sugar industry, although Franklin Knight noted that growth in the sugar industry gained "discernable momentum" after 1775; see Knight, "Origins of Wealth and the Sugar Revolution," *HAHR*, LVII (1977), 253. For the rise in the number of enslaved Africans and sugar plantation in Cuba, see García Rodríguez, *La aventura de fundar ingenios*, 12; de la Fuente, "Esclavitud," in Naranjo Orovio, ed., *Historia de Cuba*, 144–145. According to the census of 1792, the population of Havana and its surroundings was more than one-third enslaved Africans and one-half black. The town of Santiago de las Vegas, on Havana's fertile plain, was composed of almost half enslaved Africans at this point; see Ramón de la Sagra, *Historia económica-política y estadística de la isla de Cuba* (Havana, 1834), 4.

wealth being created by these new elites was so considerable that the crown had no choice but to acquiesce.[33]

Now that their industry had gained traction in Cuba, the group of elites writing from Havana identified themselves in their letter as the sugar planters of Havana. Like their counterparts in Caracas, Louisiana, and Puerto Rico, these planters argued that the code was too lenient and enacting it raised the threat of both economic ruin and slave rebellion. In a letter written by the owners of the largest sugar plantations in Havana to the Conde de Florida-blanca in January 1790, the authors sought to suspend the application of the code. As these plantation owners avowed, and the governor agreed, the practices of Cuban slavery were already comparatively mild and humane. Among other items, planters objected to limiting the number of lashes slaveowners were allowed to deliver to their human property to twenty-five, with a soft instrument. As they explained to political authorities in Madrid, *bozales* were "savage, cheeky, ungrateful . . . good treatment makes them insolent." In closing, they argued, these kinds of laws were best made municipally, according to what was customary in that region.[34]

As a rationale for their stance, the Havana planters evoked the slave rebellion that had occurred more than sixty years before, in 1727, when the British admiral Francis Hosier's ships threatened offshore of Havana. Occurring in the heat of Anglo-Spanish warfare, this rebellion had been blamed at the time on the British asiento factors. Allegedly, one of the enslaved Africans the factors had sold to the island had been directed to incite an uprising in coordination with the attack by Admiral Hosier. In their 1790 letter, the planters returned to this rebellion with a different interpretation of what had happened. The precipitant had not been the British enemy offshore but a benevolent gesture on the part of the planter. In an act of Christian humility, he had invited twelve of his enslaved workers to eat with him in a reenactment of the Last Supper. In response, his workers had lost the will to work and later had risen up in rebellion, a rebellion so shocking—said to be the first of its scale

---

33. Ferrer, *Freedom's Mirror*, 26–29. Technically, the Cédula de Aranjuez was suspended without being revoked, as it had not been previously sanctioned by the king. The next set of slave laws in Cuba would not be enacted until 1842: see Josep M. Fradera, *Colonias para después de un imperio* (Barcelona, 2005), 31, 265. For indigenous people in Cuba and often elsewhere, it was their land that was a greater point of conflict than their labor, and they wouldn't fully lose many of those traditional *fueros* (rights) until the national period or the expansion of the sugar frontier near their pueblos.

34. "Carta de los Sres. Marqués de Cárdenas de Monte Hermosos y Don Miguel José Peñalver y Calvo, Apoderados del Cuerpo del hacendados de dueños de ingenios de fabricar azúcar, al Conde de Floridablanca," Feb. 5, 1790, AGI, Estado, 7, nos. 4, 5; Ferrer, *Freedom's Mirror*, 26–29. For the text of the planters' letter, see Lucena Salmoral, *Los códigos negros de la América española*, 95–123 (quotation on 113), 115, 279–284.

in Cuba—that the plantation owner had razed the *ingenio* to the ground and established a town of white settlers in its place, Santa María del Rosario. From the perspective of 1790, the sugar planters of Cuba took this act of humility as a sign of the great dangers of treating bozales too well. The enemy was no longer the enemy offshore, but the enemy within.[35]

Cuban slaveholders' argument for a firm hand and local control over the enslaved gained traction from the violence that broke out in 1791 in Saint Domingue, when people of African descent rose up in arms to end slavery and, ultimately, colonial rule. Yet the planters' rejection of this Spanish legal code in 1790 demonstrated that, even on the eve of the Haitian Revolution, creole slaveowners' governance over their enslaved Africans trumped the crown's over its enslaved subjects. Already the language being used to refer to people of color in Cuba and the modes of African slavery on the island had begun to resemble what had reigned in the British and French West Indies during the peak of sugar plantation slavery. Soon Cuba would be launching itself in the direction of a more industrial slavery and the hardening of the institution in ways that would lead to new and brutal repression of free and enslaved blacks.[36]

Given the transformation Cuba had undergone in such a short time, it seemed a good moment to look back and take stock. Francisco de Arango y Parreño, signatory to the letter contesting the Cédula de Aranjuez and co-owner of the largest sugar plantation in the world at the time, did exactly that, crediting the British occupation as Havana's crucial moment of commercial awakening. In his influential *Discurso sobre la agricultura de La Habana y medios de fomentarla* (1793), this powerful spokesman at the Spanish court described the occupation that followed Havana's tragic surrender as "the true era of [its] resurrection." Suffering from restrictive Spanish commercial policies and the monopoly of the Royal Havana Company, Havana had "advanced very little"

35. This argument parallels Alan Taylor, *The Internal Enemy: Slavery and War in Virginia, 1772–1832* (New York, 2013). This 1727 rebellion inspired the Cuban film *The Last Supper* (1976).

36. In French Saint Domingue, racial lines also hardened after the Seven Years' War. For the impact on free people of color, see, for example, Stewart R. King, *Blue Coat or Powdered Wig: Free People of Color in Pre-Revolutionary Saint Domingue* (Athens, Ga., 2001); John D. Garrigus, *Before Haiti: Race and Citizenship in French Saint Domingue* (New York, 2006); and Dominique Rogers, "On the Road to Citizenship: The Complex Route to Integration of the Free People of Color in the Two Capitals of Saint-Domingue," in David Patrick Geggus and Norman Fiering, eds., *The World of the Haitian Revolution* (Bloomington, Ind., 2009), 65–78. On the particularly brutal repression after the 1844 insurgency of La Escalera, see Robert L. Paquette, *Sugar Is Made with Blood: The Conspiracy of La Escalera and the Conflict between Empires over Slavery in Cuba* (Middletown, Conn., 1988); Michele Reid-Vazquez, *The Year of the Lash: Free People of Color in Cuba and the Nineteenth-Century Atlantic World* (Athens, Ga., 2011); Aisha K. Finch, *Rethinking Slave Rebellion in Cuba: La Escalera and the Insurgencies of 1841–1844* (Chapel Hill, N.C., 2015); and Landers, *Atlantic Creoles*, 204–230.

in 1760, according to Arango. But the British occupation gave Havana new life with the great quantities of enslaved Africans, goods, and cloths that arrived in just one year of commerce with Great Britain. "With their slaves and their free commerce," Arango wrote, "the British did more in one year than we had in the sixty before."[37]

New times called for new histories. Just as the planters had remade the memory of the 1727 slave rebellion, now Arango did the same with the British occupation of Havana. Arango had been born after the siege and got his information secondhand, perhaps from Father Thomas Butler's famous letter. But his interpretation has gone on to be extremely influential, casting a long shadow over understandings of the occupation to the present day. Little did it matter to Arango that Albemarle himself imposed a monopoly on slave trading in British Havana. Arango portrayed the occupation as another "happy time" similar to Ribera's description of the War of Jenkins' Ear — a gold rush of wealth creation and free trade. Arango's major concern was to further open up Cuba's trade, and from his vantage in the 1790s crediting Britain's model made sense. It certainly was more viable than the French model at this juncture, given the political upheaval in France and its Caribbean colonies, but there were other reasons. In crediting the occupation, he was also crediting the "Enlightened" Spanish reforms that followed. As Arango rightfully pointed out, the British occupation had drawn Spain's attention to Havana and made the government give it more attention and care. Arango used his *Discurso* to express gratitude to the Spanish crown for dismantling Havana's monopolies, and he urged additional such policies. From "a fledgling," Arango marveled, Havana had been transformed into a great city of commerce, exporting goods to other Spanish American territories, and to Iberia, all the sugar that it needed.[38]

37. "Discurso sobre la agricultura de La Habana y medios de fomentarla," in Francisco de Arango y Parreño, *Obras*, ed. Gloria García Rodríguez, I (Havana, 2005), 146, 148, 159–160; Leida Fernández Prieto, "Crónica anunciada de una Cuba azucarera," 41–54, Rafael de Bivar Marquese, "Comparando impérios: o lugar do Brasil no projeto escravista de Francisco de Arango y Parreño," 67–84, Mercedes García Rodríguez, "De productores empíricos a hacendados ilustrados: El mundo del azúcar que precedió a Francisco de Arango y Parreño," 85–104, and, in particular, José A. Piqueras, "Los amigos de Arango en la Corte de Carlos IV," 151–166, all in María Dolores González-Ripoll and Izaskun Álvarez Cuartero, eds., *Francisco Arango y la invención de la Cuba azucarera* (Salamanca, Spain, 2009); Antonio Santamaría García and Sigfrido Vázquez Cienfuegos, "El *Discurso* de Arango en su contexto histórico: Un proyecto económico para Cuba o la redefinición de su equilibrio de poderes y relación colonial desde una *praxis* competitiva, 1790–1820," in Juan Bosco Amores Carredano, ed., *Los tiempos de Espada: Vitoria y La Habana en la era de las revoluciones atlánticas* (Bilbao, Spain, 2014), 253–294.

38. As Moreno Fraginals pointed out, Arango was against monopolies and portrayed the British occupation as a "happy time" when they were busted open; see Moreno Fraginals, *El Ingenio*, I, 36. Eric Williams used a similar metaphor to Arango, perhaps riffing off the *Discurso* when he described Cuba before its sugar boom as "an ugly duckling" not yet turned into "a beautiful swan"; see Williams, *Capitalism and Slavery* (1944; rpt. Chapel Hill, N.C., 1994), 114.

What had power for Arango was the memory of the occupation of Havana; as far as the defense against British attack went, he had no use for it. In a sign of how swiftly things had changed, in his 1793 *Discurso* and later correspondence, Arango also suggested that the time had come to disband Cuba's black militias. His proposal was not heeded, but colonial authorities considered it, which was a striking development given their long history of relying on these soldiers. Just thirty years before, black soldiers' accomplishments had been celebrated in verse in both Havana and Madrid. Even just twenty years before, the Havana city council was still writing the Council of the Indies to defend the institution of African slavery in Cuba as an improving institution, which taught Christianity and Hispanic culture and language to its charges and thus made them useful subjects for the crown. But, again, this was a new era. In 1799, the Havana *consulado* (merchant and planter guild) echoed Arango's request that the Spanish crown "diminish or extinguish the militia of color, or at least the black." Whereas before Cuba's slaveowners relied on people of African descent in myriad roles, the sugar boom made them seek to narrow categories of blackness to the controlled and the enslaved.[39]

Even Arango acknowledged Havana's black militias as "without a doubt some of the best soldiers in the world." But, rather than emphasize the benefits of free blacks to the Spanish empire, Arango came to characterize them — especially free blacks trained at arms — as a potential liability. No doubt with unfolding events in Saint Domingue in mind, Arango felt that it "was not the armed battalions that most frightened" him, but militia veterans who were no longer attached to a specific unit or company and had "retired in the countryside." In his report and correspondence, he warned that, whether free or enslaved, "they are all blacks, and more or less have the same complaints and the same motives for living angry with us." Black militias were no longer necessary or safe in a world where the internal enemy (black uprising) now outweighed the risks of the external one (foreign attack). By this point, the Haitian Revolution had broken out, only affirming Arango's fear. Just three years before, in 1792, the census had recorded the population of African descent in Cuba as larger than that of European descent, perhaps an augur of trends to come.[40]

39. "Recurso que hace el cabildo de la ciudad de la Havana a S.M. sobre la venta y libertad de los negros y mulatos esclavos de los vecinos de ella," 1772, AGI, SD, 2211. As part of this appeal from the city council, see also Actas Capitulares, 1772–1773, Archivo del Museo de la Ciudad de la Habana. For the Havana consulado's recommendation, see "Representación dirigida por el Real Consulado de la Habana al ministro de Hacienda en 10 de julio de 1799," reprinted in José Antonio Saco, *Historia de la esclavitud de la raza africana en el Nuevo Mundo* (1879; rpt. Havana, 1937), V, 136–137; Childs, *The 1812 Aponte Rebellion*, 90–91.

40. "En relación con el fomento y agricultura de Cuba con necesidad de esclavos negros se considera la reforma de las milicias de negros y mulatos libres," 1795, AGS, Guerra Moderna, 6854, exp.

As a result of modernization, free trade, and "Enlightened" reform, Cuba went from a more cosmopolitan, diversified economy of exchange to a more stratified, slave-labor-powered monoculture. Its elites went from a varied group of merchants and landholders with diversified portfolios, who often asserted their wishes by evasion, to a solidified "sugarocracy" who could determine their own laws. Across this time, slavery and racial categories in Cuba became less fluid. The Spanish monarchy's multifaceted response to the shock of the loss of Havana and the heightened imperial rivalry of the late eighteenth century had led to a contradictory legacy on the island of Cuba of more war, more trade with English speakers, and more slavery.[41]

Impacts on the Free Militias of Color

All people of African descent in Cuba experienced the pain of these social and economic shifts, but perhaps no group in Cuba felt more acutely their disorienting speed than members of Havana's free population of African descent. Within that group, black soldiers were among those who suffered the most and, among black soldiers, the moreno militia perhaps most of all.

Militia members and their families, especially pardos, were some of the "most whitened" individuals in Cuba's population of African descent, sometimes using the honorific "don" before their names. Before the Aponte Rebellion, there was little to indicate they felt common cause with enslaved Africans. During times of peace, when the free militias of African descent were not busy with other duties, they sometimes captured *cimarrones* (escapees from slavery) for authorities, and their duties even entailed escorting African bozales from slave ships to the barracoons. In the final decades of the eighteenth century, however, the climate for all people of African descent in Cuba shifted, driven by changes in both Spanish imperial policy and local patterns of war and trade that led to an influx of bozales for sale and the expansion of sugar plantation slavery. With the strengthening of local control over the institution of slavery came the hardening of slaveowners' enforcement of racial hierarchy. What resulted was a harsher reality for all people of color on the

---

32, 10r. On Arango's concerns about retired militia in the countryside, see Childs, *The 1812 Aponte Rebellion*, 90–92. The population of African descent had likely outnumbered that of European descent at other times in Cuba's past, but this was the first time a census had recorded it. More whites in Havana expressed concern about instructing blacks on using weapons as part of their militia service, yet they continued to permit it.

41. Moreno Fraginals first used the term *"sacarocracia"* / "sugarocracy" for Cuba's planter class (Moreno Fraginals, *El ingenio*). On the impact of the larger transitions of this era on the black militias in Cuba, see Landers, *Atlantic Creoles*, 138–174, 204–230.

island, but particularly for darker-skinned free blacks who closely resembled the majority of the enslaved. In the wake of the American Revolution, men who formed part of the moreno militia became involved in several disputes over their treatment.[42]

In the 1760s and 1770s, however, this was not yet the case. The city's soldiers of African descent still basked in the glow of the honors, recognition, and praise they had rightfully received for their bravery defending Havana during the British attack. Cuba's military *reglamento* of 1769, written by Alejandro O'Reilly and later exported to the rest of Spanish America, stipulated that militia members of color be "treated with esteem." The reglamento decreed that no insults in word or deed would be permitted against the officials of the battalions of pardos and morenos, and they should be "distinguished and respected" among those of their respective classes. The reglamento also demarcated the salaries due to these militia members while they were deployed and described the uniforms they would proudly display when mustered in Havana. Beneath banners that proclaimed, "Always forward in glory" (pardos), and, more fiercely, "Victory or death" (morenos), the militias of color drilled once a week on Sundays, parading their elegant uniforms before a crowd of onlookers.[43]

In the wake of the siege, the *fuero militar* was extended to all officials of color in the militias, in reward for their service and as a recruitment tool to bring in more of their numbers. According to its terms, all militia members and their families were exempt from public prisons and civil courts and would instead be tried by special military tribunals. Officers would not have to pay certain taxes. They and their mothers or widows and orphans were designated a pension in the event of their death in combat or retirement after twenty years. Inspired by these benefits and the example of the veterans of the siege who walked Havana's streets, free people of African descent joined the mili-

---

42. María del Carmen Barcia, *Los ilustres apellidos: Negros en la Habana colonial* (Havana, 2009), 233, 241; Pedro Deschamps Chapeaux, *Los batallones de pardos y morenos libres* (Havana, 1976), 22–23; Landers, *Atlantic Creoles*, 138–144, 151. On "whitening" and free people of color in the eighteenth century, see Ann Twinam, *Purchasing Whiteness: Pardos, Mulattos, and the Quest for Social Mobility in the Spanish Indies* (Stanford, Calif., 2015). On free people of color owning property, see Johnson, *Social Transformation*, 66–68. According to the 1792 census, less than 10 percent of pardo men in Havana and its immediate hinterland were enslaved; by contrast, more than 75 percent of *negro* men in the same area were enslaved; see Sagra, *Historia economico-politica y estadistica de la isla de Cuba*, 4.

43. "Reglamento para las milicias de infantería y caballería de la Isla de Cuba," 1769, AGI, IG, 1885: "Los oficiales de los batallones de pardos y morenos serán tratados con estimación. A ninguno se permitirá ultrajarlos de palabra, ni obra; y entre los de sus respectivas clases, serán distinguidos y respetados." See also Deschamps Chapeaux, *Los batallones de pardos y morenos libres*, 37–46; Childs, *The 1812 Aponte Rebellion*, 86; Barcia, *Los ilustres apellidos*, 250–252.

tias in great numbers during the two decades after the British siege of Havana. According to census data from 1776, two-thirds of all free people of color in Havana between the ages of fifteen and fifty volunteered as soldiers.[44]

Havana's newly expanded black militias had multiple opportunities to serve on Spanish military expeditions abroad and further burnish their reputation at arms. In 1769, members of the black militias sailed to Louisiana with Alejandro O'Reilly to put down a rebellion against the new Spanish governor, Antonio de Ulloa, who came into office after the territory's transfer from France to Spain at the end of the Seven Years' War. Of the Cuba militia who accompanied the expedition, more than half (160 of 280 men) were pardos and morenos. Afterward, several members of the moreno and pardo militia who were dual veterans of Havana in 1762 and Louisiana in 1769 received medals with the king's image as honorifics. Many decades later, during routine reviews of troops, pardo and moreno militia members would continue to refer to O'Reilly, beloved for his military reforms, as *"Excelentísimo"* ["most excellent"] when they recounted serving in the Louisiana expedition under his command.[45]

When Spain intervened in the American Revolution in 1779, the militias of African descent in Cuba continued their tradition of fighting against Britain on behalf of the Spanish crown. Even as Spain was sending an expedition to West Africa to expand its slave trading and Juan de Miralles was tightening commercial ties with North America that would tip the island further toward plantation slavery, black militias were sailing north from Havana to risk their lives in this North American war. In fact, two veterans of the siege of Havana petitioned the crown to raise additional companies of pardo and moreno soldiers at their own expense in order to serve the king on Bernardo de Gálvez's campaign to the Gulf Coast. The moreno Josef Uribe and the pardo Pedro Oporto sold many of their own possessions in order to raise companies that

44. Joseph P. Sánchez, "African Freedmen and the *Fuero militar,*" *Colonial Latin American Historical Review*, III, no. 2 (Spring 1994), 165–184; Lyle N. McAlister, *The "Fuero Militar" in New Spain, 1764–1800* (Gainesville, Fla., 1957). Census data for 1776 also reveals whites in Havana serving in the militias at a high rate, but closer to 40 percent; see Johnson, *Social Transformation*, 63; Childs, *The 1812 Aponte Rebellion*, 82–83, 87.

45. Kuethe, *Cuba*, 90–92. Kuethe writes that this is the first episode of forces sent from Cuba to effective action in North America, but that practice goes back to the War of Spanish Succession. The militia fought alongside 1,847 royal troops; see Troop Registers Signed by Alejandro O'Reilly, June 27, 1769, AGI, Cuba, 1055; Herbert S. Klein, "The Colored Militia of Cuba, 1568–1868," *Caribbean Studies*, VI, no. 2 (July 1966), 17–27, esp. 20. One individual who received a medal for his service in New Orleans was Pedro de Menéndez, mentioned in Chapter 5: see El Rey to the Governor of Havana, July 16, 1771, AGI, Cuba, 1140. María del Carmen Barcia writes that Juan Bautista Lobaynas, another comandante in the battalion of pardos libres and veteran of both Havana in 1762 and New Orleans in 1769, was recognized at the same time; see Barcia, *Los ilustres apellidos*, 269.

had the honor of serving alongside the professional soldiers from Spain in the company of volunteers of Cataluña.[46]

The American Revolution provided ample opportunity for the black militias to serve. Because Spain staged its entry into the war out of Havana, both professional and militia troops from Cuba composed a significant portion of the men in the defense of Nicaragua (1780), Gálvez's expedition up the Mississippi (1779), and the captures of Mobile (1780), Pensacola (1781), and the Bahamas (1782). During the siege of Pensacola, which successfully won Florida back for Spain, there were 139 pardo and 139 moreno militiamen, 100 pardo and moreno artillerymen, and 100 enslaved fortification workers from Cuba in a force of more than 7,000 Spanish troops. These soldiers of African descent composed a smaller proportion of combatants than they had been in battles fought on their own turf in Cuba. But they were tested and true battalions enthusiastic about proving themselves in battle and gaining revenge on Spain's British foes. Gálvez employed these black militia troops on the front lines of his military operations and confirmed their skill in his correspondence with the king and Cuba's captain general.[47]

In return for their service, the king continued to insist that his militias of loyal black subjects be treated well. To encourage and reward volunteering for the militias the Spanish king re-extended the military fueros in 1778 and 1780, the text of which insisted that his soldiers of African descent be accorded proper respect. The fuero of 1778 commanded that Cuba's officers in the pardo and moreno militia be regarded "as nobles." The fuero of 1780 went even further, making a striking call for black equality couched in the language of Christianity. Issued by Charles III in Spain, its text commanded that the officials of Cuba's battalions of pardos and morenos be extended the same privileges conferred upon the king's white armies. Why would God have created two classes of men, it asked, one of whites and the other of blacks, "when the scriptures teach us that there was no more than one Adam from which we all came"? Such language was more easily pronounced in Spain than in Cuba's

46. Uribe and Oporto did not have enough time to raise the full one hundred men for each company before they were despatched to take part in the Pensacola expedition; see AGI, SD, 2548, no. 16, fols. 519, 1029–1032. In his report about deaths in the Pensacola campaign, Gálvez listed ten moreno and pardo militiamen and eleven men total from all the other companies of militia and professional soldiers sent from Havana. Their higher death rate reflects their deployment on the front lines of the battle. See "Relación que manifiesta los individuos de los cuerpos que se hallan de guarnición en esta plaza y fallecieron en la conquista de Penzacola," Bernardo de Gálvez to Josef de Gálvez, Nov. 9, 1781, AGI, SD, 2548, no. 1.

47. Kuethe, *Cuba*, 106–107; Gustavo Placer Cervera, *Ejército y milicias en la Cuba colonial, 1763–1783* (Havana, 2015), 182. As they had in prior wars, members of the black militia protected Havana in order to enable its professional troops to serve abroad, and they also went to sea on warships and privateering vessels as well.

multiracial, slave-dependent economy, and there is little to show that it was in any way honored in practice. Slaveholders like Arango would soon warn of the dangers of extending messages of Christian universalism to the enslaved. The king's invocation of this language, however, showed his persistent commitment at least in word to preserving the traditional compacts forged with his humblest vassals. In turn, they invoked his royal proclamations to lobby for better treatment in the shifting racial landscape on the island to which they returned from foreign wars.[48]

After the American Revolution, black veterans arrived home to a city that was rapidly transforming itself and less in need of their military services. The disappearance of the specter of British fleets on the horizon, haunting the island with the threat of attack, had profoundly negative consequences for Cuba's black militias. During the American Revolutionary War, there had been talk of invading Jamaica — a Spanish emissary even made clandestine overtures to the maroons for their support — but no expedition materialized. A Spanish attack on Gibralter (as well as plans against Belize and even Britain itself) also came to naught. Postwar there was no prospect of future foreign engagements for Cuba's militias to participate in or threats of invasion to protect against. After the resolution of the American Revolution, Britain's imperial priorities had shifted to new horizons, and an influx of slaving vessels began to appear on Havana's horizon instead. Without the British navy menacing Havana, the sense among whites in Cuba of the urgency of black political loyalty and the necessity of black military power diminished. Consequently, the population of African descent lost leverage, and concerns arose about the threat they posed. Broader geopolitical developments had undercut their ability to play competing empires off against each other to their own advantage. In losing the opportunity to serve in foreign wars, free people of color's lives in the shifting socioeconomic conditions of Havana became more imperiled.[49]

In the 1780s, the climate for free pardos and morenos in Havana began to change, reflecting both these internal dynamics and broader geopolitical shifts. Over the two decades that followed Spain's entry into the American Revolution, it was becoming increasingly evident that the commercial gains made by men like Juan de Miralles had eroded the ground black soldiers stood upon in Cuba's social worlds. Free trading during the war had brought many thousands more enslaved Africans into Havana's ports on French, British, Spanish, Danish, and U.S. slaving ships — fifty-seven thousand enslaved Afri-

48. "Dios que crió dos clases de hombres, una de blancos y otra de negros cuando las escrituras nos enseñan que no hubo más que un Adán de donde todas provenían": quoted in Barcia, *Cuba*, 141–142 (quotation on 141), 149–150.

49. On overtures to the Jamaican maroons, see AGI, SD, 2084; and Kuethe, *Cuba*, 128.

cans in total between 1775 and 1792. In this context of heightened trafficking in enslaved laborers, local authorities began chipping away at traditional rights and privileges of its population of African descent, including pathways available to freedom. A royal decree in 1789 mandated that escaped slaves from rival colonies were no longer automatically granted their freedom but instead were put to agricultural labor under supervision. Another royal decree that same year restricted a mother's long-standing right to buy the freedom of her own child through the process of *coartación*. During these immediate postwar years, soldiers in the moreno militia of Havana launched an unsuccessful campaign for equal pay with pardos (they received two pesos less at every rank), and their leaders became embroiled in a series of disputes with their white commander.[50]

In 1789, the same year that Spain declared "free trade in slaves" and issued its short-lived Cédula de Aranjuez meant to limit the cruelties of Spanish slavery, a member of the free black militia of Havana was viciously whipped to death by a white man. According to a group of seven officers from the moreno batallion, who wrote a letter of protest to the Council of the Indies, Joseph Antonio Colón, a grenadier and veteran of the battle of Pensacola, had been tied to a post in the house of a wealthy merchant and whipped three thousand times by five different men over the course of five hours, "until his flesh began to fall to parts." Their battalion's commander, Antonio Seidel, a career military officer from Barcelona who habitually treated them, in their own words, "worse than slaves," had done nothing in response.[51]

The merchant, Antonio de Quintanilla, claimed that Colón had raped his wife. Across all this time, it is impossible to know what actually happened. Did Colón merely look at her askance? Did an act of consensual sex occur? Was it rape? Whatever the truth of the matter, it was not Colón's guilt or innocence that made up the substance of the complaint but his horrific punishment and the lack of recourse. According to the reglamento of 1769, he was owed a military tribunal for his alleged crime, not vigilante justice and a public spectacle of human torture. The Cédula de Aranjuez had aspired to curtail owners' power of the whip by permitting only twenty-five lashes with a soft instrument for enslaved Africans. As Colón's murder indicated, local whites were stepping up their efforts to treat all people of African descent as slaves —

---

50. Childs, *The 1812 Aponte Rebellion*, 91. On this limitation of the traditional right of Catholic asylum for the enslaved, see Amores, *Cuba en la época de Expeleta*, 167. On the change to *coartción*, see "Real cédula sobre esclavos," Apr. 21, 1789, AGI, Cuba, 1433B.

51. Quejas contra Antonio Seidel, 1788–1795, AGS, Guerra Moderna, 6853, exp. 53. On Seidel's brief service in Mexico before Cuba, see "Libro de servicios del batallon de morenos libres de La Habana," 1791, AGI, Cuba, 1491A.

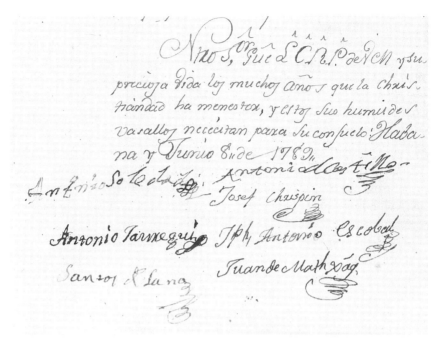

FIGURE 34 The Signatures of the Leaders of the Free Moreno Militia in Havana on the Letter of June 8, 1789, Protesting Their Treatment to the Council of the Indies in Spain. Soledad was seventy-three or seventy-four years old at this point and had served in the militia for fifty-two years. His handwriting reveals his age. Several of his fellow signatories were advanced in years, as their signatures reflect. Courtesy, Archivo General de Simancas, Spain, Guerra Moderna, 6853, exp. 53

or far worse — and resisting royal attempts to limit their power. The message Colón's murder sent was clear: any moreno who got out of his place, militia member or otherwise, could expect immediate, stunning, life-extinguishing punishment, enacted with impunity.

Among the signatories to this letter of protest over Colón's murder was Antonio de Soledad, veteran of the siege of Havana and one of the two commanders of the free black militia who had been sent to Madrid in 1763 by the Conde de Ricla to perform a display of arms before the king (see Figure 34). At least five of the six other officers who lodged the complaint were also veterans of the siege. As these men reminded the Council of the Indies in their letter, their loyalty, discipline, obedience, and military prowess were well known in Havana and even the royal court, where Soledad — "who exists to this day," as they wrote — had been a source of admiration for his dexterity and skill. These men were proud veterans of the siege of Havana who had fought with Bernardo de Gálvez in "the conquest of Pensacola" and even been afforded the great honor of being the first to open fire during that battle. And now, this? With language that echoed the military fuero of 1780, they affirmed their shared Christianity with their audience and appealed to its universalism; they complained it was "as though the life of a man, even if black, had not cost Jesus Christ the same as that of a white man." As they continued in righteous indignation, "In Havana they call blacks dogs, and treat them as such, even though they wear the uniform Your Majesty gave them."[52]

What these men's letter captures, with such a sense of pain, betrayal, and indignation, is the suddenness of the shift experienced in their lifetime, even within the span of their military careers. In the twenty-five years since they had defended Havana from British attack and their commander Soledad had been sent to Madrid and celebrated at the royal court — decades during which their battalion had performed equally brave exploits in defense of Spanish territories against the same British enemy — the treatment men of their stature and profession could receive in Havana had changed unthinkably. The professionalization of the military in Cuba meant that they now had a white commander from Spain who not only refused to protect them from an increasingly hostile environment in Havana but also added his own abuse.

According to the appeals of these black soldiers, their commander Seidel regularly imprisoned them, threw them in the stocks, and beat them, despite clear prohibitions against beating militiamen in O'Reilly's reglamento. Seidel had even let his assistant go unpunished after striking a soldier so hard for stepping out of line during drill that he killed the man. As the moreno soldiers who authored this letter put it, their commander liked to "roughly" ask them if they thought they were someone and tell them that they were "only a black," and he was their boss ("Jefe"). In part, they blamed Seidel's behavior on the influence of the Marqués de Jústiz de Santa Ana, whose niece he had married. The marqués was one of Havana's wealthiest residents, a plantation owner and large-scale slaveholder who in 1763 had lent his enslaved Africans out to defend Havana from British attack. Through marriage, Seidel was now invested

52. "Representación de los oficiales del batallon de morenos y la de Don Ygnacio Ortiz de Luna su apoderado," June 8, 1789, AGS, Guerra Moderna, 6853, exp. 53, 54v. The other officers who were signatories include: Antonio del Castillo, see "Libro de servicios del batallon de morenos de La Habana," June 1765, AGI, SD, 2093; Josef Chrispin, see Alejandro O'Reilly's review of the militia of morenos libres, Dec. 6, 1763, AGI, SD, 2078; José Antonio Escobal, see "Libro de servicios del batallon de morenos de La Habana," June 1765, AGI, SD, 2093; Antonio Jarregui, see "Libro de servicios del batallon de morenos de La Habana," June 1765, AGI, SD, 2093, and "Relación de batallon de morenos libres que gozen sueldo," 1790, AGI, Cuba, 1433A; for (Joseph) de los Santos de Luna, see Alejandro O'Reilly's review of the militia of morenos libres, Dec. 6, 1763, AGI, SD, 2078. I could not locate Juan de Mathias in troop records. For Soledad's longevity in the militia, see "Libro de servicios del batallón de morenos libres de La Havana," 1791, AGI, Cuba, 1491A.

in sugar plantations and slaves, and, apparently, the marqués had spread the message to his son-in-law that all blacks required violent treatment. Pointedly, the militiamen asked that Seidel be replaced by another Spaniard, and not a creole, whom they distrusted.[53]

As this episode captures in the extreme, even before the Haitian Revolution the expansion of the slave trade and the remaking of Cuba's political economy had unleashed an assault on the traditional rights of free blacks in Havana. Despite the long history of exemplary and essential service by the free militias of color, men who wore the uniform of the crown now could see members of their militia murdered in the most savage ways, with no recourse. This shift occurred even though the increase of Africans on the island was designed in part in response to the essential role free people of color had played, alongside the enslaved, serving their sovereign by defending at home and projecting abroad Spanish imperial power. Spanish policies that privileged and rewarded the military service of free and enslaved blacks also opened up commercial transformations that undermined the place of people of African descent in colonial society. Despite a lengthy inquiry that moved between Cuba and the Council of the Indies, by 1791 the new captain general, Luis de la Casas, and Antonio Seidel purged all the complaining officers from the moreno militia— minus Soledad, whose celebrity, it seems, made him alone untouchable.[54]

When the Haitian Revolution broke out, its reverberations in Cuba transformed the racial landscape and led to repressive measures for all people of African descent on the island. In the thirty years after Spain's new policy of "free trade in slaves," approximately 325,000 enslaved Africans arrived on the island. This was the steepest moment of the ascent of the trade throughout Cuba's history. In the altered sociopolitical environment of the island, slaveholders perceived a sizable population of free people of color as a threat to their ability to control the their human chattel. As unrest roiled Cuba, free people of color were required to carry licenses and treated with suspicion. Because of the fear of political contagion, Cuba's black militias had not been deployed to fight alongside Spain's black allies in its military intervention in the Haitian Revolution. Instead, they served only on privateering vessels in a more limited role. Now Arango, the most powerful man on the island aside from the governor, was questioning the very existence of the militias, and

53. Quejas contra Antonio Seidel, 1788–1795, AGS, Guerra Moderna, 6853, esp. 53; Kuethe, *Cuba*, 123–126; Marqués de Jústiz de Santa Ana to Arriaga, Dec. 17, 1763, AGI, SD, 1506.

54. Quejas contra Antonio Seidel, 1788–1795, AGS, Guerra Moderna, 6853, exp. 53. Six of the seven complainants are listed as officers in the moreno militia in 1789, and only one (Soledad) remains in 1791 (AGI, Cuba, 1433A, and AGI, Cuba, 1491A). On Soledad's celebrity, Matt Childs has pointed out that he was listed as the commander of the black battalion in the Guía de forasteros of Havana, notably for 1795; see Childs, *The 1812 Aponte Rebellion*, 81.

their members found themselves deprived of the fuero and forced to labor alongside the enslaved in work camps as one of their assigned duties. Indeed, after a long tradition of military service in wars both at home and abroad, these free men of color were suddenly experiencing attacks on their traditional rights, privileges, and very persons. Havana's elites—if not the king himself—seemed to have forgotten their valiant service defending Havana from foreign attack. Members of the moreno militia continued to petition the Spanish crown against incidents of mistreatment, persisting in their campaign for equal pay with pardos and even whites, but they had lost the leverage to do so effectively. Without the threat of foreign invasion or the possibility of being deployed on behalf of their king, in this new climate their petitions fell on deaf ears.[55]

The Aponte Rebellion

Amid this radically altered landscape in Cuba, in the spring of 1812 the Aponte Rebellion broke out. Over the course of two months, this coordinated series of slave rebellions spanning the island left thirteen whites dead. According to the trial that followed, this was a moreno movement. Ninety-six percent of those arrested, questioned, imprisoned, punished, or executed in its wake were morenos as opposed to pardos. More than three quarters of those caught within the investigation's net were enslaved. At first glance, it might seem that authorities scapegoated Aponte, their alleged leader, to enact a purge on Havana's morenos libres, a population they had come to regard as troublesome. Yet analysis of the trial testimony has led scholars to believe Aponte was indeed the leader of this rebellion, at least in the Havana vicinity, if not across the entire island. There is a rich body of scholarship, relied on here, that insists that, despite all that has been uncovered, there are limits to what we will ever know about the historical figure Aponte and the rebellion that bears his name. That said, multiple strands of evidence indicate that the movement was shaped at least in part by the memory of the siege of Havana and the experience of soldiers in the moreno militia in the decades immediately afterward.[56]

55. Childs, *The 1812 Aponte Rebellion*, 70, 91–92. On the multifaceted political and economic impact of the Haitian Revolution in Cuba, see Ferrer, *Freedom's Mirror*.

56. "Appendix: Biographical Database of the Aponte Rebels," in Childs, *The 1812 Aponte Rebellion*, 189–215. Matt Childs comes to the conclusion that Aponte led the island-wide rebellion; Ada Ferrer argues that he at least led the part that took place near Havana; and Stephan Palmié contends that he did not lead the uprisings. See Childs, *The 1812 Aponte Rebellion*; Ferrer, *Freedom's Mirror*; Stephan Palmié, "'For Reasons of History': José Antonio Aponte and His Libro de Pinturas," in Palmié, *Wizards and Scientists: Explorations in Afro-Cuban Modernity and Tradition* (Durham, N.C., 2002), 79–158.

Rereading the Aponte Rebellion in relation to the history and memory of the siege of Havana—alongside the Haitian Revolution and the immediate context of 1812—provides insights into the impacts of the siege and the context and causes of this multifaceted movement. The Aponte Rebellion reveals the persistence of the memory of the siege of Havana among free blacks in Cuba, even in a time of sugar boom and hardening white supremacy. Aponte both invoked a particular memory of the siege of Havana and connected his movement to the promises made by the king to his loyal black vassals in the decades that followed the siege. As was all too clear in Havana in 1812, these promises had been betrayed by powerful local forces and the unfolding impact of reforms the Spanish crown set into motion.

The roots of the insurgency reached at least as far back as the defense of Havana fifty years before. The military acumen men of African descent had acquired through their decades of service helped coordinate the rebellion, which, in its early stages, sought to target Havana's military arsenals to procure weapons. Aponte himself had been placed in the public jail for allegedly trying to steal weapons from the arsenal as early as 1800. In January the following year, Antonio Seidel forced Aponte to retire from his position as a captain in the moreno militia. Aponte had served for more than twenty years, including in the capture of the Bahamas during the American Revolution. More than a decade before the rebellion, Aponte already had a volatile combination of personal grievance and plans.[57]

Aponte's movement had connections with the moreno militia's conflict with Seidel and colonial authorities in the 1780s. During a search of Aponte's house, authorities found handwritten copies of the military fueros of 1778 and 1780. Judicial officials demanded Aponte explain how he received copies of these fueros and whether others had knowledge of them. Even just repeating these fueros, which insisted on equal treatment for officers of color in Havana, had become an act of sedition in Cuba's changing racial landscape. When questioned, Aponte claimed to have obtained copies of the documents from "José Domingo Escobar, a retired sergeant of the black battalion," and had given them to his apprentice to copy. According to Aponte's testimony, Escobar had received the decrees from black militia captain Cristóbal de Zayas, an officer in the moreno militia and a veteran of the defense of Havana in 1762. According to Aponte's testimony, Zayas had them because of "a dispute about

57. Carlos de Ayala to Marqués de Someruelos, Dec. 23, 1800, AGI, Cuba, 1679. The reason cited for Aponte's forced retirement after twenty-three years of services was that he was *"cansado,"* or lacking strength; see "Relación de morenos que gozan el fuero," signed Antonio Seidel, Jan. 15, 1801, AGI, Cuba, 1667. On this point, see also Childs, *The 1812 Aponte Rebellion,* 84, 94, 233 n. 45, 236 n. 107.

the formation of the regiment"—perhaps the purges enacted by Seidel or one of the moreno militia's petitions for equal pay.[58]

There are even more direct links between the Aponte Rebellion and both the siege of Havana and the subsequent struggles of the island's moreno militia, but they require some parsing. In Aponte's house, in a wooden box with a sliding top that was hidden in a trunk of clothes, investigators found a so-called *libro de pinturas*, or book of paintings, now made famous by scholars. Although this book of paintings and collages has been lost to posterity, it may be reconstructed from the hundreds of pages of testimony in which Aponte and his accused conspirators explained its images and their meanings to questioners. As their testimony revealed, Aponte regularly showed the book—part inspiration, part recruitment tool—to members of the free black militia in Havana and other individuals during meetings at his house. Colonial officials considered it a "blueprint for revolution"; contemporary scholars have subsequently deemed it "the most powerful document we have of the imaginary of radical antislavery in the Caribbean." This book contained military maps; drawings of incidents from Aponte's life; Greek, Roman, and Egyptian gods; biblical figures; portraits of popes and Ethiopian kings; and an image of two black soldiers being honored by the Spanish king.[59]

When questioned, Aponte identified these two black soldiers by name: Antonio de Soledad and Ignacio Albarado. According to Aponte's testimony, in this painted version of Soledad and Alvarado's appearance at the royal court, the king was placing his hand on Soledad's forehead, insisting that he need not remove his hat in His Majesty's presence. Protocol around the removal of hats had been a point of conflict between the moreno militia and the white officials assigned to their battalion in the wake of the Seven Years'

---

58. Asuntos Políticos, 12, no. 17, fols. 75–75v, 95–95v, ANC; Franco, *Las conspiraciones de 1810 y 1812*, 168–169; Childs, *The 1812 Aponte Rebellion*, 84. Cristobal de Sayas is also said to have fought in the defense in "Libro de servicios de los morenos," 1774, AGI, Cuba, 1136A.

59. Childs, *The 1812 Aponte Rebellion*, 4 ("blueprint"); Sibylle Fischer, "The Deadly Hermeneutics of the Trial of José Antonio Aponte," in Fischer, *Modernity Disavowed: Haiti and the Cultures of Slavery in the Age of Revolution* (Durham, N.C., 2004), 41–56 ("radical" on 43). On the book of paintings or pictures, see also Linda María Rodríguez, "Artistic Production, Race, and History in Colonial Cuba, 1762–1840" (Ph.D. diss., Harvard University, 2012); Gloria García, *Conspiraciones y revueltas: La actividad política de los negros en Cuba (1790–1845)* (Santiago de Cuba, 2003); Jorge Pavez Ojeda, "The 'Painting' of Black History: The Afro-Cuban Codex of José Antonio Aponte (Havana, Cuba, 1812)," in Adrien Delmas and Nigel Penn, eds., *Written Culture in Colonial Context: Africa and the Americas, 1500–1900* (Leiden, 2012), 271–303; Ernesto Peña González, *Una biblia perdida* (Havana, 2010); Juan Antonio Hernández, "Hacia una historia de lo imposible: La revolución haitiana y el 'libro de pinturas' de José Antonio Aponte" (Ph.D diss., University of Pittsburgh, 2005); and Palmié, "'For Reasons of History,'" in Palmié, *Wizards and Scientists*, 79–158. See also Digital Aponte, http://aponte.hosting.nyu.edu.

War. Moreno militia soldiers were always required to remove their hats in their white commanders' presence, even though no other militia members had to do so. In 1805, a captain of the moreno militia had been thrown in jail for eleven days for failing to remove his hat while addressing the company's white attendant during drill. Moreno militia members protested his imprisonment, arguing that an officer could hardly stop to remove his hat while leading military exercises, particularly before another member of the army who ranked no higher. In Aponte's re-imagining of Soledad and Alvarado's meeting with the Spanish king, the king himself had asserted the nobility and status of these two moreno soldiers by refusing to allow them to remove their hats in his presence. Adapting the history of the siege to the times in which it was written, Aponte made abundantly clear that men who had met the king and been treated as his equal should not have to humble themselves before ordinary white men in Cuba.[60]

Another image in the book of pictures depicted Aponte's grandfather Joaquín fighting in the defense of Havana in 1762. According to his testimony, one of the drawings of his grandfather portrayed him in battle against British troops, with the ships they had just disembarked in the background. The rest of the company of morenos was also visible in this image, along with its banner. Aponte identified by name specific members who had fought in the siege as well as others who had not. In the former category was sublieutenant José Antonio Escoval, who had been one of the moreno captains eliminated from the militia for coauthoring the letter of complaint about Colón's murder. In the latter category was Aponte's father Nicolás, who had served in the militia but, according to military records, not necessarily in the siege. Including family members who had not necessarily fought widened the circle of honor of moreno veterans of the siege. In this image, as well as one other in the book of pictures, moreno soldiers formed a cavalry unit, even though people of color were barred from riding horses in war. As Aponte stated, the goddess of war in her chariot was pointing to Captain Joaquín de Aponte, who was battling and capturing six hundred men and killing "un Milor" ("My Lord," an English officer or gentleman) who wore bloody clothes.[61]

---

60. For Lámina 31 in the libro de pinturas, see Jorge Pavez Ojeda, ed., "Expediente sobre José Antonio Aponte y el sentido de las pinturas que se hayan en el Libro que se le aprehendió en su casa, 1812," *Anales de Desclasificación*, I, *La derrota del área cultural*, no. 2 (2006), 717–768, esp. 731; Childs, *The 1812 Aponte Rebellion*, 81–82; Ferrer, *Freedom's Mirror*, 316–317. In the background of Lámina 31 stood the next king of Spain, Carlos IV, and "the infante Don Antonio" along with "trophies of war." For mention of the 1805 imprisonment, see "Los capitanes y subalternos del mas respetuoso y humilde batallon de morenos libres de la Havana," May 28, 1812, AGI, Cuba, 1798.

61. For Láminas 18–19, see Pavez Ojeda, ed., "Expediente sobre José Antonio Aponte," *Anales de*

Military records confirm that Captain Joaquín de Aponte served along-side Soledad and Albarado and distinguished himself during the defense of Havana in two separate actions protecting the western approach to the city. In the encounter evoked in Aponte's painted history, at Puentes Grandes, the militia of free blacks of Havana did indeed kill a British captain and take many prisoners — forty-five, according to a journal of a Spanish officer. Aponte's version magnified events that had taken place, just as an oral history augments the history it repeats and all histories tailor events to the time of their recount-ing. Now Aponte's book of pictures confirmed the ability of a small number of blacks to capture and overpower a much larger number of whites, even powerful and high-ranking ones, perhaps serving as a plan of action for the rebellion. It also commemorated the brave actions of the ancestor of this man who presumed to lead his fellow blacks into war. Another image in the book of pictures depicted the medal with the king's effigy that had been awarded to Aponte's grandfather after his service in O'Reilly's expedition to New Orleans. Aponte's own self-portrait depicted him as a humble carpenter, not a soldier, but against the backdrop of a scene of his service with the moreno militias leading the assault on the Bahamas during the American Revolution.[62]

Men of African descent in Havana did not have to imagine foreign lands like Haiti or older histories like that of Ethiopia to conjure up images of black men triumphant at arms. They already had their own history of heroic black soldiers who had led them in a campaign killing and capturing whites, even and especially powerful ones (*milores*). Alongside imaginings of Haiti, a place he had never visited, Aponte could also draw on a family history in the place where he and his co-conspirators lived. The presence of Joaquín de Aponte in his grandson's book of pictures serves as an important reminder that this local history still had salience. In addition to the inspiration of Haitian gen-erals, Cuba had its own black military tradition, one that still resonated where it had taken place. All Aponte had to do was to remember his grandfather dur-ing the most important battle ever fought in the city where he lived. In one of

---

Desclasificación, I, *La derrota del área cultural*, no. 2 (2006), 727–728. On Nicholas and Joaquín de Aponte, see Childs, *The 1812 Aponte Rebellion*, 25.

62. For Joaquín de Aponte's military records, see "Libros de servicios de los diferentes batallo-nes de Cuba," 1771–1775, AGI, Cuba, 1136A, fol. 636; and AGI, SD, 2117, fol. 656. For the encounter during the siege at Puentes Grandes, see Pedro Manuel de Olañeta, "Diario del sitio y rendición de la plaza de la Habana al Ingles," June 17, 1762, Miscellaneous Manuscripts, MS 352, XV, box 83, folder 1662, Sterling Memorial Library, Yale University; Gustavo Placer Cervera, *Inglaterra y La Habana, 1762* (Havana, 2007), 184. Placer writes that the skirmish took place June 21–25, 1762. For the sec-ond image of Joaquín de Aponte, see Láminas 32–33, and for José Antonio Aponte's self-portrait, see Láminas 24–25, in Pavez Ojeda, ed., "Expediente sobre José Antonio Aponte," *Anales de Desclasifi-cación*, I, *La derrota del área cultural*, no. 2 (2006), 729–730, 731–733.

the images in the book of pictures, as Aponte described it, the city of Havana, portrayed as a woman, presented herself before officials of the moreno militia in memory of those that had defended her.[63]

A subterranean oral history of the siege of Havana surfaced in this rebellion in nineteenth-century Cuba and played a role in its construction. Many veterans of the siege of Havana lived into a surprisingly old age and would have kept the memory of their exploits alive. Thirty years after the British invasion, in the 1793 review of the battalion of morenos libres of Havana, there were still twelve veterans of the siege serving as officers, including Commander Antonio de Soledad at the impressive age of seventy-eight. During each review of troops, they reminded officials of the role they had played during specific skirmishes of the siege, identifying each encounter with the enemy by precise location and date. Indeed, without their detailed accounts, insisting on the importance of their role, year after year, in so many routine reviews of troops, their accounts of siege might have been lost, and this book would have been less able to reconstruct their stories.[64]

At first glance, a British occupation of a Spanish colonial city and its return at a peace treaty at the end of a war may not seem a redemptive story of black power and liberation, able to help galvanize a revolutionary movement. But the invasion and occupation of Havana—as it was fought, remembered, and recreated by these men in Havana—was exactly that. By 1812, the siege of Havana had become a reminder for the conspirators in the Aponte Rebellion of a time when the Spanish king honored black men of arms. This memory was all the more poignant in an increasingly racialized regime of large-scale plantation slavery where the population of African descent found its rights under assault. Now that the British enemy had become an ally against Napoleon in 1808, and a free black republic had arrived next door, Cuba's slaveholders perceived men of African descent wearing the king's uniforms and carrying weapons as a threat. Under these conditions, Aponte and his collaborators responded in kind, turning their military training and experience against the most powerful plantation owners on the island. At the end of his trial, local

63. See Láminas 18–19, in Pavez Ojeda, ed., "Expediente sobre José Antonio Aponte," *Anales de Desclasificación,* I, *La derrota del área cultural,* no. 2 (2006), 727–728.
64. "Libro de servicios del batallon de milicias de los morenos libres de La Habana," December 1793, AGI, Cuba, 1492B. In December 1811, the battalion of pardos libres had two veterans of the siege in their late sixties still serving as captains. See "Libro de servicios de pardos libres de Havana," 1811, AGI, Cuba, 1773A. Capitan de granaderos José del Castillo (sixty-nine years old) had defended Havana against the British landing at Cojímar and also served at Pensacola during the American Revolution. Capitan José Escobar (sixty-four years old) had served in the defense, in the expedition to Louisiana in 1769, and as a privateer on the *Galga.* On Aponte as a historian constructing a prestigious past for men of African descent in Havana, see Barcia, *Cuba,* 137–145; and Barcia, *Los ilustres apellidos,* 290–298.

authorities executed Aponte on the same plaza where the Conde de Ricla had gathered enslaved veterans of the British siege to manumit them in honor of their service in 1763. Nevertheless, both the struggle for which Aponte fought and the black military tradition of which he was a part would live on.

Conclusion

In response to the embarrassing loss of Havana, Spain dove headfirst into the project of developing a transatlantic slave trade and expanding agricultural slavery in its overseas territories. This project formed part of the renewed pact it forged with its wealthiest subjects in Havana in the wake of the British occupation. Breaking into the slave trade was a global operation that drew Spanish officials' attention to West Africa and the Philippines in pursuit of the tools, goods, and outposts it lacked. Some efforts met with success, while others failed spectacularly. Yet, by the 1790s and early 1800s, the Spanish monarchy had succeeded in opening the slave trade to Spanish America and widening the stake of Spanish and Spanish American merchants in it.

Spain's drive to acquire its own slave trade occurred before the height of the sugar boom in Cuba. It also took place before the Spanish crown was under any kind of pressure to stop the slave trade from British abolitionism or the Royal Navy's campaign to intercept slave ships. Together these two facts reinforce how deeply the trade was tied up in eighteenth-century imperial competition and Spain's quest for greater sovereignty over its overseas territories. Over many decades, Spanish officials worked assiduously to wrest control over the Spanish American slave trade from its most vexing enemy's hands. The results of these efforts were never exactly as desired, or even that close to how they were imagined, but their impact was enduring. Spanish reformers' belief in the connection between slavery and modernity engendered a political economy of exploitation that persisted and expanded into the nineteenth century, the century of abolition but also the apex of slavery and the slave trade.

In the decades after the Seven Years' War, Spain's twin policies of more slave trading and more war with Britain remade the island of Cuba. More enslaved Africans for sale and more wartime free trading enabled the rapid ascendance of a powerful agricultural sector and sugar elite in Havana. The American Revolution further stimulated the sugar industry by providing more commerce and slave trading as well as lucrative new outlets for Cuba's sugar exports. From the perspective of the 1790s, Cuba's most powerful sugar planter, Francisco de Arango y Parreño, could look back with gratitude at Cuba's rapid transformation and locate its beginnings in the British occupation of Havana. In 1762 and 1763, the relationship between the crown and its elite subjects in Havana had been broken, but now it was remade in the most mutually beneficial way.

The Spanish king's new bargain with his wealthy white subjects in Cuba sold out the black soldiers who had defended Havana from British attack. The descent into large-scale slave trading and the remaking of Cuba's political economy undermined the place of those who had been the most loyal to Spain during the British siege. As Havana's largest slaveholders launched the island in the direction of export commodity agriculture, they sought to restrict the rights of all black subjects on the island. Even worse, men like Arango worked to eliminate the black soldiers who had nearly saved Havana from a lethal attack and been honored by a king for doing so.

In Cuba in 1812, the reigning climate of racial oppression, inequality, and enslavement alone might have been enough to inspire the Aponte Rebellion. The news of racial insurgency in Cuba's neighbor to the east and rumors of impending liberation elsewhere certainly helped. The Aponte Rebellion drew inspiration from the Haitian Revolution but also recent history in Havana. The gap between the promises the king had made to his black vassals and their prevailing treatment stung. In the 1780s, officers of the moreno militia had petitioned in protest, and the petitioners had been largely removed from their positions of authority. These experienced officers had reason to think themselves equal to a white man, if not better, and yet they were treated like dogs. In this context, the memory of the siege of Havana became a symbol of a lost age that had come before. In Spain's rush to copy its British rival, the monarchy had risked losing the allegiance of a group that had been a cornerstone of its empire.

Conclusion

A History That Haunts

The memory of the British invasion and occupation of Havana has haunted the island of Cuba throughout the 250 years since these events transpired. The seizure of Havana by English-speaking forces has had this uncanny and enduring effect because of its resonance with Cuba's subsequent history and the island's fraught political and economic relationship with the United States. Across the generations, the specter of invaders on the horizon has retained its power, even as evocations and interpretations of this eighteenth-century attack have twisted in the shifting winds of Cuba's relations with Spain and the Anglo-American commercial system. Yet, as much as the British invasion and occupation of Havana is a history that haunts, it ought to haunt us further still.[1]

People of African descent, the institution of racial slavery, and imperial rivalry over the transatlantic slave trade shaped the invasion and occupation of Havana; however, that is not the way these events have been remembered. The crucial role played by people of African descent—so clear to those involved at the time—has been lost from the story. In the nineteenth century, decades after the siege, their place in this history became an uncomfortable truth that flew in the face of newly evolving racial ideologies and political projects, and it was erased. Instead, subsequent generations of historians, writers, and politicians, both on and off the island of Cuba, silenced this history in the pursuit of their own national and imperial agendas.

In Spain and Cuba, the military history of the siege endured in popular memory, but in whitewashed form. There it emerged as a valiant but ill-fated

---

1. On haunting, history, and the memory of slavery in the United States, see Avery F. Gordon, *Ghostly Matters: Haunting and the Sociological Imagination,* new ed. (Minneapolis, Minn., 2008); Saidiya Hartman, *Lose Your Mother: A Journey along the Atlantic Slave Route* (New York, 2007); and Tiya Miles, *Tales from the Haunted South: Dark Tourism and Memories of Slavery from the Civil War Era* (Chapel Hill, N.C., 2015).

FIGURE 35 *Defensa del Moro contra el ataque inglés.* By Rafael Monleón y Torres. 1873. Oil on canvas. Monleón painted this image in the decades before the U.S. invasion of 1898. Like Dominic Serres, Monleón emphasized naval aspects of the siege of Havana rather than the land battle. In this exaggerated scene, Spanish cannon fire from the Morro has destroyed a British warship. Courtesy, Museo Naval de Madrid, Spain / Bridgeman Images

defense of *patria*—Spanish or Cuban, depending on the point of view—against the forces of Anglo and Anglo-American advance. Cuba's wars of decolonization in the nineteenth century first framed interpretations of the events of the Seven Years' War (see Figure 35 [Plate 12]). To Spanish historian Jacobo de la Pezuela, writing in the 1860s, the emphasis was on loyalty. The events of the British siege proved the strength of the bonds that tied the Havana populace to the Spanish king, the Catholic religion, and Hispanic culture and values. To contemporaries Pedro José Guiteras and Antonio Bachiller y Morales, two historians of Cuba forced into exile from their native land by anti-Spanish conspiracy and warfare, the defense of Havana from British attack revealed a proto-Cuban nationalism emerging under the rule of Spain.[2]

2. Pezuela's account singled out Sebastián de Peñalver y Angulo and Gonzalo Recio de Oquendo as two of a small group of traitors who betrayed a loyal populace; see *Como vio Jacobo de la Pezuela la toma de la Habana por los ingleses: Cuatro capítulos de su Historia de la isla de Cuba y un fragmento de su diccionario geográfico, estadístico, histórico de la isla de Cuba* (Havana, 1962). See also Pedro J. Guiteras, *Historia de la conquista de la Habana por los ingleses* (Havana, 1962); and Antonio Bachiller

During these same fraught decades of the nineteenth century, a particular memory of the occupation resonated with commercial interests in Cuba
that favored closer political and economic ties, under relations of autonomy
or annexation, with the United States. They followed the model of Francisco
de Arango y Parreño, who famously wrote of the occupation as "the true era
of Havana's resurrection." For sugar planters like Arango and nineteenth-
century separatists from Spain, the British occupation provided a convenient
origin story for the economic interdependence of Cuba and British North
America, later the United States. In all of these cases, the contest over Cuba's
nineteenth-century destiny cast its shadow over interpretations of the events
of the century before.[3]

During the twentieth century, in the era of the Cuban Revolution, the
memory of the defense of Havana from British attack aligned with the tropes
of Cuban nationalism, though, again, in whitewashed form. The popular
memory of these events had nothing to do with people of African descent.
In the 1960s, Cuban historians seized on the figure of the humble creole from
Guanabacoa, Pepe Antonio, in the search for predecessors for Fidel Castro,
Ernesto "Che" Guevara, and the other valiant defenders of the fatherland at
the Bay of Pigs invasion. By design, the Bay of Pigs invasion was, after all, nothing other than another attack on Havana. President John F. Kennedy's original plans plotted a massive force meant to land on Cuba's southern coast and
take Havana by storm, liberating Cuba's oppressed opposition as they moved
overland. In light of these events, historians in Cuba lauded the heroic Pepe
Antonio as a mythic, protonationalist figure who stood up to the English-
speaking imperialist aggressors. That Pepe Antonio was in fact a slaveowner
who died of disease early in the siege did not seem to matter. Nor have popular accounts of his protagonism been deterred by the much lesser celebration
for him at the time compared to the men of African descent he fought along-

y Morales, *Cuba: Monografía histórica que comprende desde la pérdida de la Habana hasta la restauración español* (Havana, 1883).

3. Francisco de Arango y Parreño, "Discurso sobre la agricultura de La Habana y medios de fomentarla," in Arango, *Obras*, ed. Gloria García Rodríguez, I (Havana, 2005), 146. Following Arango,
Antonio Bachiller y Morales called the British invasion and occupation of Havana "the most important episode in the history of Cuba." "It awakened Cuba," he wrote, "from a sleep of several centuries"; see Bachiller y Morales, *Cuba*, 5, 131. In the 1930s, Cuban historian Herminio Portell-Vilá
credited the British occupation with redirecting the path of Cuba's evolution "and especially Havana
along the path of progress"; see Herminio Portell-Vilá, *Historia de Cuba en sus relaciones con los Estados Unidos y España*, I (1515–1853) (Havana, 1938), 59. Writing from a different political perspective in
1978, Marxist historian Manuel Moreno Fraginals shared this interpretation of the economic effects
of the British occupation, as a launching pad for Cuba's sugar and slavery complex of the nineteenth
century, in a text first published in Havana in 1978; see Moreno Fraginals, *El ingenio: Complejo económico social cubano del azúcar* (Barcelona, 2001), 15–59.

side. A machete that supposedly belonged to him is on display to this day in a museum in Guanabacoa.[4]

On an island infused with militarized political language, popular memory of the siege of Havana thus became a place to fight other wars and to celebrate an undying defense of Cuban *patria*, constantly under siege. These other narratives have retained their urgency across time, but they also obscure key dynamics of the original events that inspired them and their enduring consequences. The remembering of this history has been predicated upon the forgetting of the inconvenient parts that exist outside the contours of a raceless Cuban nationalism. Recent generations of scholarship have nuanced these portraits, but their general outlines endure in popular consciousness. In a telling example, a phrase born of the siege, *"la hora de los mameyes,"* continues to be used in the Cuban vernacular. Mameyes, a tropical fruit that is red on the inside, were used to refer to the British in their red coats; thus, it means the hour of attack, a "do or die" or decisive moment, of the kind that seem to abound in Cuban national history.[5]

In Britain and the United States, the afterlives of these events have taken different forms, but the process of erasure and remaking in the nineteenth century has been essentially the same. For Britain, the occupation of Havana was a historical dead end, soon surpassed by subsequent events and then faded from memory. Plans of attack conceived in earlier wars, developed and honed over the centuries, came to fruition in Havana's capture, thus proving the unequivocal ascendance of British land and sea power in the era of the Seven Years' War. But, by the time Britain's combined forces had the acumen, experience, and good luck to succeed in taking Havana, the British empire's changing political landscape had rendered it no longer desirable. In the wake of Havana's capture and return, Britain's thirteen North American colonies won their independence against its weakened army, Britain's opportunistic

---

4. Juan Florencio García, *Pepe Antonio: Biografía del héroe popular cubano Don José Antonio Gómez de Bullones* (Havana, 1962); Marcos A. Rodríguez Villamil, *Apuntes para una biografía de Pepe Antonio* (Havana, 2004). For novels about Pepe Antonio, see Álvaro de la Iglesia, *Pepe Antonio* (Havana, 1979); and Antonio R. Viñes, *Pepe Antonio* (Miami, 1995). On the Bay of Pigs invasion, see Lars Schoultz, *That Infernal Little Cuban Republic: The United States and the Cuban Revolution* (Chapel Hill, N.C., 2009), 142–169; Jim Rasenberger, *The Brilliant Disaster: JFK, Castro, and America's Doomed Invasion of Cuba's Bay of Pigs* (New York, 2011); and Peter Kornbluh, ed., *Bay of Pigs Declassified: The Secret CIA Report on the Invasion of Cuba* (New York, 1998). Pepe Antonio's machete may be found at the Museo Histórico de Guanabacoa, Havana.

5. On race, nation, and nationalism in Cuba, see, for example, Alejandro de la Fuente, *A Nation for All: Race, Inequality, and Politics in Twentieth-Century Cuba* (Chapel Hill, N.C., 2001); Karen Y. Morrison, *Cuba's Racial Crucible: The Sexual Economy of Social Identities, 1750–2000* (Bloomington, Ind., 2015); and Devyn Spence Benson, *Antiracism in Cuba: The Unfinished Revolution* (Chapel Hill, N.C., 2016). For "la hora de los mameyes," see https://www.ecured.cu/La_hora_de_los_mameyes.

attempt to seize the rebelling French colony of Saint Domingue failed, and its imperial horizons shifted to other oceans. As the British nation sought to reclaim its moral authority through international abolitionism, acquiring Spain's key to the Indies lost its compelling logic. The capture of Havana fit neatly into narratives of the rise to global dominance of the British navy, but otherwise the brief, faltering incorporation of western Cuba into the British empire and the ten thousand lives extinguished to that end constituted a history that went nowhere, overtaken by other developments even before its culmination. Consequently, British Havana fell off the map.[6]

Instead, Britain's centuries-long obsession with possessing the island of Cuba became the political and cultural inheritance of the United States. In the cauldron of nineteenth-century politics, the memory of Havana's capture and its regrettable return to Spain at the end of the Seven Years' War haunted the nation to Cuba's north. In altered form, it continues to do so to this day. What endured in the United States, though, was not a memory of the events as they unfolded; it was a lingering sense of loss associated with the island, accompanied by the false belief that re-acquiring it would be easy. Five U.S. presidents tried to purchase the island, beginning with Thomas Jefferson's first offer in 1808. If purchase was not possible, then perhaps another invasion would do. During the War of 1812, Andrew Jackson considered the option of invading Cuba. U.S. filibusters' designs on the island during the 1840s and 1850s and the interest in Cuba of southern proslavery groups are relatively well known, but their roots go farther back than most realize. They have their origins in British and British American slave trading and war making with Spanish America in the late seventeenth and early eighteenth centuries.[7]

6. In a similar move to what happened in Havana, Britain attributed its defeat in Saint Domingue, not to the skill of the black generals and soldiers fighting against them, but to yellow fever alone; see Michel-Rolph Trouillot, *Silencing the Past: Power and the Production of History* (Boston, 1995), 99; David Patrick Geggus, *Slavery, War, and Revolution: The British Occupation of Saint Domingue, 1793–1798* (New York, 1982). On the moral imperative of British abolitionism in the wake of the loss of the thirteen North American colonies, see Christopher Leslie Brown, *Moral Capital: Foundations of British Abolitionism* (Williamsburg, Va., and Chapel Hill, N.C., 2006).

7. On American presidents' attempt to buy Cuba, see Hugh Thomas, *Cuba; or, The Pursuit of Freedom* (1971; rpt. New York, 1998), 88. In addition to Thomas Jefferson, the others were James K. Polk, James Buchanan, Ulysses S. Grant, and William McKinley. On Andrew Jackson and Cuba, see Harold D. Moser, David R. Hoth, and George H. Hoemann, eds., *The Papers of Andrew Jackson*, IV, *1816–1820* (Knoxville, Tenn., 1994), 60, 352; and Frank R. McCoy, Third U.S. Cavalry, unpublished manuscript, 1898, Miscellaneous Collection, William L. Clements Library, Ann Arbor, Mich. On filibustering and southern U.S. slaveholders' imperialist designs on Cuba in the 1840s and 1850s, see Herminio Portell Vilá, *Narciso López y su época (1848–1850)* (Havana, 1952); Lester D. Langley, *Struggle for the American Mediterranean: United States–European Rivalry in the Gulf-Caribbean, 1776–1904* (Athens, Ga., 1976); Tom Chaffin, *Fatal Glory: Narciso López and the First Clandestine U.S. War against Cuba* (Charlottesville, Va., 1996); James E. Lewis, Jr., *The American Union and the Problem of*

For most of the nineteenth century, U.S. journalists, writers, and statesmen conceived of the island's annexation as a natural and necessary process, part of the nation's manifest destiny. The most potent encapsulation of this U.S. policy toward Cuba derives from a famous letter to the U.S. minister in Spain written by John Quincy Adams in 1823. "There are laws of political as well as of physical gravitation," Adams wrote, "and if an apple, severed by the tempest from its native tree, cannot choose but fall to the ground, Cuba, forcibly disjoined from its own unnatural connexion with Spain, and incapable of self-support, can gravitate only towards the North American union, which, by the same law of nature, cannot cast her off from its bosom." Inherent in Adams's thinking and that of other U.S. pro-annexationists are many of the same assumptions that had shaped plots against Havana a century before: namely, Spain was an incompetent colonial master, Cuba was incapable of self government — a racialized assumption — and the island would naturally migrate into the U.S. orbit because of its strategic geographic location and the strength of its trading ties. All that remained was to wait until the fruit was ripe; Adams predicted it would take no more than fifty years. Although matters did not develop as he imagined and the U.S. Civil War intervened, Cuba's fight for independence from Spain rekindled U.S. interest in the British occupation of Havana as a precedent, historical lesson, and justification for its own intervention in Cuba in 1898. Subsequent U.S. military interventions in 1906 and 1917 and the attempted Bay of Pigs invasion in 1961 repeated a similar logic, whether or not they explicitly invoked the history that had come before.[8]

In all these national histories, the role of people of African descent and the geopolitics of the slave trade were written out of the narrative. Once Brit-

---

Neighborhood: The United States and the Collapse of the Spanish Empire, 1783–1829 (Chapel Hill, N.C., 1998); Rodrigo Lazo, *Writing to Cuba: Filibustering and Cuban Exiles in the United States* (Chapel Hill, N.C., 2005); and Walter Johnson, *River of Dark Dreams: Slavery and Empire in the Cotton Kingdom* (Cambridge, Mass., 2013), 303–365.

8. John Quincy Adams to Hugh Nelson, Apr. 28, 1823, in U.S. Congress, House of Representatives, *Island of Cuba*, 32d Congress, 1st session, Executive Document No. 121 (Washington, D.C., 1852), 7. For Adams's letter and analysis of the discourse in the United States about Cuba's annexation, see Louis A. Pérez, Jr., *Cuba in the American Imagination: Metaphor and the Imperial Ethos* (Chapel Hill, N.C., 2008), 25–42, esp. 30. For the revival of U.S. interest in the siege of Havana in 1898, see Asa Bird Gardiner, *The Havana Expedition of 1762 in the War with Spain*, Rhode Island Historical Society (Providence, R.I., 1898), 167–189; Robert Burton, "Siege and Capture of Havana in 1762" (1899), *Maryland Historical Magazine*, IV (1909), 321–335; Edward Everett Hale, *The Capture of Havana in 1762 by the Forces of George III: Being Two Authentic Reports of the Siege and Capture of Havana by the Combined Forces of Great Britain and the American Colonies . . .* (Cambridge, Mass., 1898); James Otis, *At the Siege of Havana: The Experience of Three Boys Serving under Israel Putnam 1762* (New York, 1899); James Otis and J. Watson Davis, *The Navy Boys at the Siege of Havana: The Experience of Three Boys before Moro Castle* (New York, 1899); McCoy, unpublished manuscript, 1898, Miscellaneous Collection, Clements Library.

ain had restyled itself as an international beacon of abolitionism, the way that slave trading had driven the rapid expansion of its polity would just as soon be forgotten. At the same time, the crucial importance of people of African descent in the battle for Havana became discordant with the prevailing racial attitudes and social hierarchies of the nineteenth century, at the pinnacle of plantation slavery and scientific racism. Indeed, to those most invested in Cuba's sugar and slavery regime, the very notion that people of African descent had played a variety of roles in Spanish colonial society was anathema. This shift in attitudes was so dramatic it may even be seen erupting on the page in Spanish documents from the period.

The Havana creole Nicolás de Ribera's description of the island of Cuba preserves a poignant example. Written in 1757, his manuscript was altered in subsequent years. Where Ribera extolled the virtues of black militiamen, claiming that over time African-born *bozales* could "become like Spaniards" and free blacks would even manage to get rich, a later reader scrawled, "What portion of lies! And infamies!" For the generations that followed Ribera, statements attesting to the humanity, intelligence, and elite status of people of African descent in Cuba were shocking and objectionable. In the context of both virulent racism and the threat of abolition, this history had no place.[9]

What was lost in this erasure was more than just the memory of the military participation of free and enslaved people of African descent in the attack and defense of Havana. What was forgotten was the knowledge that the Spanish colony of Cuba was kept afloat by people of African descent—by their labor, sacrifice, and struggle to improve their lives. What was obscured was a story of black political loyalty to a Spanish king, who rewarded many of his servants with their freedom, on an island crucial to the king's ambitions. And, finally, what went unacknowledged was the role of black military power helping to take down a massive British army and strike fear in the hearts of all foes. This proud memory lived on in oral histories and political imaginaries on the island, such as José Antonio Aponte's subversive book of pictures, the Escalera conspiracy of 1844, and the enduring military tradition of men of color in colonial Cuba. But it was dropped from national histories, which sought more comfortable truths, with less direct implications for the rights of former soldiers and slaves in the postwar period.[10]

9. Nicolás Joseph de Ribera, *Descripción de la isla de Cuba* (Havana, [1975]), 143; Olga Portuondo Zúñiga, ed., *Nicolás Joseph de Ribera* (Havana, 1986), 164–165.

10. On black political loyalty in nineteenth-century Cuba, see David Sartorius, *Ever Faithful: Race, Loyalty, and the Ends of Empire in Spanish Cuba* (Durham, N.C., 2013). On the Escalera rebellion, see, for example, Robert Paquette, *Sugar Is Made with Blood: The Conspiracy of La Escalera and the Conflict between Empires over Slavery in Cuba* (Middletown, Conn., 1988); Michele Reid-Vazquez, *The Year of the Lash: Free People of Color in Cuba and the Nineteenth-Century Atlantic World* (Athens,

By obscuring this history, we lose an understanding of the key role that the invasion and occupation played in a series of political and economic shifts that followed. We also conceal a central truth about imperial power in the Atlantic world. As I have argued throughout this book, people of African descent and the transatlantic slave trade played a constitutive role in Atlantic empires and the rivalries between them. The colonial spaces of the eighteenth-century Greater Caribbean region were built by people of African descent, interconnected by African diaspora, and enmeshed with one another by networks of contraband and the slave trade. Britain and Spain fought several wars over the terms of that integration, relying on enslaved Africans and soldiers of African descent, along with European and Euro-American soldiers and sailors, in doing so. At the end of the Seven Years' War, the loss of Havana to the British was so profoundly felt by Spain that it determined to launch a new offensive to break into transatlantic slave trading and wrest control of the trade from Britain. As a result of events in Cuba, Spanish political authorities came to the realization that the expanding slavery and increasing populations of African descent in its colonies were essential to the modernization of its empire in the face of intense competition and threat.

In some respects, the shift that followed the loss and return of Havana should not be surprising. This book may seem to chart a familiar story of how the rigid racial hierarchies of the nineteenth century replaced the greater flexibility and fluidity of the eighteenth century. Elsewhere in the Americas that transition is often mapped as one between an older world of competing empires and a newer one of rival nation-states. With the consolidation of nation-states and the loss of competing empires, people of color lost their ability to play rival imperial regimes against one another to their own advantage. The broader chronological arc of this shift holds true for Cuba, even though the timeline for Cuban nationhood—which was not achieved until 1902, in a compromised, neocolonial form—does not align with the rest of the hemisphere. But, even if Cuba's transition fits a recognizable pattern, it would be wrong to think that it was solely the product of disembodied economic or political forces, rather than the contingent result of a chain of human actions and reactions.[11]

Ga., 2011); and Aisha K. Finch, *Rethinking Slave Rebellion in Cuba: La Escalera and the Insurgencies of 1841–1844* (Chapel Hill, N.C., 2015).

11. On the broader shift between worlds of competing empires and those of rival nation-states and their impacts on people of color, see Jeremy Adelman and Stephen Aron, "From Borderlands to Borders: Empires, Nation-States, and the Peoples in between in North American History," *American Historical Review*, CIV (1999), 814–841; and Daniel K. Richter and Troy L. Thompson, "Severed Connections: American Indigenous Peoples and the Atlantic World in an Era of Imperial Transformation," in Nicholas Canny and Philip Morgan, eds., *The Oxford Handbook of the Atlantic World,*

Instead, the precocious Cuban elite, whose wealth was built on selling the diversified products of slavery—hides, tobacco, sugar, and urban services—in an integrated Atlantic economy of maritime exchange, pushed and lobbied to expand Cuba's slave trade and regional commerce. In the wake of Havana's capture and return to Spain, they were successful. Havana was of such strategic importance to Spain, and the blow of its loss had been so great, that Spain was willing to do whatever it took to placate the island's elite and thus tie them more effectively to their sovereign. These efforts became an urgent matter as Spain struggled to respond to British competition and rivalry. After nearly three centuries without their own slave trade, Spanish authorities initiated new policies to expand and enhance the trade in enslaved Africans to its overseas territories, just as the forces of slave trade abolitionism were gaining traction in Britain and the United States. At the same time, government reforms opened further avenues for the island to participate in Atlantic commerce. The results of these reforms remade the island and more severely restricted the traditional privileges of free black soldiers and all people of African descent.

This history should haunt us because it is a story of broken promises that has implications for the present day. The people on whose backs empires and nations were constructed found themselves denied the just rewards of their labor and sacrifice. As a result of the cascading set of changes put into motion by the British occupation of Havana, Africans and their descendants in Cuba ended up forsaken by the monarch whose empire they had built and defended. Spain's twinned response of more slave trading—under its own flag, apart from British traders—and more war with Britain ultimately led to greater local autonomy in Cuba and increased commercial interdependence with the Anglo-American system. These developments helped drive the dramatic expansion of sugar plantation slavery, the hardening of racial hierarchy on the island, and the rise of a sugarocracy committed to retaining its wealth and power.

Colonial Cuba was an island where warfare and geopolitical confrontation cast a long shadow, and this historical dynamic had given men of African descent the opportunity to fight their way into social positions with greater

---

1450–1850 (New York, 2011), 499–515. This transition has also been delineated as that from societies with slaves to slave societies. For the derivation of these terms and an argument about the North American case, see Ira Berlin, *Many Thousands Gone: The First Two Centuries of Slavery in North America* (Cambridge, Mass., 1998). Jane Landers has also charted this transition for populations of African descent in Cuba; see Landers, *Atlantic Creoles in the Age of Revolutions* (Cambridge, Mass., 2010), 170–174, 204–236. Political independence in the Caribbean was a vexed and contested process. As other plantation societies demonstrate, decolonization could be both early (Haiti) and late (Puerto Rico, Martinique, and Guadeloupe, which are still overseas territories of, respectively, the United States and France).

rights and privileges for themselves and their families. In the wake of Havana's restitution to Spain after the Seven Years' War, Charles III honored black veterans for their achievements; however, the future that veterans of the siege and their families had been promised—greater rights and privileges in exchange for their vital military service to the crown—did not come to pass. At the same time that Cuba was turning to increased slave trading and plantation slavery, Spanish military victories against Britain finally extinguished Britain's quest to gain control of the island. The loss of the long-standing threat of British attack undercut the position many free people of color had managed to carve out for themselves in local society. In the aftermath of the siege of Havana, that pathway to a better life was gone.

Although the Spanish king would not always honor his promises to his vassals, they would consistently have the last say. In 1812, during the Aponte Rebellion, a group of men that included several descendants of black veterans of the siege of Havana precipitated Cuba's first major rebellion against slavery and colonial rule. Later in the nineteenth century, the *mulato* general Antonio Maceo and thousands of black soldiers would help bring Spanish empire in Cuba to its knees. The struggle of Maceo's generation to convert their wartime service into full citizenship would take place in the context of the new Cuban republic, formed under an occupying army from the United States. In that island nation, Maceo's unfulfilled quest retains its symbolic meaning to the present day. But those are other eras, with similar but separate battles, and that is the history of another war.

Acknowledgments

The rest of the world has had an enduring fascination with the island of Cuba for a very long time, which means that the documents, objects, and artwork associated with its history are scattered far and wide, particularly for the colonial period. This made the research necessary for this book both costly and fun. None of it would have been possible without funding from the following sources, which supported research, writing, and revision at critical junctures of the project: the National Endowment for the Humanities, the Omohundro Institute of Early American History and Culture, the Hellman Fellows Fund, the Townsend Center for the Humanities, the Institute for International Studies at the University of California, Berkeley, the William L. Clements Library at the University of Michigan, the John Carter Brown Library at Brown University, the Program in Early American Economy and Society at the Library Company of Philadelphia, the McNeil Center for Early American Studies, the Princeton Program in Latin American Studies, the Princeton Institute for International and Regional Studies, and the Departments of History at Princeton University and UC Berkeley.

This book began as a dissertation at Princeton University, the idea for which first emerged during a meeting in Jeremy Adelman's office in the spring of 2006. I can't imagine a more brilliant, generous, and inspirational adviser than Jeremy. At Princeton I also benefited from the expertise and exacting standards of professors Colin Palmer, Linda Colley, Emmanuel Kreike, Dan Rodgers, Peter Silver, Philip D. Morgan, and Josep Fradera. Vera Candiani, Antonio Feros, and Ada Ferrer generously agreed to serve as members of my dissertation committee and made important interventions in the project at early stages. My fellow Princeton graduate students Hannah Weiss, Paul Ocobock, Chin Jou, and Jason Sharples made for great companions and colleagues. While at Princeton I had the opportunity to participate in New York University's community of Latin Americanists and Atlanticists by taking a class with Sinclair Thomson and becoming a regular at Karen Kupperman's fantastic Atlantic World Workshop, which helped shape my thinking immeasurably. From my New York years, I am also indebted to Christopher Schmidt-Nowara, my neighbor in Brooklyn (twice, in two different apartments), who took me under his wing as one of the many side-mentoring projects that were typical of his bottomless generosity and energy. Chris, your loss is immense. We mourn you still.

Cuban historians have made my work possible through their rich tradition of scholarship and the advice many of their ranks extended to me during my trips to Havana, especially that first one when I had no idea what I was doing. First and foremost, I want to thank my Cuban *padrino* and the *padrino* to many a historian of Cuba, Enrique López Mesa. Enrique has enriched my life and work with his wry sense of humor, warm friendship, and vast knowledge of Cuban history and archives. I am looking forward to our next eight-hour conversation in Havana huddled in front of the air conditioning. I also wish to thank friends and colleagues Mercedes García Rodríguez, Reinaldo Funes, Urbano Martínez Carmenate, Gustavo Placer Cervera, and Marial Iglesias Utset. The work of César García del Pino, María del Carmen Barcia, Olga Portuondo Zúñiga, the late Francisco Pérez Guzman, and the late José Luciano Franco have been foundational for this book. In Havana I owe many thanks to my friends and adoptive family Yamira Rodríguez and the beloved Lillian Lechuga. Ada Ferrer, Rebecca Scott, Hansel Hernández, and Alysa Nahmias all provided crucial introductions on my first trip to Havana. Showing my students Alysa's fantastic documentary about the National Arts School in Havana, *Unfinished Spaces,* is a highlight of every semester. Through her, I had the great honor of getting to know Luz María Collazo and the late Roberto Gottardi, who added much to my trips to the island. To my fellow researchers in Havana, including Anne Eller, David Sartorius, Enver Casimir, Frances Sullivan, Cherina Mastratones, and Marianne Samayoa, I cannot thank you enough for your camaraderie, support, and friendship.

Like all historians, I relied heavily on the work of many archivists, librarians, and fellow scholars and researchers who offered advice during the time I spent circulating to archives for this book. In Spain I would like to extend special thanks to Isabel Aguirre Landa at the Archivo General de Simancas. In Seville G. Douglas Inglis shared with me a wealth of research on eighteenth-century Cuba culled from British and Spanish archives; I hope he doesn't find my own findings too off the mark. In Seville I enjoyed great conversations over *café* with fellow researchers at the Archive of the Indies and the benefits of research assistance from my good friend Pepa Robles. Brett Rushforth and Fabian Klose generously took research photos for me in the National Archives in Ottawa and Kew, respectively. James Robertson provided a very helpful introduction to the National Archive at Spanish Town in Jamaica. I had extraordinary hosts in Kingston—a huge thank you to Candice Hoyes and her marvelous family, Charles, Betty, and Lisa Williams. I thought I knew curry goat, but not until I got to your house.

The McNeill Center for Early American Studies provided an important space for me early in the journey of this book. I matured as a scholar and also made fantastic friendships there, especially with the brilliant Dawn Peterson, Alyssa Mt. Pleasant, Joe Rezek, and Paul Conrad. At the John Carter Brown Library and at Brown University, I learned so much from many great conversations with Valerie Andrews, Ken Ward, Adrian López-Denis, and my stellar fellow fellows Christian Crouch, Kaja Cook, Jorge Cañizares-Esguerra, Jesse Cromwell, Nuala Zahadieh, and Charlie Foy.

Fredrika Teute encouraged me to apply to the Omohundro Institute postdoctoral fellowship and helped me figure out what my book was about when I was most in the dark with it. I kept referring back to her feedback on my manuscript and notes I scribbled down during our conversations long after I left the Institute. During my two years in Virginia, I benefited from the input of a host of scholars and made a number of great friends. My heartfelt thanks to Molly Warsh, Brett Rushforth, Nadine Zimmerli, Greg O'Malley, Alexandre Dubé, Paul Mapp, Antonio Espinoza, Kim Borchard, and Carlos Gálvez Peña. While I was at the Omohundro Institute, John Garrigus and Stuart Schwartz offered extensive feedback on my dissertation, some of it bracing, which provided an invaluable road map for the revision process. I also want to thank Ronald Hoffman, Sally Mason, Karin Wulf, and Melody Smith for their warm welcome and stewardship in Williamsburg.

Portions of this work have been presented and received valuable feedback at too many venues to list, but I would like to extend particular thanks for invitations from Alison Games at the Georgetown Early Modern Global History Seminar Series, Cathy Matson at the University of Delaware, Peter Silver at Rutgers University, Kathleen Wilson at Stony Brook University, Martin Bowen at New York University, Phil Stern at Duke University, Kristie Flannery at the University of Texas at Austin, Carla Pestana at the University of California, Los Angeles, Adrian Finucane at the Early Modern Studies Institute at the University of Southern California, Greg Downs at the University of California, Davis, and Mikael Wolfe at Stanford University. The Association of Caribbean Historians and the Forum on European Exchange and Global Interaction were also favorite annual conferences where I received helpful feedback and useful critiques.

Many, many scholars helped shape this project through their ideas and advice. Because I sought to connect both Latin American and British Atlantic history, I perhaps needed more help than others. Those I have not yet mentioned include but are not limited to Ernesto Bassi, José Luis Belmonte Postigo, Alex Borucki, Marcela Echeverrí, Ada Ferrer, Sibylle Fischer, Pablo F. Gómez, Evan Haefeli, Jane Landers, Kris Lane, Melanie Newton, Juan José Ponce Vásquez, Rebecca Scott, Stephanie Smallwood, Cristina Soriano, Sinclair Thomson, Barbara Weinstein, and David Wheat.

Thank you to my fiercely intelligent colleagues in the Department of History at UC Berkeley, without whom this would have been a lesser book. For their crucial feedback on early drafts, I would like to single out Victoria Frede Montemayor, Carlos Noreña, Mark Peterson, Caitlin Rosenthal, Abhishek Kaicker, and, especially, Rebecca McLennan, Brian DeLay, and Margaret Chowning. Brian and Margaret helped me think through how to reorganize the book, and Rebecca helped me to understand better what I had done in doing so. Rebecca, Abhishek, and Mark all assigned the manuscript to their graduate seminars, and their students provided me with sharp insights and feedback. In particular, I would like to thank Nicole Viglini, Matty Enger, and Maria Barreiros Almeida Reis. Berkeley graduate students Clare Ibarra, Corinne Stoffler, and Raphael Murillo did fantastic work for me, as did Amanda Mosler, undergraduate research assistant extraordinaire.

I was the lucky beneficiary of a manuscript conference held in December 2015 at UC Berkeley. At that event, Matt Childs and James Sweet provided an abundance of feedback and critiques and shared generously of their own ideas. I would also like to thank my UC Berkeley colleagues who took part: Daylet Domínguez, Yvonne del Valle, Raúl Coronado, Julia Lewandowski, Toby Liang, Stephanie Jones Rogers, Rebecca Herman Weber, Maureen Miller, Brian Wagner, Mark Peterson, Daniel Sargent, Rebecca McLennan, and Yuri Slezkine. Dear and talented friends and colleagues Christian Crouch, Molly Warsh, Ignacio Gallup-Díaz, Kym Morrison, Adriana Chira, Alejandra Dubcovsky, Anne Eller, and Sarah Pearsall all read chapters or other related work and provided crucial feedback that shaped this project. Julie Ericksen Hagen did inspired work to help make my prose its best self.

Paul Mapp and Nadine Zimmerli graciously shepherded this book through the publication process and provided the push I needed to articulate my argument more powerfully and to balance the historiographical and human stories. I especially appreciated their calm guidance during moments of peak stress. Virginia Montijo Chew, with the assistance of William & Mary graduate students Morgan McCullough and Kasey Sease, hit my footnotes like a Virginia summer storm. I thank them for their incredible energy, hard work, and commitment to getting them right. Ginny was a gracious shepherd of the book through the production process and an excellent hand reigning in sometimes rambling prose. She caught many errors for which I am grateful. I would also like to thank the helpful insights and extensive substantive feedback of David Sartorius and the other reviewer for the Omohundro Institute.

This book could not have been written without the brilliant and inspirational women of the Berkeley Quilters' Collective, who actually do no quilting. Its members include Charisma Acey, Lisa Trever, Caitlin Rosenthal, Karen Tani, Carolina Reid, Karen Trappenberg Fick, Elena Conis, Andrea Sinn, and Anna Brand. I've learned so much from all of you about how to be a writer, scholar, and rising female academic with a sense of humor. In particular, I would like to thank Caitlin Rosenthal for being a fantastic interlocutor, a deft editor, and an ideal companion on this California life journey.

My dearest friends are spread too far and wide, but they all played a hand in helping me through this project. My main regret is all the time it took away from my being able to spend it with all of you. In California, I would like to thank the incomparable Chereesse Thymes, Meghna Mahjumadar, Rucker Alex, Rebecca McLennan, Rebecca Groves, David Henkin, Catherine Flynn, Vanessa Ogle, Bernie Palau, Nelson Enriquez, Ribhu Kaul, Pierre Theodore, Caille Milner, Shimeko Franklin, Taylor Shogren, Bill Charman, Miguel Vargas, and Charles Fisher. On the East Coast and farther afield, I send my love and forever thanks to my dear, dear friends Christina Wilson, Candice Hoyes, Sarah Jacoby, Nancy Meakem, Betsy Herbin, Christian Crouch, Dawn Peterson, Adriana Chira, Anne Eller, Kelly Bregou, Carrie Gibson, and Toby Liang.

My family has suffered the most during the writing of this book, but it's also in part their fault I chose this life path. They have been there behind the scenes making it all possible. I lost two grandmothers since I started this project, Yvonne Schneider and Mary Lawrence, both strong, intrepid women. My love of history and wandering spirit is no secret: it comes via Mary Lawrence and my mother Fidela. Thank you to Steven Schneider and Leslie Krinsk, my brother John, his wife, Jenny, and their fantastic children, Madeleine and Christopher, who provided love and joy at the holidays and any other chance we got. The deepest and most profound thank you to my parents, Ted and Fidela, who raised me in a house full of books and inspired me with their passion for borderlands and for history. Their unending love and support on this twisting path has made it all possible. Fidela even graciously tried her hand at line editing with this manuscript and in the process discovered a serious gift for the art (thanks, Mom!). For all that and everything else, I dedicate this book to you both.

Index

Page numbers in italics refer to illustrations.